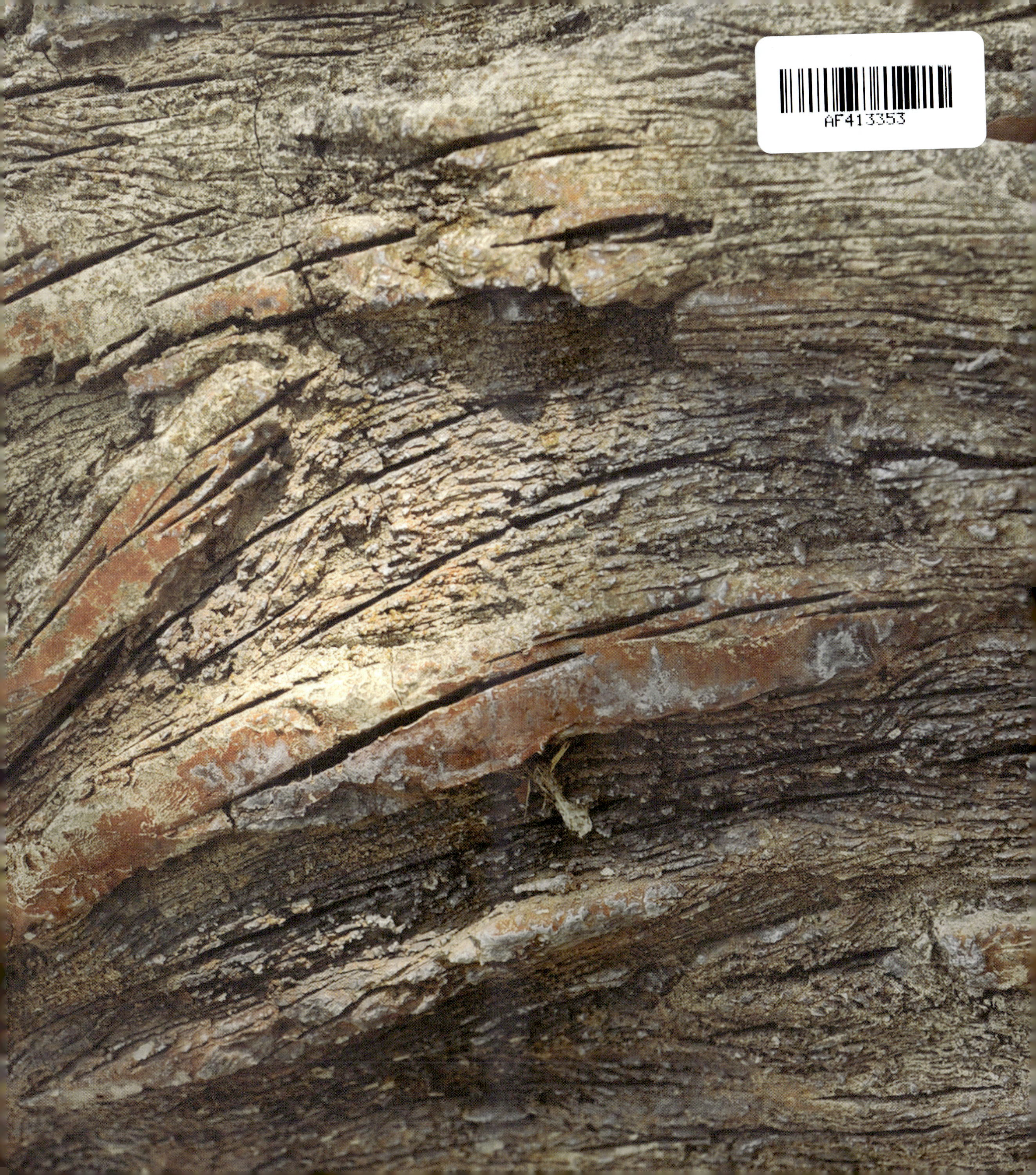
AF413353

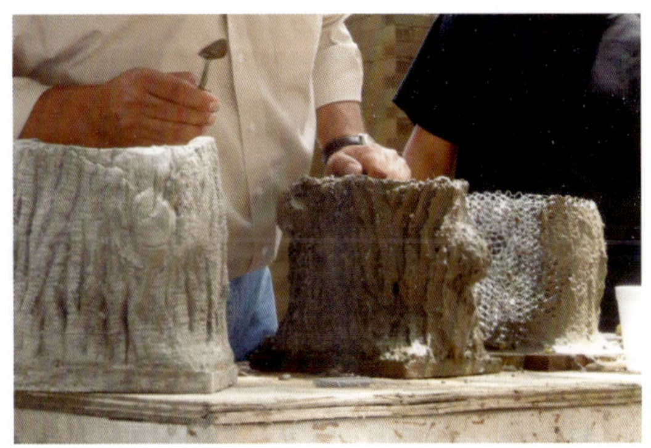

ARTISANS OF Trabajo Rústico

Number Nineteen

Rio Grande / Río Bravo Borderlands Culture and Traditions

Norma E. Cantú, *General Editor*

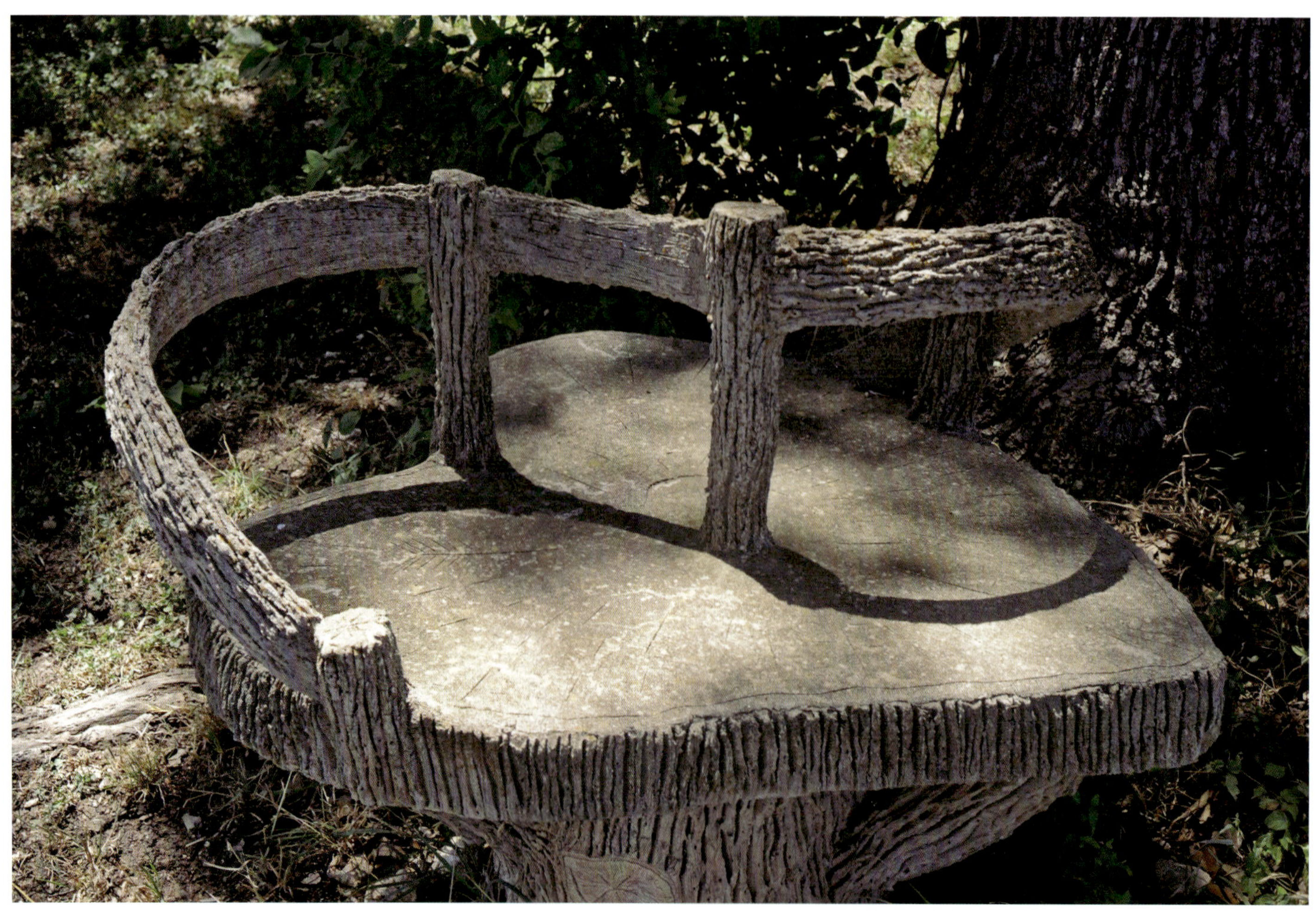

Artisan unknown. Boerne, TX. Collection of Carolyn and Larry Biedenharn. Photo by Kent Rush.

Artisans of Trabajo Rústico

The Legacy of Dionicio Rodríguez

Patsy Pittman Light

Photographs: Kent Rush

Texas A&M University Press
College Station

This paper meets the requirements of ANSI/NISO Z39.48-1992
(Permanence of Paper).
Binding materials have been chosen for durability.
Manufactured in Canada by Friesens

Library of Congress Cataloging-in-Publication Data

Names: Light, Patsy Pittman, author. | Rush, Kent, photographer
(expression) | Jasper, Pat, writer of preface.
Title: Artisans of trabajo rústico : the legacy of Dionicio Rodríguez /
Patsy Pittman Light ; photographs by Kent Rush.
Other titles: Rio Grande/Río Bravo ; no. 19.
Description: First edition. | College Station : Texas A&M University Press,
[2021] | Series: Rio Grande/Río Bravo, Borderlands culture and
traditions ; number 19 | Includes bibliographical references and index.
Identifiers: LCCN 2020053643 | ISBN 9781623497668 (cloth) | ISBN
9781623499136 (ebook)
Subjects: LCSH: Rodríguez, Dionicio, 1891–1955—Influence. | Popular
culture—Mexico—Influence. | Artisans—Texas—San Antonio. | Decoration
and ornament, Rustic—Texas—San Antonio—Themes, motives. | Concrete
sculpture—Texas—San Antonio—Pictorial works. | Outdoor
sculpture—Texas—San Antonio—Pictorial works. | Garden ornaments and
furniture—Texas—San Antonio—Pictorial works. | Nature in popular
culture. | Nature in art.
Classification: LCC NB237.R635 L535 2021 | DDC 730.74/764351—dc23
LC record available at https://lccn.loc.gov/2020053643

DESIGNED BY *Barbara Mathews Whitehead*

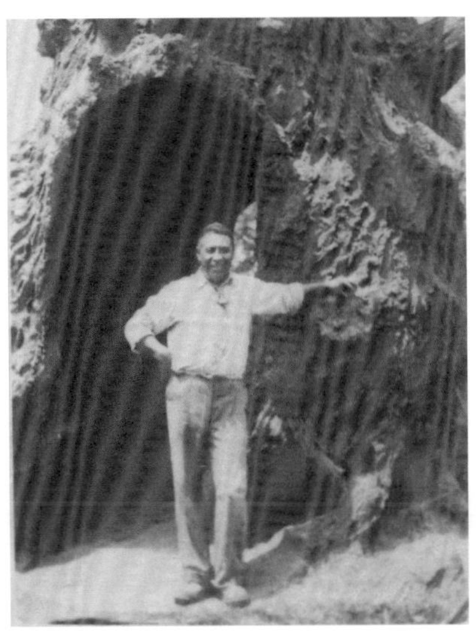

This book is dedicated to
the Trabajo Rústico artisans,
past and present,
whose creations continue to enchant us
with their inspired images
of art in nature.

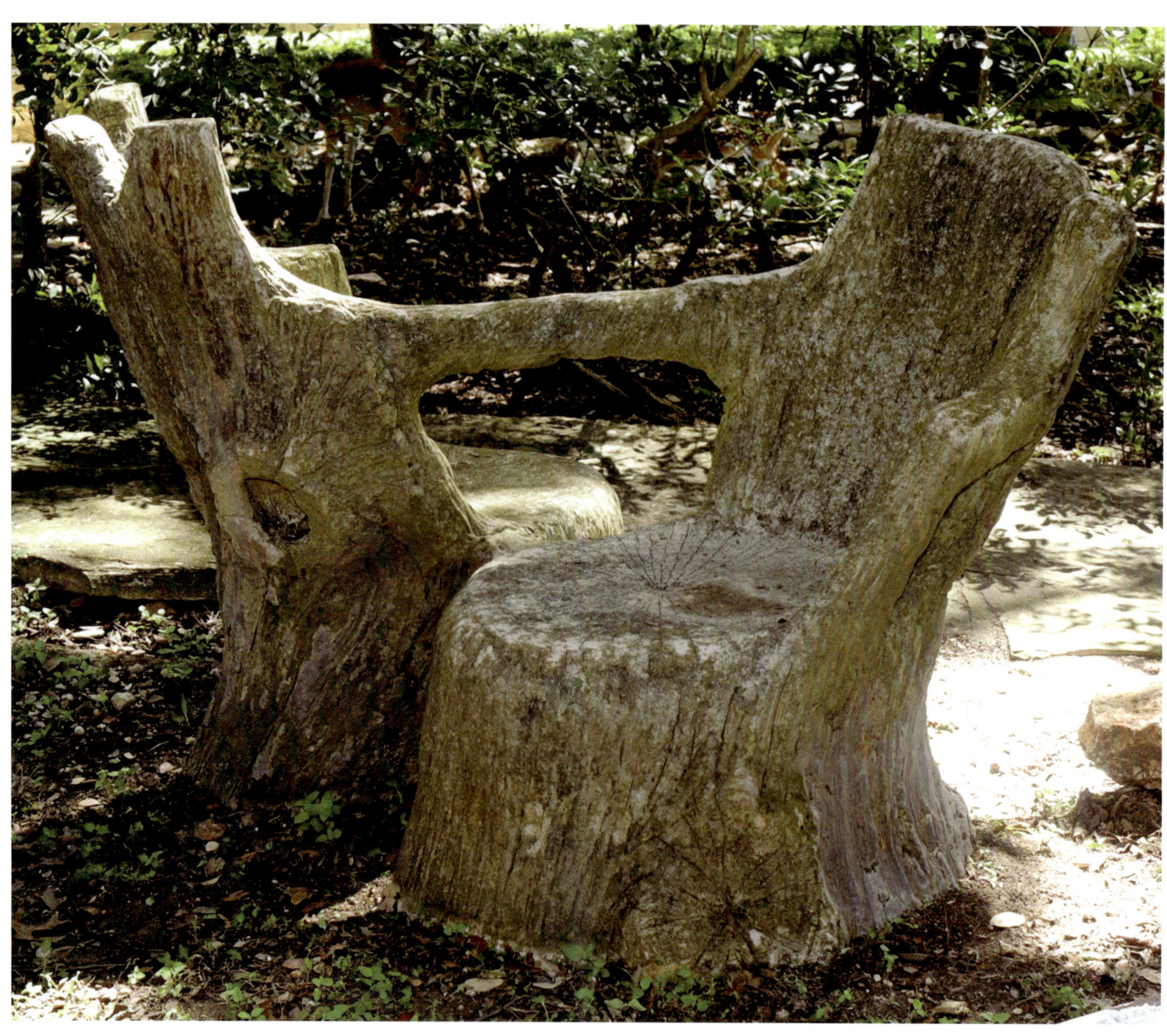

Carlos Cortés. New Braunfels, TX. Private collection. Photo by Kent Rush.

Contents

Acknowledgment of Donors

Generous grants from friends, foundations, and organizations
made this book possible:
The Conservation Society of San Antonio
Walter S. Light Jr.
The Summerlee Foundation

WE ARE GRATEFUL FOR THE SUPPORT of our families: Myssie Light Acomb, Laurie Light Saunders, Walter Scott Light, Walter S. Light Jr., and Haydeé Victoria Suescum. We also appreciate the support of the contemporary *trabajo rústico* artisans and descendants of early artisans. Thanks go to many friends for their support and encouragement: Rene Paul Barrilleaux, James A. Broderick, Kay Hindes, Sarah Westkaemper Lake, Cappy and Suzy Lawton, Marion Oettinger Jr., Ansen Seale, Scott Sherer, and Kathy Vargas. The research assistance that we received from Tom Shelton, photo archivist at The University of Texas Institute of Texan Cultures; from our editors, Sally Antrobus, Pat Clabaugh, Thom Lemmons, and Helen Skeldon, who made our text readable; and the elegant arrangement of the photographs by designer Barbara Whitehead were all outstanding. We especially appreciate Pat Jasper's preface, who creatively describes the inspiration that drove our work.

We are grateful for the privilege of visiting institutions, residences, and other sites, public and private, for the permission to use photographs of trabajo rústico collections, as well as the permissions granted by those in other locations. This assistance made it possible for us to research and document important works of art. We also want to thank artisans, private collectors, and those in multiple locations whose names are withheld for reasons of privacy.

Our special thanks to:
Proprietors, Benedictine Sisters of Boerne, Texas
Boydell & Brewer Ltd.
Bridgeman Images
Angelina Casarez, Chief Public Affairs, 302nd ABW, JBSA Lackland, Texas
City of Alamo Heights, TX
City of San Antonio, TX
City of Uvalde, TX
CLR Design, Inc. under direction of Gary Lee; fabrication by Cemrock Landscape Inc.
Cool Crest, LLC
David J. Culver
Dover Publications-A. J. Downing: Landscape Gardening and Rural Architecture 1991
©Miquel Tres Lopez
©Marco Merola
María Fernanda Vargas Mesén, La Paz Waterfall Gardens
Musée des Comtes de Provence, Brignoles, France
Painshill Park Trust, Ltd., UK
Queen of the Holy Rosary Catholic Church, Hostyn, TX
©Michel Racine
Patti Roetmon, A Little Nature Store
Tammy Russell, Manager, Candlelight Coffee House
St. Matthew's Sports Complex
San Antonio Housing Authority
San Antonio Museum of Art
Gregory Smith, Texas Historical Commission
Mary Ann Sullivan, Bluffton University
Anne L. Cook, Texas Department of Transportation Division 15, Headquarters,
San Antonio
University of North Carolina Asheville, Park Memorial Public Library,
North Carolina Collection.
University of North Carolina Asheville, Richard Pearson Collection, Special
Collections, Ramsey Library, Asheville, North Carolina
The University of Texas at San Antonio Institute of Texan Cultures
The University of Texas at San Antonio Special Collections
San Antonio Express News/San Antonio Light, ZUMA Press
Mark Wolfe, Executive Director, Texas Historical Commission

Foreword

IT IS SELDOM that one person manages to mark, alter, and embellish an urban landscape in an enduring way, especially if the skill involved is of a human or natural scale. Notable architects and famous planners and their works are sometimes associated with a particular city, painters may memorialize a place in canvas after canvas, and prominent landscapers can manicure major swathes of parkland much admired within a community. But an adornment so local that it is sometimes invisible or seems merely a part of the scenery, something taken for granted and almost overlooked, yet that in the long run serves to distinguish a place, give it an indelible character, and set it apart—accomplishing that is an unusual feat

Such is the work of Dionicio Rodríguez in the city he changed through his work: San Antonio. Patsy Light published a full treatment of his work (*Capturing Nature: The Cement Sculpture of Dionicio Rodríguez*). Although the present book reaches beyond Rodríguez, it is nevertheless true that the reason for authoring *Artisans of Trabajo Rústico* would not exist without his singular efforts and contributions. Through apprentices, family members, co-workers, and admirers, his influence is visible in trabajo rústico works throughout the city, the region, and in many other places in the United States.

In a sense this book is a family tree that leads back to or branches out from this seminal craftsman, and that is its central achievement. This is not to say that there weren't other colleagues whose work was of similar or equal quality or selected individuals who extended the technique in a unique and extraordinary manner. One who was Rodríguez's peer and frequent partner was Máximo Cortés. His continuing importance is seen in the exquisite and practiced work of Máximo's son, Carlos, who has carried that family's name forward in the art. Beatrice Ximénez, on the other hand, did not necessarily stand out in the trabajo rústico tradition. She learned it alongside her husband, who was taught by Rodríguez's former helper Sam Murray, but she flexed her understanding of the technique to create a genre of her own, fashioning fantastical cement sculptures of cartoon characters, movie monsters, and animals she saw in books. Her *rústico* pieces were almost an afterthought.

Still, with a few exceptions, Rodríguez is the crucial figure inspiring the practice of this tradition as it is explored in *Artisans of Trabajo Rústico*. He did not invent the technique, but he clearly mastered the craft before bringing it with him to San Antonio. Once in the city, he set out to construct an entire career around it. He introduced it in works found throughout the region and carried this expertise to other metropolitan areas in the United States. Even when he did not directly touch the lives of the craftspeople included here, his impact is evident in his works and sometimes in the those of artisans who came to the tradition later. This book, then, is a dual homage: to the practitioners who helped spread the work and to those who continue to practice it today. Despite its ubiquity, the virtuosity of Rodríguez's work—both in the past when he was making it and in the present as its value has been rediscovered—fuels appreciation of his followers and his followers' followers. Rodríguez captured nature in his work, but he also captured our imagination. And to its credit, *Artisans of Trabajo Rústico* makes what was once almost invisible become fully visible to us all.

—Pat Jasper

Independent Folklorist, Houston, Texas
Co-Curator, Art among Us/*Arte entre osotros*
Mexican American Folk Art of San Antonio
San Antonio Museum of Art, 1986

Preface

WITH ITS LARGE deposits of limestone from which cement is produced, South Texas was ideal for artisans who used this local material in creating metal-reinforced concrete artistic works, many as garden furniture and decorations. In 2004 Maria Pfeiffer and I (Patsy) researched and wrote the National Register of Historic Places listing "The Cement Sculpture of Dionicio Rodríguez in Texas," which included the names of many artisans, some his assistants and others working independently. This research also revealed who assisted him in Texas and who accompanied him to work in other states.

Dionicio Rodríguez enlisted the aid of others, primarily Mexican men. Some had recently arrived from the home country and brought knowledge of the technique with them, while others learned from him. Several artisans were family members who continued working with him for years. Some began their own concrete sculpture businesses, and many shared their expertise with others, thus creating a new group of craftsmen—uniquely—in the San Antonio region. In 2008 my book *Capturing Nature: The Cement Sculpture of Dionicio Rodríguez* documented Dionicio's life's work, again mentioning many of his fellow workers.

In the spring of 2016 artist and photographer Kent Rush, professor emeritus of art at The University of Texas at San Antonio, suggested that the work of these other talented artisans merited documentation, along with that of those who now carry forward this lasting art form. He has spent more than forty years photographing examples of trabajo rústico. A skilled and talented woodworker and builder of small boats, he understands the techniques artisans use to mimic the construction methods craftsmen use. In addition, his having worked as a reinforcing steel detailer augments his knowledge of reinforcement. Thus began a partnership resulting in the documentation of more than one hundred sites, some representing collections of works, some with single pieces, some hidden from view in overgrown backyard gardens, and others in well-known civic and public places. In our collaborative project, I contributed historical details and researched photographic examples worldwide, and Kent provided technical explanations and photography. Together we researched historical and existing works and traveled many miles to document them. Chapter 1 introduces the art form and its history. Chapter 2 describes techniques, illustrating them with drawings and photographs. Brief biographies of twenty artisans are presented in Chapter 3, and Chapter 4 is a photo gallery of works from known and unknown artisans.

It is our sincere hope that this book will serve as a lasting record of the artisans of the mid-1920s and 1930s and others who continue to practice the fascinating endeavor of imitating nature.

—Patsy Pittman Light
Kent Rush

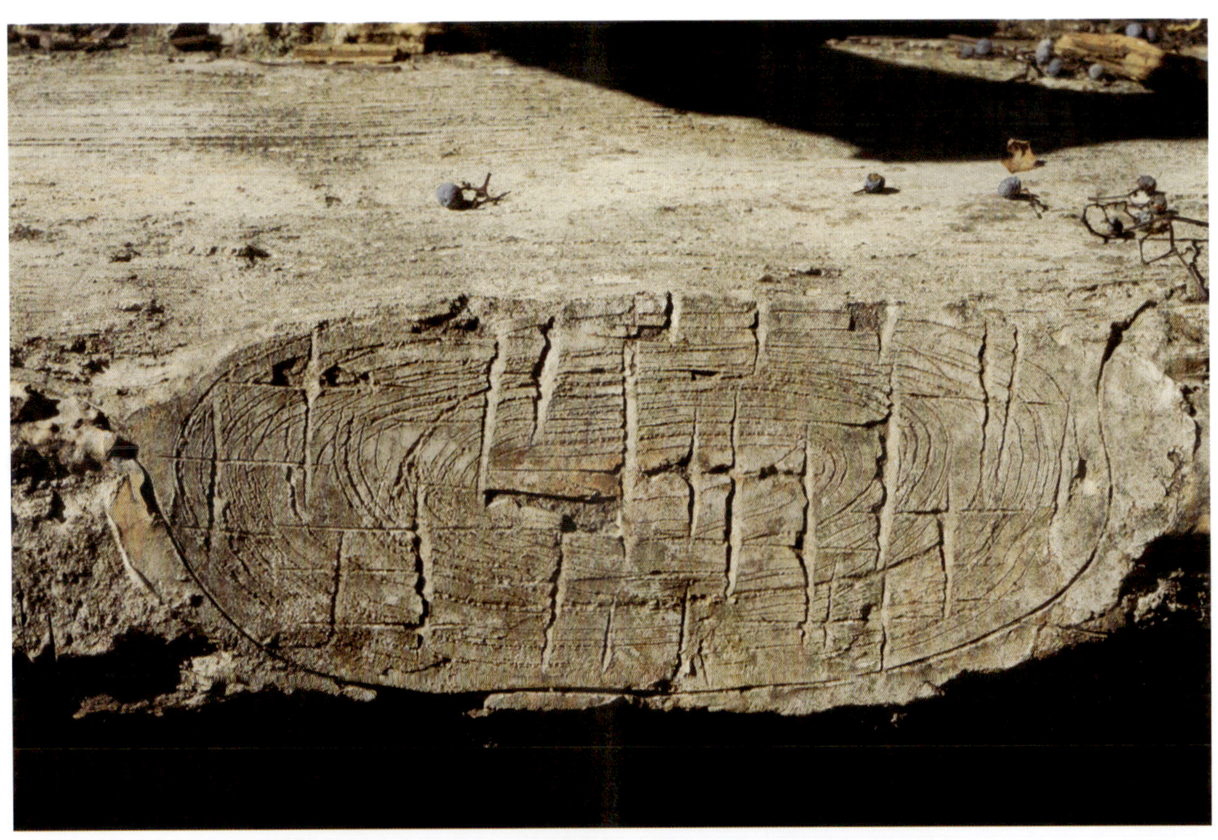

Artisans of Trabajo Rústico

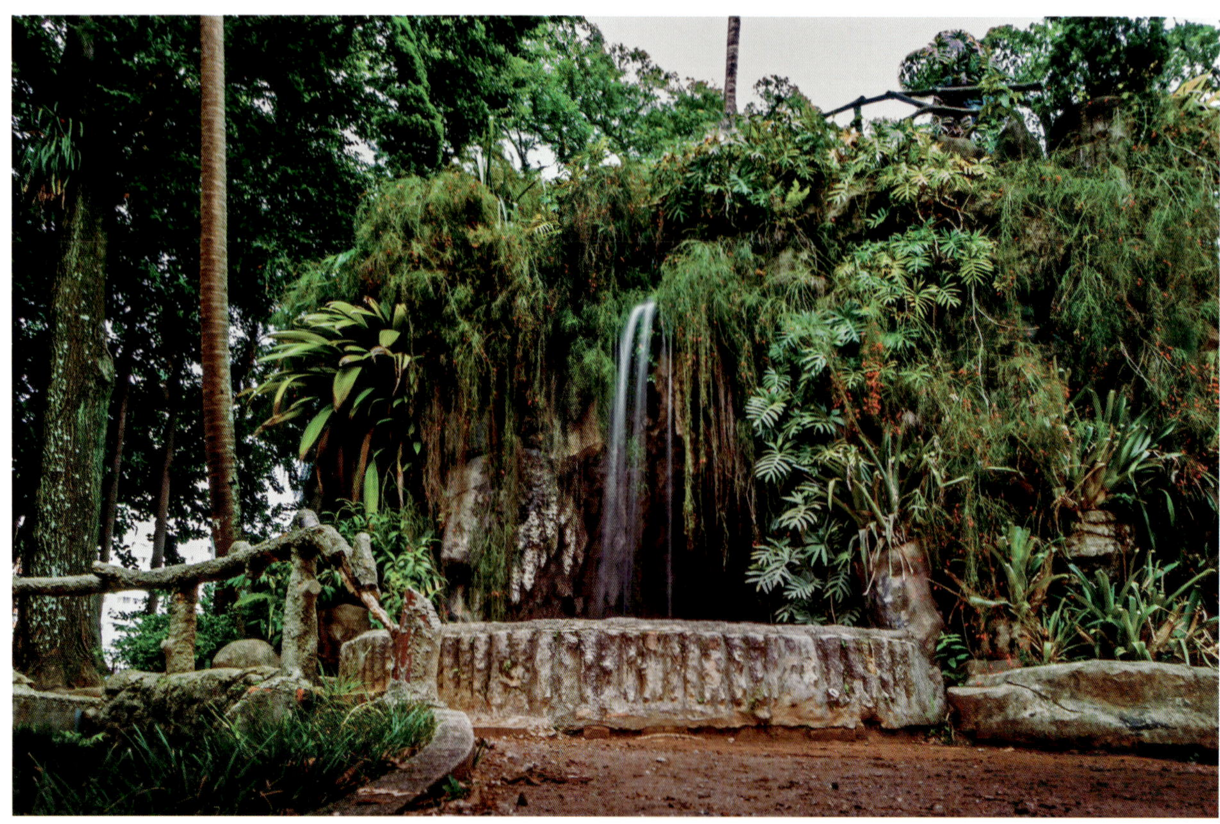

Above: *Artisan unknown. São Paulo, Brazil.*
Parque Jardim da Luz. Fountain.
Photo by Armando Bruck.

Right: *Artisan unknown. El Valle de Antón,*
Coclé, Panama. Golden Frog on a tree.
Photo by Kent Rush.

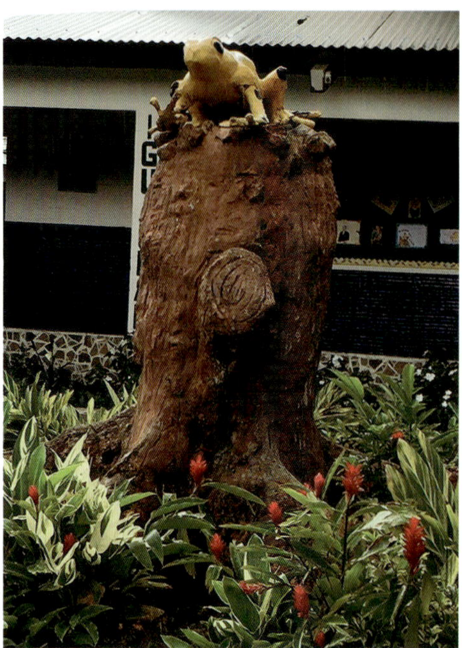

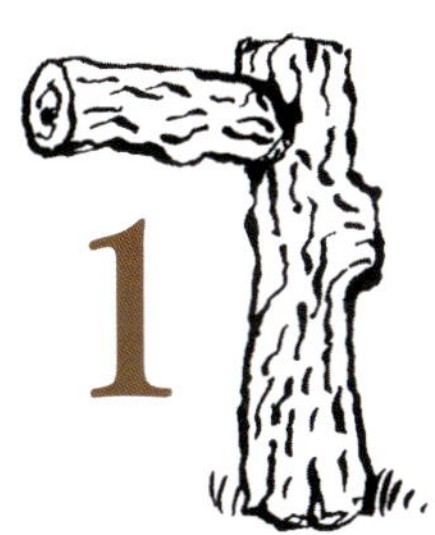

Background and History

DECORATIVE ART FORMS created in concrete and cement, reinforced with steel, are identified in many widely used terms: *trabajo rústico*, Spanish for rustic work, and ferro-cement for iron and cement. As this art form spread, artisans and the public added more terms to describe the works: *giboku* (Japanese), garden yard art, arboreal masonry, and additional French words, *ciment armé, faux bois*, and *art rustique*. Trabajo rústico, which appeared in Texas in the early 1920s, is used throughout this book.

Ramón Magriña, Architect. Havana, Cuba. Los Jardines de la Tropical. Photo by Rosa Lowinger.

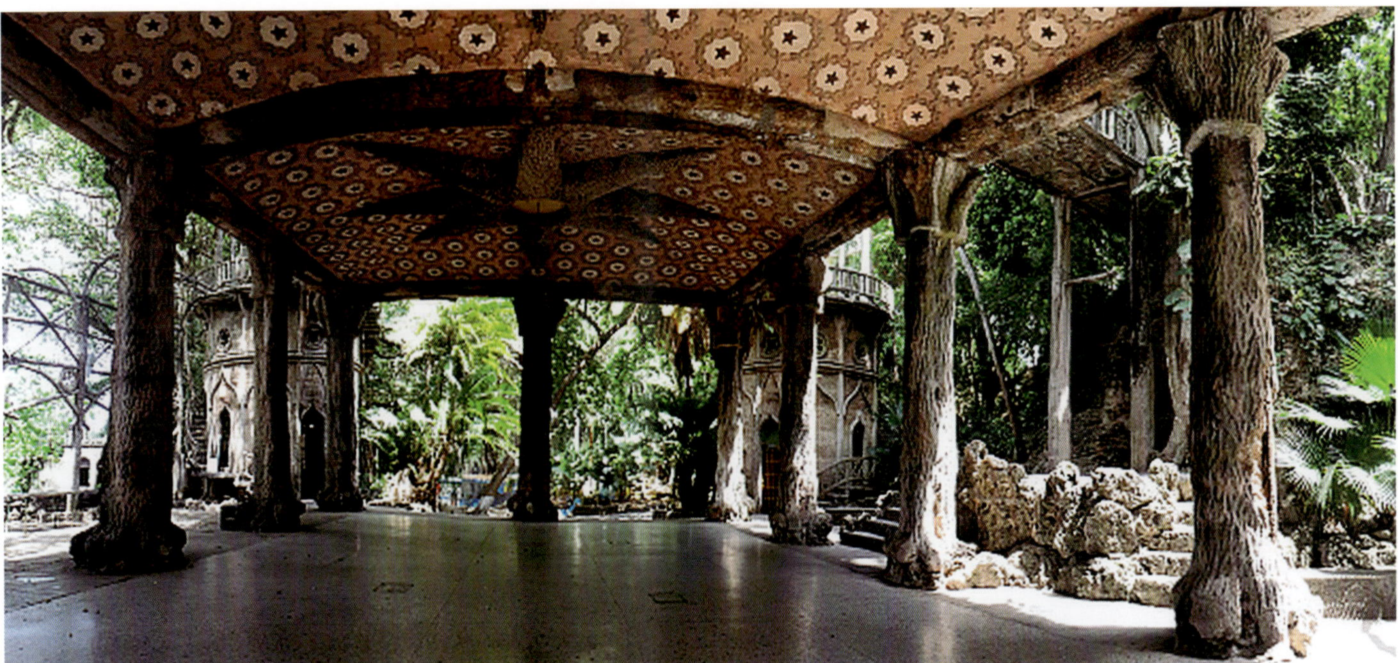

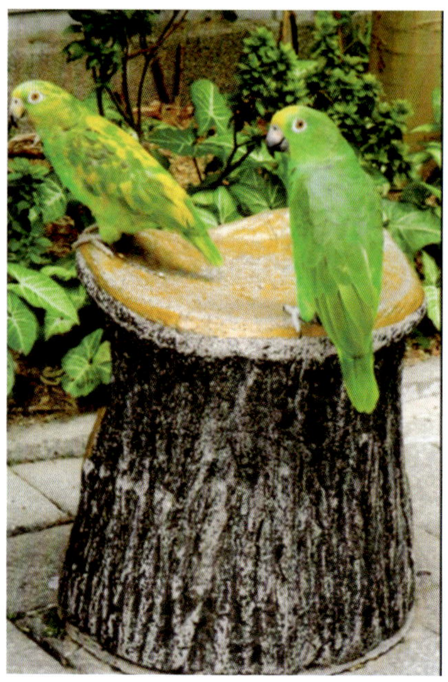

Above: Artisan unknown. Hong Kong, China. Bird market stump with parrots. Photo by Myssie Light Acomb.

Right: Artisan unknown. Sorrento, Italy. Planter. Photo by Walter Scott Light Jr.

The genre had its genesis in France in the mid-1800s with the development of portland cement and inexpensive steel, and eventually appeared throughout Europe, Asia, Central and South America, and the United States. The art form was found in Brazil in 1870, followed later in Argentina, Cuba, Panama, and Mexico.

Trabajo rústico can also be classified as folk art, which has several different meanings, including that it "may be learned formally or informally . . . [and] may also be self-taught." Additionally, "it may be decorative or utilitarian"[1] as were many objects created by craftsmen working with reinforced concrete, including arbors, *palapas* (shade structures), birdbaths, furniture, and aviaries. As an art form that has been passed from one generation to the next, trabajo rústico is an example of our tangible cultural heritage.

> Objects are important to the study of human history … and their preservation demonstrates recognition of the necessity of the past and other things that tell its story.[2]

This chapter is a brief history of
- concrete, cement, and inexpensive steel,
- evolution of garden design and historic examples of garden decoration,
- the spread of reinforced concrete used in trabajo rústico,
- explanation of the technique and materials, and
- earlier proponents and contemporary artisans and their work.

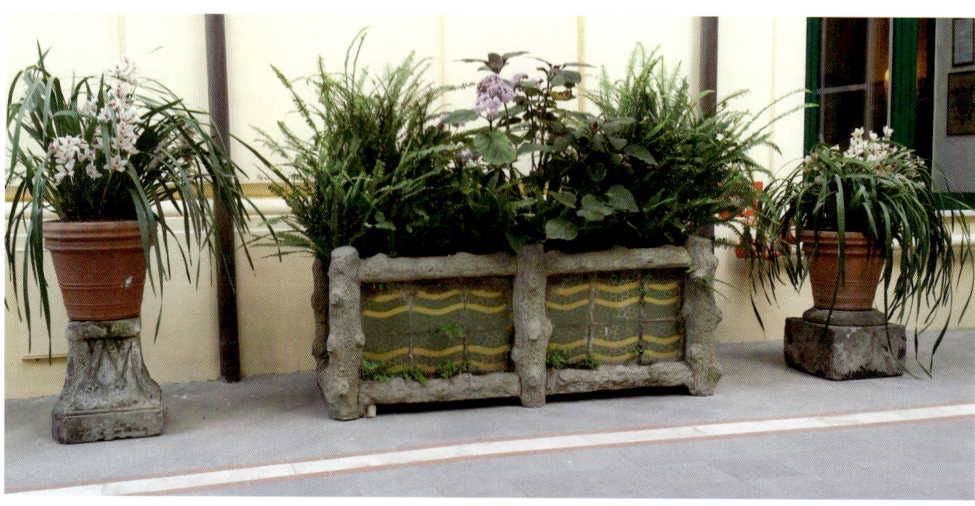

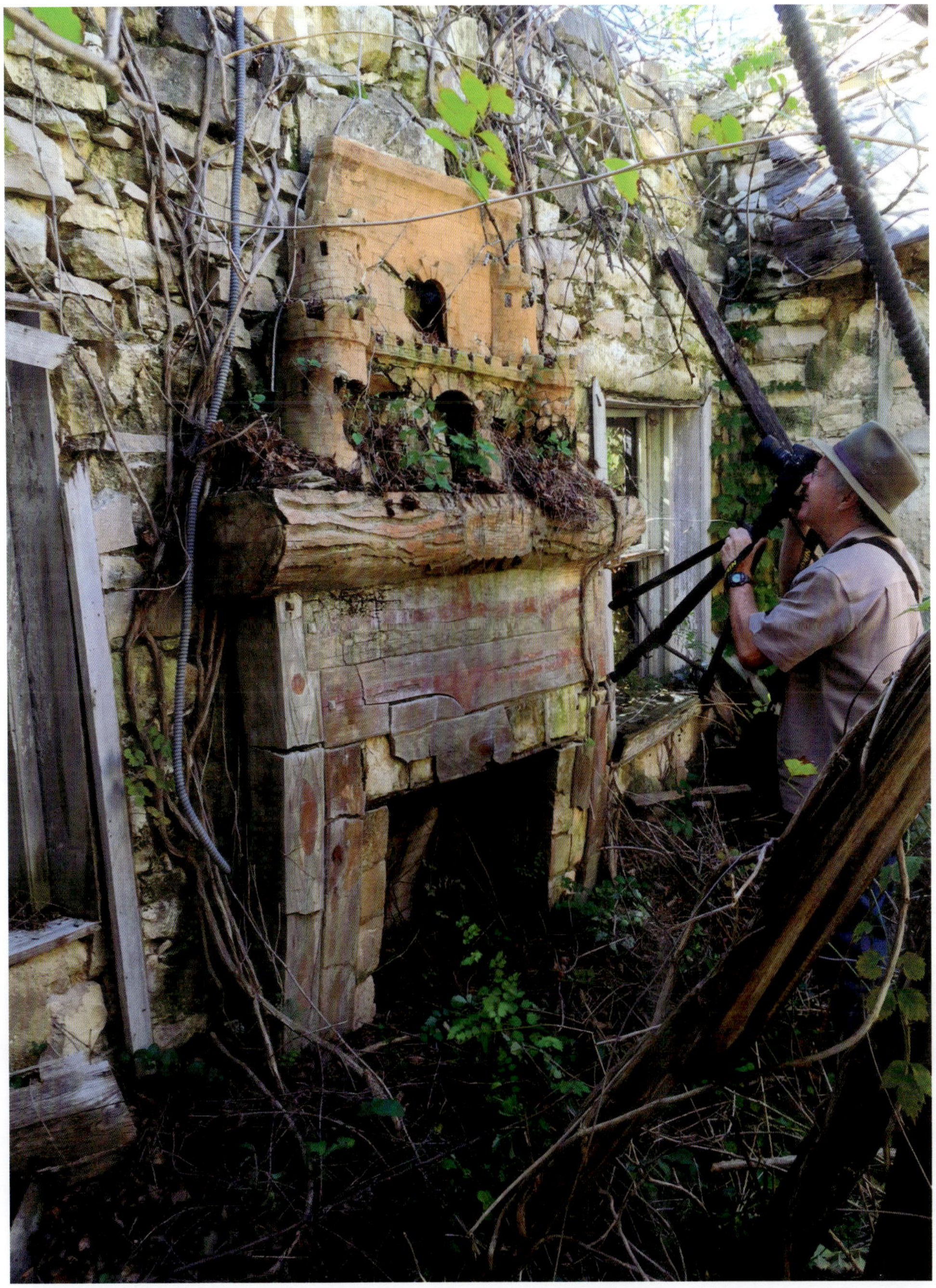

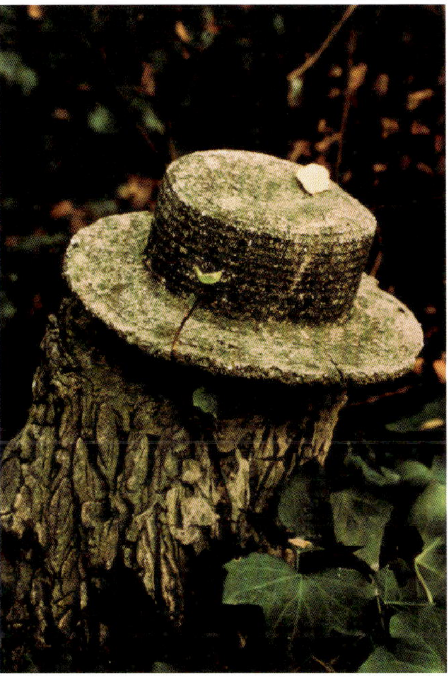

Artisan unknown. Marseille, France. Photo by ©Marcel Racine.

Artisan unknown. Kent Rush photographing at Panther Springs Ranch. Bexar County, TX. Camp Bullis Military Training Reservation. Photo by Patsy Pittman Light.

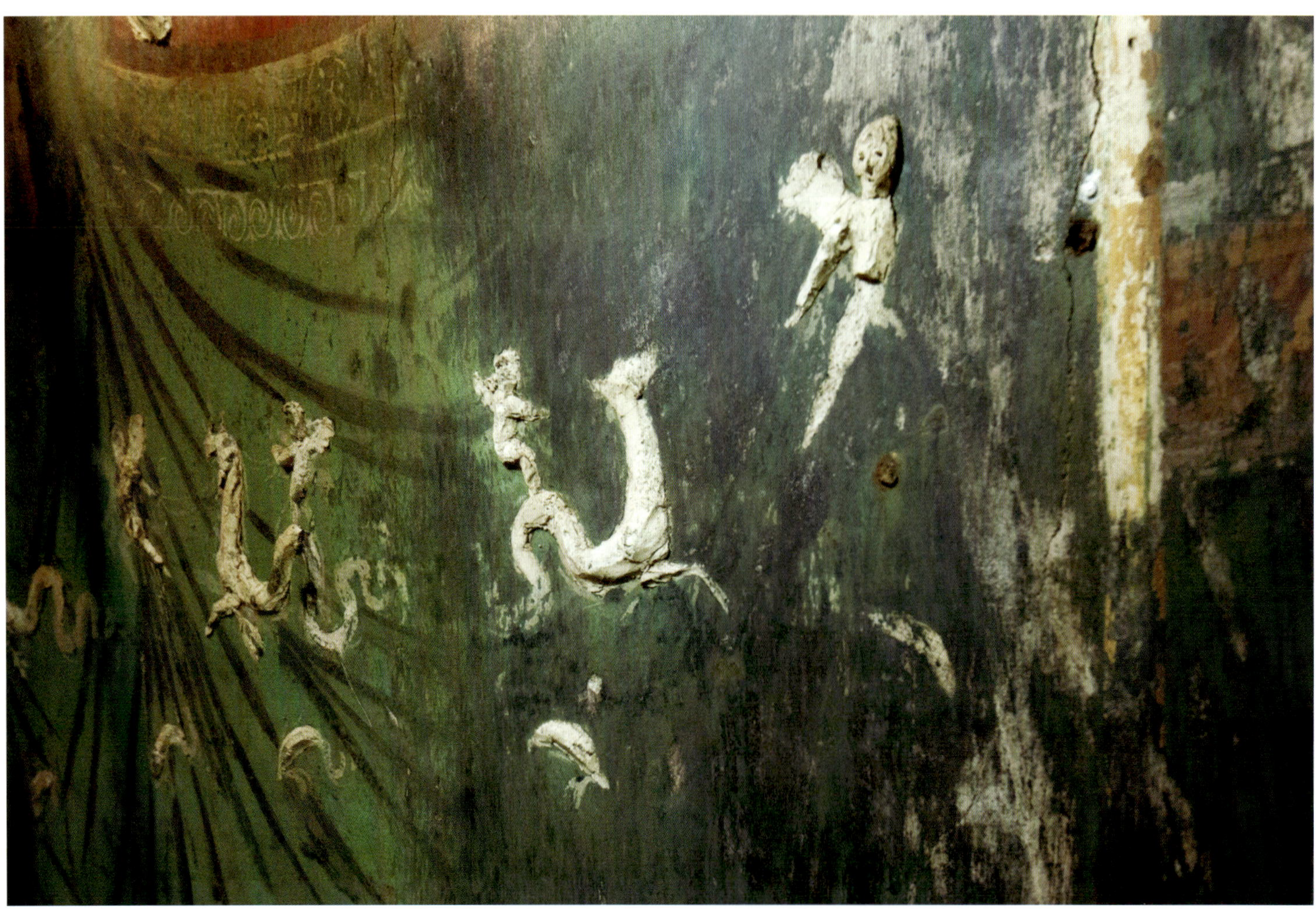

Artisan unknown. Positano, Italy. Stucco wall decorations at Roman villa ruins. Photo by ©Marco Merola.

Trabajo rústico, the technique brought to the United States by Dionicio Rodríguez in 1924, uses a combination of various formulas of concrete and cement. Although the words are often used interchangeably, concrete and cement are different materials that share some commonalities.

Concrete is defined as a "hard, strong building material made by mixing a cementing material (such as portland cement) and a mineral aggregate, such as sand and gravel, with sufficient water to cause the cement to set and bind the entire mass."[3] Cement, the binding material, is "a powder of alumina, silica, lime, iron oxide, and magnesium oxide burned together in a kiln and finally pulverized and used as an ingredient of mortar and concrete."[4] Another word that defines trabajo rústico is ferro-cement, which is "any cement-based material . . . generally concrete . . . internally reinforced with some form of ferrous metal (iron, steel)."[5]

Following the development of portland cement in the mid-1800s, artisans have used various formulas of concrete and cement applied over a metal armament (usually rebar) wrapped with metal lath and a hand-applied surface texture.

Antecedents in History

Some of the major ingredients of concrete and cement ingredients have existed for millions of years. In Israel, 12 million years ago, "natural deposits were formed by reactions between limestone and oil shale that were produced by spontaneous combustion."[6] Around 6500 BC, Bedouins or Nabataean traders, who occupied areas in Syria and Jordan, built structures of material similar to concrete. They later developed "cement that hardens under water."[7] It has been discovered that around 5600 BC homes were constructed with concrete floors "along the Danube River in the area of the former country of Yugoslavia."[8] Beginning around 3000 BC, the Egyptians used a mixture of gypsum and lime, a primitive form of concrete, as a mortar for setting the mud and straw bricks on the surface of the pyramids. The Chinese used glutinous, sticky rice as a key ingredient in the mortar for their bamboo boats and the Great Wall.[9] In 700 BC, the Nabataean traders heated material in kilns used to fire their pottery and produced mortar to coat the floors and walls in their rock houses and waterproof their underground cisterns. Their ability to conserve water helped them survive in desert conditions.[10]

By 600 BC, the Greeks discovered a "natural pozzolana . . . that developed hydraulic properties when mixed with lime," but were not as successful as the Romans, whose temples, aqueducts, and roads have endured for centuries.[11]

Mayan settlements in Mexico (particularly those situated in the Petén-Yucatan platform) possessed large deposits of limestone from which they built magnificent temples and pyramids. The Mamon culture (600-400 BC) crafted a powder for plaster in a very complicated process. First, they chipped the limestone and layered it with wood.[12] After inserting a cylinder or pipe up the middle, the stack of limestone and wood was ignited and burned, producing a powder. By combining the powder with water,[13] the Chicanel (300 BC-150 AD)[14] used the mixture in their elaborate architectural detailing to plaster the outside of their buildings, apply a layer to floors, and create sculptures.[15]

Recent research in southern Italy has revealed that the concrete used in Rome and southern Italy was made of lime and volcanic rock. This mortar, known as *pozzolana*, was mixed with seawater which "hydrated the lime and reacted with the ash

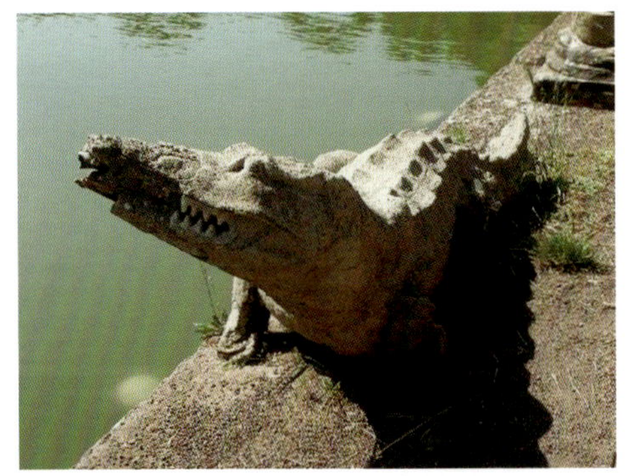

Artisan unknown. Tivoli, Italy. Hadrian's Villa crocodile. Photo by Mary Anne Sullivan, Bluffton University.

to cement everything together."[16] Researchers have concluded that this formula for Roman concrete was exceptionally strong and could replace the use of portland cement for present day construction.[17] The Romans also developed *harena fossicia* cement "made from naturally reactive volcanic sand" for their land structures that required more durability. Both mortars "added animal fat, milk, and blood." Romans also used two "artificial pozzolana-calcined kaolinitic clay and calcined volcanic stones."[18]

Although statuary in Greek and Roman gardens and public sites was primarily made of marble and bronze, an archeological investigation in 2015 revealed a wall fresco that was buried thirty-nine meters deep when Mount Vesuvius erupted in 79 AD. About forty miles away from this eruption, one wall of a wealthy Roman's villa near Naples was decorated in stucco with a scene of flying dolphins and winged cherubs riding horse-like animals. It is evident that the Romans knew the components of stucco, which is similar to pozzolana and was "usually composed of cement, sand, and hydrated lime mixed with water and laid on wet."[19]

Ancient Gardens

British archeologist, Maureen Carroll, author of the most complete story of ancient gardens, related that archeological excavations in Greece and Italy in recent years have revealed more about ancient gardens than previous knowledge found in "literary and archival sources."[20] Archeologists have found Egyptian wall reliefs that depict gardens: Some appear utilitarian, landscaped with food items and trees; others served as pleasure gardens for the wealthy. Temple gardens were landscaped with trees, many with pools. Funerary temple gardens, as exemplified by the garden of Queen Hatshepsut, were planted with imported trees. Embellishments included peristyles with supporting columns, but there is little evidence of decorative statuary, although some containers for plants were evident.[21]

According to some historical sources, Greek agoras (large public spaces), surrounded by colonnades housing shops, were planted with trees and decorated with statues, altars, and fountains.[22] Hellenistic period houses were spaced close together with enclosed courtyards paved with mosaic floors.[23]

Romans imitated many Greek artworks for garden decoration as exemplified by the pool in the Canopus of Hadrian's Villa in Tivoli, which is surrounded by sculpture of heroes and features a crocodile at the edge. Garden paintings depicting

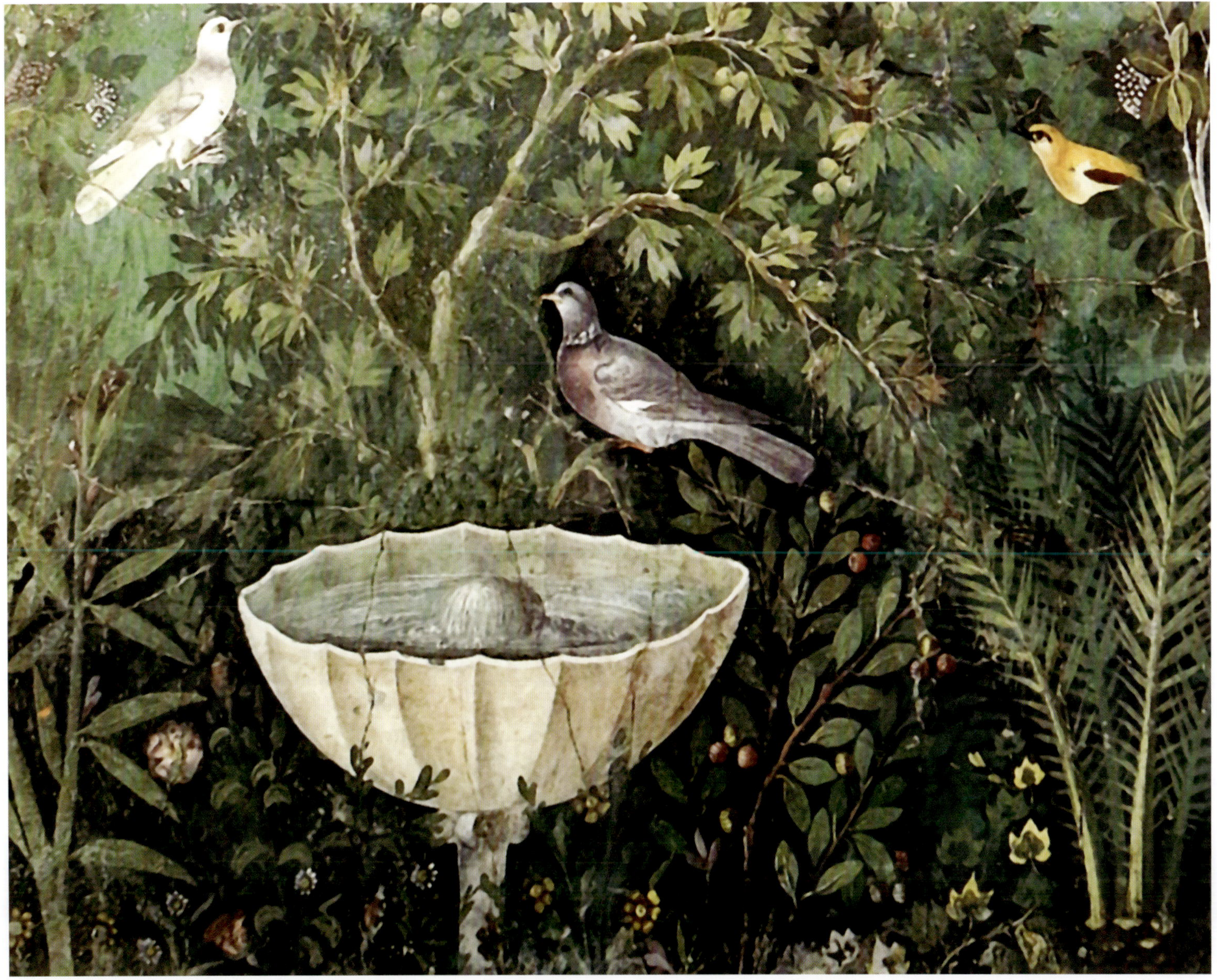

sculpture, fountains, plants, and pillars called herms are found on the walls of the interior and exterior of some Roman houses. The painting of the marble birdbath on a wall in a room in the Casa del Bracciale d'Oro in Pompeii and the crocodile at Hadrian's Villa in Tivoli are similar to designs later executed by Rodríguez and his followers.

Artisan unknown. Pompeii, Italy. Detail, House of the Golden Bracelet, 1st century. Permission of Samuel Magal, Sites and Photos Ltd., Bridgeman Images.

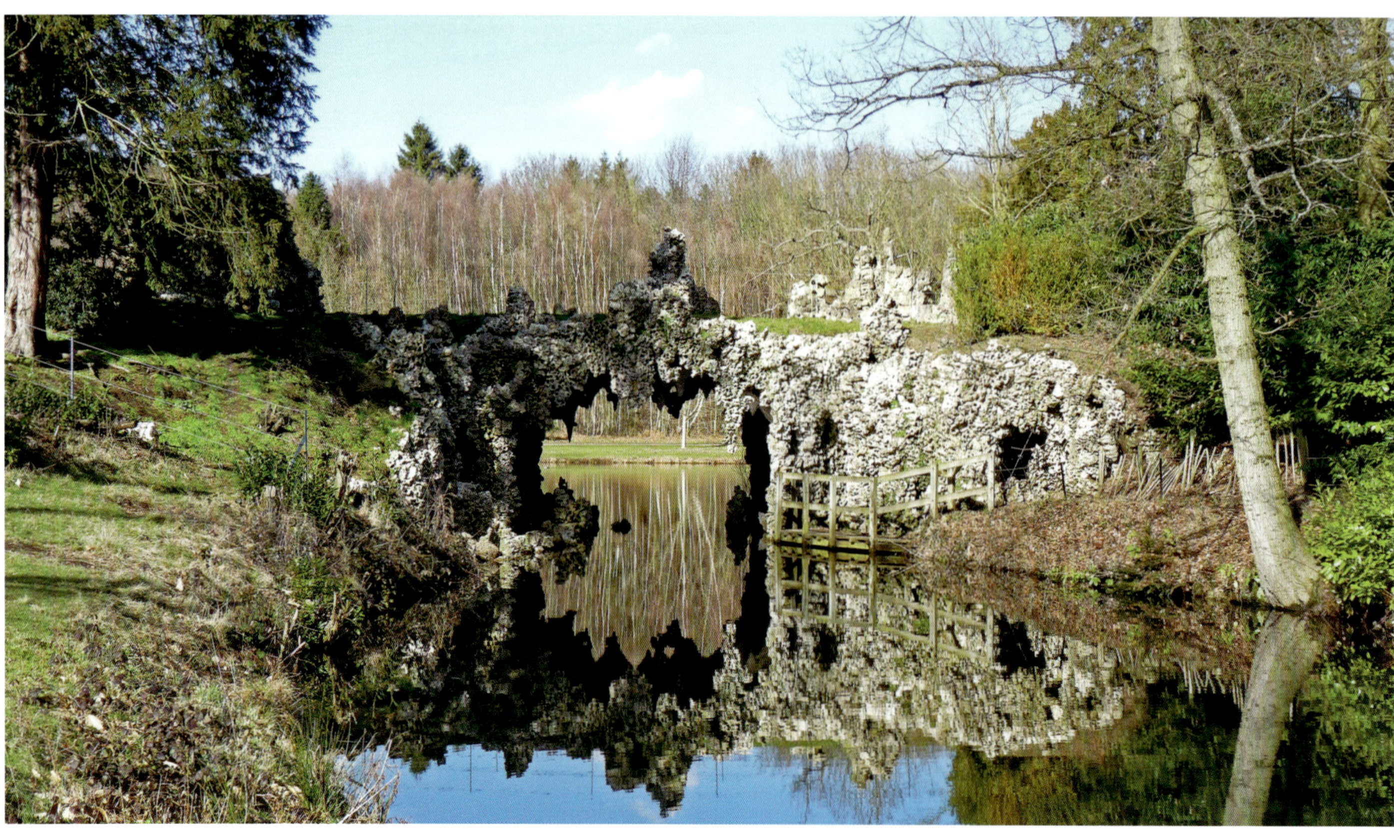

Joseph Lane. Painshill Park, U.K. Bridge and grotto. Photo by Geoff Scotton, Painshill Park Trust Ltd.

"After the fall of the Roman Empire (400 AD to 476 AD)," the methods for making pozzolana cement were lost.[24] Manuscripts written in 1414 mentioning the techniques used by the Romans aroused interest in using concrete for building, but it would be three hundred years before anyone would rediscover how to make concrete.[25]

Garden Design in England and France

Several factors influenced garden design beginning in the 1700s. Trade with China had begun that generated interest in travel books illustrating Chinese gardens, and there was a renewed interest in the Gothic period. Travel by wealthy young noblemen educated in the classics facilitated the spread of styles in England and France. According to Sarah Rutherford, young English noblemen who traveled to Italy returned home "full of enthusiasm for an idealized past and were keen to evoke it and their own properties," involving both the architecture of Andrea Palladio and the landscape. They were also influenced by the peaceful rural landscape paintings of Claude Lorraine, Nicolas Poussin, and Salvador Rosa's depictions of "rough, wild landscapes of witches, banditti, mountains and forests."[26]

English architect and landscape designer, Lancelot "Capability" Brown, is credited with "more than 250 sites across the UK."[27] He continued the trend begun by his father-in-law, William Kent, and others, replacing more formal geometric landscapes with sweeping vistas and "scenes focused on Palladian temples, classical monuments, and bridges."[28] The Chinese influence appeared in the reproduction of pagodas. Also featured were contrived ruins of buildings or Gothic-style structures.

Brown's style was defined as *picturesque*: "It was said . . . so closely did he copy nature 'that his works will be mistaken.'"[29] Often, he designed the grounds around an existing manor house, resulting in two distinct areas: parkland and a pleasure garden. The two areas were separated by a ha-ha, a man-made feature introduced earlier by William Kent, that substituted for walls or fences. The ha-ha "defined the English Landscape Garden," and Brown was a master of its use which "came from the defensive sunken fortifications used in wars of the previous century, adapted to keep out sheep and cattle as the 'enemy.'"[30] Retaining walls of stone or brick built on the side of the pleasure ground were invisible. It was possible to view the park

Artisan unknown. Painshill Park, U.K. Engraving from Thomas Whately's book, Observations on Modern Gardening. *Photo reprinted by permission of Boydell & Brewer Ltd.*

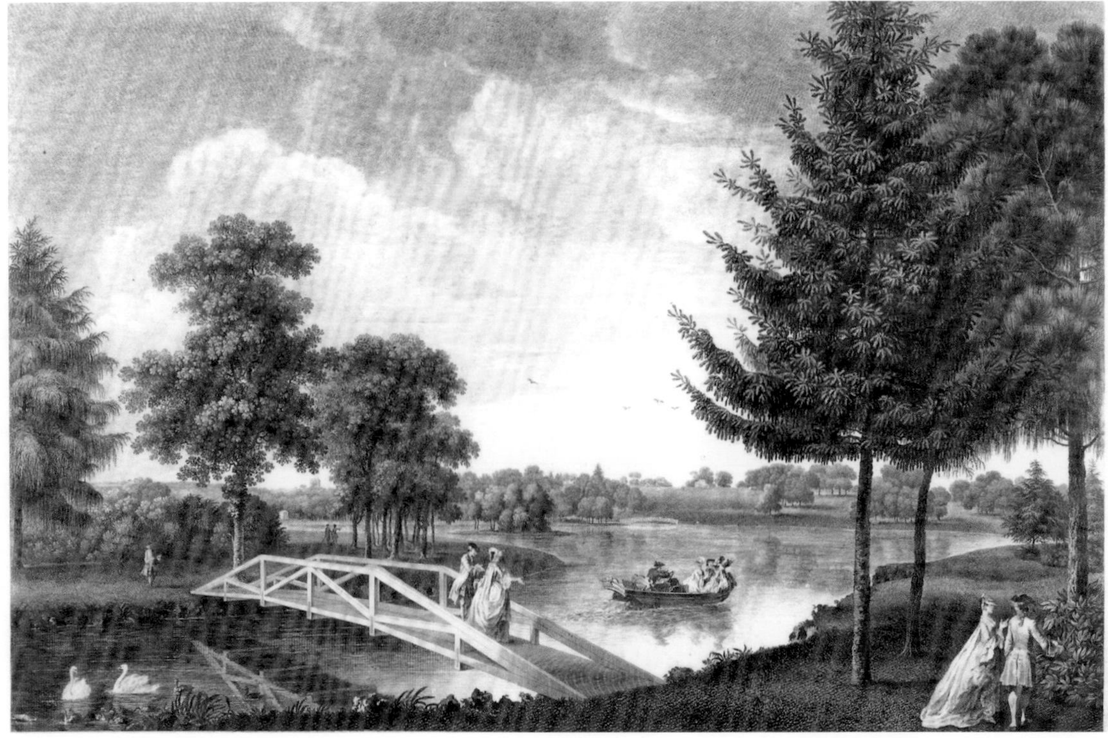

over a ditch. The pleasure gardens occasionally included whimsical structures---grottos, animal and bird menageries, and sculptural pieces usually to the taste of the landowner (more often Greek or Roman).[31] Landowner Charles Hamilton of Painshill, an example of the landscape park, engaged a famous grotto maker, Joseph Lane, to create a striking grotto in 1760.[32]

A former Brown foreman, Thomas Wright, started out on his own, designing smaller gardens in contrast to Brown's sweeping vistas. Wright's gardens can be classified as rococo not only by their smaller size, but also by the inclusion of artifacts that were "often ephemeral, rapidly constructed and relatively inexpensive."[33] He built grottoes and hermitages made of tree-trunks and branches, sometimes occupied by resident hermits hired to entertain visitors.

The influence of the English garden style in France, where LeNôtre's Versailles and Vaux le Vicomte's formal designs required vast amounts of maintenance, can be partially attributed to Thomas Whatley's *Observations on Modern Gardening,* a 1770 English publication, later translated into French. As a member of Parliament and Secretary of the Treasury, Whately was known for his political life but also possessed an interest in gardens. In his introduction to the 2016 reissue of Whately's book, Michael Symes wrote that his

> ideal gardens are firmly based on Whig notions of property and freedom—freedom, that is, to follow nature unconstrained by the geometry associated principally with France, where the formal garden was seen as representing the tyranny and absolutism of the monarchy.[34]

Instead of writing a how-to book, Whately described gardens of the period, not in guide-book style, but with descriptions of various elements in these gardens, such as bridges, cascades, lakes, rocks, trees, and shrubs.

The element of whimsy (realized as follies) in French gardens, illustrated by Marie Antoinette's bucolic Petite Trianon at Versailles, was evidence of early interest in the rustic style. Later follies influenced by the English tradition included Baron Berlinger's grotto, built in a fake mountain with a salon for bathing and storage for ice, and the hermitage of rock and straw built by the Marquis de Girardin.[35] Those two are non-extant examples, but Parc Monceau in Paris, originally designed in 1773 "as an elaborate entertainment facility" by Louis Carrogis Carmontelle for the duc de Chartres, possesses some remnants of his fantasy. It was the modern theme

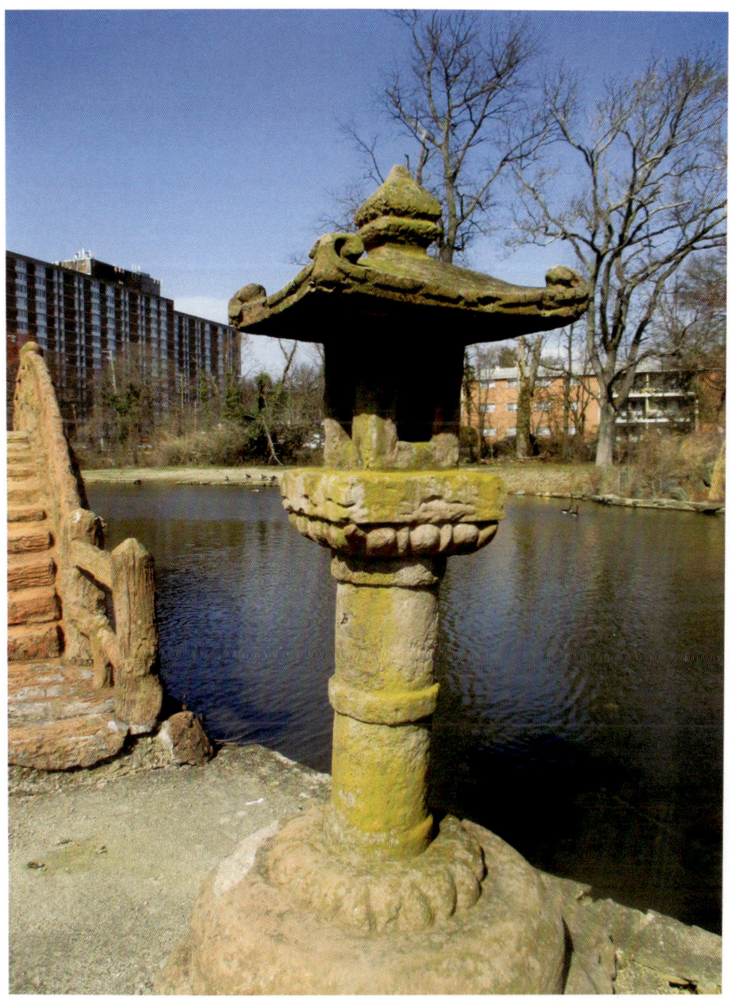

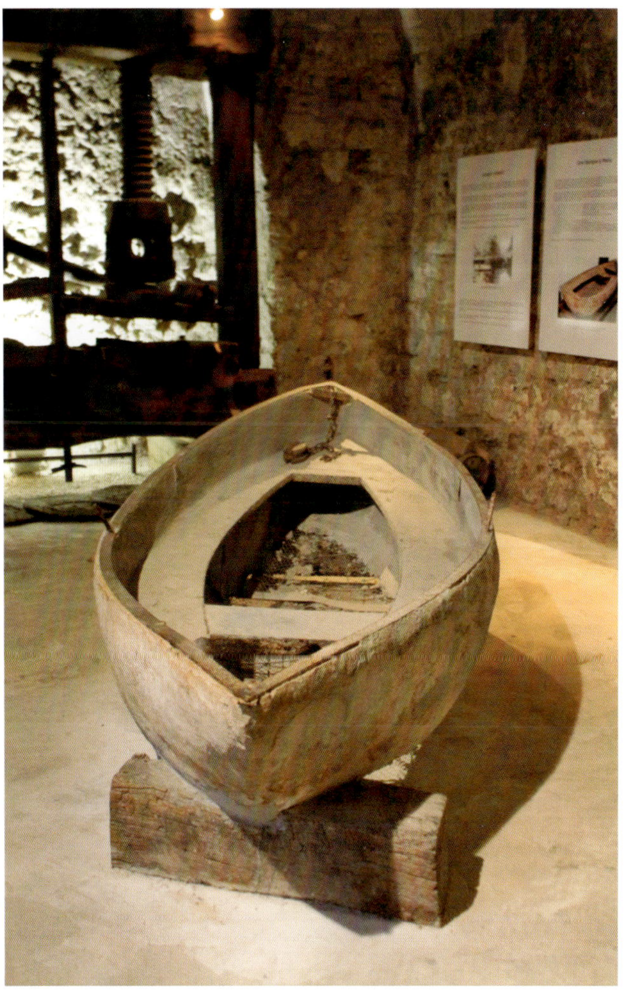

park of its day and original follies remaining include a pyramid, a lake surrounded by a Roman colonnade, and a Japanese stone lantern.[36] It is interesting to note that in 1936 Dionicio Rodríguez included a similar lantern at Cedar Hill Cemetery in Suitland, Maryland.

John Beardsley wrote that the transition to the less formal style of the English continued into the early 1800s as evidenced by pattern books printed in England and in Europe providing instructions on how to build rustic structures, including "rude wooden shelters, log and rock bridges, and naturalistic grottoes made from stone and tree roots."[37]

Above left: *Artisan unknown. Suitland, MD. Cedar Hill Cemetery. Photo by Kent Rush.*

Above: *Joseph Lambot. Brignoles, France. Musée des Comtes de Provence. Boat, ca. 1850-1856. Photo courtesy of Musée des Comtes de Provence.*

11

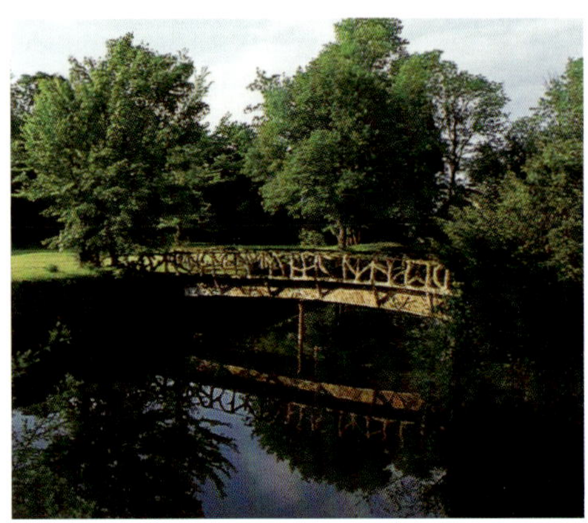

Joseph Monier. Chazelet, France. Bridge at Château de Chazelet. Photo by ©Michel Racine.

Rediscovery of Portland Cement

It was not until 1793 that Englishman John Smeaton rediscovered how to make hydraulic cement that hardened in water.[38] Several individuals were later responsible for developing portland cement, which became one of the world's most important manufactured materials.

In 1817, French engineer Louis Vicat received a commission to build the Souillac Bridge spanning the Dordogne River. He invented, but did not patent, his formula for artificial cement. He heated crushed limestone mixed with clay in a furnace, ground it into a powder, and mixed it with water, thereby creating a material similar to Portland stone and enabling him to build his bridge that would set "after being submerged in water for several days." Vicat's bridge "was the first bridge to be built using artificial cement."[39]

In 1824, Englishman Joseph Aspdin developed a cement by heating ground chalk and clay to high temperatures in a kiln. The resulting product was called "Portland" cement, as it had a texture similar to that of limestone used for building in Portland, England.[40]

Development of Inexpensive Steel

The combination of steel in the form of rods and mesh and concrete are important components of trabajo rústico that creates shapes imitating nature; however, the two basic materials were not combined until the mid-1800s. Englishman William Wilkinson and four Frenchmen, Jean Louis Lambot, Francois Coignet, Joseph Monier, and Francois Hennebique, were among the first to use the technique that paved the way for new artistic works and significantly changed construction methods. Wilkinson, a plasterer, built a two-story servants' cottage in 1854, "reinforcing the concrete floor and roof using iron bars and wire rope."[41] Lambot used "iron bars and wire mesh" to reinforce concrete boats in the 1850s, and in 1856, he applied for a patent in France and Belgium. Several of his boats actually floated.[42]

Also in 1856, Francois Coignet patented his method of reinforcing concrete with metal. He built the first iron reinforced concrete house (a four-story structure), still extant and declared a historical monument in 1998.[43] He had an exhibit at the Paris Exposition Universelle in 1867, the same year as Monier. Coignet's other projects included the lighthouse at Port Said, Egypt, and the high walls at the Trocadéro and Passy cemeteries in Paris.[44]

Frenchman Joseph Monier is more widely known as the inventor of ferro-cement. Although he was not the first to combine steel and concrete, he combined them "in such a way that the best qualities of each were brought into play." Concrete is easy to shape and has "compressive strength," but is "weak in tensile or pulling strength." With the reinforcement of steel bars, concrete's strength increased.[45] Although Monier and others developed both ferro-cement and reinforced concrete technologies, reinforced concrete is a process whereby the concrete is poured *into* a form as opposed to ferro-cement when it is applied *onto* a form.

Monier, a gardener, was responsible for the Orangery at the Tuileries Gardens near the Louvre in 1846. In 1850, to make more durable pots to replace ceramic ones for the orange trees that had to be moved to greenhouses in the winter, he combined steel and concrete. He patented his work in 1867 and exhibited at the 1867 Paris Exposition Universelle. Subsequently, he obtained more patents for "iron reinforced cement pipes and basis (1868); iron-reinforced cement panels for building facades (1869), bridges made of iron-reinforced cement (1873); reinforced concrete beams (1878)."[46] Monier designed the first iron-reinforced *béton armé* bridge at the Château de Chazelet.[47]

François Hennebique saw Monier's reinforced tubs at the 1867 Paris Exposition and was inspired to apply the technique to methods of construction. In 1879, he developed floor slabs of reinforced concrete and by 1892, he patented a system of utilizing "beams of concrete reinforced with stirrups and longitudinal bars designed to resist the tensile forces against where original concrete was weak."[48] He built his home of concrete with hanging gardens and an irrigation system[49] and is credited with building 1,200 concrete structures worldwide reinforced with steel.

The systems developed by Monier and Hennebique differed and descriptions of both techniques were published in magazines. Monier's patent was purchased by a German company, Wayne and Fretag, active in Austria, Germany, and Central Europe, and it published 10,000 copies of the *Monier Brochure*. Hennebique's marketing of 6,000 to 10,000 copies of *Le Béton Armé* extended to France and elsewhere in Europe, Buenos Aires, Indochina, and New York. Although many companies were competing in the market at this period, the two dominated "the market of reinforced concrete for the first decade of the twentieth century."[50]

Prior to 1856, steel was expensive and difficult to manufacture. Mass production of steel was possible after Sir Henry Bessemer invented a converter that led to the production of steel from pig iron (which is not as malleable as steel), and in 1876, he added limestone to iron ore which led to the production of cheap steel.

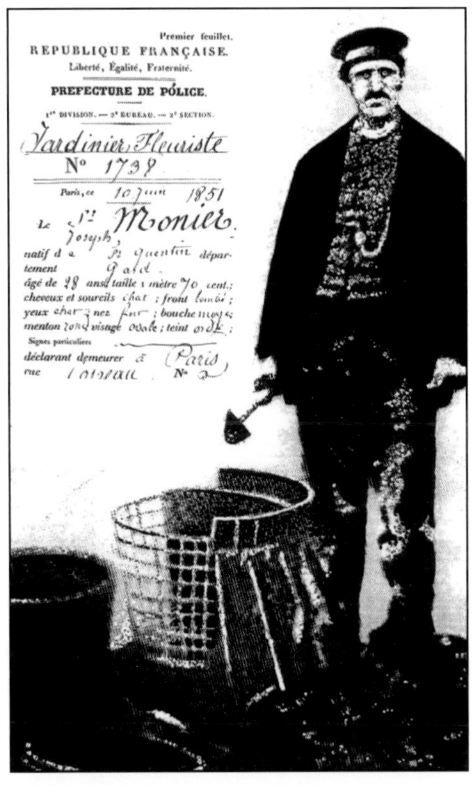

Artisan unknown. Paris, France. Joseph Monier's Permit #1738 as landscaper, florist, plant expert, dated June 10, 1851. Courtesy of Jacques Degenne.

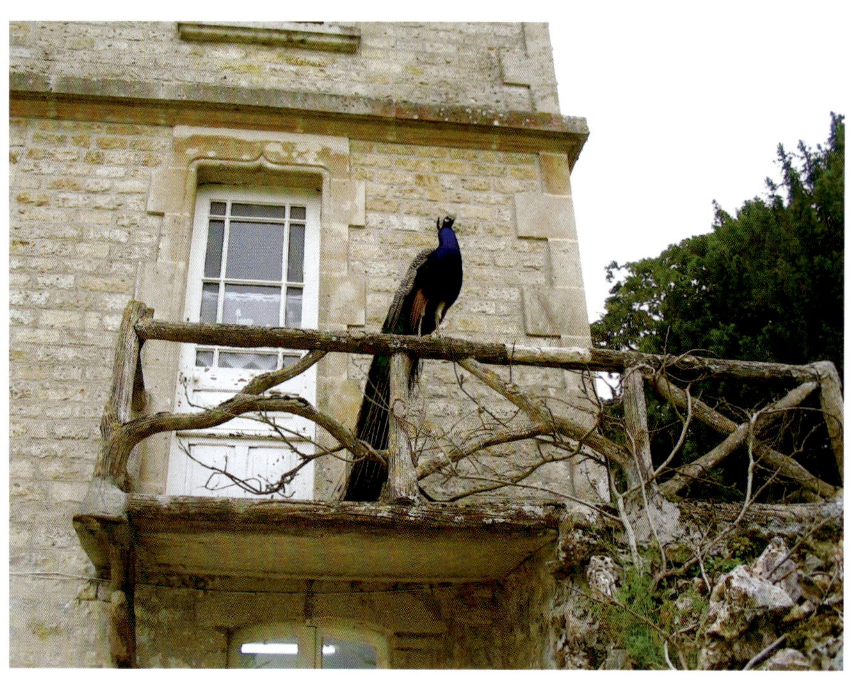

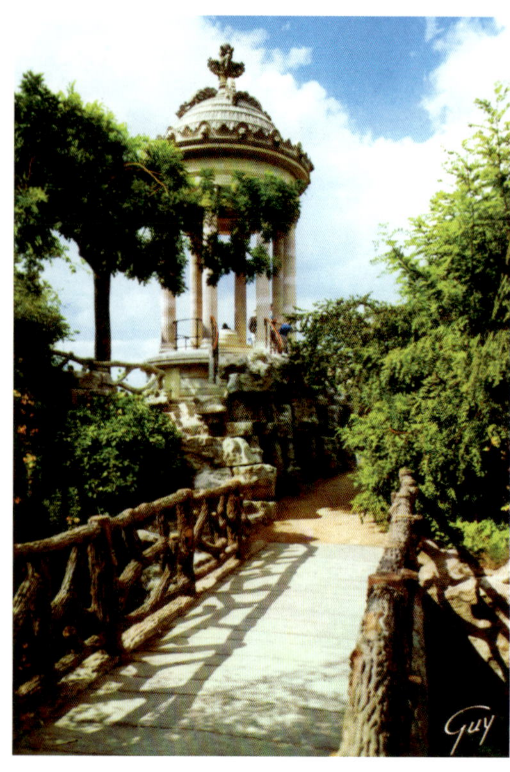

Above: *Artisan unknown. Normandy, France. Balcony railings. Photo by Barbara Whitehead.*

Above right: *Artisan unknown. Paris, France. Parc des Buttes-Chaumont. Archival postcard. Collection of Kent Rush.*

Bessemer held 100 patents. Two additional processes produced a much less expensive steel. English inventor Robert Mushet added manganese, iron, and carbon (known as spiegel); and Sidney Gilchrist Thomas, a Welshman, added limestone in 1876. After these processes were added, steel prices fell dramatically, causing a huge reduction in the production of iron for many uses.[51]

A reinforced concrete home was built by William Ward, an electrical engineer in Port Chester, New York, in 1875. Because a relative was afraid of fire, it was built out of concrete that Ward created to appear as a stone façade.[52]

The development of portland cement and its use as a component along with aggregate and inexpensive steel for construction projects resulted in the filing of many patents. In 2021, reinforced concrete using portland cement continues to be an important material for "buildings, bridges, floors, pavement, and pre-cast concrete products."[53]

Although it is difficult to know exactly when construction methods evolved into smaller scaled projects, concrete artisans known as *rocailleurs* enjoyed great popularity in France for almost one hundred years. During the years 1840–1925,

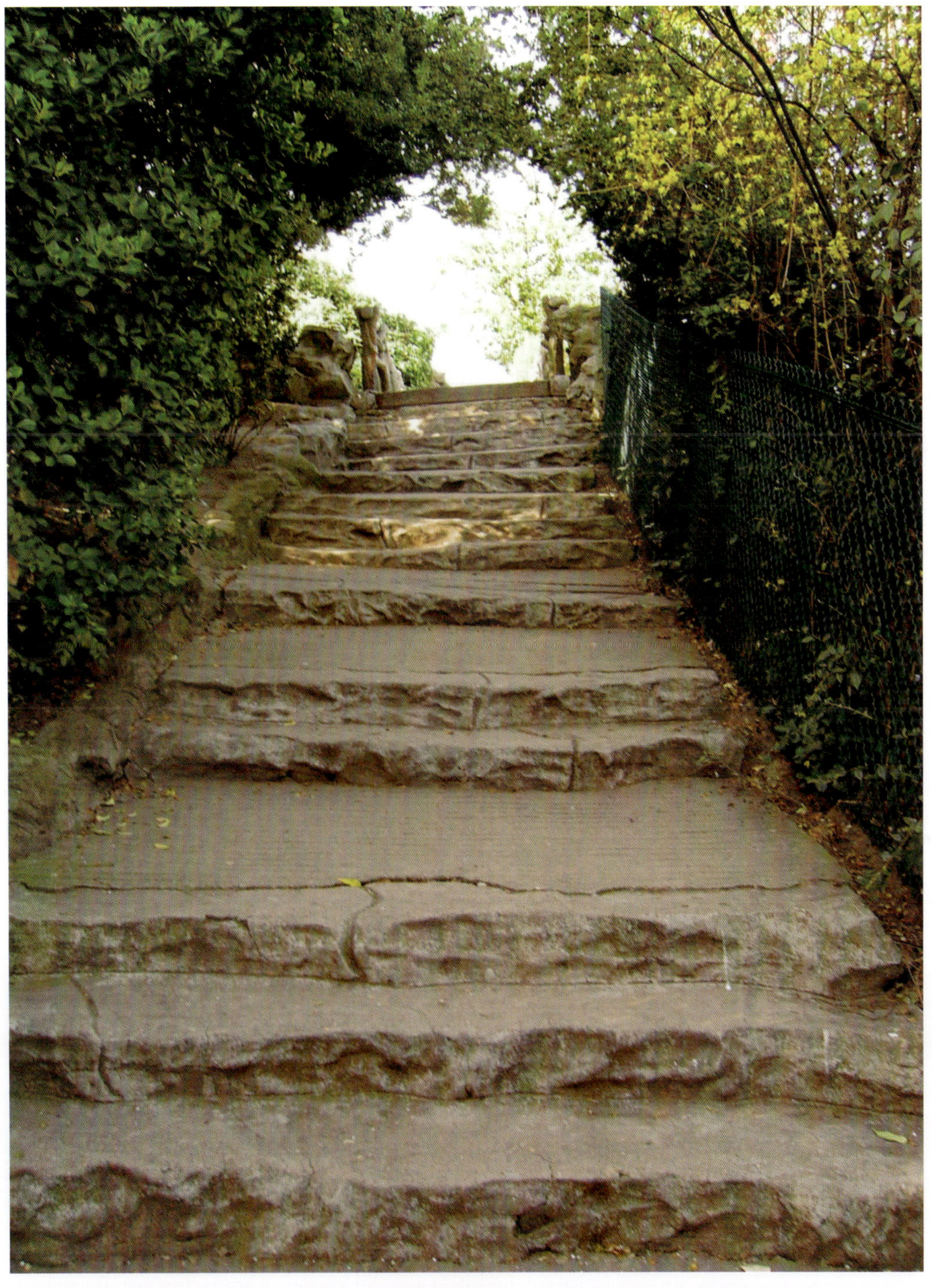

Jean-Charles Adolphe Alphand, engineer. Paris, France. Parc des Buttes-Chaumont. Steps. Photo by Ann E. Komara.

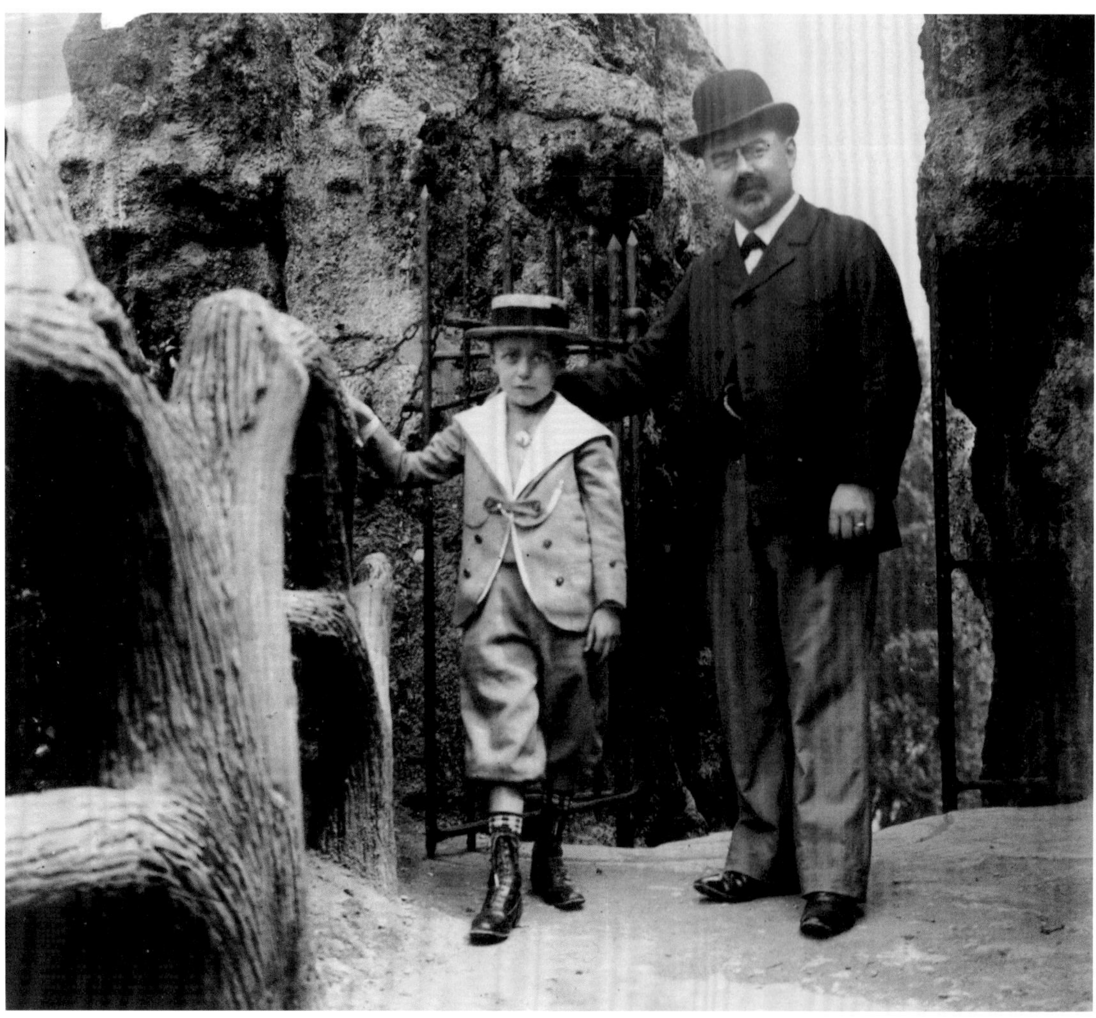

Michele Racine writes there were approximately one hundred *rocailleurs* and other concrete artisans working in Paris and in other areas of France.[54]

Important examples of the use of ferro-cement are found in the work of landscape architect Adolphe Alphand. A major park in Paris, Parc des Buttes-Chaumont, originally a lime quarry and later a dumping ground, was designed by Baron Haussmann and Alphand and developed during the years 1863-67. Gustave Eiffel designed the suspension bridge leading to the belvedere, and Gabrielle Davioud was the architect for the classical elements,[55] including the Temple of Venus (modeled after the Temple of Venus in Tivoli, Italy) which was added in 1869.

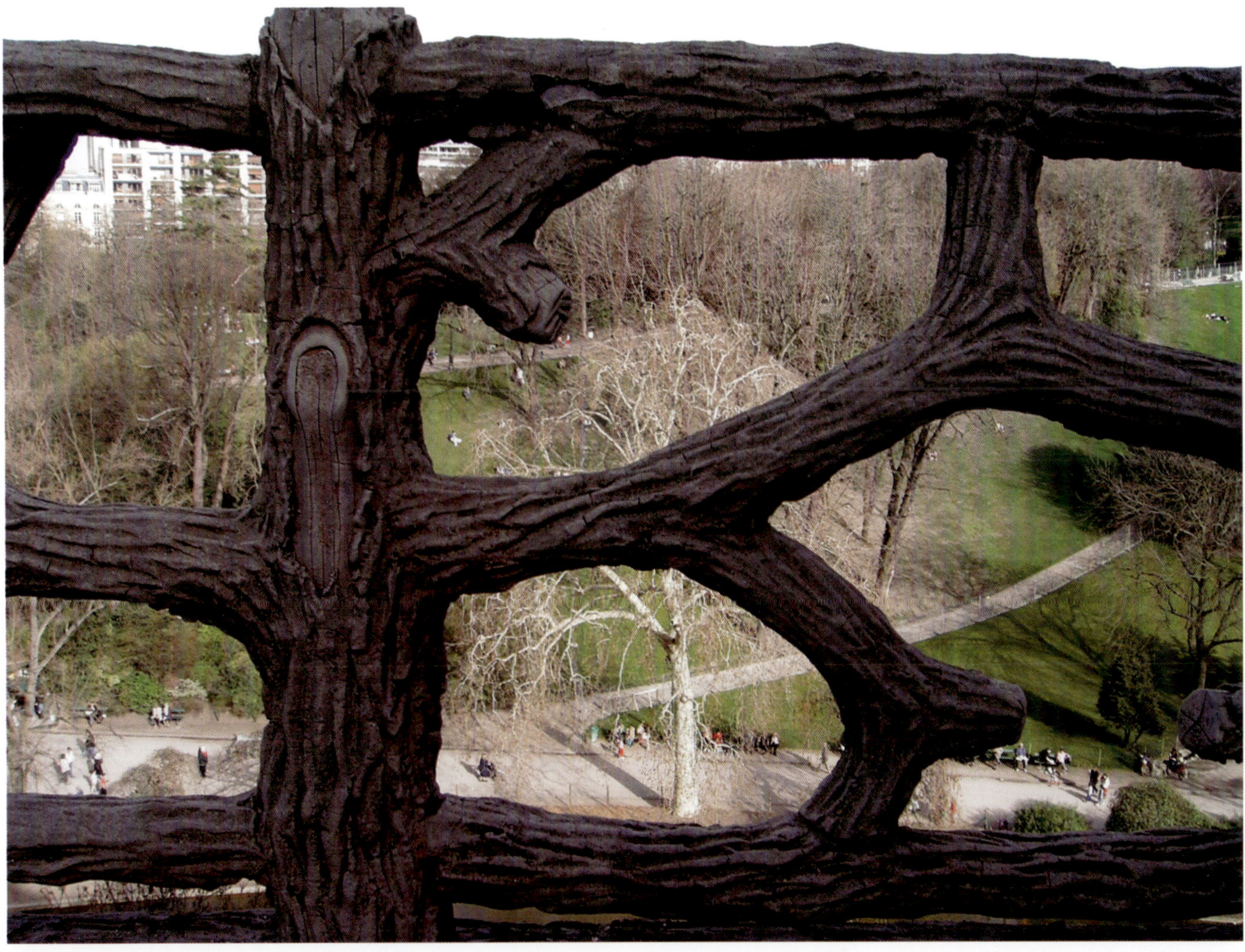

Jean-Charles Adolphe Alphand, engineer. Paris, France. Parc des Buttes-Chaumont. Railing detail. Photo by Ann E. Komara.

Ann Komara wrote that "the park demonstrated advances in landscape design through numerous innovations in construction and materials, particularly concrete." She stated that the park was "an engineered landscape," using three types of concrete *(béton)* application: "impervious lining for water rills and the lakebed, decoratively as stucco cement *(stuc ciment)* embellishments, and structurally as reinforced concrete *(béton armé)* for numerous features and design elements." She further noted that "Artisan Hilaire Muzard created many detailed artificial rockworks of *stuc ciment* to blend with natural areas of rock."[56] Komara concluded that many of these railing details were produced with a "repeat molding" technique, perhaps

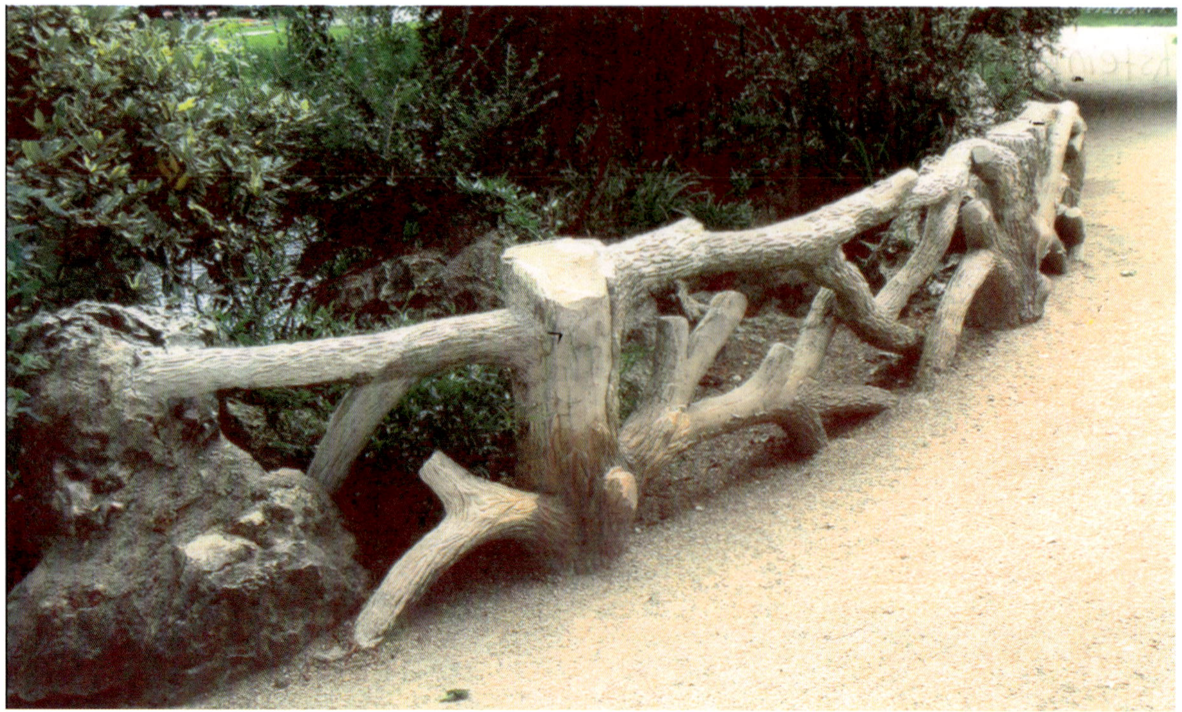

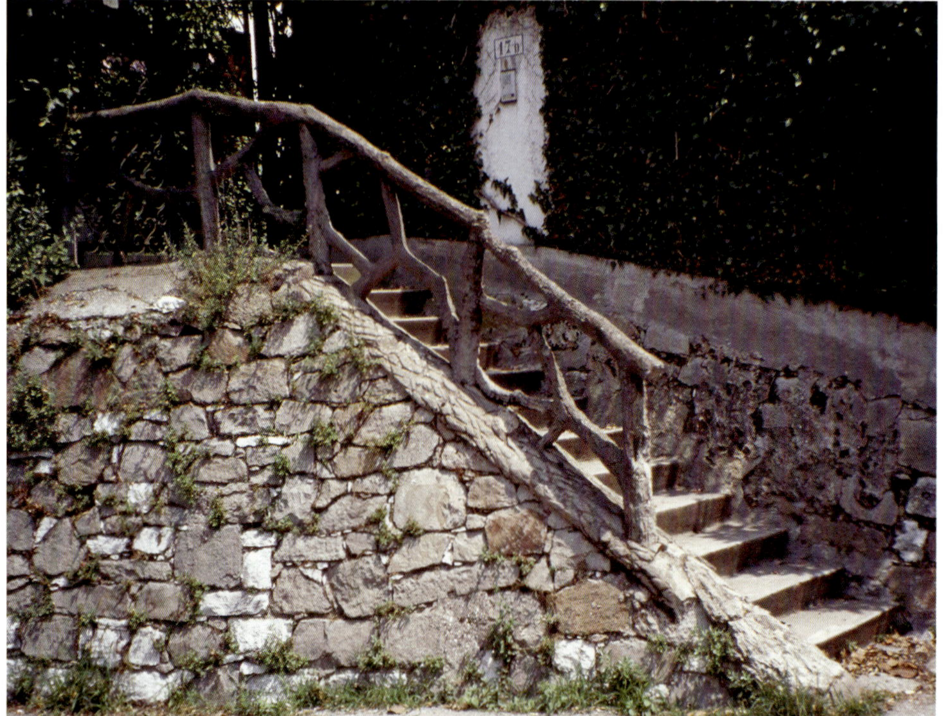

Above: *Artisan unknown. Dijon, France. Parc de l'Arquebuse. Photo by Nina Ekstein.*

Right: *Artisan unknown. Lido di Venezia, Italy. Handrails. Photo by Kent Rush.*

18

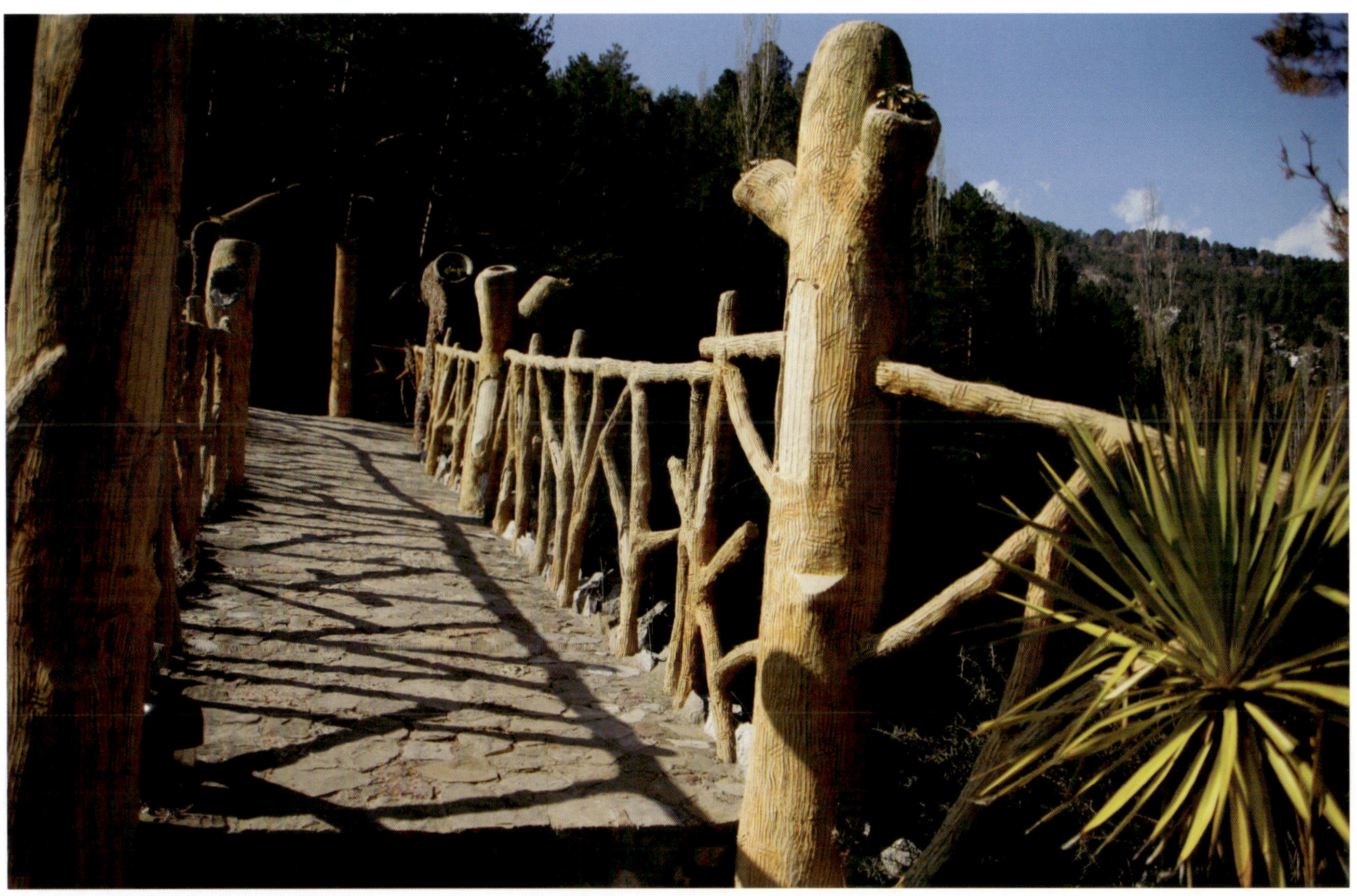

Antoni Gaudí. La Pobla de Lillet, Spain. Artigas Gardens. Photo by ©Miquel Tres.

in situ rather than in the factory. The difficulty in finding the joints between the molded parts shows the high caliber of technical craftsmanship-or artistry-employed in producing these rails.[57]

While rustic features and objects were made of wood in eighteenth century gardens, Alphand worked with the newly developed industrial technique using cast iron and portland cement to create picturesque elements. It is possible that Alphand was an early exponent of the use of the technique described by Englishman William Robinson, who, when writing about the parks and gardens of Paris in 1878, noted that the Parc des Buttes-Chaumont was "the boldest attempt at what is called the picturesque style that has been made in any Paris or London gardens."[58] To facilitate walking on the various levels of the park, five miles of paths were lined with handrails and stair risers of a simulated bark texture. Similar stair railings can

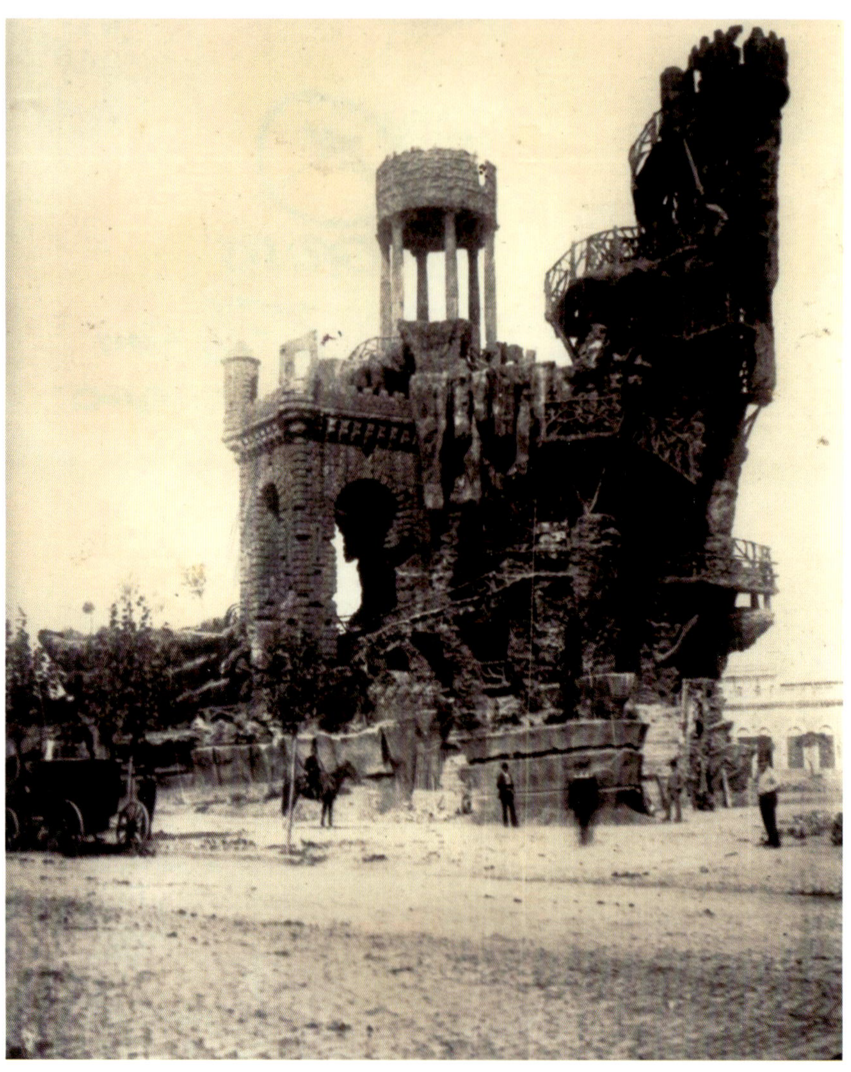

Eugenio Courtois. Buenos Aires, Argentina. Constitución Grotto, Plaza Constitución. Photo courtesy of Daniel Schávelson.

be seen throughout France and in almost all of Alphand's parks in Paris: Boulogne, Vincennes, Monceau, and Montsouris. These railings in the Parc des Buttes-Chaumont provide stylistic elements in one type of French garden that Elizabeth Barlow Rogers referred to as "like theatrical scenery, usually rustic in style."[59]

The spread of the genre throughout Europe is evidenced by works of artisans found in Italy and Spain. Antoni Gaudí is known for his large-scale works of concrete for many of his projects. He was commissioned to plan a landscaped park for the Artigas Garden at the textile factory in La Pobla de Lillet, which is filled with trabajo rústico bridges, handrails, planters, and seating.

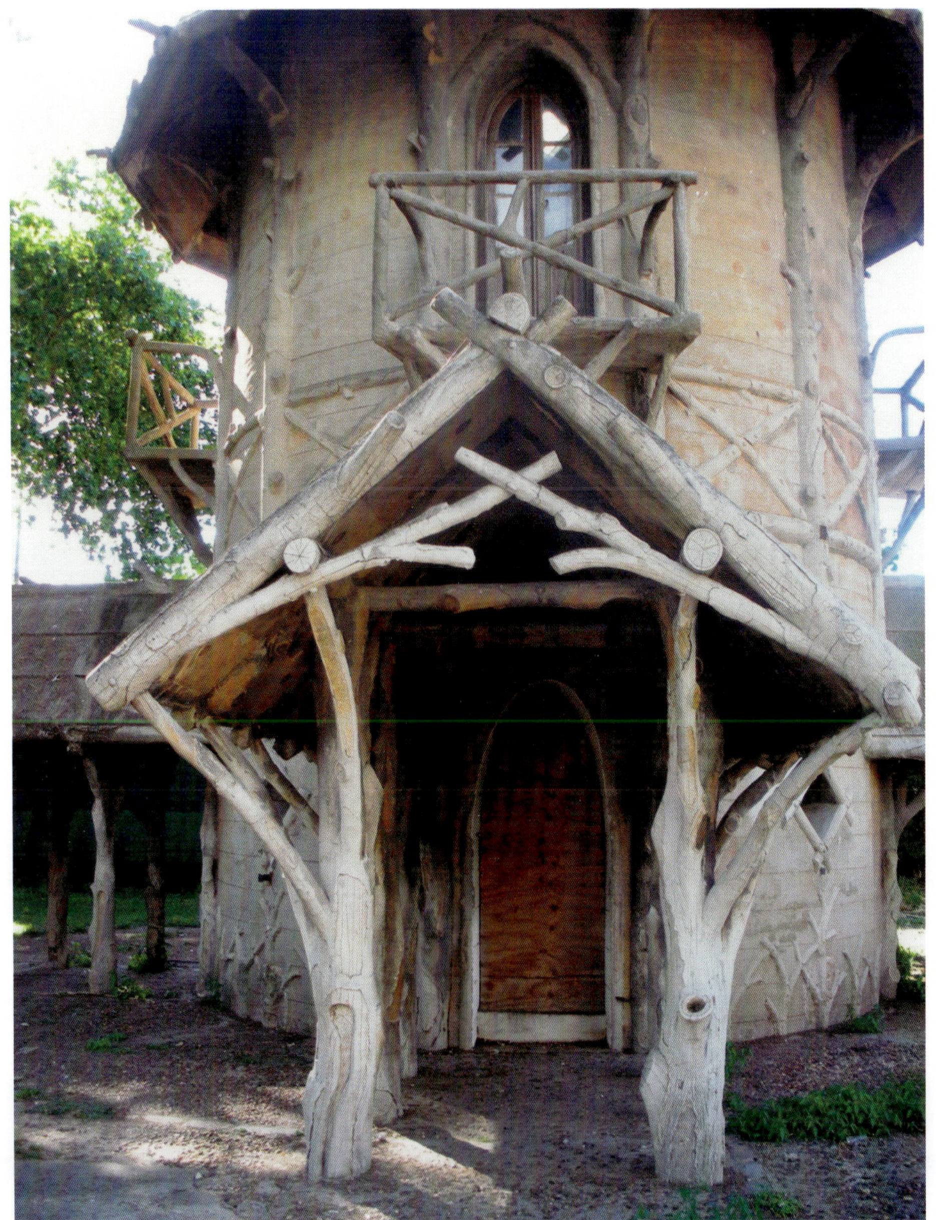

Artisan unknown. Buenos Aires, Argentina.
Zoological Gardens. Photo: Kathleen Trenchard.

Arrival of Trabajo Rústico in the Western Hemisphere

Beginning in the late 1800s, immigrants to Argentina from Germany, England, Italy, Spain, France, and other European countries outnumbered native Argentineans. The influx of French and Italians in Argentina contributed to the spread of trabajo rústico in the Americas. Development of the infrastructure and the installation of

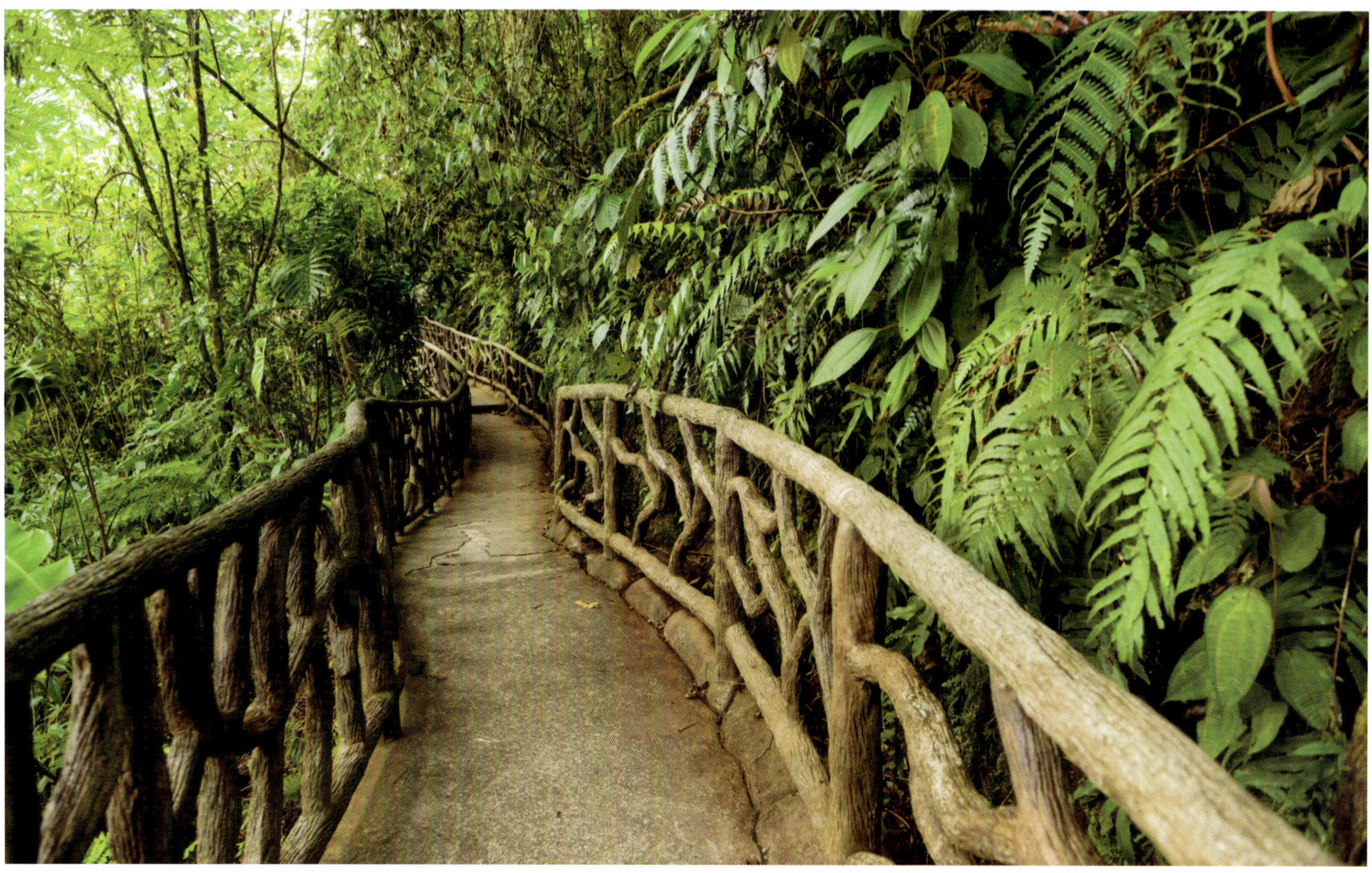

"running water and sanitation sources" by European technologists was accompanied by the building of plazas and parks.[60]

The models of Baron Haussmann of France strongly influenced French landscape designers Eugenio Courtois and Carlos Thays in their work in Argentina. Argentinean architects Daniel Schávelzon and Francisco Girelli wrote about the flourishing of the Parisian styles of landscaping art and architecture created by the "Generation of 1880," which lasted for thirty or forty years.[61] Large public projects in plazas and parks as well as private house facades and gardens exhibited examples of trabajo rústico.

In 1882, Courtois was commissioned to design the grotto of Retiro, a park that included a ruined castle with a lookout, a lake, a waterfall, an artificial mountain, trabajo rústico tree trunks, and concrete rocks. In 1886, Courtois was again commissioned to design the Constitución Grotto in Buenos Aires, with two towers topping an enormous cement structure and a winding staircase with trabajo rústico railings ascending to the top. It also included a bridge made of artificial logs which crossed over a small lake. The remarkable structure was demolished in 1914 when the French influence fell out of fashion.

Schávelzon's book, *El Árbol de Cememto: Arquitectura de Rocallas*, illustrates archival photos of work throughout Argentina and Latin America, including single objects and architectural embellishments.[62] Several buildings in the now closed Buenos Aires Zoological Gardens were designed by Domingo Selva in his early years.

Frenchman Carlos Thays arrived in Argentina in 1889. He was appointed Director of Parks and Walkways and designed the Botanical Gardens which adjoin the Zoological Gardens. Thays' influence is reflected where he incorporated trabajo rústico details in other areas of Argentina and work in Chile, Uruguay, and Brazil.[63]

Other Frenchmen had arrived earlier in Brazil, beginning around 1860–70. Among these early immigrants was Botanist Auguste François Marie Glaziou, who promoted the remodeling of gardens from the more geometric European style to a more natural style.[64] These new gardens were filled with imitations of "natural elements, such as rock, tree trunks, caves, and waterfalls which were described as . . . rustic works." Artisans who created these works were referred to as "rockers" and Frenchman Paul Villon, along with several others, advertised themselves as "rockers" in Buenos Aires newspapers.[65]

Another name given to these artisans in Brazil was *cascateiros*. Portuguese-born Francisco da Silva Reis, known as Chico Cascateiro, worked in the southern part of Brazil. His works "can easily be confused with natural elements."[66]

Beginning in the 1990s, Don Bernardo Picado constructed his trabajo rústico pieces including the walkway above one of the waterfalls in the La Paz Waterfall Gardens near Vara Blanca, Heredia, Costa Rica. Don Picado continues as the master builder for the gardens in 2021.

Recent projects by artisans in other countries include the work by architect/engineer Raimon Díaz Mariño, who was commissioned by the town of La Massana, Andorra, in 2002 to create a concrete sculpture of roots for a church wall in the center of the town.[67]

Rustic Influence in the United States

Early designs for rustic wooden structures for New York's Central Park designed by Calvert Vaux and Frederick Olmsted were published in Vaux's *Villas and Cottages:*

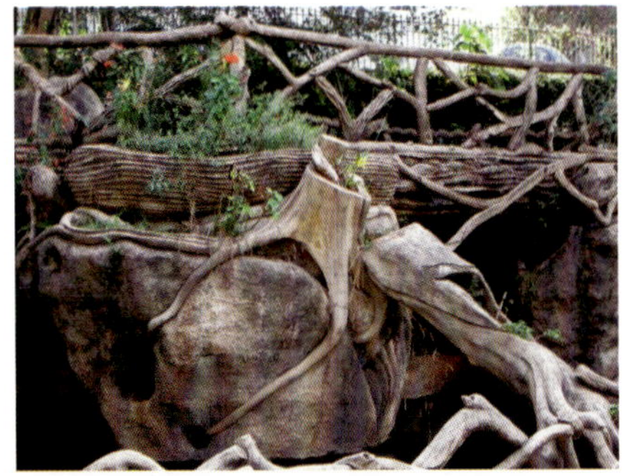

Fernando da Silva Reis. Minas Gerais, Brazil. Parque das Águas de Caxambu. Belvedere, artificial cave, small lake. Photo by Christiane Maria Magalhães.

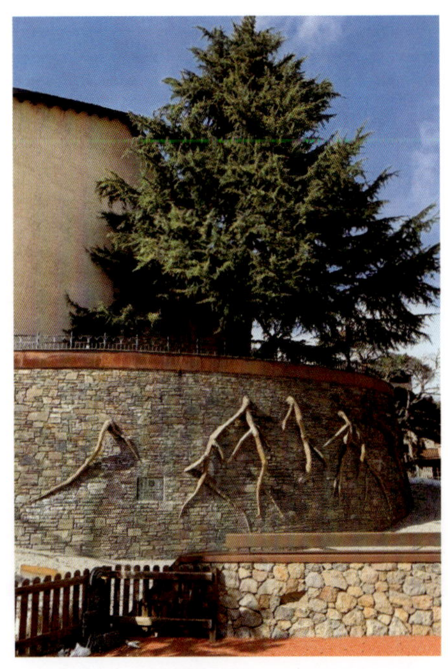

Raimon Díaz Mariño. La Massana, Andorra. Eglésia de Sant Iscle i Santa Victòria. Roots on garden wall. Photo by Adrienne Atwell Bogaerts.

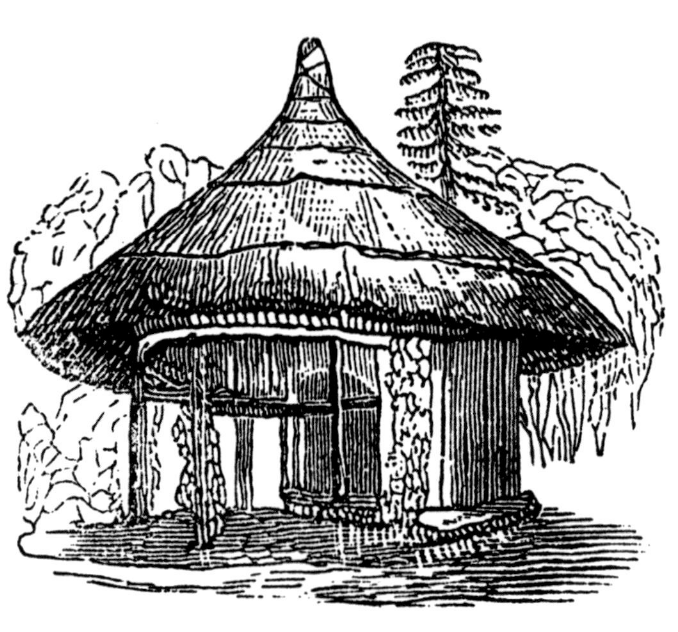

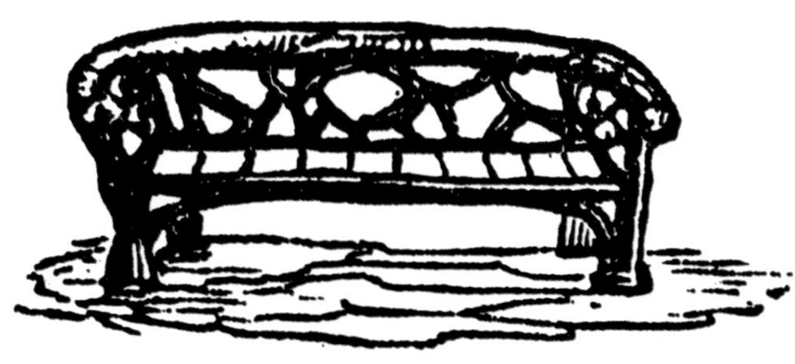

Above: *A.J. Downing.* Landscape Gardening and Rural Architecture, *1991. Permission of Dover Publications.*

Above right: *Woodward's* Architecture, Garden Landscaping and Rural Art No. 1-1867, *p.1.*

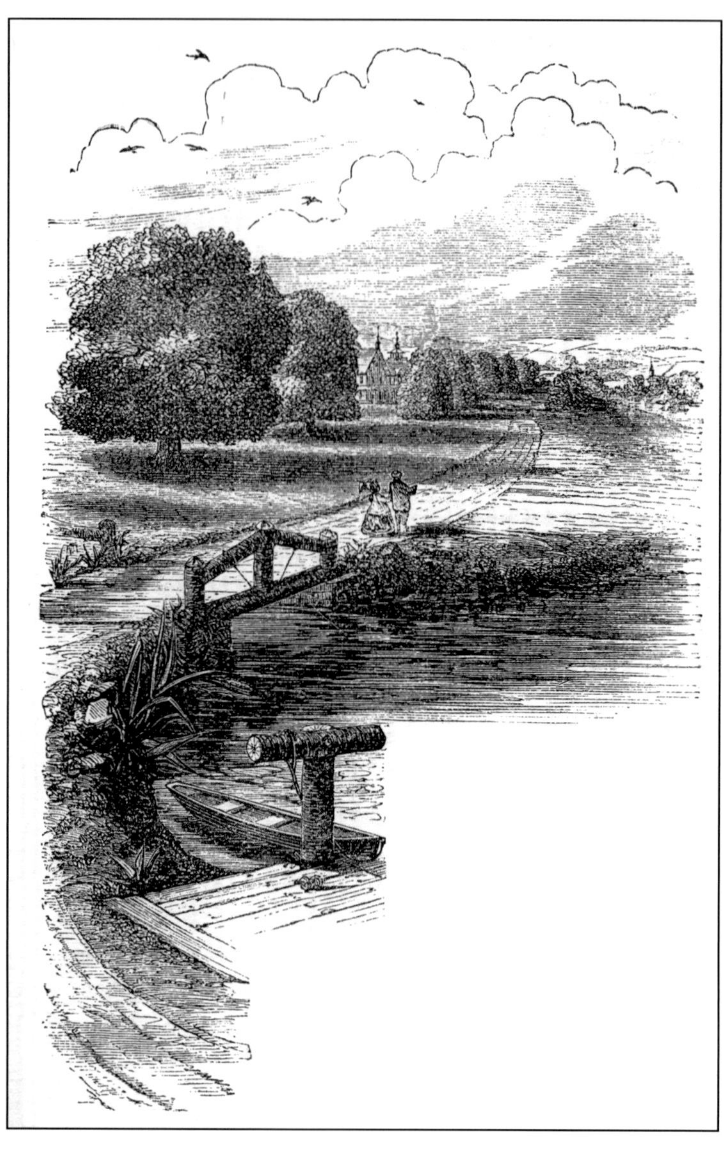

A *Series of Designs.* By the mid-1800s, naturalistic landscaping and the rustic influence in the United States were promoted by American landscape designer A. J. Downing in his 1840 book *Landscape Gardening and Rural Architecture.* In the chapter "Embellishments," Downing described and illustrated rustic seats, arbors, and summerhouses made of maple, larch, hazel, and white birch. George Woodward, landscape engineer, published drawings of wooden seats and a bridge in his *Architecture, Garden Landscaping, and Rural Art* in 1867, along with more than fifty

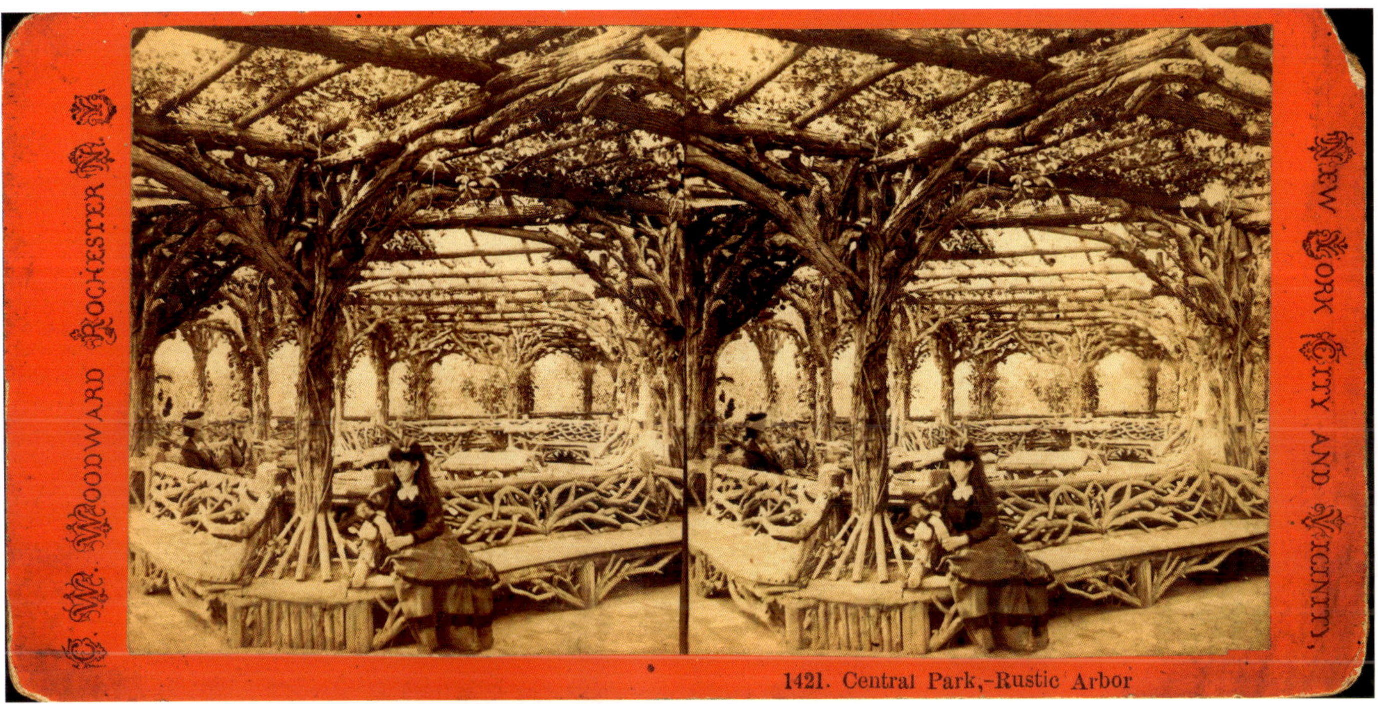

additional designs for plots of land, including cottages, barns, chicken coops, well-houses, a piggery, an icehouse, smoke houses, and a horse stable.[68]

Daniel Mack, rustic furniture maker and author, noted that wealthy New Yorkers, Duran, Morgan, and Vanderbilt, who visited Central Park and Prospect Park (both designed by Vaux and Olmsted) "carried these rustic furniture ideas with them to create their own rustic worlds at their great summer homes" in the Adirondack Mountains. Carpenters in the area made rustic Adirondack furniture: beds, tables, and chairs.[69] Mack also wrote that families in the Appalachian Mountains began building "fanciful rockers and other rustic pieces"; southern rural families made willow furniture; and hickory tree farms were planted in the Midwest to supply material for the furniture.[70] As an indication that rustic garden influence was not confined to any specific geographic area, Mack included an illustration in his book of a gazebo made of oak limbs in a private home in Asheville, North Carolina.

With this interest in rustic furniture, it is easy to understand the use of rustic furniture or objects as studio props by late nineteenth century portrait photographers. With the advent of cabinet cards in the 1880s, which had larger formats than earlier photographic portraits, there was a need to fill in open spaces in the photographs.

Calvert Vaux. New York Central Park Rustic Arbor. Stereoptic card of The Kinderberg. New York Public Library, the Miriam and Ira D. Wallach Division of Art, Prints and Photographs, Photography Collection. Photographers: J. W. and J. S. Moulton, ca. 1878. Photo of card from the Collection of Daniel Mack.

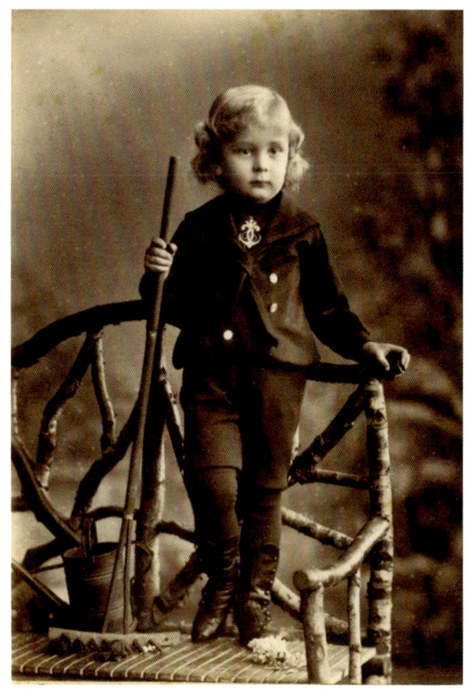

Above: *Artisan unknown. Child with rustic wooden furniture. Archival photo: Collection of Kent Rush.*

Right: *Artisan unknown. Asheville, NC. Summerhouse at Richmond Hills. Photo courtesy of Richmond Pearson Collection, Special Collections, Ramsey Library, University of North Carolina Asheville.*

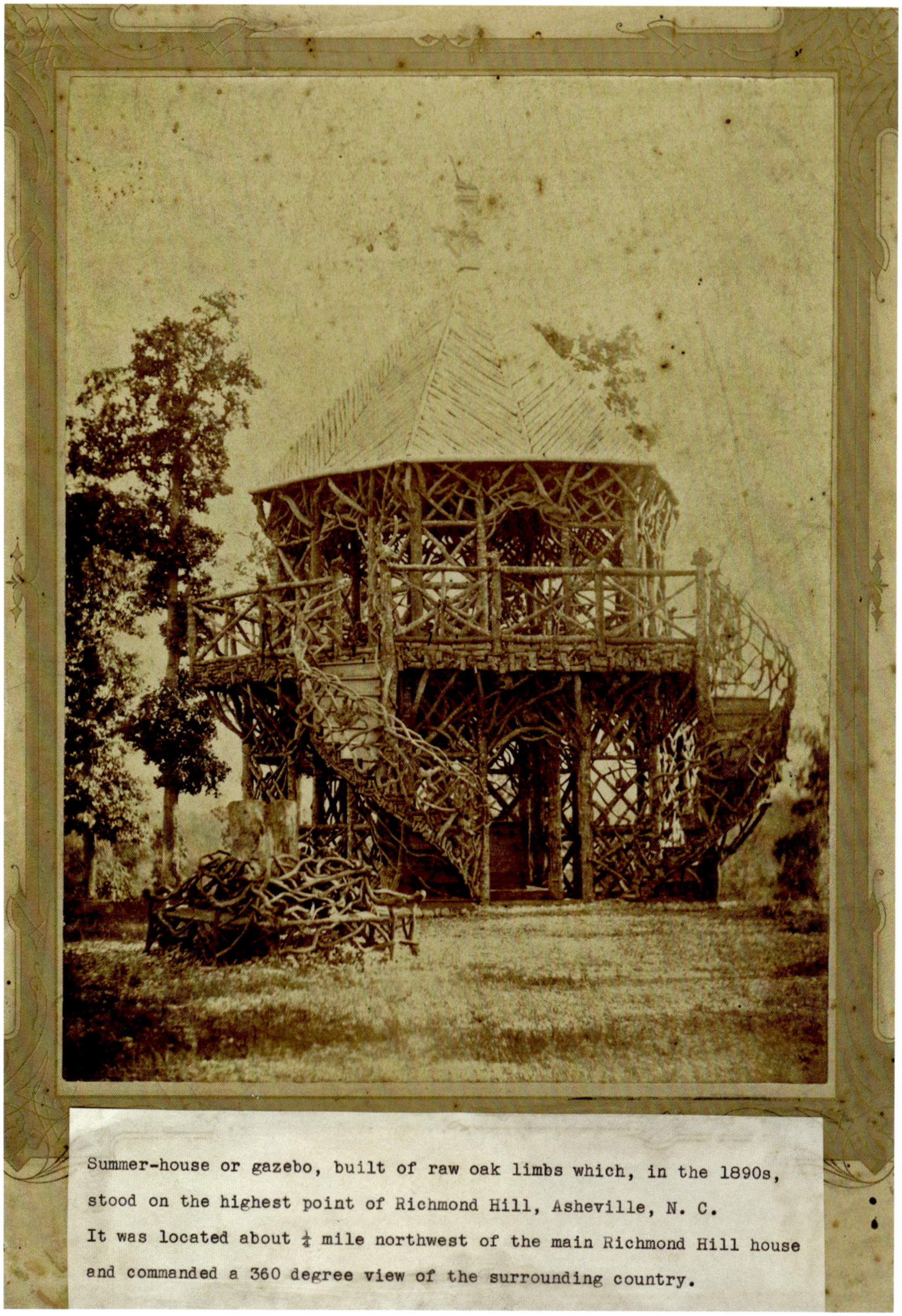

Summer-house or gazebo, built of raw oak limbs which, in the 1890s, stood on the highest point of Richmond Hill, Asheville, N. C. It was located about ¼ mile northwest of the main Richmond Hill house and commanded a 360 degree view of the surrounding country.

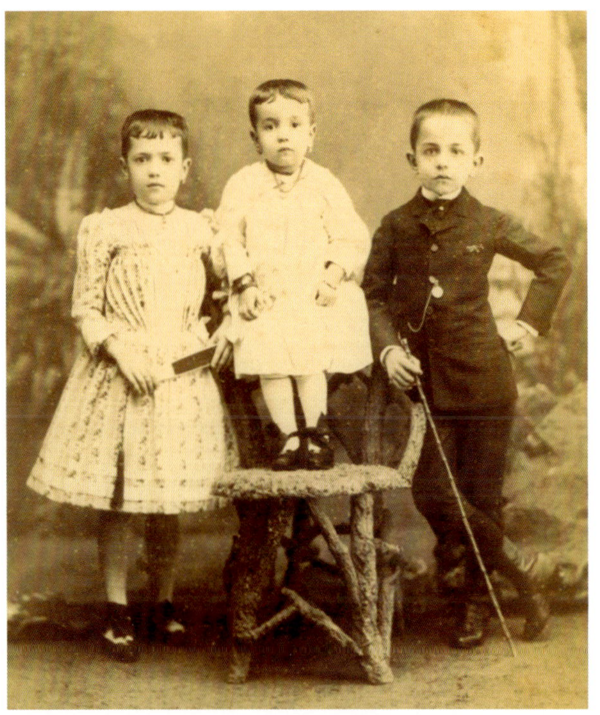

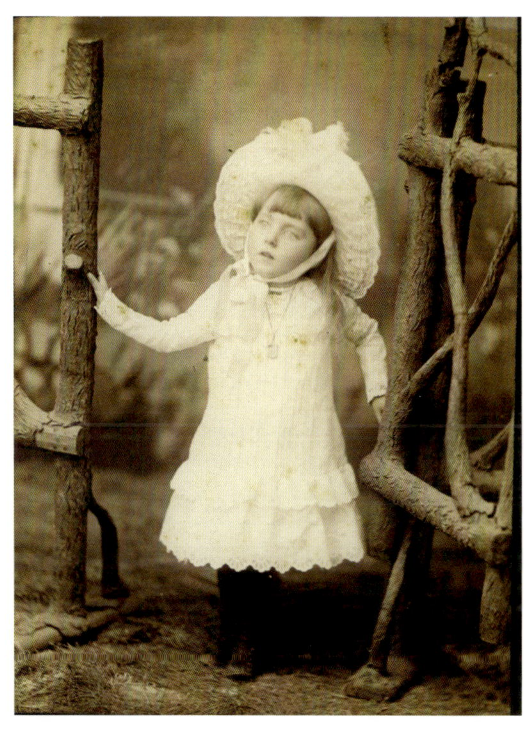

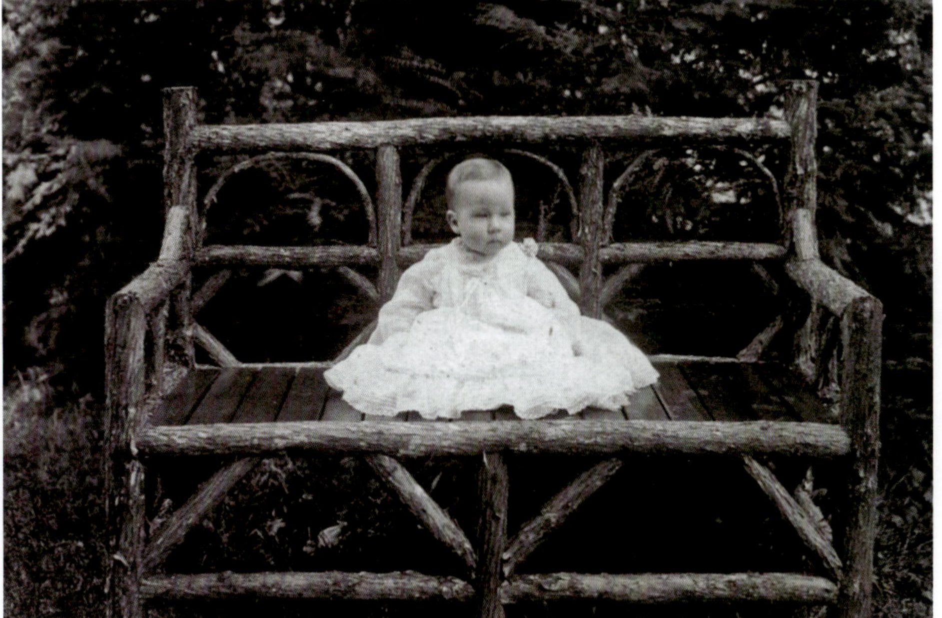

Above right and left: *Artisans unknown. Photographs with rustic wooden furniture. Archival photos: Collection of Kent Rush.*

Left: *Artisan unknown. Archival photograph with rustic wood furniture. Collection of Daniel Mack.*

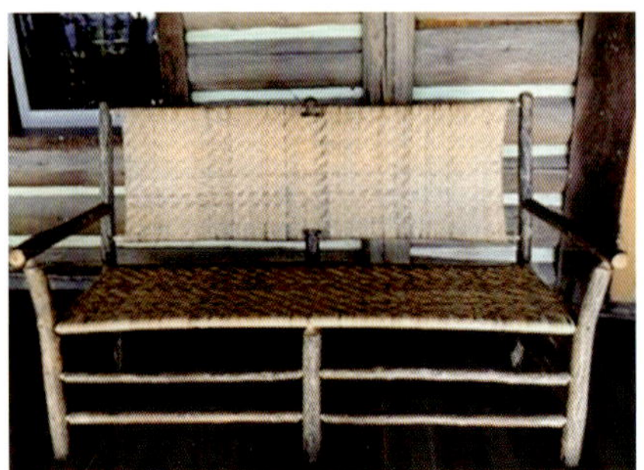

Artisan unknown. Hickory chair made in Indiana. Photo by Myssie Light Acomb.

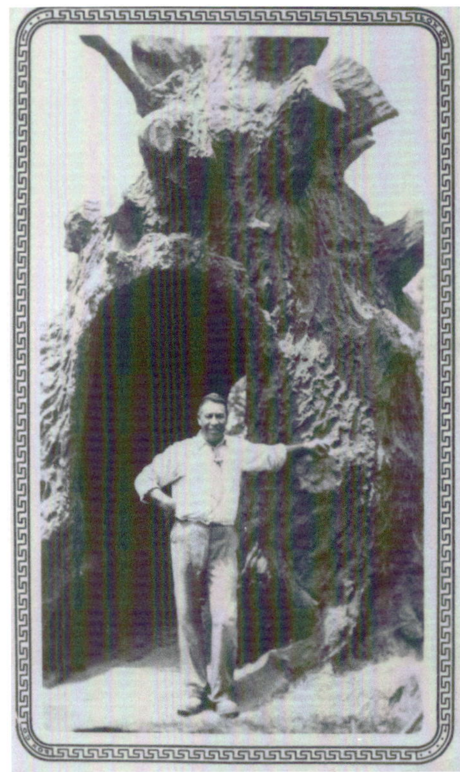

Dionicio Rodríguez. Memphis, TN. Memorial Park Cemetery. Photo from The University of Texas at San Antonio Special Collections.

According to Gary W. Clark, professional photographer and author, studio props used were rustic walls, rocks, chairs, and other objects, constructed of papier-mâché.[71] From observation of photographs, it is possible that some of these props were made of stucco or wood.

The interest in rustic furniture waned with the advent of new materials at the turn of the century, but there was a revival of interest in the 1930s during the Great Depression when people wanted inexpensive furniture. Among environmentally sensitive groups, which still exist into 2021, rustic yard furniture is popular.

Several companies (including Amish communities) continue to make handmade furniture of hickory saplings that can be shaped to fit body contours and often have seats and backs of inner bark strips woven in a herringbone pattern. A company in Shelbyville, Indiana, which was incorporated in 1899, made hickory chairs for Adirondack parks and resorts and National Park lodges. The company has been making chairs since 1904 for the Old Faithful Inn in Yellowstone, where they are still in use today.[72]

Arrival of Trabajo Rústico in San Antonio

Portland cement, one of the basic ingredients in the making of trabajo rústico, was discovered in San Antonio at about the same period as it was discovered in Europe. Its manufacture in San Antonio can be traced to an Englishman William Lloyd, who went hunting in 1879 "in what is now Brackenridge Park. He literally stumbled over a piece of what he thought was cement rock."[73] He took samples to be analyzed by George Kalteyer, a chemist and owner of a drug store. Kalteyer "heat-tested the materials and found it was cement rock, probably the finest in this area."[74] The first of eight cement quarries situated on the Balcones Fault from San Antonio to Austin, Alamo Portland and Roman Cement was founded near Lloyd's discovery in 1880.[75] It was providential that the source of portland cement would be readily available for the trabajo rústico artisans, who began working in San Antonio in the mid-1920s.

Early work and contemporary projects by present-day individuals can be seen in public areas around the city. Visitors to San Antonio are often told that they "were made by that man from Mexico." In a sense, this is correct, as the work was introduced in the city by one individual, Dionicio Rodríguez, whose first work in the United States was in San Antonio.

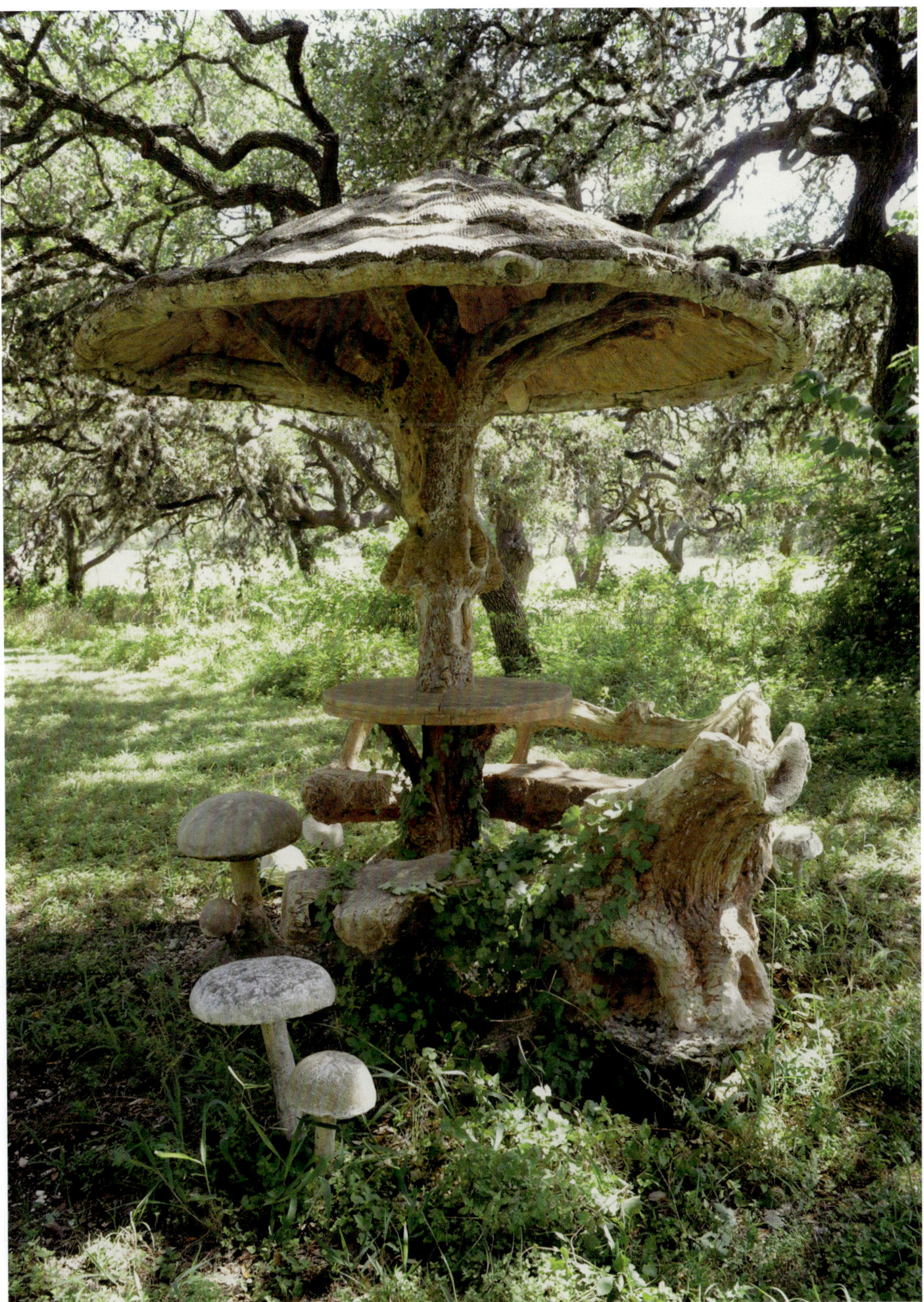

*Dionicio Rodríguez. Boerne, TX.
Collection of Carolyn and Larry
Biedenharn. Photo by Kent Rush.*

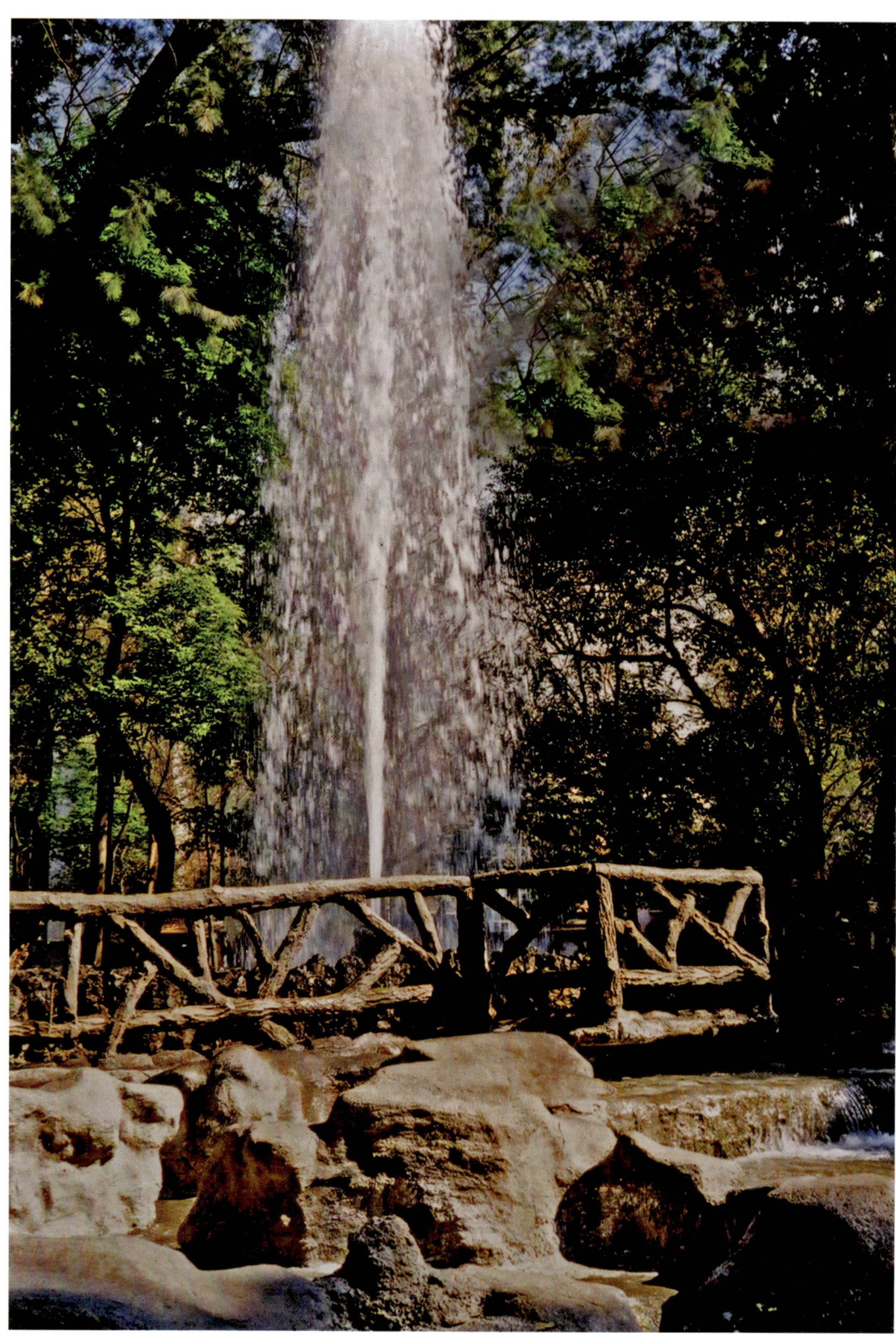

Artisan unknown. Mexico City, D.F., Mexico. Parque Mexico. Fountain and railing. Photo by Patsy Pittman Light.

Although Rodríguez was the original artist, a prodigious amount of work was achieved with the assistance of others, primarily men from Mexico who worked with him, learned the technique, and continued as his assistants. Some began working on their own and still others, self-taught, copied the technique. This book documents the lives and work of these early individuals as well as contemporary artisans who continue the tradition. Rodríguez's work is found in eight states, and 21 projects are listed on the National Register of Historic Places. As a result of Rodríguez's influential work, the City of San Antonio, Texas, can boast of possessing the largest number of trabajo rústico works found in any city in the United States.

Much of the work in Texas and other states is credited to Rodríguez and his followers: tables, benches, thatched roof shelters (known as *palapas*), hollow tree houses, stairs and railings, bridges, grottos, birdbaths, fountains, shrines, barbeque ovens, gazebos, details of façades and interiors of homes, and even some animals.

It is interesting to note that Rodríguez and his followers must have been introduced to pictures of Roman garden decorations, work in French parks and gardens, and the work by Gaudí in Spain. They constructed bridges and grottoes similar to those seen in images of Capability Brown's gardens and in those of rococo designer Thomas Wright. Recently, notes, drawings, and clippings were found in a trunk belonging to Rodríguez, offering proof that he did not work totally from imagination.[76]

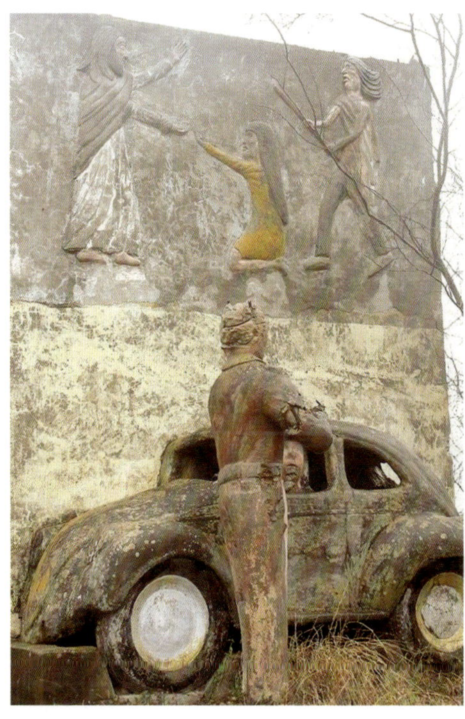

Don Catariño Hernandez. Rancho Orizatlán near Reynosa, Mexico. Volkswagen and figure. Photo by Jorge Eduardo Sanchez Martinez.

The Legacy of Dionicio Rodríguez

Dionicio Rodríguez was born in Toluca, near Mexico City, in 1891. We have only a patchwork of information about his life before he immigrated to the United States. Rodríguez worked with his father making bricks in Mexico City. Interviews with his niece, Manuela Theall, revealed that he would have used different types of firewood for the brick kilns; therefore, he would have observed the textures and coloration of the wood.[77] There are letters of recommendation for him from two engineers in Mexico City; one is from Luis Robles Gil,[78] a contractor specializing in reinforced concrete works mimicking rocks and wood. Gil is believed to have learned the technique in Spain.[79] *Parque México* in Mexico City possesses one hundred trabajo rústico *palapas* (all very similar to *palapas* made by Rodríguez at sites around the United States) as well as a large cascading fountain, but their provenance is unknown.[80]

Other work is found in the Mexican cities of Zacatecas;[81] Toluca, Rodríguez's birthplace; and Reynosa, where in 1966, Don Jeronimo Monterrubio Cervantes hired Don Catariño Hernández to build fifty concrete sculptures, many historically themed. Subjects included Adam and Eve, Maximillian and Carlotta, a large Mexican eagle, Hernándo Cortez, Emiliano Zapata, and a huge pyramid. The property, known as Lago Orizatlán, Hidalgo, was sold in 1976 for a school of veterinary medicine, which was not successful. Some of the sculptures were moved to other sites, others were demolished, and the property is now deserted with only a few pieces remaining.[82]

Rodríguez arrived in San Antonio in 1924 and began to work for Dr. Aureliano Urrutia. The Mexican Revolution caused many refugees from the struggle to flee to San Antonio including Urrutia, who was exiled from Mexico for his participation in the conflict.[83] He left escorted by the American general, Frederick Funston.[84] The doctor, a renowned surgeon with a clinic in Mexico City, established a practice in San Antonio, built a Mexican-style house, and designed a private garden, Miraflores, reminiscent of Xochimilco, the floating gardens in Mexico City.

Based on correspondence, Urrutia was familiar with work credited to Rodríguez in Mexico City, including the fountain and artificial rocks at *Lago de Chapultepec*.[85] Rodríguez created ten trabajo rústico works for Miraflores, a Texas Historic Landmark, and a bridge in Brackenridge Park, now listed in the National Register of Historic Places. Later, through written and word-of-mouth references, he received commissions for additional work in San Antonio, throughout Texas, and in seven additional states.[86]

For these extensive travels, he bought a new car every year. According to his niece, who spent a year visiting many of the projects sites with him, these recurring purchases were attributed to the fact that he knew little about cars.[87] Various relatives and others traveled to commissions with him from 1924 to the 1950s. At other times, he would hire locals to assist him.

It was shortly after Rodríguez arrived in Texas that he enlisted the assistance of Máximo Cortés, with whom he had previously worked in Laredo. Artisans who were early helpers included Cortés's brothers, Ruben and Carlos, and father-in-law, Julius Tobar; Armando Silva; and Mauro Del Toro and his wife, Guadalupe. Additional practitioners of the work were Bacilio Aguilar, Sam Murray, Antonio Lopez, Modesto Dena; Dionicio Rosales; Ralph Corona and George Cardosa; J. M. Martinez and C. Ramirez; Eliseo Alvarado, who sculpted animals; Julian Sandoval, who made molds for other artisans; Floresville residents, Beatrice and Pedro Ximénez (who learned from Sam Murray); and Houstonian Vidal Lozano.

Although Corona and Cardosa worked mainly on sites in San Antonio and around Texas, they completed several projects in Michigan, some with Rodríguez's involvement, including McCourtie Park in Somerset Center, Michigan, where they made *seventeen* trabajo rústico bridges and two bare tree trunks, and the Slayton Arboretum at Hillside College.[88] Corona was quoted in an interview saying that he and/or Cardosa "worked several other sites in the region . . . including at least one tree sculpture at the Detroit Zoo [indicating that they/he assisted Rodríguez on that project] and at Our Lady of Lourdes Convent in Sylvania, Ohio."[89] Corona was also assisted by his teacher, Rodríguez, with the St. Joseph Church and Shrine in the Township of Cambridge, Michigan. Eventually Cardosa returned to Texas, and Corona remained in Michigan, where he worked on additional projects.[90]

This art form has been passed down by some artisans to family members and by others, to their assistants. The scope and diversity of the styles of these individuals is evidenced by their existing work. Many assistants and followers exhibited special talents in mimicking textures of wood, thatch, and rocks, although Rodríguez's style has been credited as the most realistic. On many major projects, it is apparent that Rodríguez was given individual credit as the one who received the original commission. Gene Fowler wrote of Donald Tucker's explanation:

> The distinguishing factor of North American *trabajo rústico*—as pioneered by Rodríguez-is the finish coat. The historic French work is a sanded mortar aggregate that limits the amount of detail. Rodríguez's version utilizes portland cement and water, without any aggregate and is very difficult to master.[91]

Today, the technique continues through apprenticeships, self-instruction, and, more recently, the work of the late Donald Tucker, a self-taught artisan.[92]

Rodríguez and his helpers worked in eight cemeteries, but they did not construct concrete grave markers at these locations. Although some identifiable artisans created individual concrete tombstones and a fountain in San Antonio and the surrounding area, there are numerous other graveyard objects, including two arbors and one family plot crafted by unknown individuals. Historian Terry Jordan wrote: "The widespread acceptance of cement markers by Mexican Americans began in the 1920s and has spread to all parts of the state."[93] Professionally-made grave markers of carved marble that looked like tree trunks were originally furnished to mem-

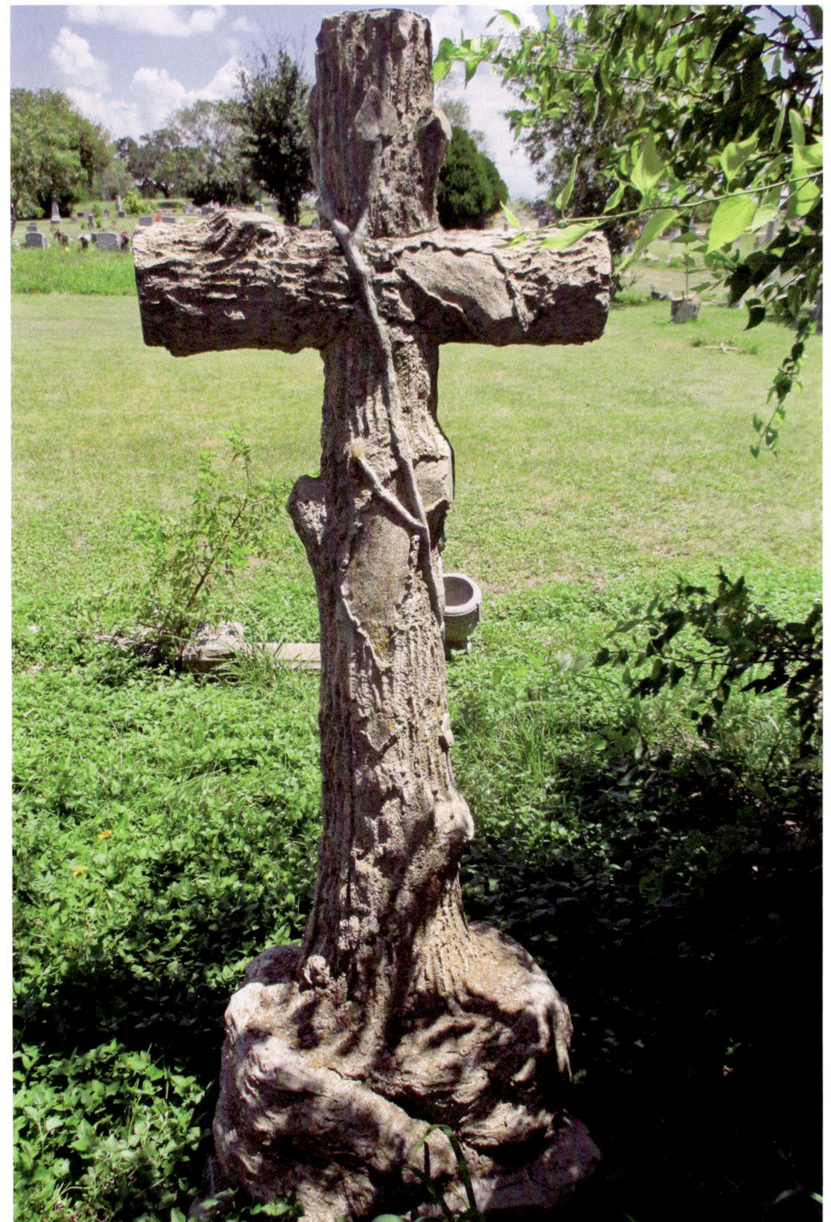

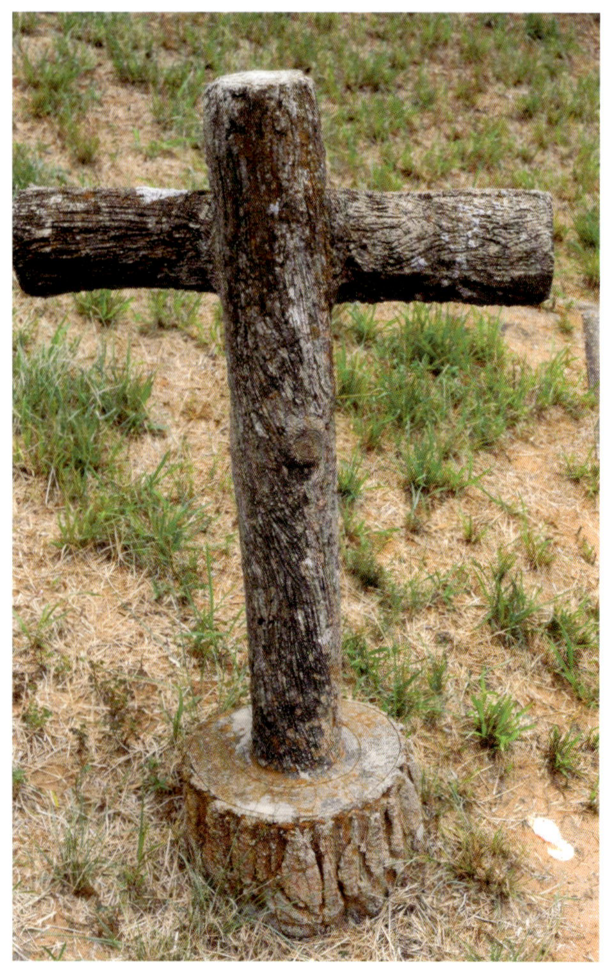

bers of the Woodmen of the World, but they were later replaced with less expensive hand-made markers with wood texture.

Another Mexican immigrant was Benjamin Dominguez, who studied at the Academia de Artes Plásticas of the National Autonomous University of Mexico. He designed the tiger and lion cages at the Chapultepec Zoo in Mexico City, and he also worked in Texas, Nevada, and California.[94]

Now deserted and outwardly dilapidated, Mexico City's La Posada del Sol, on Avenida Niños Heroes 139, exhibits the design of a nude upholding trabajo rústico examples of primal water creatures in a fountain flowing from a tall tree. The 1945 photo of La Posada designed by Fernando Saldaña Galván shows a six hundred room hotel that combines design elements of baroque colonial and modernist architecture and encompasses half a city block.

Japanese-American Ryozo Kado, an immigrant from Shizuoka, Japan, created many *faux* woodworks in Southern California before WWII and during his internment in Manazar Relocation Center.[95] Projects by unknown artisans are also found throughout California, including the wisteria arbor of oak at the Huntington Museum, which was rebuilt as trabajo rústico in 1915 after Arabella and Henry Huntington returned from a trip to Paris. Terrance Eagen restored the arbor for eight years.[96] Additional sites of unattributed work are found throughout the United States.

Restoration and Conservation

Many existing trabajo rústico works need restoration and conservation, and several methods of conservation are being explored. According to conservator Shane Winter, "restoration deals more with reworking areas of loss," while "conservation deals more with stabilization and the retarding of deterioration." He reveals that "maintenance is the most important thing . . . there is no reason to restore a piece if it can't be maintained."[97]

The fate of many old trabajo rústico pieces is uncertain. As with any art works, there are threats to both old and contemporary work. Sturdy as concrete may appear, age, environment, weather, and people are continuing problems. Historical photographs reveal work no longer existing in Texas, including garden embellishments for the John Henry Phelan mansion in Beaumont;[98] Cole Park, a public bayside park with trabajo rústico railings in Corpus Christi; and a highway roadside park near Floresville with a table, chairs, and a bench.

Perhaps the greatest threat is cracking, the result of changes in weather, vibration from nearby traffic or equipment, or from simple aging. The cracking allows moisture to penetrate the hardware cloth and rebar, causing them to disintegrate. As steel rusts and attempts to return to its natural state, it can expand its original size up to 70 percent, creating pressure from within that causes cracks. As further

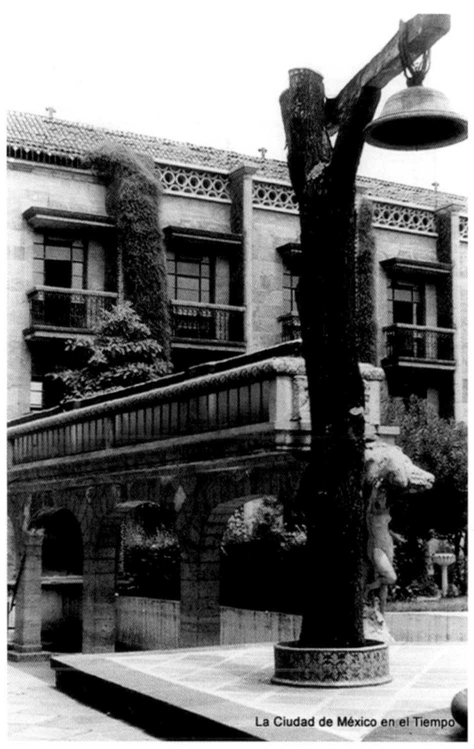

Artisan unknown. Mexico City, D.F., Mexico. La Posada del Sol ca. 1945. Photo courtesy of Carlos Villasana Suverza.

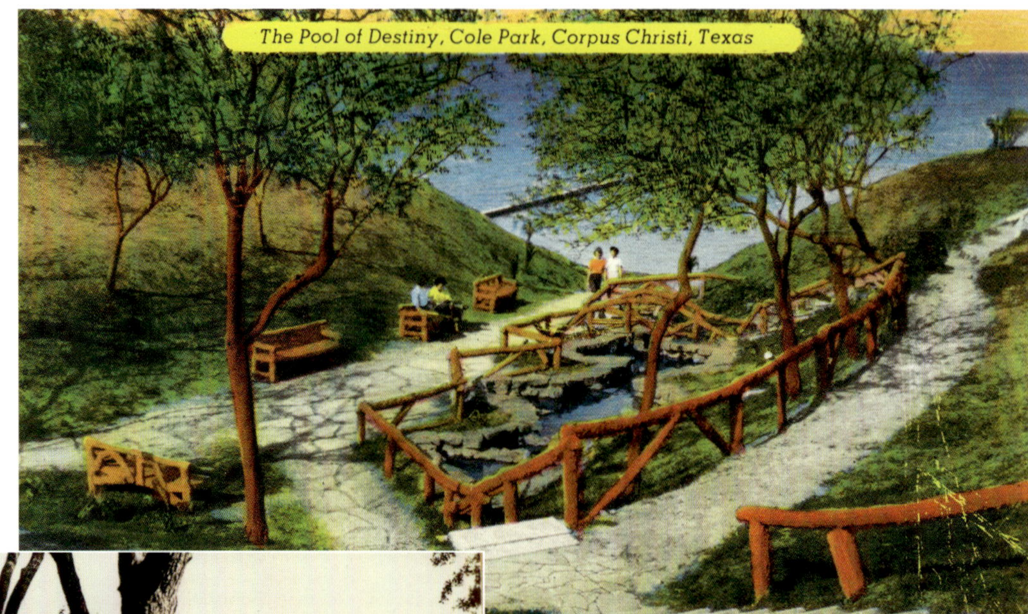

Above: *Artisan unknown. Corpus Christi, TX. Cole Park. Photo of vintage postcard courtesy of Jim Moloney.*

Above: *Artisan unknown. Picnic area in roadside park between Floresville and Stockdale, TX, Highway 97. Archival photo courtesy of Texas Department of Transportation, from Views of Division 15, San Antonio.*

explained by Winter, steel and concrete do not exist in nature, and, in oxidizing, steel is attempting to return to its low energy state (i.e., rust).

There are products that can slow deterioration. Ethyl silicate is a silicone dissolved in a solvent that can be sprayed on deteriorated stone, masonry, or concrete. As the solvent evaporates, it leaves the silicone in any voids. The exterior of the piece can then be patched and sealed with either a chemical coating such as silane or a coat of wax.[99]

The surfaces of some older pieces have been affected by pollution; others have been damaged by humans—vandalism and graffiti, particularly in public areas. Fortunately, several of the most talented artisans have applied their talents to restoration of trabajo rústico projects in public spaces.

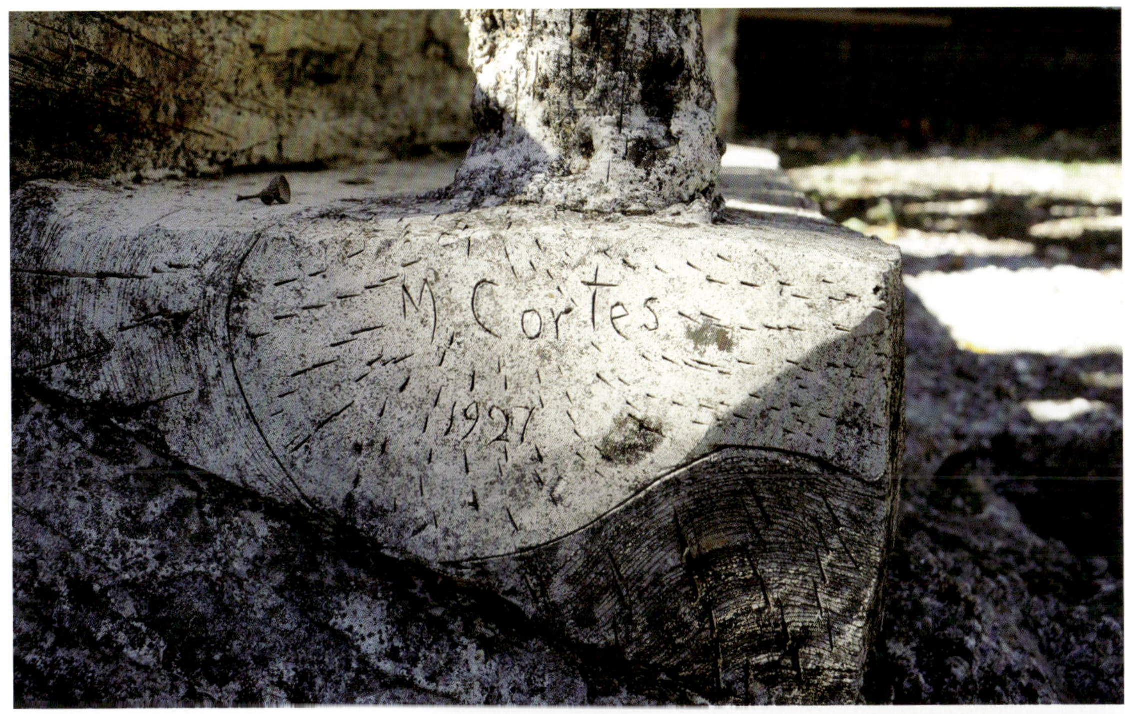

*Photographs of artisans' signatures.
Top, M. Cortés. Below, Aguilar Maker.
Photos by Kent Rush.*

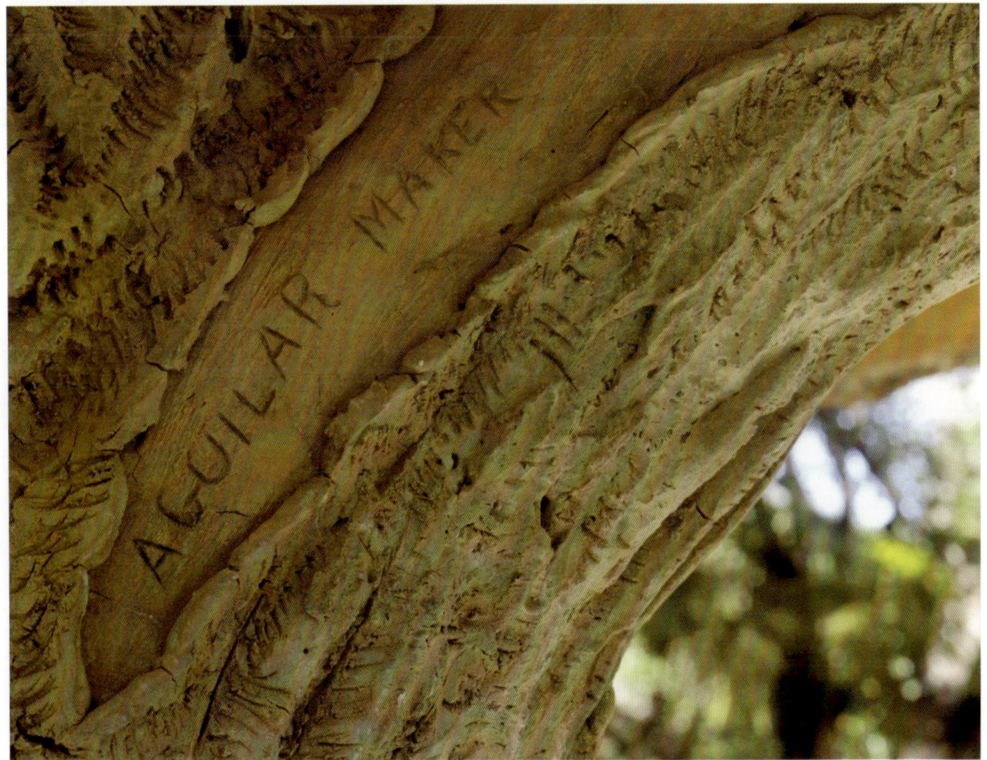

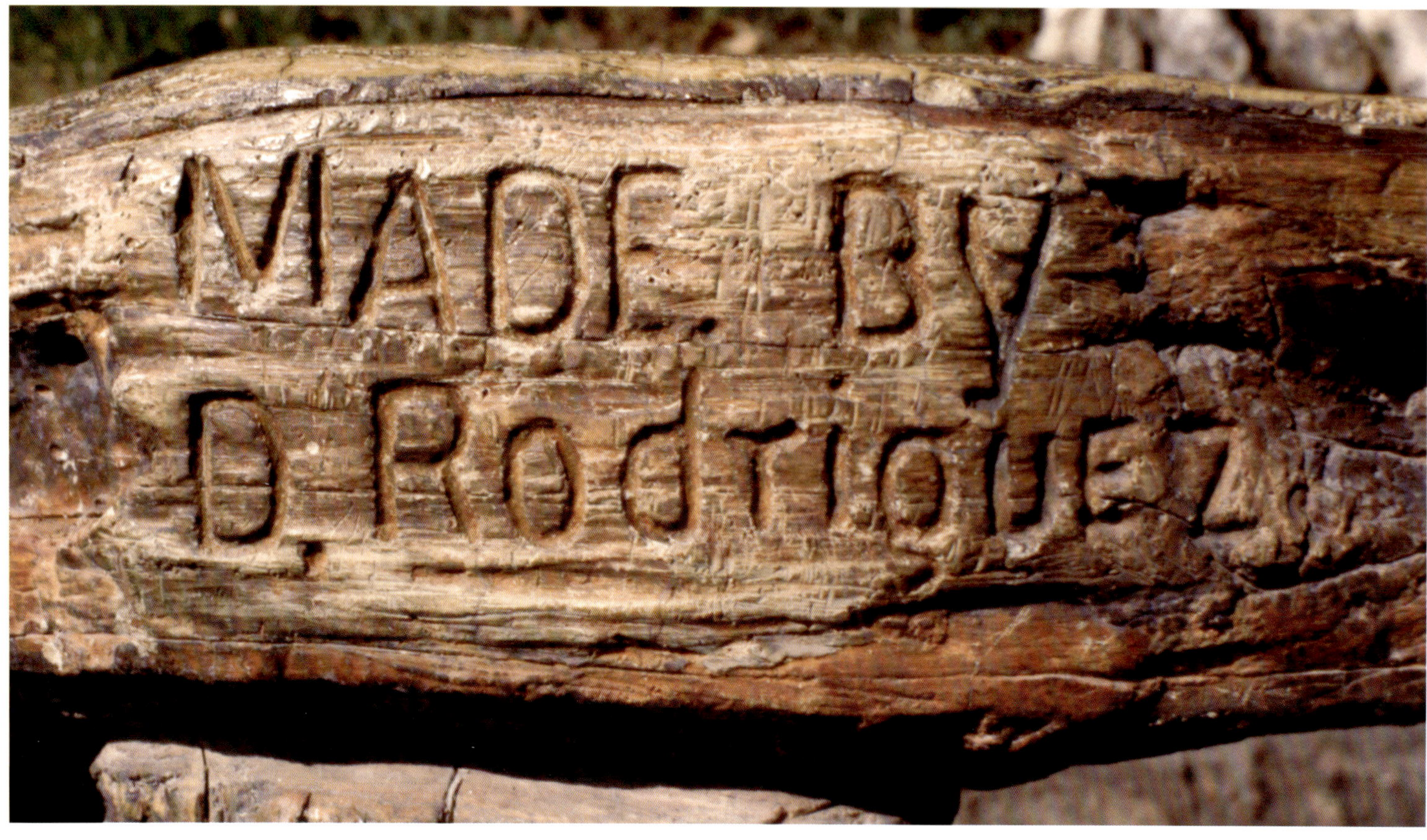

Artisan unknown. San Antonio, TX. Japanese Tea Garden gate. D. Rodríguez name as inscribed by a coworker. Photo by Kent Rush.

In her Columbia University master of science in historic preservation thesis, Suki Gershenhorn wrote:

"Luckily, trabajo rústico pieces in San Antonio have dodged neglect and demolition for several reasons. Community preservation and art historians in the city have long embraced the work as part of the city's identity. The work speaks to several aspects of San Antonio identity-its Mexican immigrant population, as well as the influence and presence of Alamo Cement Company, without which, Rodríguez's works may have never been produced."[100]

Numerous community organizations and groups have been involved in preservation and conservation of older trabajo rústico works. The Conservation Society of San Antonio (organized in 1924) has aggressively publicized and promoted conservation of older works. In 2011, they funded restoration of a Rodríguez *palapa* and grotto in Miraflores Park. The City of San Antonio through a 2012 bond issue commissioned restoration of works by Rodríguez in Brackenridge Park; an anonymous donor and Mission Heritage Partners, formerly Los Compadres, funded the replacement of wooden railings with trabajo rústico rails around the mill at Mission San Jose in 2014–15; the City of Alamo Heights (an incorporated town surrounded by the greater metropolitan San Antonio area) and the Texas Department of Safety restored the Rodríguez trolley stop; contributions to the Japanese Tea Garden include a new trabajo rústico bench donated by a private donor in 2016; and San Antonio Parks Foundation commissioned restoration of the Torii Gate, built by Rodríguez and Cortés, in 2017. By 2021, more than $277,000 has been spent, and there are plans to restore additional work.

The tradition of sculpting in concrete is an element of the tangible cultural heritage brought to Texas and other areas of the United States by immigrant Mexicans and others who were children of immigrants who had fled "during the turbulent era after the Mexican Revolution."[101]

Lack of signatures has complicated identification of the creators of many earlier pieces. Of the early practitioners, Rodríguez, Cortés, and Aguilar signed much of their work. Many other trabajo rústico practitioners did not sign their work; therefore, it is impossible to discern "who did what." Almost one hundred years later, many projects lack attribution.

In 2021, trabajo rústico continues to evolve as evidenced by new artisans who are producing their interpretations of the genre. New objects appear in the work of Carlos Cortés and Rene Romero. Frank and Jacob Tobar and Mario Flores continue to work with their relative, Carlos Cortes, on various projects. Jacob Tobar is a resident of New Mexico and is acquiring commissions on his own. Around the United States are self-taught professionals: Michael Fogg of Colchester, Connecticut; and Melinda LoPresto and her daughter, Melissa Lashaway, of Frontier, Michigan.

Artisans who continue this tradition are San Antonio resident Frank Ramos and former San Antonian Jorge Enrique Cerrato Gutierrez, now of Honduras. Others who practice trabajo rústico were former students of Donald Tucker: Marcella Marie Davis of Saint Louis, Missouri; Diane Husson of Norfolk, Virginia; Michael Palella of New Preston, Connecticut; Gregory Everingham of Villeneuve-lès-Avignon, France; and Beau Johnstone of Deniliquin, New South Wales, Australia.

In Chapter 2, Kent Rush includes important descriptions and drawings along with many of his photographs illustrating the remarkable imaginations of the early and contemporary artisans. He has amassed for the reader an intriguing story of how the artisans work to construct these amazing art forms.

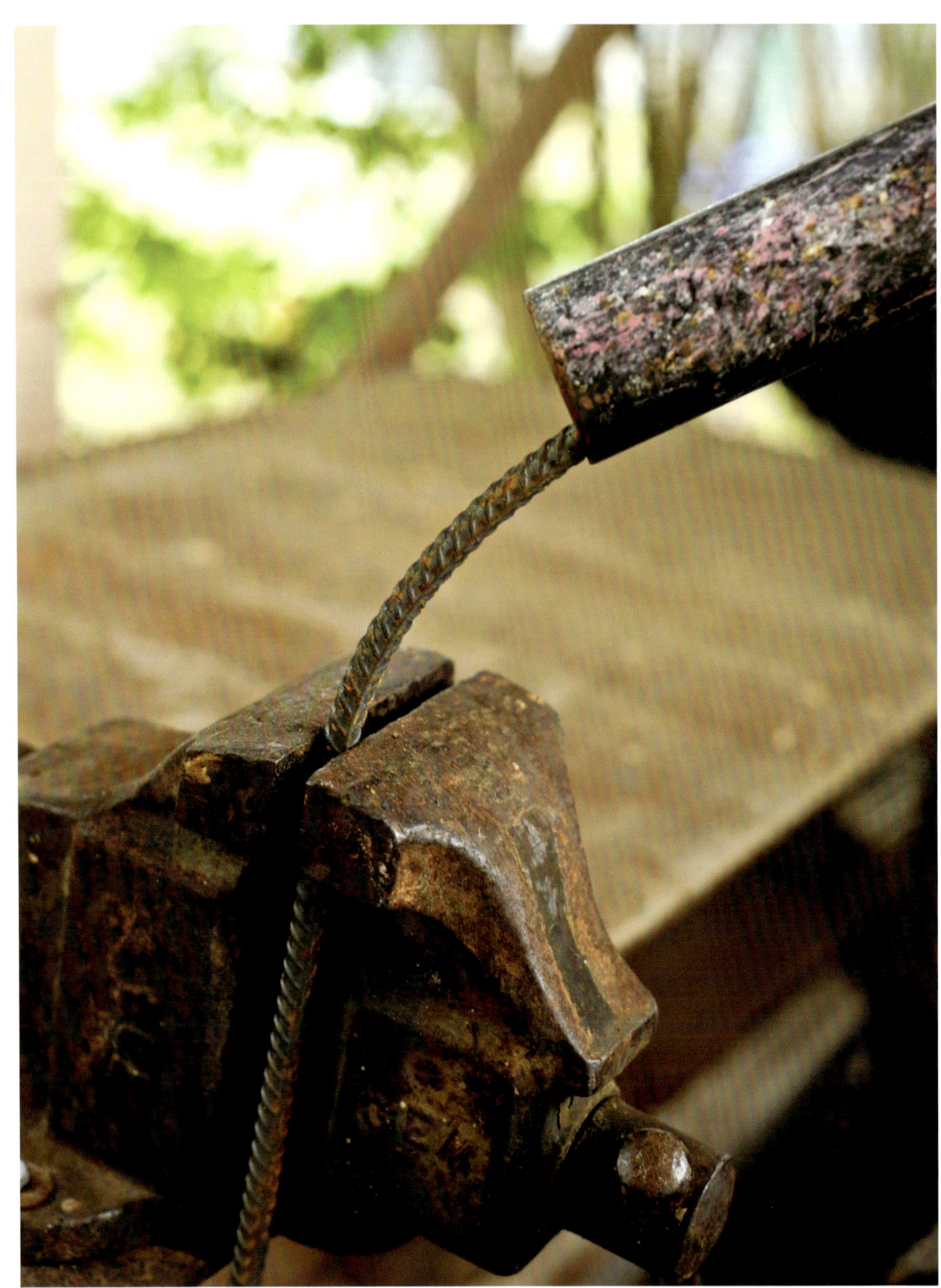

Rebar rod bent with vise and pipe. Photo by Kent Rush.

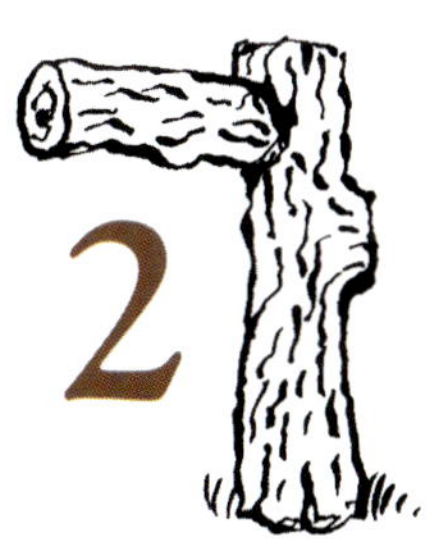

The Fabrication of Trabajo Rústico
by Kent Rush

TRABAJO RÚSTICO structures, from benches to gazebos and bridges, follow and mimic the look of traditional rustic construction used by woodcrafters, who made similar structures but from real trees: limbs, branches, logs, trunks, and stumps. This chapter relates mainly to the types of trabajo rústico mimicking tree and branch forms.

The underlying fabrication process of trabajo rústico is a method used for centuries for three-dimensional, tree/branch structures, relying on an armature defined by Merriam-Webster as "a framework used by a sculptor to support a figure being modeled in a plastic material."[1]

Although the function of the structural elements is the same in trabajo rústico and traditional tree/branch craft, the way these elements are constructed is different. In trabajo rústico, the main internal linear armature is made of a metal rod or rods – today, mostly *rebar* (reinforcing bar). These rods come in a variety of diameters and are made of soft steel that makes them easy to shape and bend and that has a *knurled* texture on the exterior, which creates a more secure bond with the concrete and provides a good grip for the wiring on of the mesh.

The bars are bent to the basic shape of the tree or branch forms and either welded together or wired securely. To add the underlying bulk form of the branches, wire mesh of various kinds, including hardware cloth, expanded metal mesh, or stucco lath, is wrapped around the rebar in a basically cylindrical shape and wired securely into place.

Once the entire armature is complete, the first two of three layers of concrete are applied onto and into the mesh and are formed roughly to the desired finished shape. These first two layers of concrete are the bonding coat, followed by the scratch coat, the latter being the thicker, sculptural one.[2] This second layer is

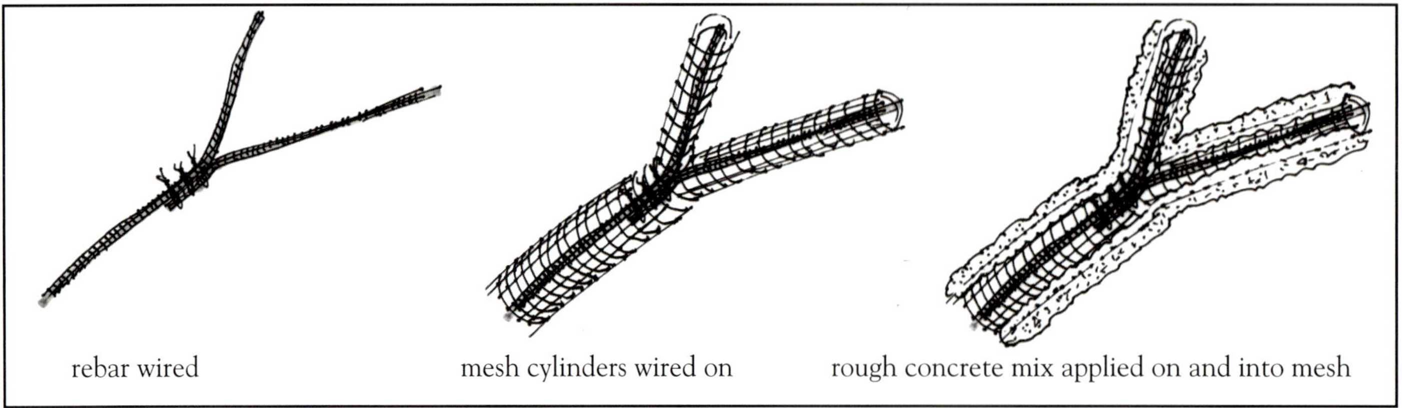

Above: *Stages of fabrication. Illustration by Kent Rush.*

Right: *Mesh wired to rebar armature. Courtesy of Studio Cortés. Photo by Kent Rush.*

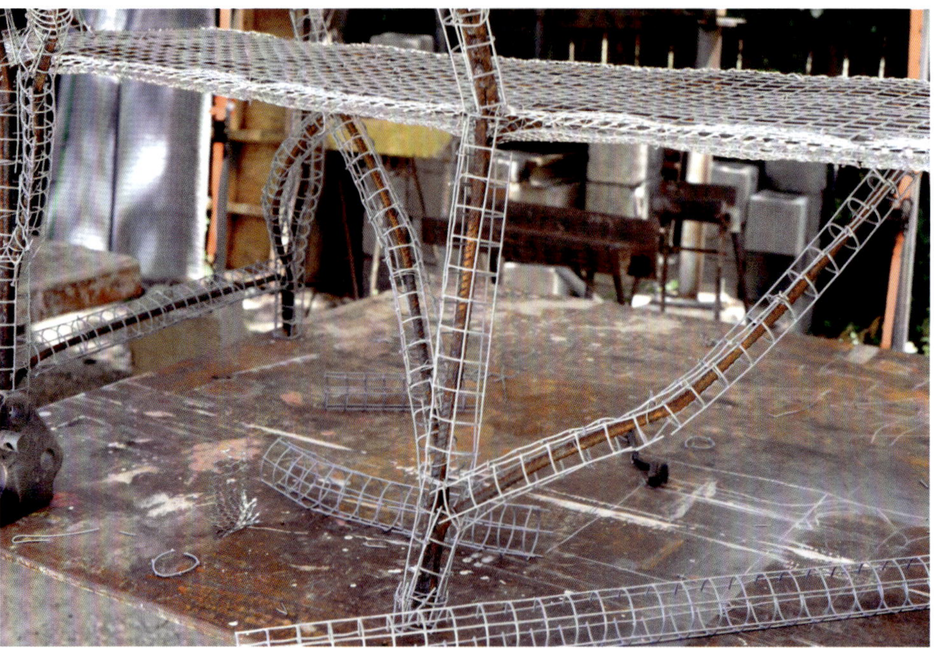

scratched with tools while still wet to provide a texture so that the final layer can form a mechanical bond.

When the bonding layer of concrete is applied, it also gets pushed into the metal fabric so that it oozes into and around the mesh, thereby trapping itself around the metal once it dries. Besides creating the basic shape, this coat provides "the bulk of the strength to the finished piece."[3] The third and final coat provides the detail in texture that gives the effect of barks and wood grains. This mix is created with a much finer aggregate, usually a fine sand, to make it more plastic. Dionicio Rodríguez

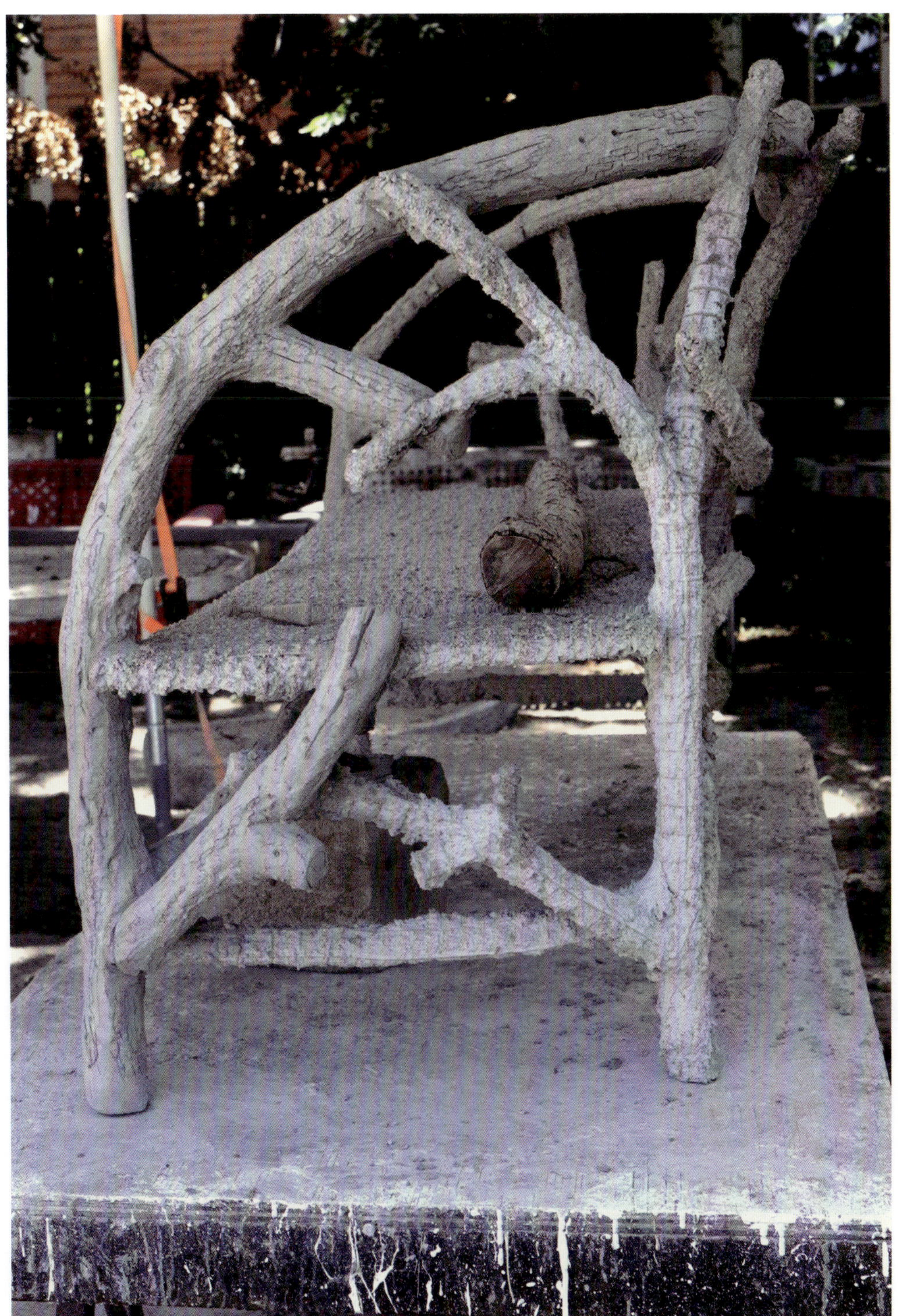

Bench with various concrete coats applied. Note: Middle branch has final, detailed coat. Courtesy of Studio Cortés. Photo by Kent Rush.

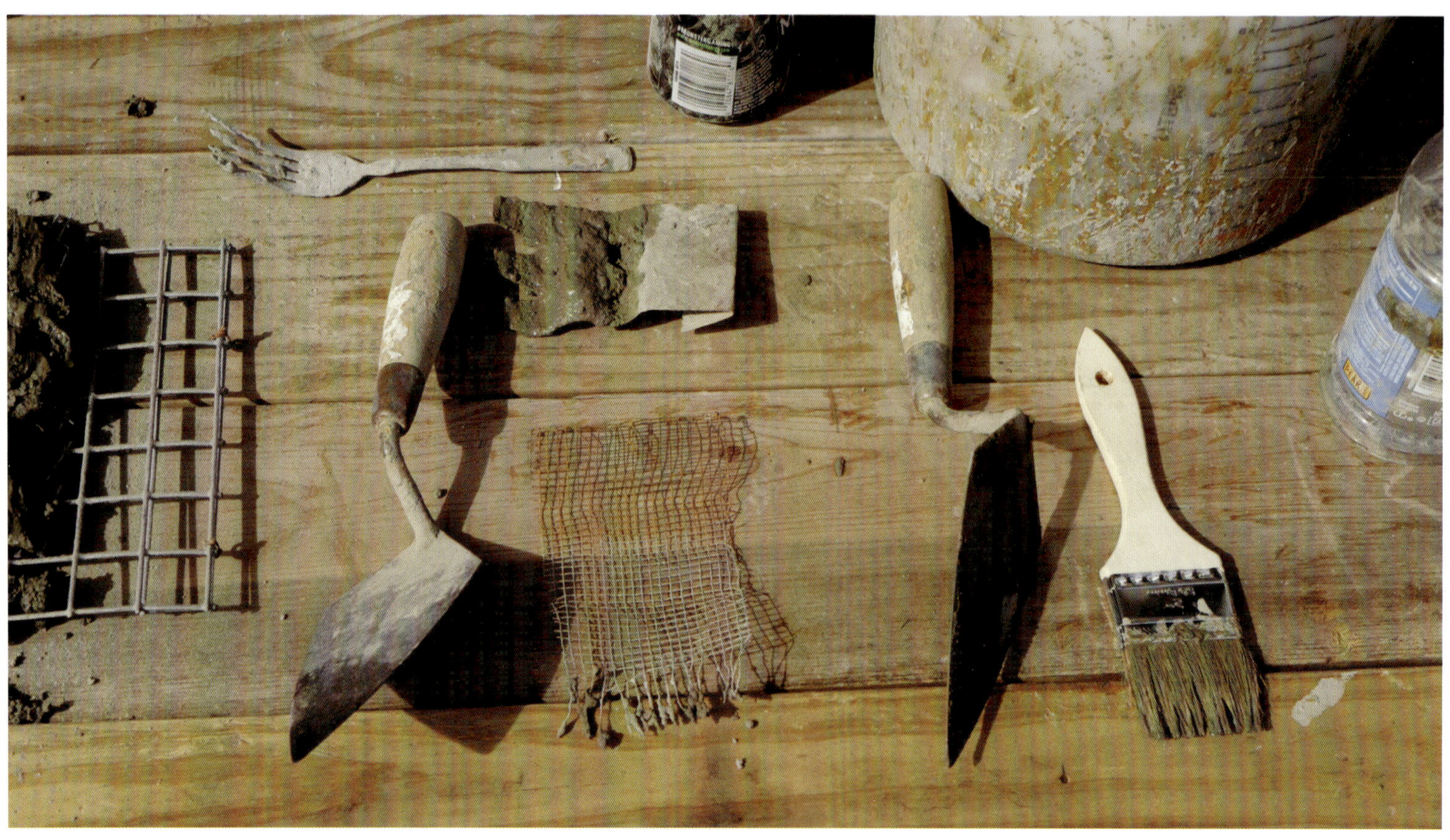

Assortment of tools used to apply and create textures in concrete. Courtesy of Rene Romero. Photo by Kent Rush.

(and possibly others) used pure cement without aggregate. It is reported that he "applied a final coat of 'neat' (pure) Portland cement to the armature directly from the bag."[4]

The details of construction can be broken down into three broad areas: (a) joinery: articulations and connections; (b) surface modeling and texturing; and (c) coloration. All these details involve the fascinating and appealing fool-the-eye representation of tree and branch formations. People unfamiliar with trabajo rústico often view these objects without realizing they are made of concrete.

Joinery: Articulation and Connections

Tree and branch joinery in trabajo rústico is not sophisticated when compared to furniture construction or even to other rustic forms, such as log cabins or heavy timber construction, especially considering that in trabajo rústico the actual joinery is that of rebar joints and not real branches. Rather, the objects imitate a type of rough work where the branches and limbs are left as they are–bark left on and branches often left splaying. Connections between these members are generally unrefined.

It is common to see one limb member lap, or cross over another, with nothing more than a metal fastening (mimicked) passing through to hold one to the other. Other connections, however, are created to represent more structurally secure articulations. The artisan has many choices and much latitude for creativity in this arena. These joints are most often shown with simulated simple metal fastenings such as bolts or spikes. They tend to be simple for the most part; however, as many structural members are round, it is difficult to compare the joinery with that of flat-sided dimensional lumber. The accompanying illustrations depict some of the most common joinery methods used in trabajo rústico.

The simplest joint is a *butt joint* where two members merely butt up against each other. A butt joint demands some sort of fastener – a dowel, screw, bolt, or metal rod to make it secure.

Notching in one form or another is one of the most basic methods of structural joinery in woodcraft trabajo rústico construction. In woodcraft construction, these more sophisticated joints are also more secure, as they relieve some of the strain on the metal fastener.

Examples of various construction and joinery methods are detailed in the following photographs and drawings.

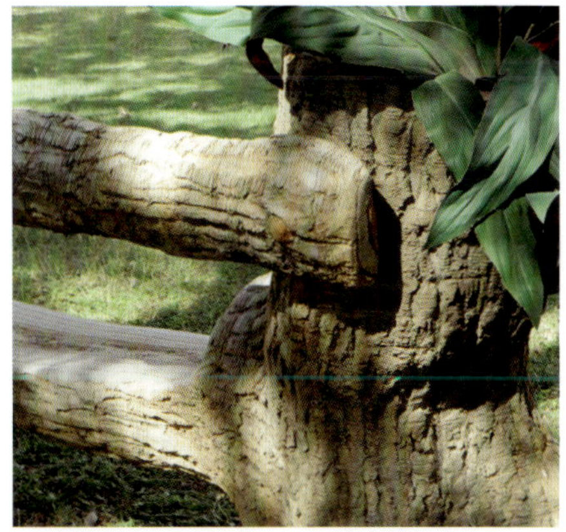

Simple notched side lap. Jorge Cerrato. Private collection. Photo by Kent Rush.

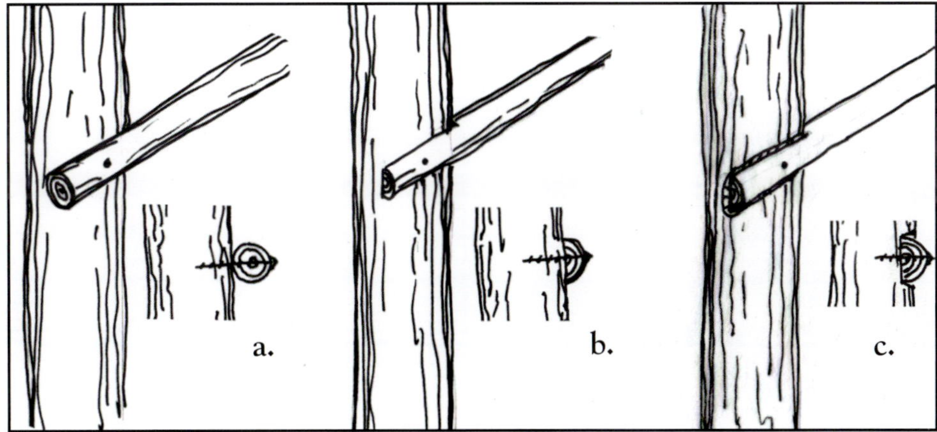

Above: *Types of laps - each shown with inset cross section: (a) Simple lap with metal fastening; (b) Lap with cross-member notched; (c) Lap with both members notched. Illustration by Kent Rush.*

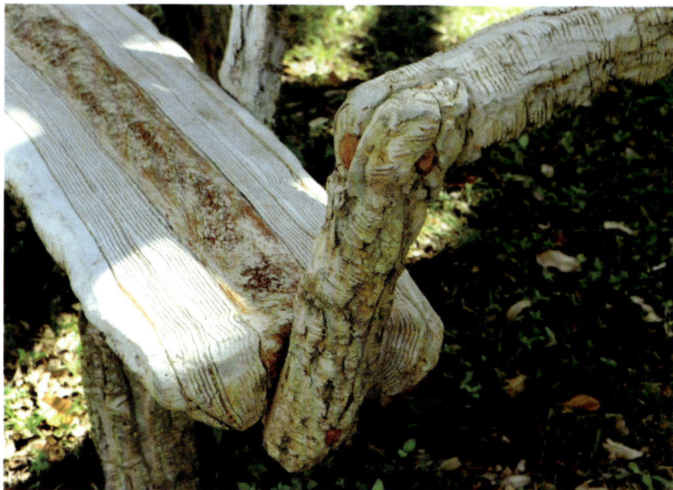

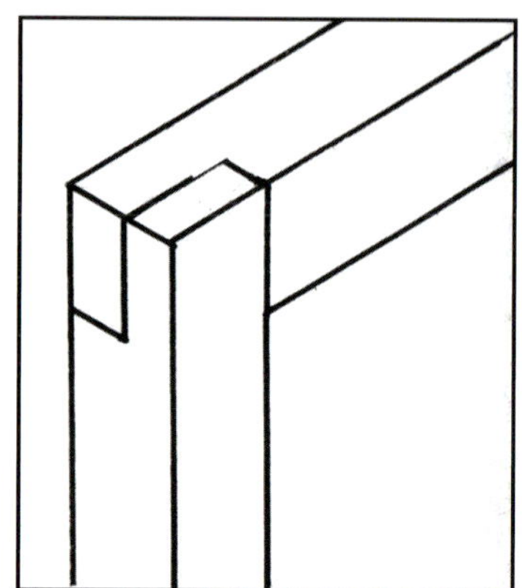

End or half lap. Jorge Cerrato. Location unknown. Private collection. Photo and drawing by Kent Rush.

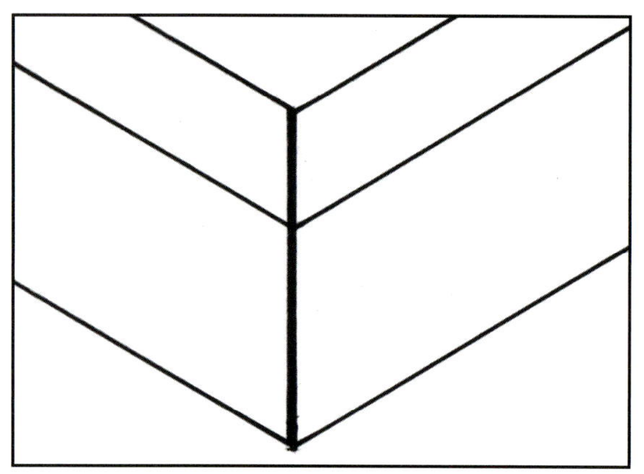

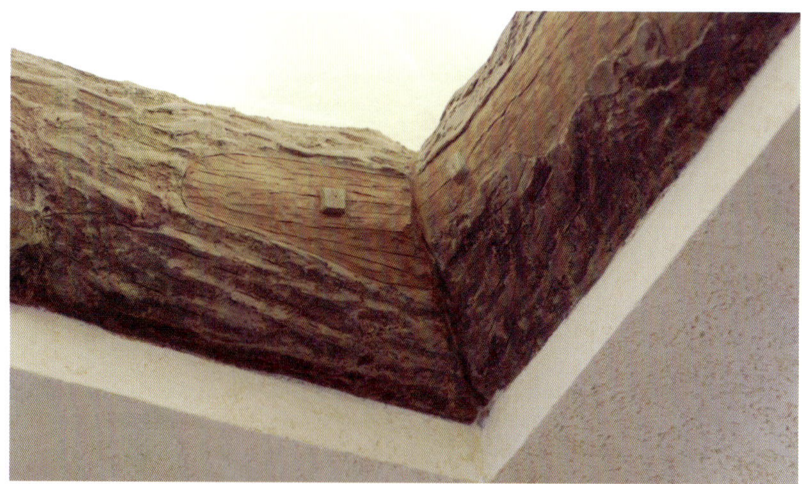

Miter. Máximo Cortés and Dionicio Rodriguez, San Antonio, TX. Private collection. Photo and drawing by Kent Rush.

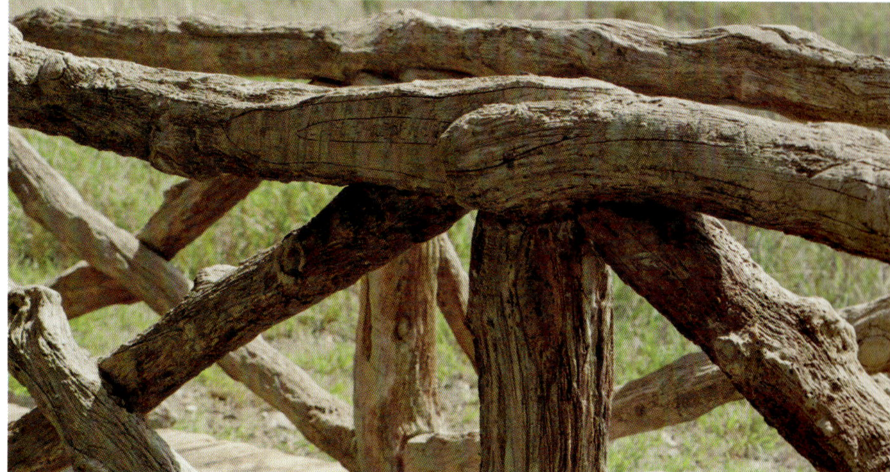

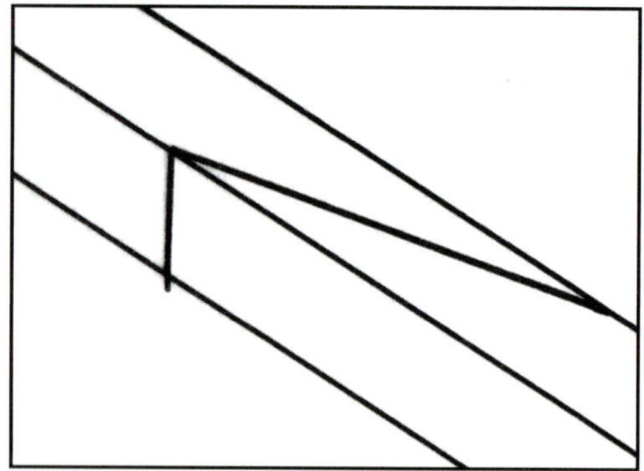

Scarf joint. Footbridge. Máximo Cortés. San Antonio, TX. Private collection. Photo and drawing by Kent Rush.

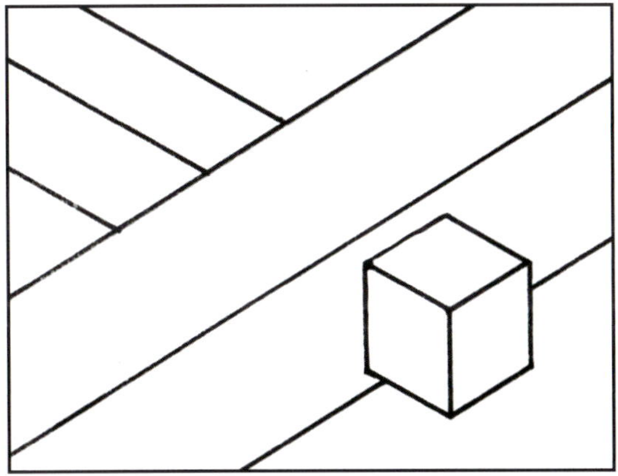

Through mortise: rectangular hole for bench seat slabs. Carlos Cortés. New Braunfels, TX. Private collection. Photo and drawing by Kent Rush.

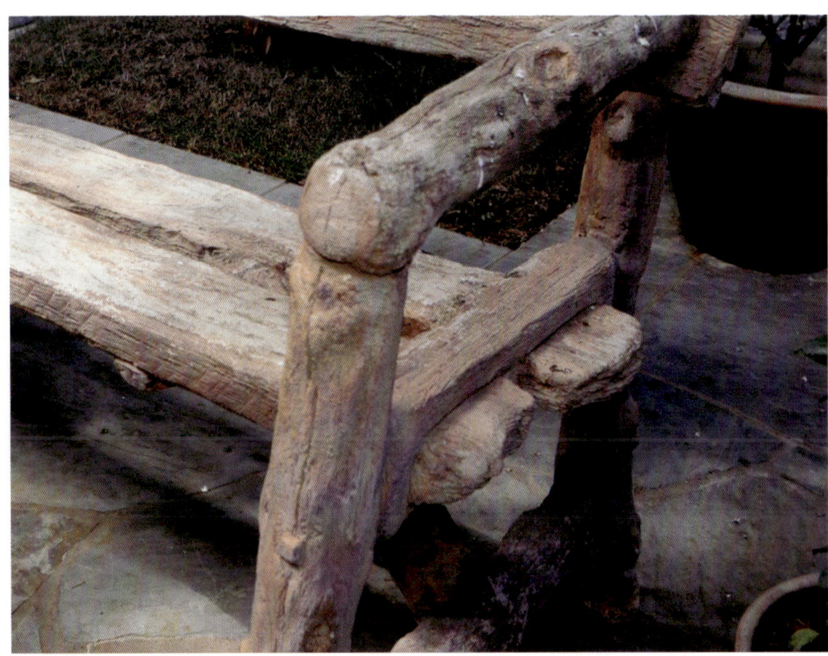

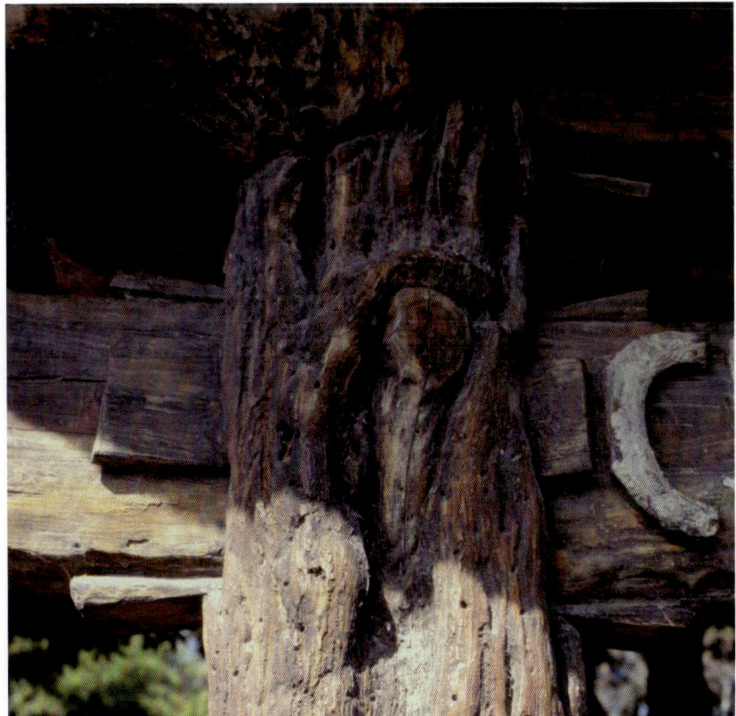

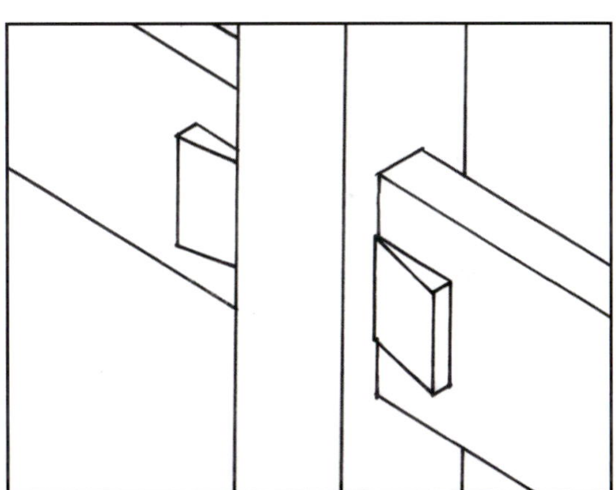

Mortised beam with wedges. Dionicio Rodríguez and Máximo Cortés. San Antonio Japanese Tea Garden. Torii gate. Photo by Kent Rush.

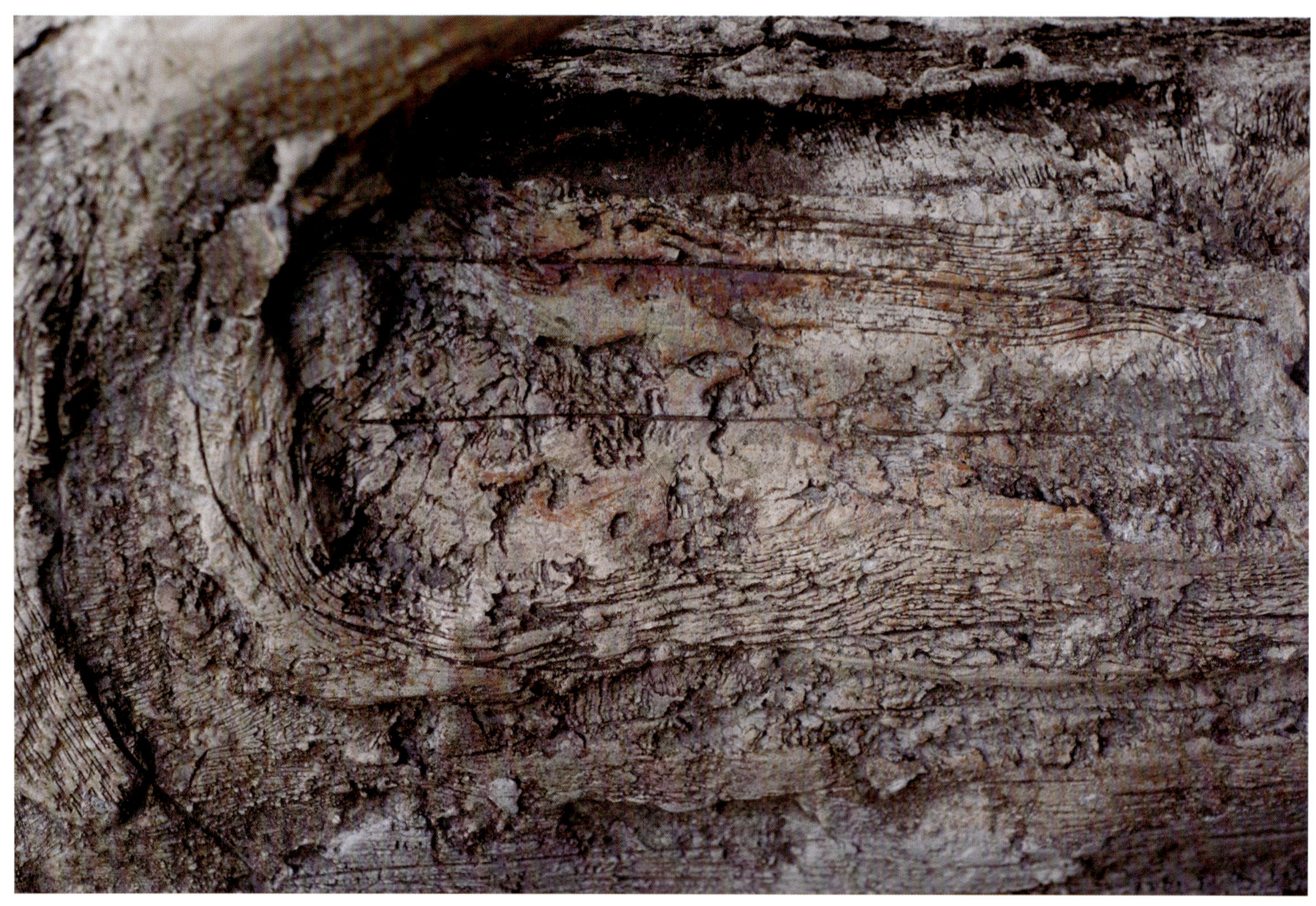

Example of modeled and pigmented tree bark. Antonio Lopez. San Antonio, TX. Private collection. Photo by Kent Rush.

Surface Modeling and Texture

The most alluring of the details that these artisans impart to their objects are the intricately elaborated surface effects and textures. Tree bark, of course, is an essential component and possibly the defining element of trabajo rústico of the tree/wood style. Even so, some talented contemporary practitioners do not routinely apply bark, or do so rarely, preferring to emphasize the intricacy of wood grains in the object.

The artisans are familiar with growth patterns of bark and how bark differs depending on the type of tree from which it originates. As told in *Capturing Nature: The Cement Sculpture of Dionicio Rodríguez*, in the 1920s, Dionicio Rodríguez created for Charles Baumberger at the offices of the Alamo Cement Company a fence that represented the limbs and barks patterns of twenty distinct trees.[5] But there are other textures rendered.

Along with the elaborate tracery of the overall forms and the details of the diverse types of connections, the multitude and variety of textures and surfaces pique our attention and keep us fascinated with the knowledge, skill, and creativity of the artisan. The tools used to create these textures, even to this day, are mundane instruments such as forks, combs, and the wiry edges of mesh. As one studies the surfaces of these pieces, one can visualize the artist, basic tools in hand, dragging, scratching, pressing, poking, dabbing, incising, smoothing, raking, slathering, and scooping the textures into existence, shaping the incredibly realistic expressions of tree wood and bark. After an appropriate curing time, coloration is applied with acid etch stains.

In a 1927 article on Dionicio Rodríguez's bridge in Brackenridge Park in San Antonio, W. E. Barker described the technique:

> The axe marks show: the growth rings can be counted on the ends of the logs; small limbs have been trimmed off, leaving chisel-shaped stubs. There are knots which growing bark has partly covered; the bark covers some logs and is partly stripped from others. Log ends have been roughly trimmed to fit against other logs and at places nails have cracked the imitation wood – nails, which, by the way, are only concrete painted a rusty brown. Closer inspection is repaid by the discovery of more clever mimicry; worm holes, a place where stripped bark exposed the channel made by some wood borer, a spot where some industrious woodpecker sought a grub.[6]

The wood of trees is often revealed, displaying where the log has been stripped of bark, hewn or sawn into a plank, or crosscut to serve as, perhaps, a tabletop or a bench seat. Renditions show the longitudinal wood grain striations or concentric circular tree rings, and interrupting knots, spike knots, and often the distinction between heartwood and sapwood. All types of wood deformities and abnormalities are also rendered, among them burls, splitting, splintering, checking, weathering, dead and decaying wood, and fire damage.

Not all artisans strive for absolute realism in their work, however. Each develops their individual sculptural tendencies; some prefer a more generic realism (e.g., "bark like" as opposed to "pine bark"), some create "shorthand" abbreviations of

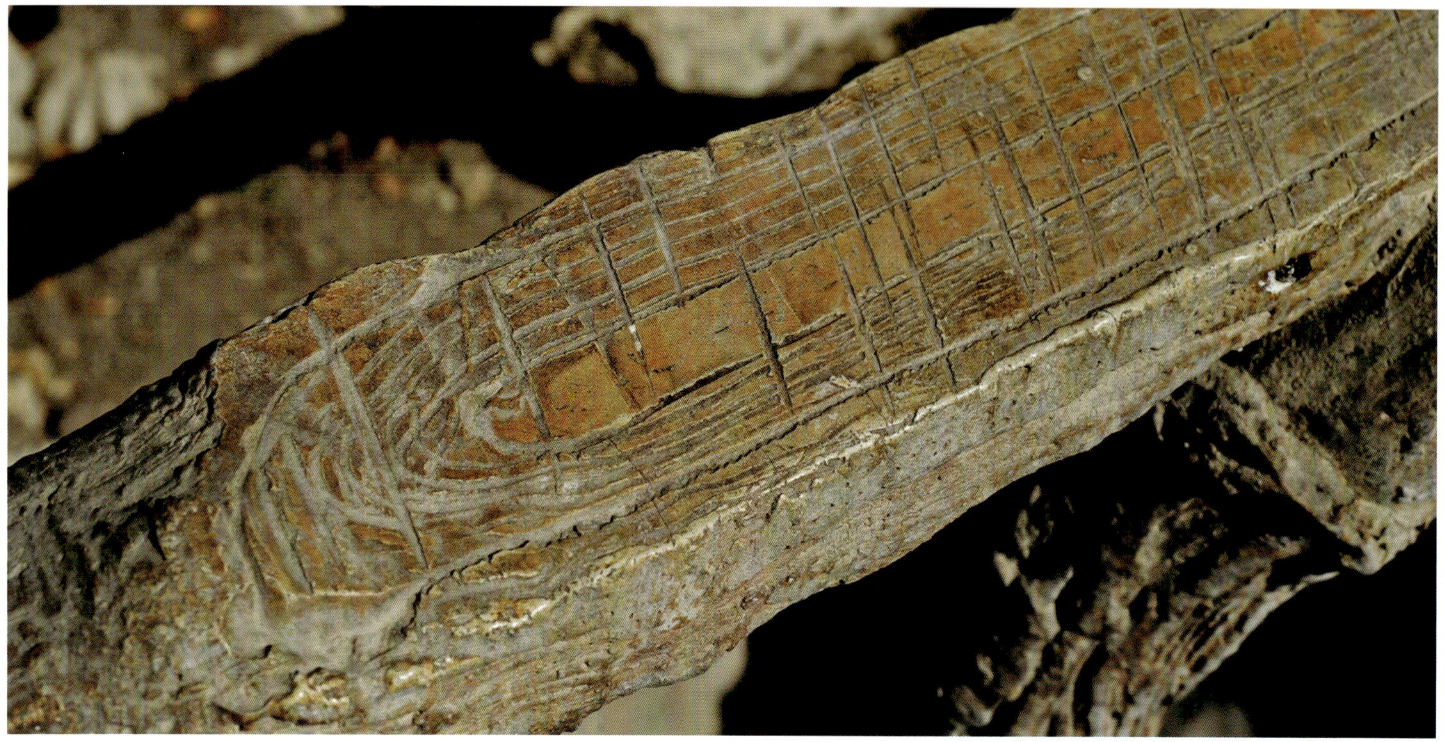

Above: *Saw marks along face of cut. Dionicio Rodríguez. San Antonio, TX. Private collection. Photo by Kent Rush.*

Right: *Artisan unknown. Bandera County, TX. Heartwood exposed chair arm. Private collection. Photo by Kent Rush.*

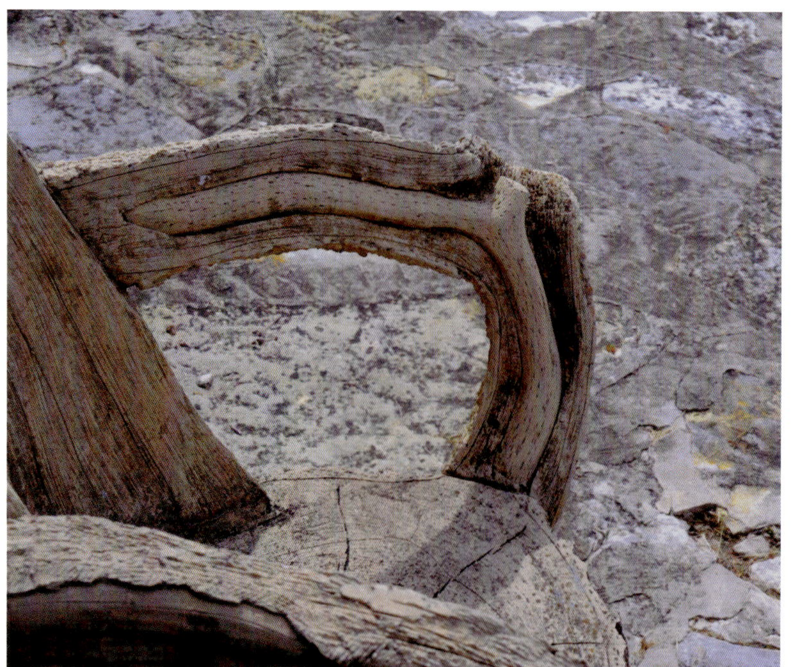

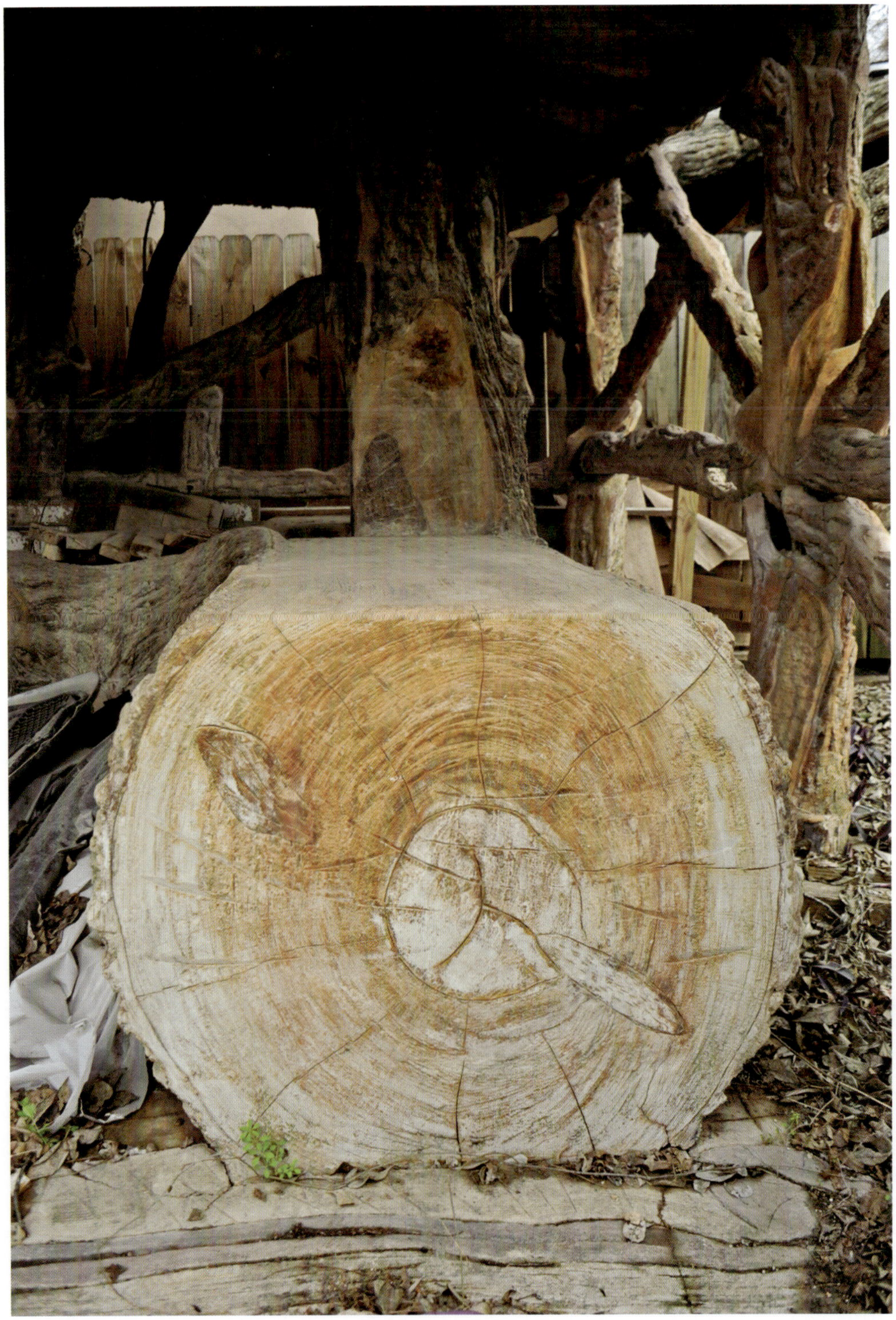

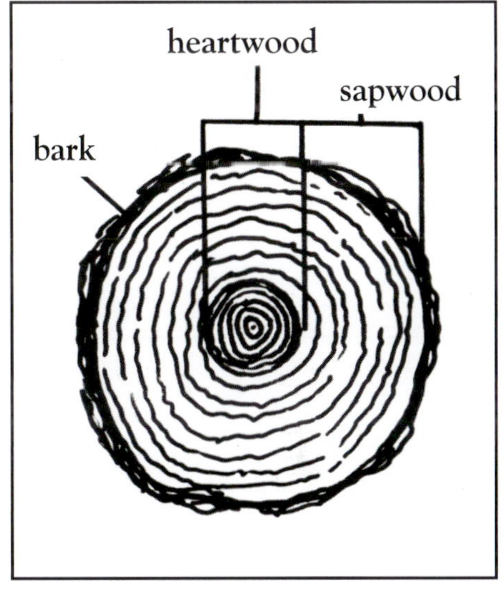

Crosscut log: bark, sapwood, heartwood. Mauro Del Toro. San Antonio, TX. Private collection. Photo and illustration by Kent Rush.

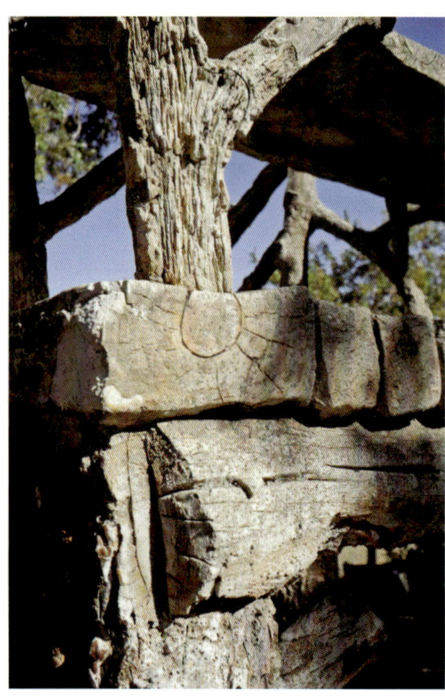

Details of complex textures: checking, splitting, crosscut, and other. Above: Maximo Cortés. Boerne, TX. Private collection. Right: Dionicio Rodríguez. San Antonio, TX. Photos by Kent Rush.

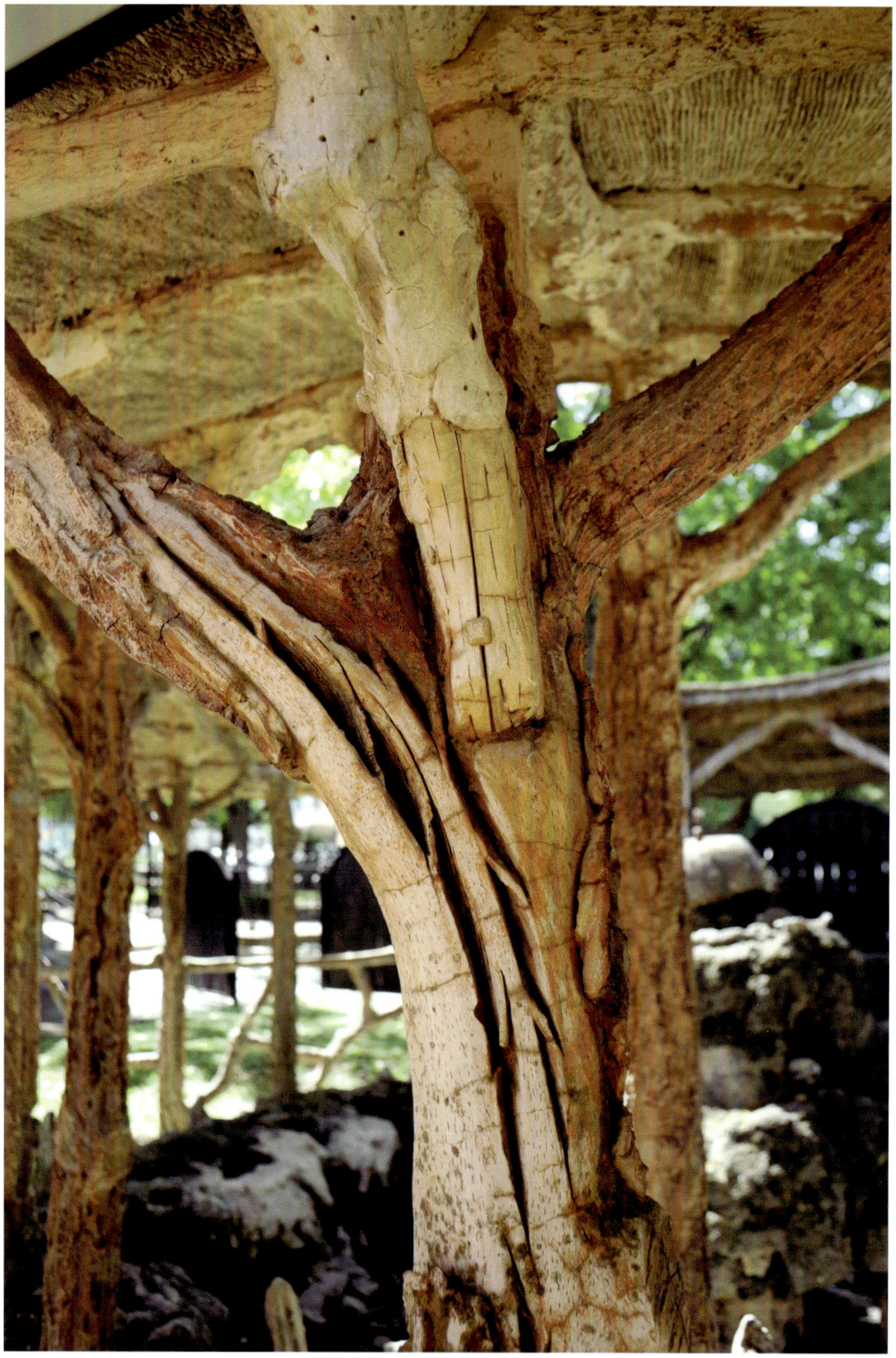

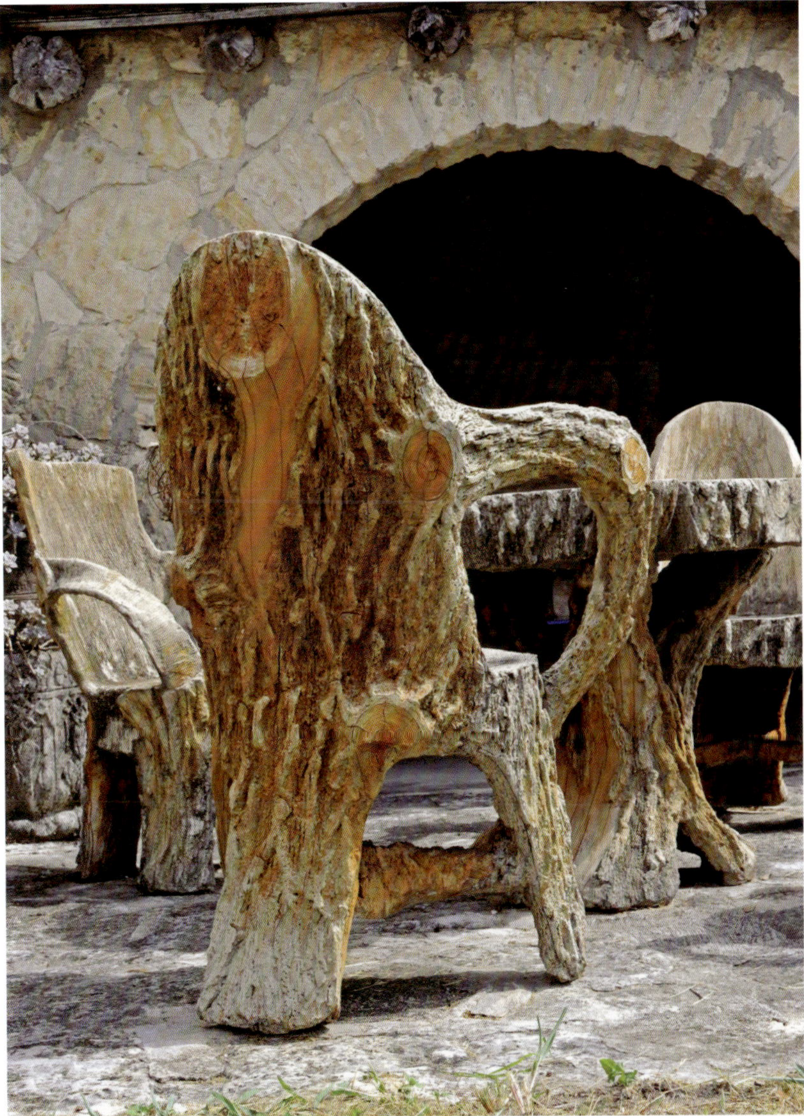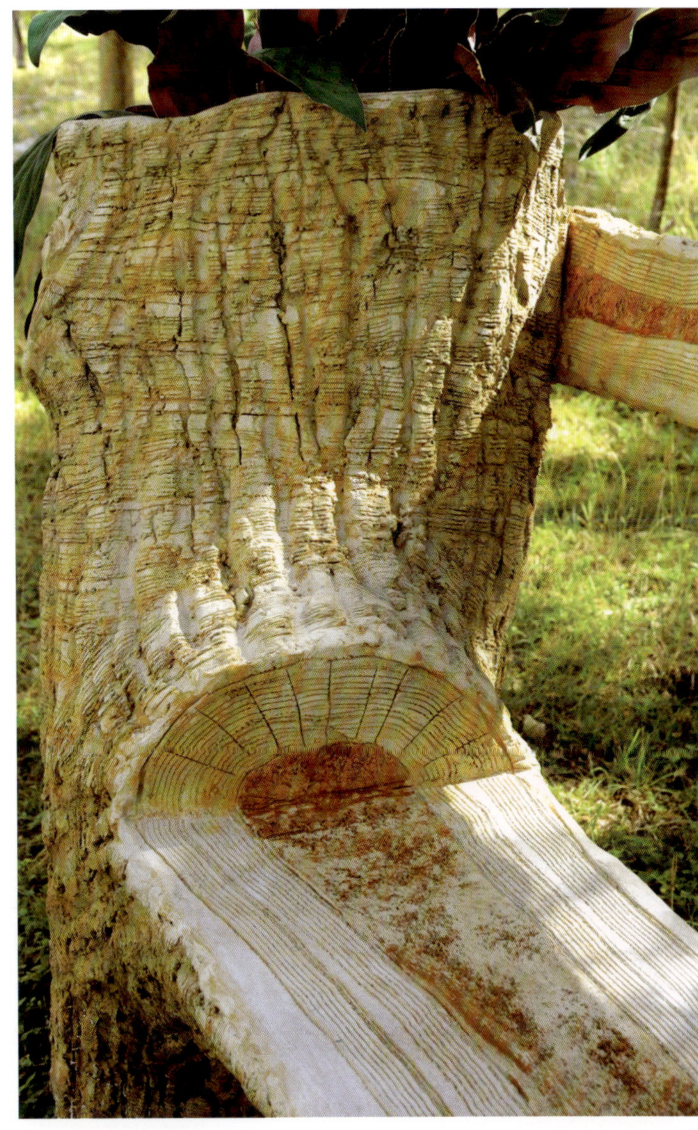

specific textures, and others, like Mauro Del Toro, emphasize a more exaggerated or surreal affectation.

Coloration

Of the three aspects of detail, color is perhaps the most problematic. The sculptural and textural aspects are relatively permanent but not so the coloration. Though the original colorants were meant to penetrate and bond chemically with the surface of the concrete to make the colors permanent, it is not surprising that after almost one

Above left: *Surface facing away from sun and weather retains original color. Unknown artisan. Bandera County, TX. Private collection. Photo by Kent Rush.*

Above: *Jorge Cerrato. Location unknown. Bench with crosscut showing sapwood in yellow and heartwood in orange. Photo by Kent Rush.*

hundred years most pieces from the earlier period have faded considerably and have taken on a bone-white to gray color in the most exposed areas. Like the Greek classical sculptures, we have come to know and think of these works in their monochromatic state.

The colors have proved to be less permanent than the concrete itself. Ultraviolet light and weather fade the colorant, and, in specimens such as the Alamo Heights trolley stop, so does the constant wear-and-tear of the public's clothing on the seating areas, eventually returning the concrete to its base color. Only the undersides or sections facing away from direct sunlight and wear-and-tear retain their color. Contemporary artisans use both water-based and acid-based tints and apply various types of sealers. It seems that some use commercially available concrete stains.

Coloration was and is used to distinguish one kind of bark from another and very often to distinguish the differing colors of the inner woods, the sapwood, heartwood, and pith from the bark where the trunk or limb had been hewn, exposing these layers. In other instances, washy variegations were used on barks where a more mottled effect was appropriate.

Even if color photographs existed of these older pieces, they would be of questionable help as a guide for restoration. Early color photography was not very accurate, and prints, negatives, and transparencies may themselves have changed hues.

In some cases, owners who were concerned about the cracking of the concrete surface (spalling) applied slurries of cement or mortar rubbed into the crevasses and wiped it back. This slurry was indiscriminate, however, and filled in some of the deep textural marks and striations, thus permanently obscuring the original sculptural detail along with its coloration.

Some of San Antonio's most beloved and publicly viewed pieces are being stabilized, repaired, and recolored by experienced practitioners as are other trabajo rústico treasures scattered across the United States. To those of us familiar with the old weathered look, the change is, at first, startling. But the look is probably much closer to its original than the grayish, weathered look to which we have become accustomed.

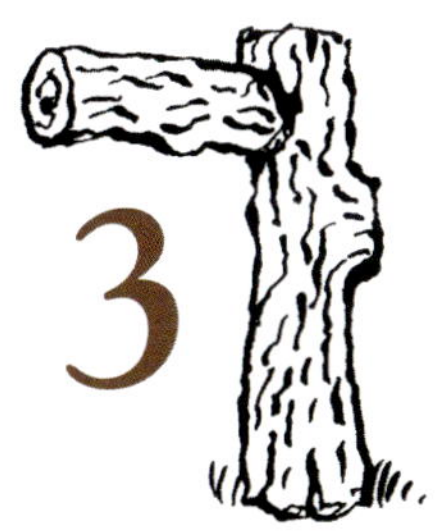

Profiles of Early and Contemporary Artisans

Recognition of the genre of trabajo rústico in the United States in recent years has been slow in comparison with its predecessor, *faux bois* or *rocaille* in France. Although imported French work began to appear in the antique marketplace during the 1970s and 1980s, US-made concrete objects and furniture that mimicked textures of tree bark and rocks were less favored, perhaps because the artisans did not advertise this form of art with regional roots.

Scholarly recognition began in the late 1900s in San Antonio in an exhibition organized by Pat Jasper and Kay Turner in 1986 at the San Antonio Museum of Art—Art among Us (*Arte Entre Nosotros*): Mexican American Folk Art of San Antonio.[1] The following year the museum's folk art curator, anthropologist Marion Oettinger, organized the permanent Mexican Folk Art Collection, *Con Cariño* ("With Appreciation").[2] Both exhibitions featured examples of trabajo rústico work, later popularized by Martha Stewart, who had discovered the work of Carlos Cortés.

In 2005, The San Antonio Botanical Garden opened an outdoor exhibit of sculptures by Carlos Cortés and Family, "Art in the Garden: Trabajo Rústico;" and in 2010, the San Antonio Conservation Society, the Department of Art and Art History at The University of Texas at San Antonio, the City of San Antonio office of Cultural Affairs, and the Alamo Cement Company sponsored a Historic Preservation Month program at the Southwest School of Art in San Antonio, "Fantasies in Cement: Trabajo Rústico," a photo exhibit of trabajo rústico artisans and a seminar that included artisan talks and a demonstration by Carlos Cortés and his helpers.

The sociocultural context of the trabajo rústico artisans in the following biographies resulted from historical events including the revolution in Mexico, which caused many families to flee to safety in San Antonio, and the Great Depression that soon followed. Of utmost importance was the arrival of one individual: Dionicio Rodríguez, who is believed to have been the first concrete artisan in San Antonio. While other immigrants brought their age-old traditional skills of leather and metal work (practiced by the Spanish and later the Mexicans), his skill was a result of industrialization, the combination of reinforced steel with concrete (beginning in France in the late 1800s).[3] Rodríguez brought his knowledge of the technique, which he had learned in Mexico City, and others, mostly Mexican immigrants or first-generation US-born, learned either by working as his assistants or as self-taught artisans.

In comparison with family groups in Mexico who have worked together for centuries creating crafts and folk art, few trabajo rústico artisans worked together as family units.[4] Exceptions were Rodríguez and Máximo Cortés, who earlier worked with various relatives in the 1920s and 1930s, and Carlos Cortés and Rene Romero, who later employed relatives for their projects. In early 2000, anthropologist Maribel Alvarez wrote of a family group that produced plaster "border-type things" for sale to tourists.[5]

Bacilio Capetillo Aguilar

BACILIO AGUILAR was born in Monterrey, Nuevo Leon, Mexico, about 1887; his birth certificate records that he was baptized in San Miguelito, San Luis Potosí.[6] He came to San Antonio from Monterrey in 1919 with his wife, Anita, his parents, and two children, and they lived in the Mexican Village, a group of cottages below the Japanese Tea Garden in Brackenridge Park.[7] The census listed his occupation as "plaster worker." According to family history, he was the first artisan to answer a newspaper advertisement seeking Mexican artisans to work in the Village.[8] He and his neighbors made items to sell to the tourists visiting the Tea Garden, and an archival photograph illustrates him with a decorative vase. Surviving in 2016 are the rock cottages and a rock kiln, where Aguilar fired ceramic objects, including chia heads (which grow chia seed as hair). Other families were the widow Guadalupe Pozos and her four children, who wove cane and *tuile* (bulrush) for furniture,[9] and the Rangel family. Mrs. Rangel made baby clothes. No longer at the site was a brush-covered arbor where the families entertained tourists with dancing and music and served Mexican dinners. The Aguilar family later moved to 2521 Guadalupe Street, and the 1940 census listed Bacilio as a sculptor.[10] His signature is found on numerous

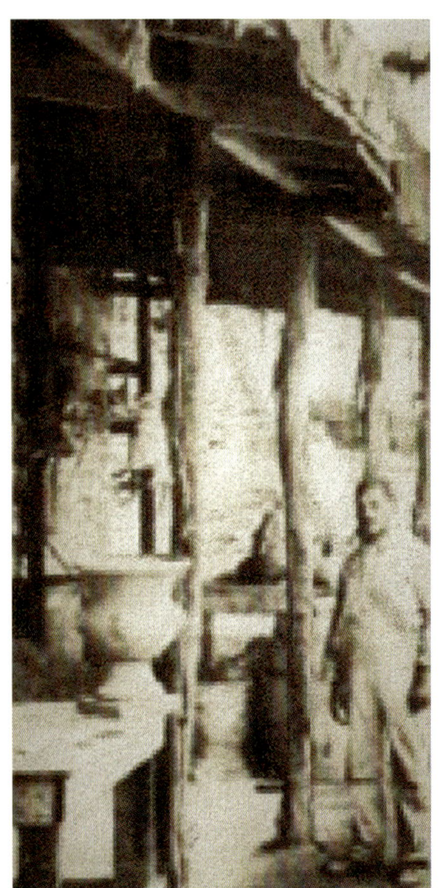

Bacillo Aguilar at work. Unknown photographer. Photo courtesy of David Culver.

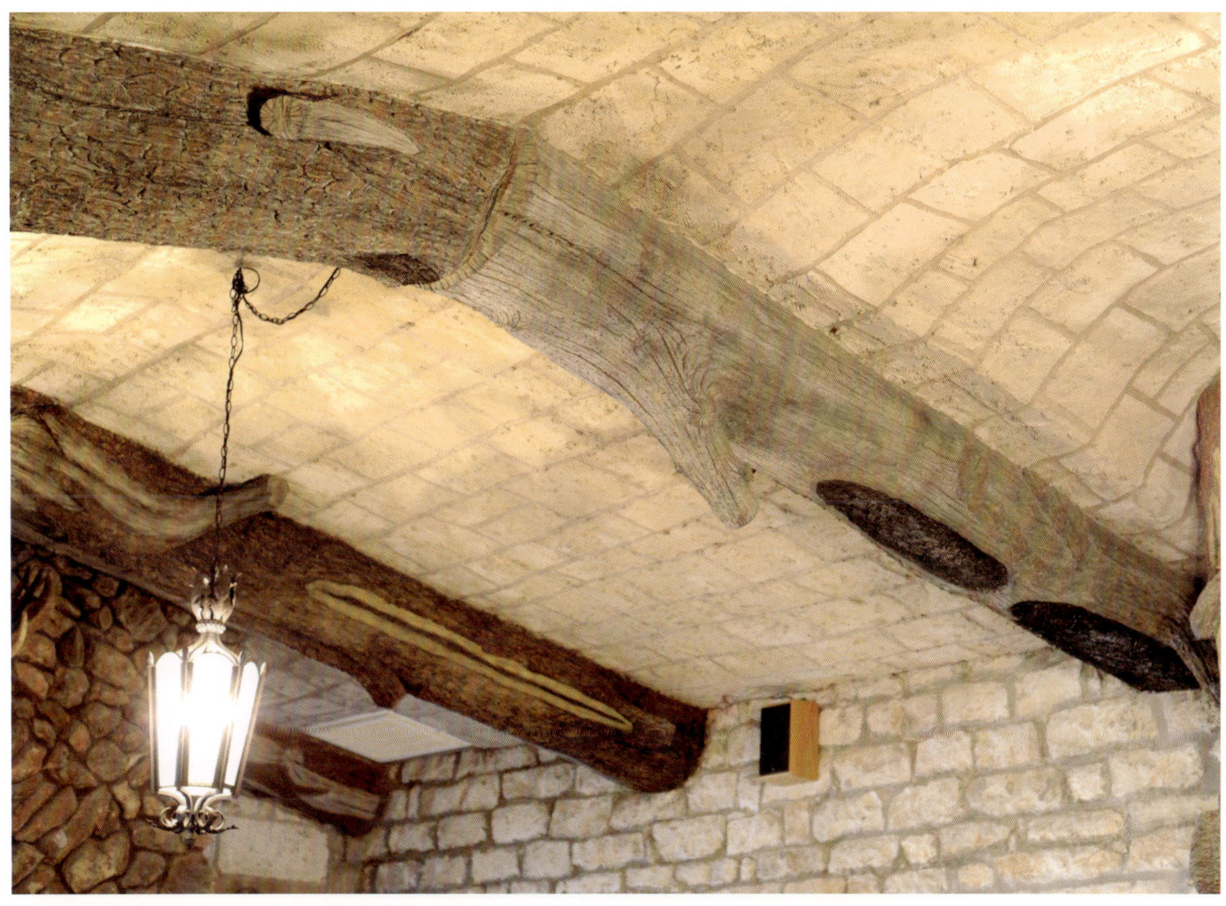

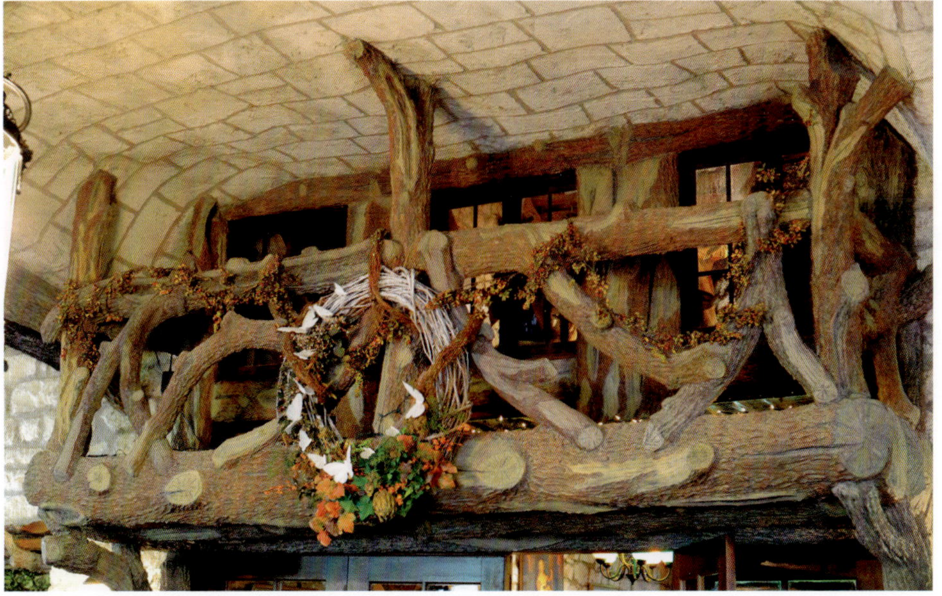

Above: *Bacilio Aguilar. Boerne, TX. Speakeasy Ranch. Beams and ceiling. Gary Devloo, owner. Photo by Kent Rush.*

Left: *Bacilio Aguilar. Boerne, TX. Speakeasy Ranch. Interior balcony rail. Gary Devloo, owner. Photo by Kent Rush.*

trabajo rústico projects for private clients, including the work commissioned by San Antonio resident Frank T. Brady, north of Boerne, Texas.

Aguilar applied trabajo rústico exterior and interior details to the previously constructed house, including window lintels, roof beams, stair rails, a built-in china cabinet, and a chandelier. Other cement objects at this site, the Speakeasy Ranch, were a wishing well, a large basket planter, and a cave-like grotto with a fishpond and dripping water. In his later years he made cement and marble tombstones and helped his son in a hardware store. Aguilar died in 1964.

Eliseo G. Alvarado

Eliseo Alvarado held a variety of jobs after he moved from La Vernia, Texas, to San Antonio in 1923, including helping to build the Kelly Air Force Base airstrip. His last job before he retired was with the City of San Antonio as groundskeeper for some city-owned golf courses.[11]

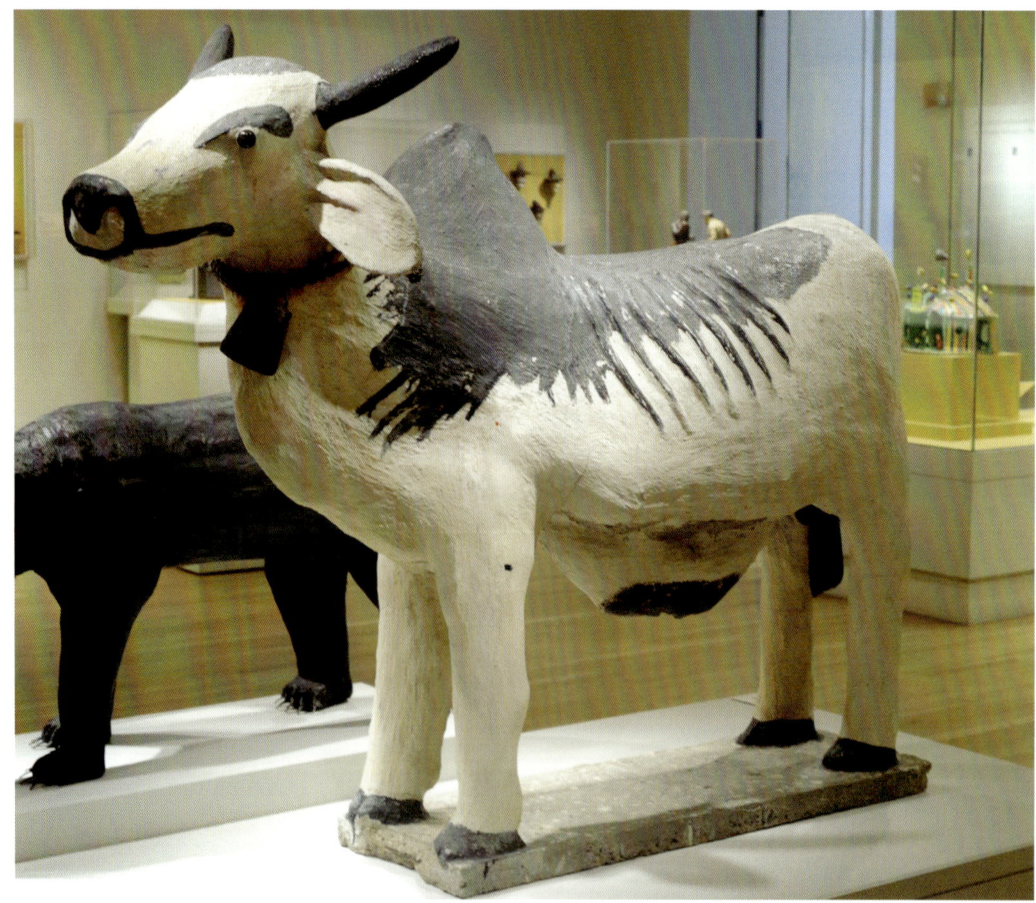

Above: *Eliseo G. Alvarado. San Antonio, TX. Photo by Ron Bechtol.*

Right: *Eliseo Alvarado. San Antonio, TX. San Antonio Museum of Art Collection. Bull. Photo by Kent Rush.*

After he retired he started building concrete sculptures in his front yard for his sixteen grandchildren "to enjoy playing with (and on) them." As a child he made animals out of mud, but as an adult he used concrete with "a base of chicken wire." Cars driving down the street would come to a stop and back up to see his sculptures. Most were animals: an elephant weighing two tons, a donkey, a giraffe almost as tall as the roof of the house, a horse, a Brahma bull, a two-humped camel, and more. The animals were described as stocky, had legs without joints, and were realistically painted. There were wishing wells, planters shaped like baskets and hats, also realistically painted, and a shrine to the Virgin of Guadalupe.[12]

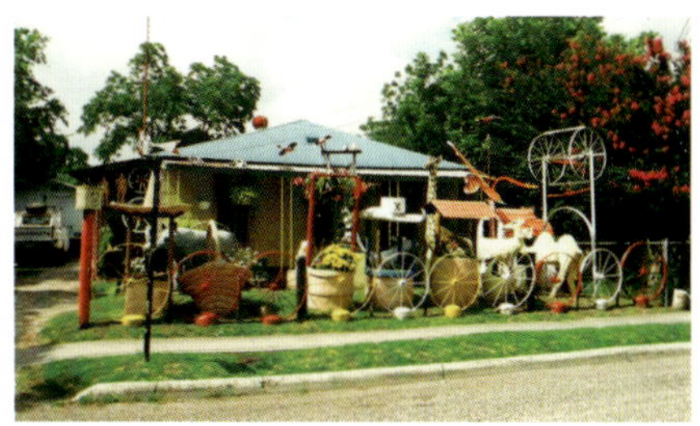

Eliseo Alvarado. San Antonio, TX. Alvarado home display. Photo by Larry Harris.

One day a passerby saw the works, got out of his car, and proclaimed Alvarado's animals "folk art." The individual (presumably a Madison Avenue art dealer) said he would get high prices for his work in New York and that the works should be in a museum. The artisan replied, "Where will the children play if I sell them?"[13] Eventually the artisan donated two pieces, the bull and the horse, to the Latin American Folk Art Gallery at the San Antonio Museum of Art. When asked by gallery curator Marion Oettinger to donate the two animals to the museum, Alvarado came up with the estimated value of the cost of wire, cement, and paint at $23.75.[14] He was never convinced that his work was art. He said, "I guess it is art. . . . If they say it is, I guess it is."[15]

Most of the remaining works were sold in 1999 to a New Braunfels collector, who used a crane to remove them. The front yard no longer features sculptures. Born in 1910, Alvarado died in 2001 at the age of ninety.[16]

Genaro Briones portrait. Courtesy of Texas Historical Commission.

Genaro Briones

GENARO BRIONES (1899–1979) was raised by an uncle in New Mexico from the age of four. When he was thirteen his uncle took him to El Paso to learn bricklaying and plastering. By the 1930s he had moved to Austin, had married Carolina Villarreal, and was working as a bricklayer and plasterer. According to Mrs. Briones, he had steady work during the Great Depression, working in Texas, California, Mexico, and Tennessee. He worked with Dionicio Rodríguez in Memphis, Tennessee, probably assisting with building structures at Memorial Park Cemetery, where, along with two other artisans, George Cardosa and Ralph Corona, he learned about Rodríguez's acid-based color formulas: copperas, sulfuric acid, muriatic acid, iron oxide, saltpeter, and lampblack. According to Briones, these colors were "clear

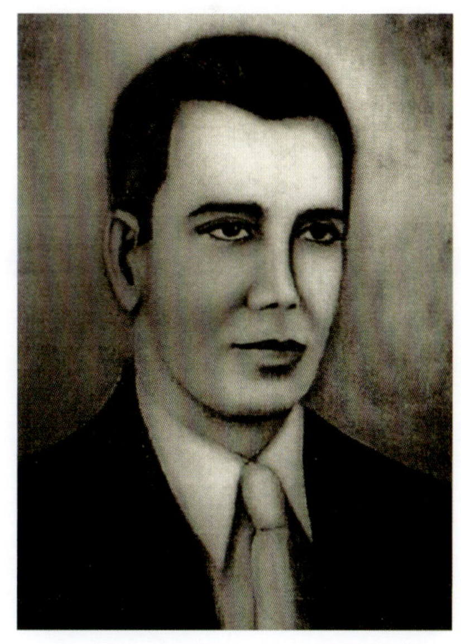

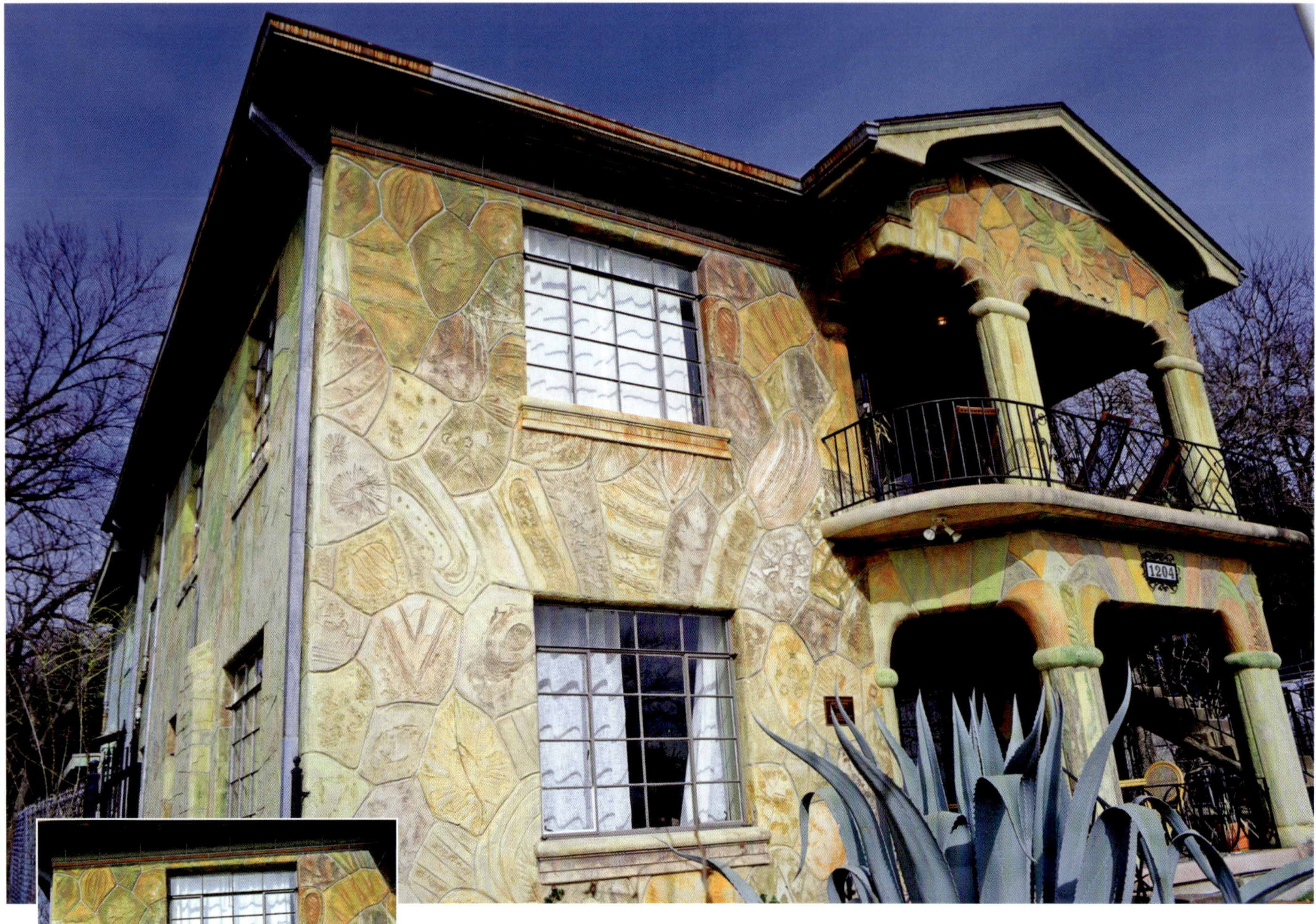

Above and left: *Genaro Briones. Austin, TX. Briones house. Above, front view; left, front façade. Laurie D. Marchant and Robert L. Marchant, owners. Photos by Kent Rush.*

as water" when applied to the wet cement. For the colorant to penetrate the cement, it was necessary to apply strong pressure with a brush and soon colors began to appear on the surface.

Briones owned a house at 1204 East Seventh Street in Austin, which he rented to tenants, but in 1947 he demolished the structure and poured a foundation for his two-story duplex. Working nights and weekends, he finished the upstairs portion of the structure in 1951, and he and his wife and mother-in-law moved in. By 1953 he had completed the downstairs.[17]

Built of concrete block, the house is reminiscent of Art Deco and features designs with bright colors, in contrast to Rodríguez's colors, which imitated the more subdued shades of nature. The works in the yard—the table, chairs, settee, basket and planter, and flamingos—were made in the style of Rodríguez, who visited the site during its construction; they were no longer extant in 2021.[18]

Briones applied his decorative cement designs to other buildings in Austin, including a bank in South Austin, which by 2018, had been either remodeled or demolished, with the exception of Vikashimo's Lounge at 1405 East Sixth Street. He created exhibits for the Texas Parks and Wildlife Department in its former headquarters in Austin, destroyed in 1956, and also built a decorative house for Elisio de la Peña in San Antonio. His own home is still on its original lot in Austin and retains much of its joyful coloring. The Briones House was listed in 1995 on the National Register of Historic Places.[19]

Carlos Cortés

Born in 1958 in San Antonio, Carlos Cortés helped his father Máximo (see following profile) in his younger years, but did not initially aspire to follow in his father's footsteps as a sculptor. Carlos planned a career in medicine, but while at St. Mary's University, he began drafting for a civil engineering company, which later proved helpful with his large-scale concrete projects.[20]

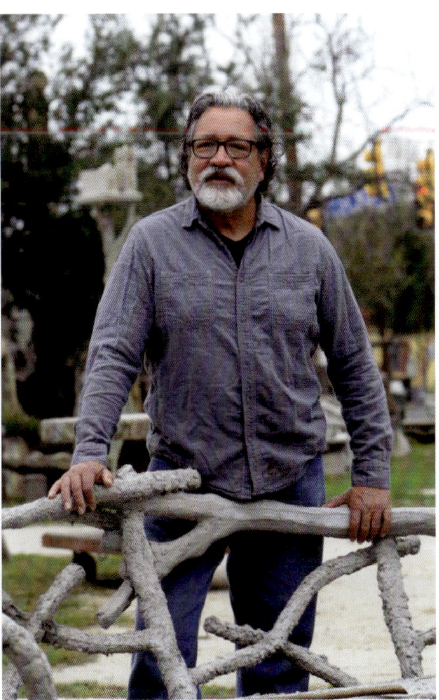

Above: *Carlos Cortés. San Antonio, TX. Photo by Kent Rush.*

Left: *Carlos Cortés. San Antonio, TX. Landa Library pavilion. Photo by Kent Rush.*

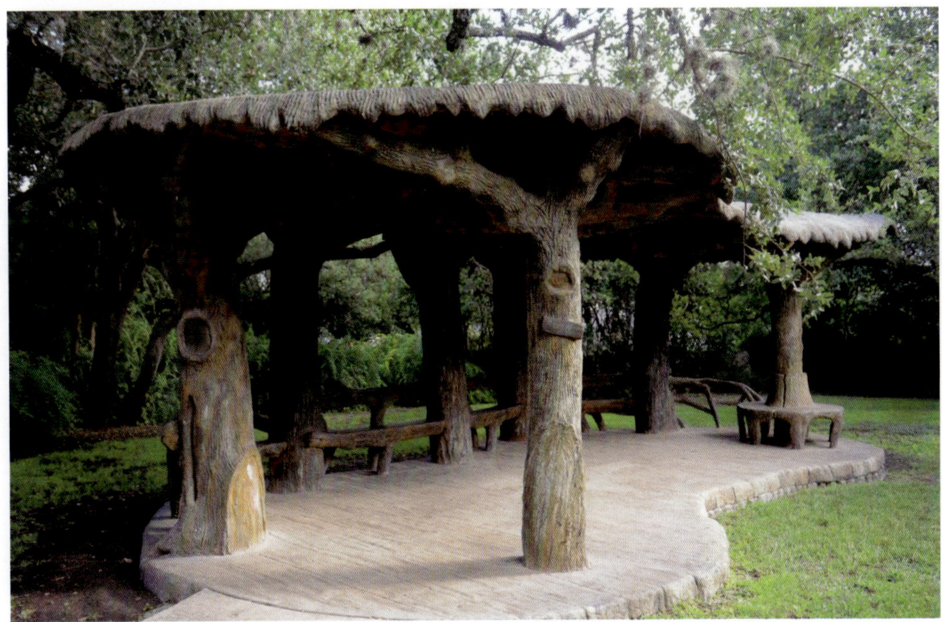

Carlos Cortés. San Antonio, TX. San Antonio River Walk. Arbor. Photo by Kent Rush.

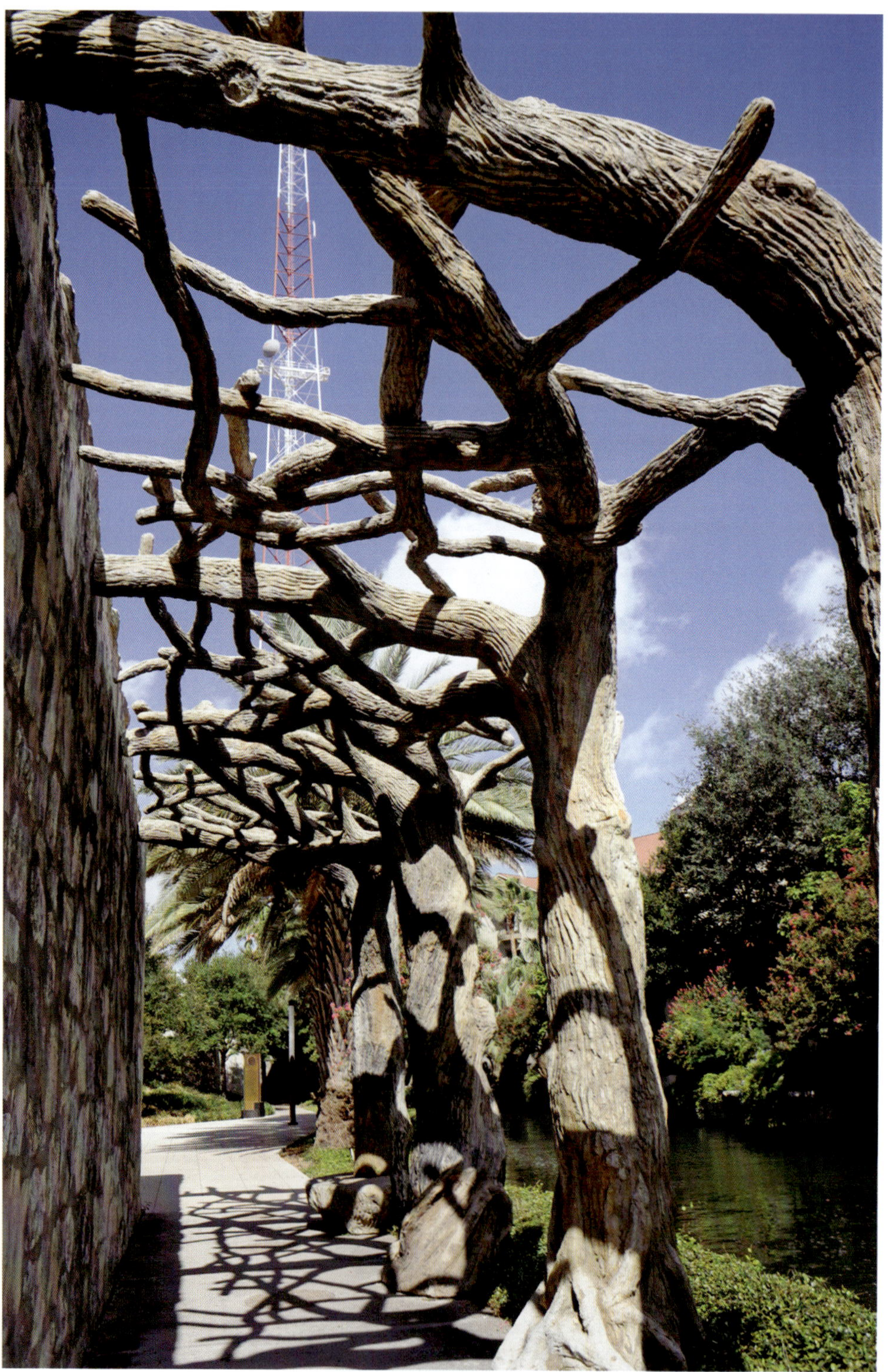

In mid-1980s, Carlos quit his desk job in Dallas and returned to San Antonio to follow in his father's footsteps from whom he had learned the trabajo rústico techniques. He began making benches, birdbaths, and other small objects. During the last thirty years, he has received many private and public commissions for large works, including bridges, arbors, a bus stop, and a grotto on the San Antonio River Walk Museum Reach.[21] History of the development of the genre in San Antonio reveals that Carlos has continued the tradition of employing extended family members as helpers. He is considered an expert in restoring works by Rodríguez, his father, and Ralph Corona and George Cardosa (both of whom worked in Michigan). His studio in San Antonio is a veritable museum featuring collected works by his father, his great uncle (by marriage) Dionicio Rodríguez, J. M. Martinez, Sam Murray, and Julian Sandoval.

Cortés was awarded the Lynn Ford Craftsman Award by The San Antonio Conservation Society in 1998 and the Artisan Award by the Texas Society of Architects in 2004. The "domestic diva" Martha Stewart, a collector of antique French pieces and of his work, has featured him and his projects in her *Living* magazine and on her television program. She also launched a line of trabajo rústico–inspired designs that has influenced many other designers of lamps, linens, tableware, and numerous other products.[22]

Máximo Cortés Cortés

Máximo Cortés Cortés was born in Monterrey, Nuevo Leon, Mexico, in 1903.[23] His father Carlos, who made altars, columns, monuments, grave markers, and grottos,[24] offered Dionicio Rodríguez employment as Rodríguez traveled through Monterrey on his way to San Antonio. The elder Cortés suggested that Rodríguez go to Laredo and work with his son Máximo, who was making plaster ornaments for a school. Máximo later encountered Rodríguez while visiting in San Antonio and was invited to work with Rodríguez. Máximo arrived in San Antonio in 1925.[25]

He learned trabajo rústico from Rodríguez, and they worked together on the footbridge in Brackenridge Park, the trolley stop in Alamo Heights, and various additional projects until Cortés began working on his own in 1927 in a workshop on Mitchell and Flores Streets.

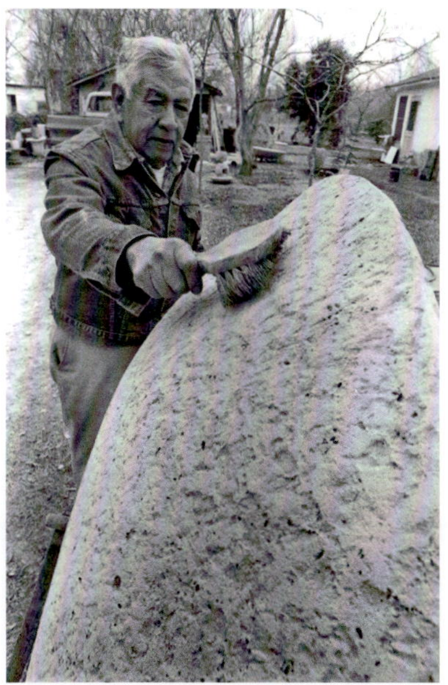

Maximo Cortes. San Antonio, TX. Photo from The University of Texas at San Antonio Special Collections. *San Antonio Express News Collection. ZUMA Press.*

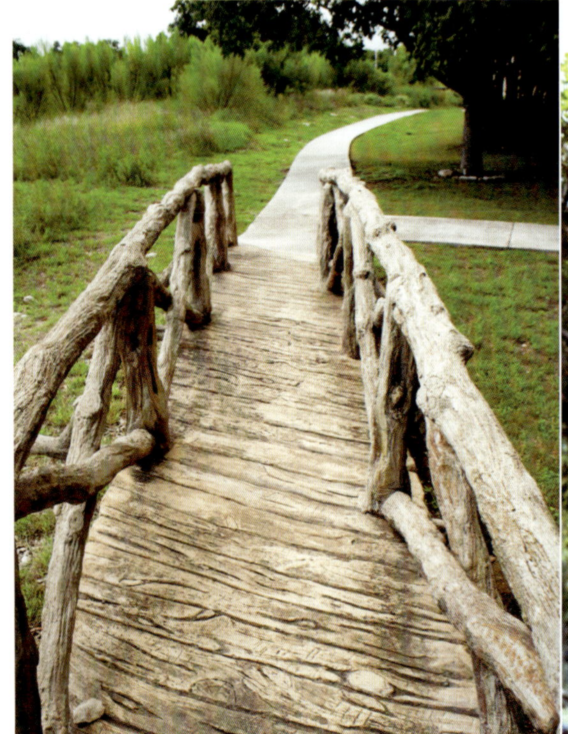

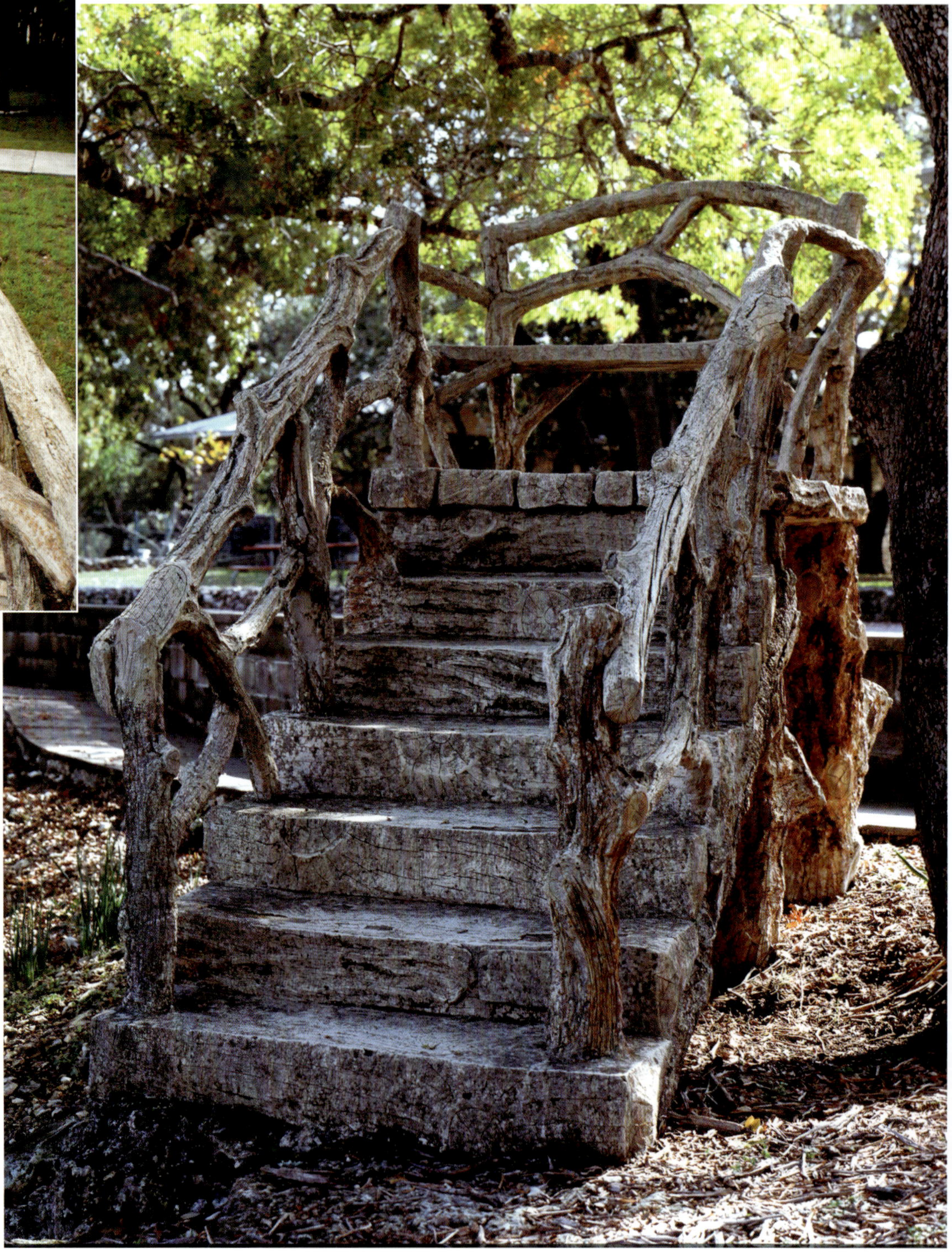

Above: *Máximo Cortés. San Antonio, TX. Private collection. Photo by Kent Rush.*

Right: *Máximo Cortés. Boerne, TX. Elevated bench. Private collection, Proprietors: Benedictine Sisters of Boerne, TX. Photo by Kent Rush.*

After a stint of working in Oklahoma, Cortés opened another shop on Roland Street. He continued to collaborate with Rodríguez for projects in San Antonio, including the Torii Gate entrance to the Japanese Tea Garden, and at several locations outside San Antonio. His work is found in many private collections. Cortés died in 1997.[26]

Marcella Marie Davis

BORN IN Inglewood, California, to an artist mother, Marcella Marie Davis (1957-2020) commented that she had memories of some old trabajo rústico, visiting the historic missions, and "hanging out with her mother's artist friends," which left a visual impact on her that would reappear in later years.

With a background of having worked for twenty years in metalsmithing, armed with a BFA degree in jewelry and metalsmithing from Missouri State University and an MFA in metalsmithing and drawing from Washington University, Marcella was already a practicing artist when she became interested in sculpting in cement.[27]

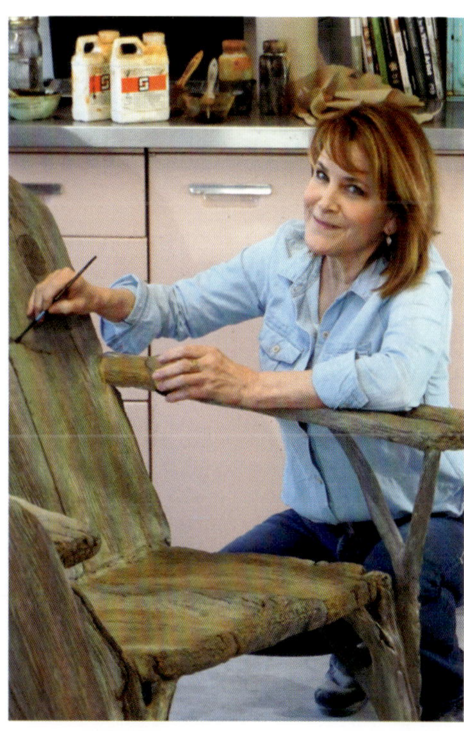

Above: *Marcella Marie Davis. St. Louis, MO. Photo by Christopher Lay.*

Left: *Marcella Marie. St. Louis, MO. Private collection. Photo by Marcella Marie.*

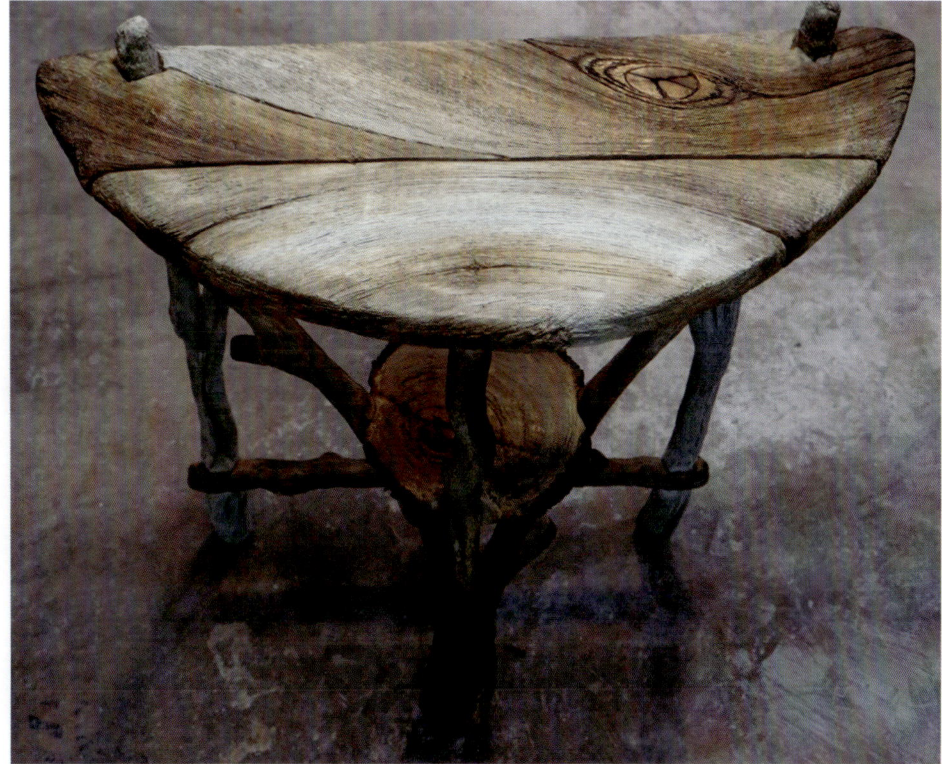

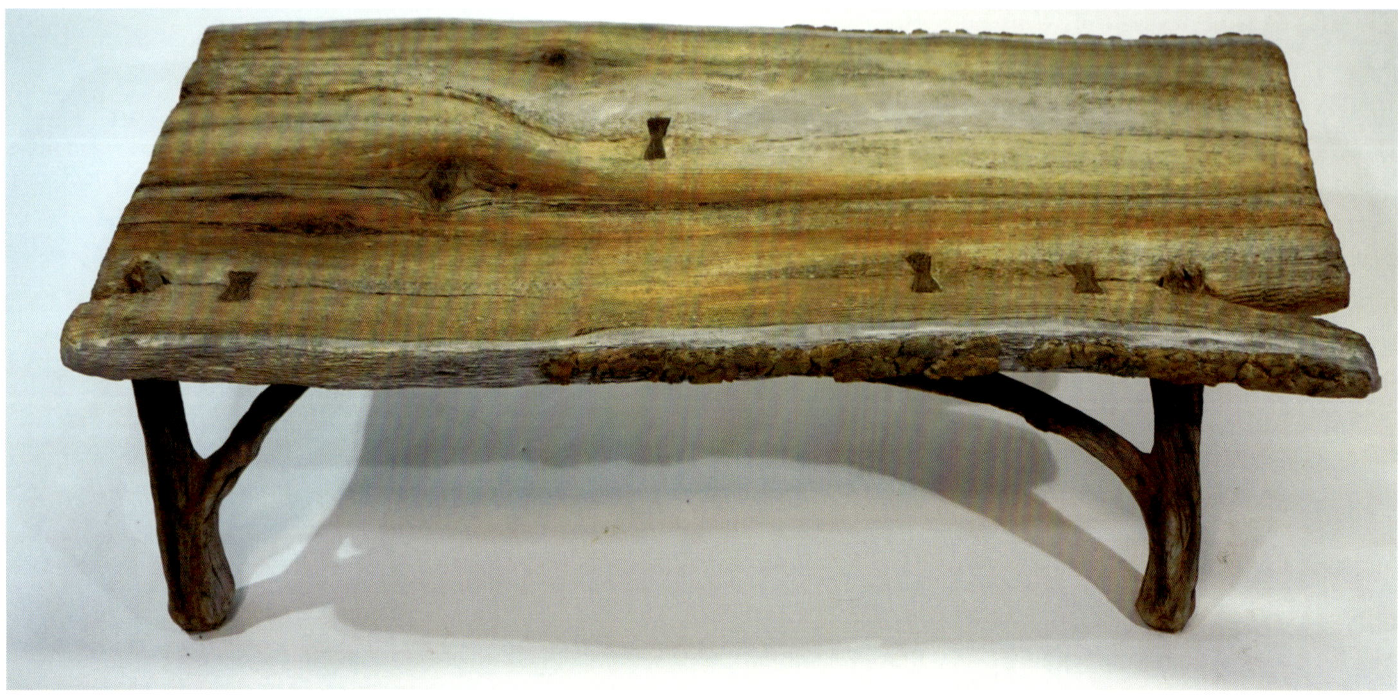

Above: *Marcella Marie. St. Louis, MO. Private collection. Photo by Marcella Marie.*

Left: *Marcella Marie. St. Louis, MO. Private collection. Photo by Marcella Marie.*

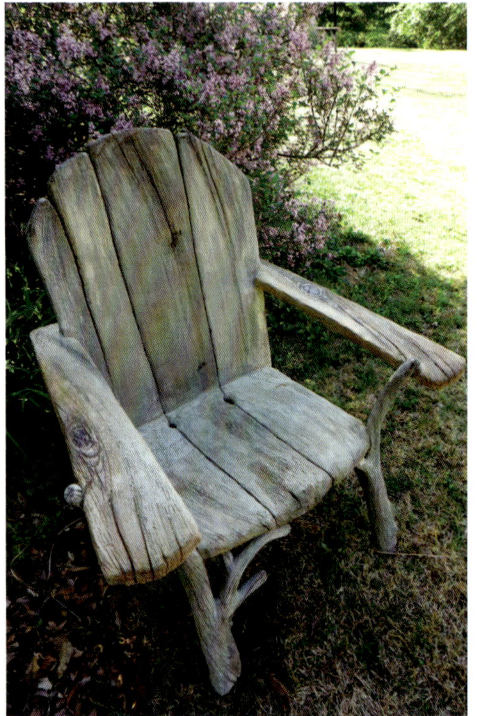

"I had visions of sculptural wood floating ephemerally through my mind's eye compelling me to sculpt."[28]

After checking out a library book on concrete art and making an unsuccessful attempt at sculpting a fish, she started to teach herself by reading anything available and asking questions of local concrete businesses. She writes, "I knew I had seen faux bois in my childhood and loved it."

She turned to Donald Tucker's book, *An Introduction to Sculpting Ferrocement Faux Bois*, which she bought online, and began corresponding with him on his blog. Marcella became his student, spending many hours in his Houston studio and serving as his teaching assistant in his trabajo rústico classes in Tennessee. She wrote that she "owes her passion and love of concrete to him."[29] Marcella's style of creating trabajo rústico without bark was similar to Tucker's in that she made wood forms without bark texture.

Each of Marcella's pieces has a bluebird attached, "representing my pure joy in sculpting faux bois."[30]

Martin Marcial Delgado

According to an article in the *San Antonio Light* of February 12, 1932, Martin Delgado, born in Elmendorf, Texas in 1907, who managed the Spanish Art Shop at 3533 McCullough Avenue in San Antonio, created a doghouse in trabajo rústico style. Accompanying the article, Delgado and his doghouse appear in a photo together with a frog mailbox designed by Antonio Lopez.[31]

The doghouse made of concrete has an artificial rock façade. Details include an awning, a stairway to the second story, and a sun deck. Lopez's frog sits on a heavily textured fake wood stump and features an open mouth to receive mail and a hole at the rear for the owner to retrieve mail.

There is no record of Delgado working on other projects, except that the article says he and Lopez are credited as designers and executors of the trabajo rústico bridge in Brackenridge Park.[32] Later research credits the bridge to Dionicio Rodríguez, who probably hired Delgado and Lopez as assistants. Lopez died in 1958.[33]

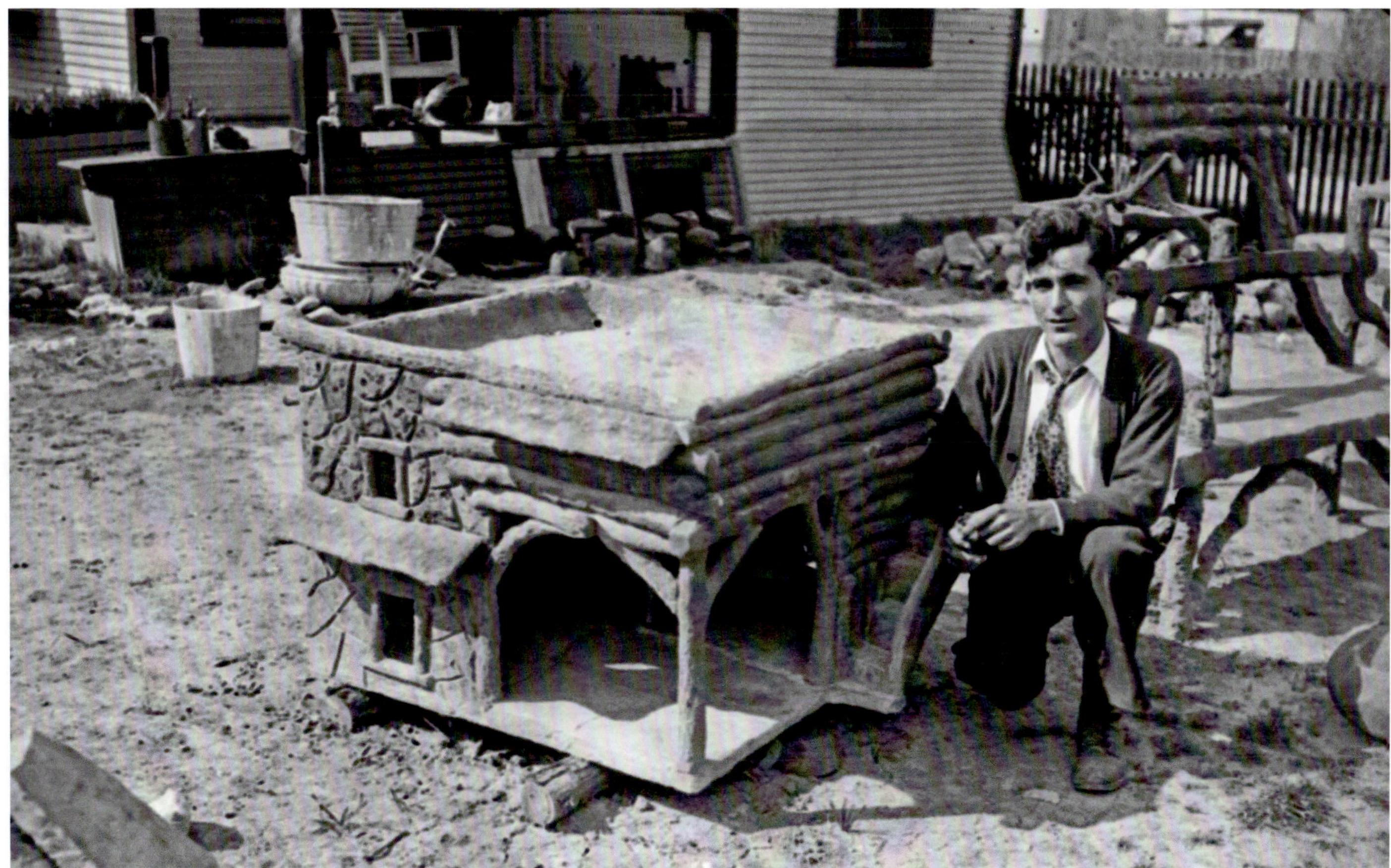

Martin Delgado. San Antonio, TX. Doghouse. Photo from The University of Texas at San Antonio Special Collections San Antonio Light Collection. ZUMA Press.

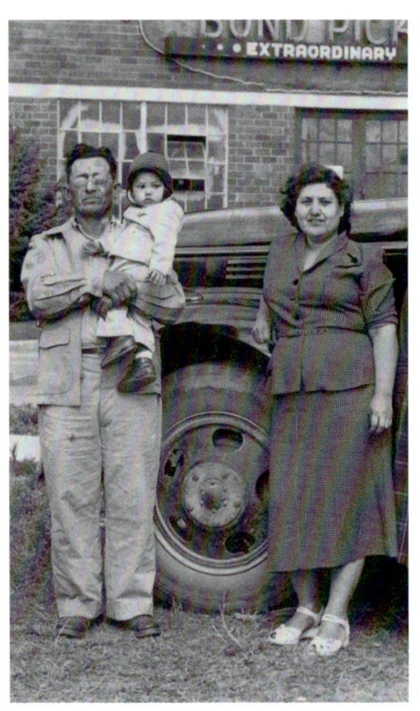

Mauro Del Toro with his wife, Guadalupe, and son, Jesse. San Antonio, TX. Photo courtesy of Yvonne Perez.

Mauro Del Toro

Bᴏʀɴ ɪɴ Candela, Coahuila, Mexico, in 1893 on a hacienda, Mauro Del Toro was one of nine children. According to his daughter, Emma Bailey, his family were "people of some means" but fled Mexico during the Revolution and settled in Agua Dulce, Texas. When Mauro was in his twenties, his father, who had previously known Dr. Aureliano Urrutia in Mexico, contacted the San Antonio doctor asking him to give Mauro a job.[34] Dr. Urrutia hired Mauro to work in his pharmacy, and Mauro and his wife Guadalupe lived with Urrutia in his home on Broadway. Urrutia asked Dionicio Rodríguez, who was working on trabajo rústico projects, to teach Del Toro the technique, and Mauro began working on Brackenridge Park projects with Rodríguez. Later he moved to Corpus Christi, where he worked in the Robert Driscoll Hotel (remodeled as Wells Fargo Tower in the 1970s).[35]

In an interview, Guadalupe related that they accompanied Rodríguez and others to Beaumont, where they both assisted him with trabajo rústico garden embellishments for the John Henry Phelan mansion (now demolished). It appears that Guadalupe knew two of the important steps of the technique: the application of color and the creating of the *mezcla*. The *mezcla* was the final coat of portland ce-

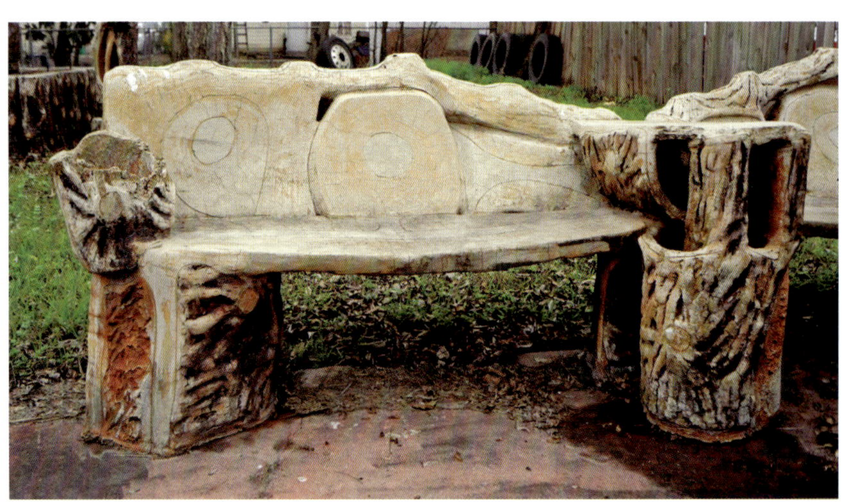

Mauro Del Toro. San Antonio, TX. Private collection. Photo by Kent Rush.

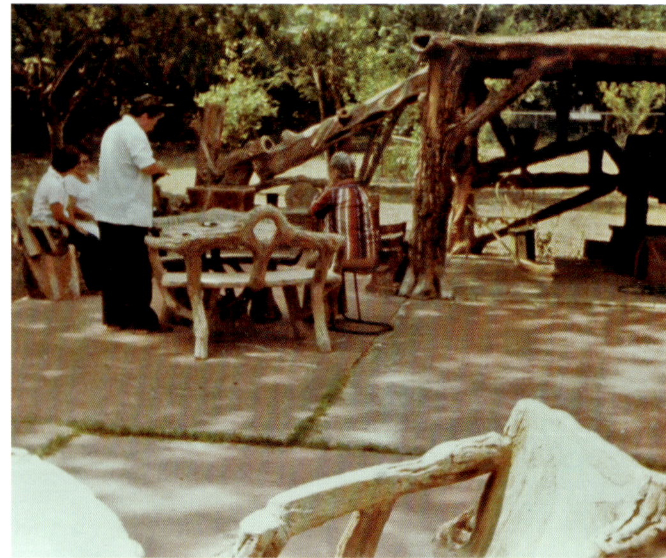

Mauro Del Toro. San Antonio, TX. Del Toro Family back yard. Courtesy of Del Toro Family.

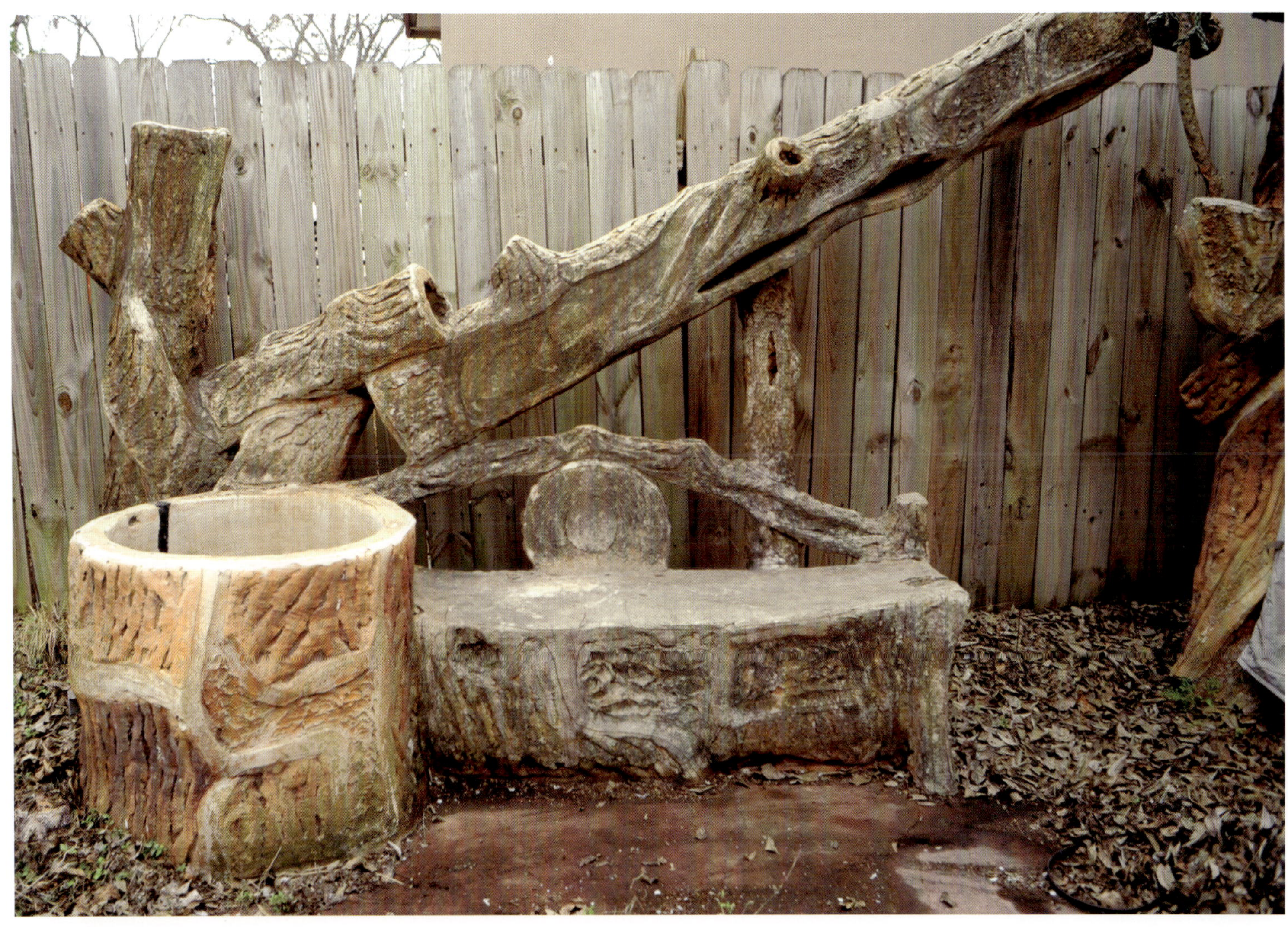

Mauro Del Toro. San Antonio, TX. Private collection. Photo by Kent Rush.

ment, which was usually applied and sculpted by Dionicio when she and her husband worked with him. In a conversation with Patsy Light, she told of the purchase of *sulfacto* (sulphur) and *polvos* (powders) and the technique of boiling them in a clay container to make the dyes. She added that they were applied with a brush, and, afterward, the finished piece was washed down with a *mangera* (hose and water).[36] Later Del Toro organized his own crew, and they traveled throughout Texas working on projects. He also built several grottos for churches. According to his granddaughter, he signed his work on these projects, but they have not been located.[37] He built unique pieces in his own backyard. Very few remain, and they are in poor condition. His work was obviously made for use by his family and friends. Del Toro died in 1967.

Michael Fogg

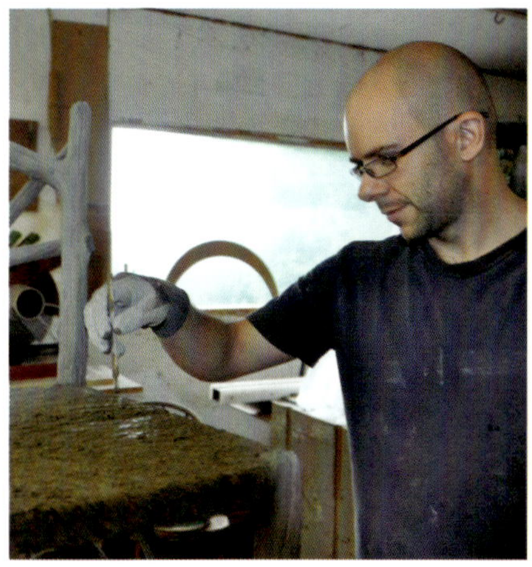

Michael Fogg. Ledyard, CT. Photo courtesy of Michael Fogg, LLC.

MICHAEL FOGG was born in Hamilton, New York, in 1975.[38] He attended Wesleyan University in 1994–98, and after working as a cabinetmaker for twenty years, he found a magazine article about Carlos Cortés, watched videos, and taught himself the craft.[39] Fogg works from pencil sketches, although he "sometimes brings a piece of bark for inspiration." He has devised secret formulas, saying, "The less water, the stronger the mix is, but the harder it is to work with. . . . I like it to be like cream cheese."[40]

Michael says he is attracted to whimsy in the execution of his pieces; he has created a chandelier with a knot that looks like a face and has made planters resembling fungus or snail shells. He aims "for a slightly lighter aesthetic than his peers." His tables appear to be supported by bonsai tree limbs, and his chandeliers have thin, graceful branches.[41]

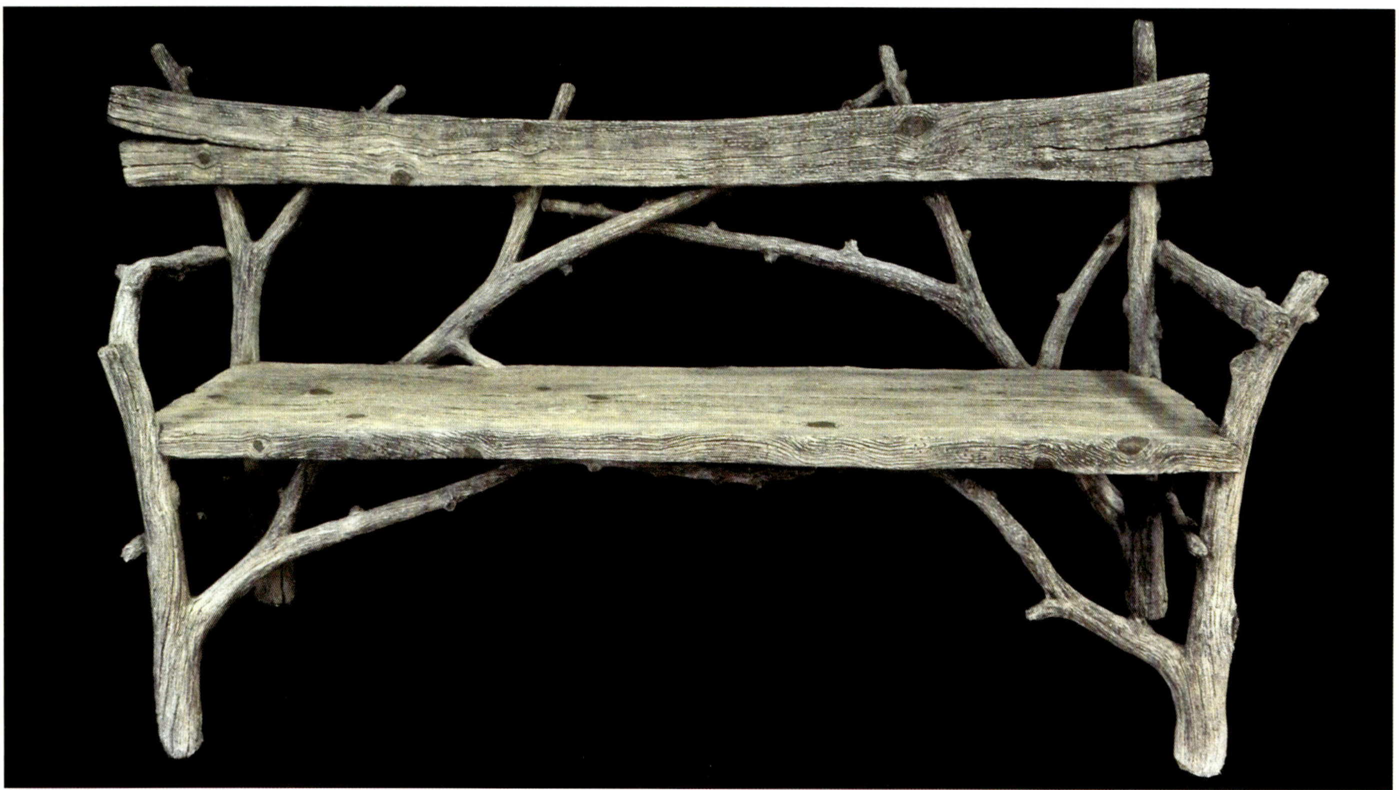

Michael Fogg. Ledyard, CT. Torii bench. Private collection. Photo courtesy of Michael Fogg, LLC.

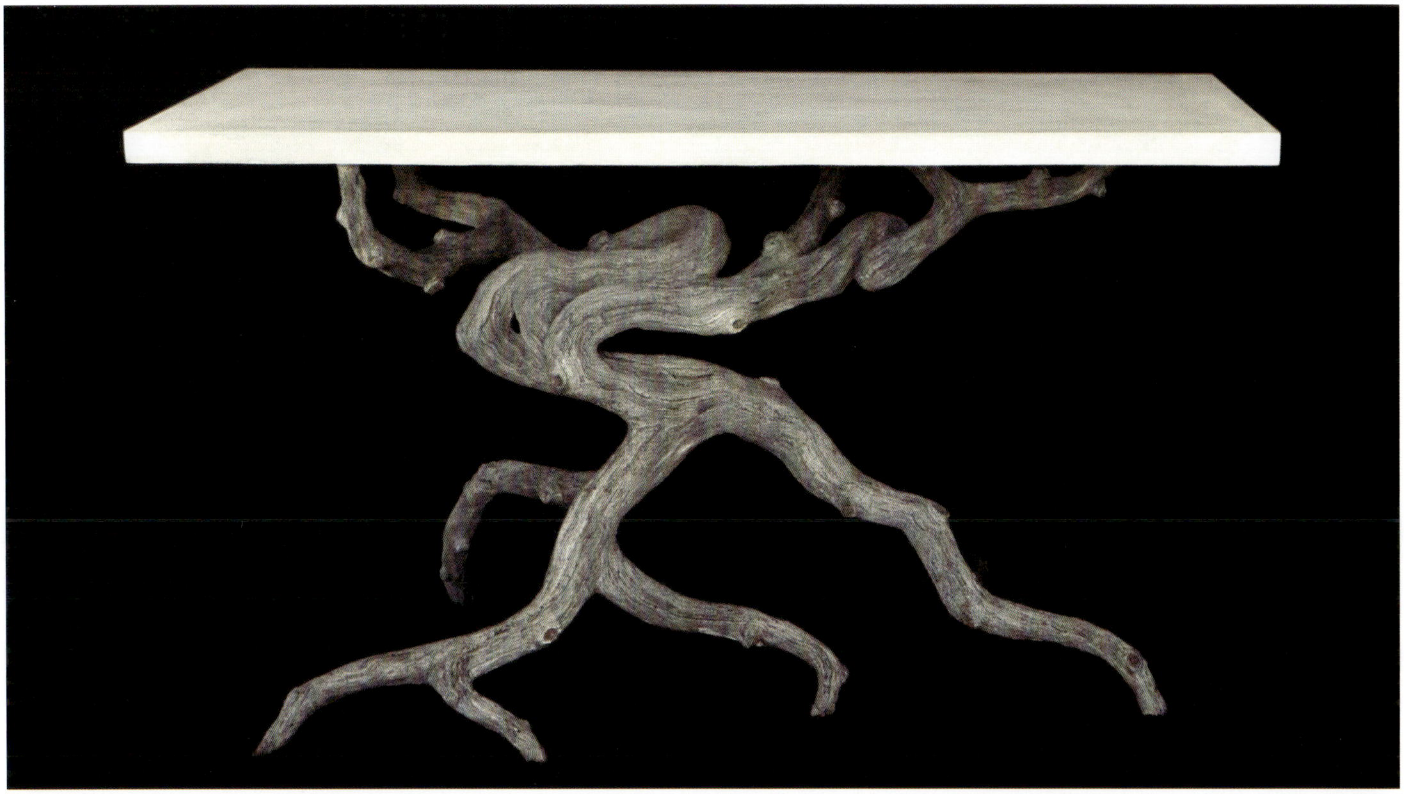

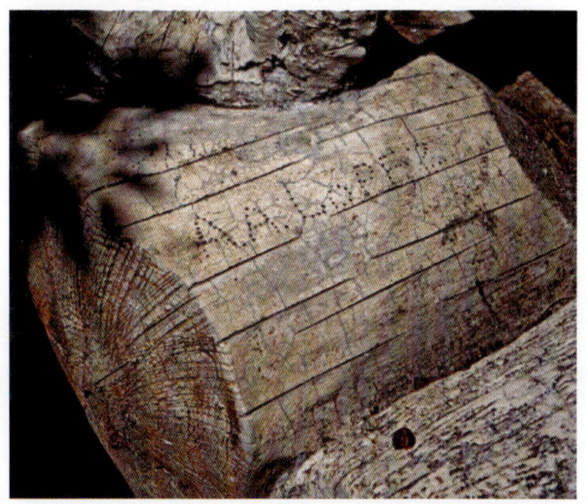

Michael Fogg. Ledyard, CT. Bonsai table. Private collection. Photo courtesy of Michael Fogg, LLC.

Antonio Acebedo Lopez

Antonio Acebedo Lopez was born in Sabinas, Hidalgo, Mexico, on September 2, 1890,[42] but it is unknown when he arrived in San Antonio. According to Esperanza Flores, he lived on Pastores Street near the zoo, in housing provided by the city. She related that the family worked for the city, and Antonio, one of several boys, worked at the zoo, feeding the animals.[43]

In 1931, he was living at 333 Cecilia Street in San Antonio with his wife, Berta, and he listed the Lopez Art Shop at 3015 McCullough Avenue as his business.[44] In 1932, the *San Antonio Light* ran a photograph of a trabajo rústico doghouse (with a sun deck or roof garden—see Delgado profile) made by Martin Delgado and A. A. Lopez at Delgado's Spanish Art Shop at 3531 McCullough. They also created a mailbox topped by a huge frog: letters were dropped into its large mouth. The newspaper article revealed that Lopez and Delgado worked on the bridge in Brackenridge Park, built in 1925, which is credited to Dionicio Rodríguez and Máximo Cortés. It appears that Lopez and Delgado assisted in its construction.[45]

Antonio Acebedo Lopez. San Antonio, TX. Bridge detail with signature. Private collection. Photo by Kent Rush.

71

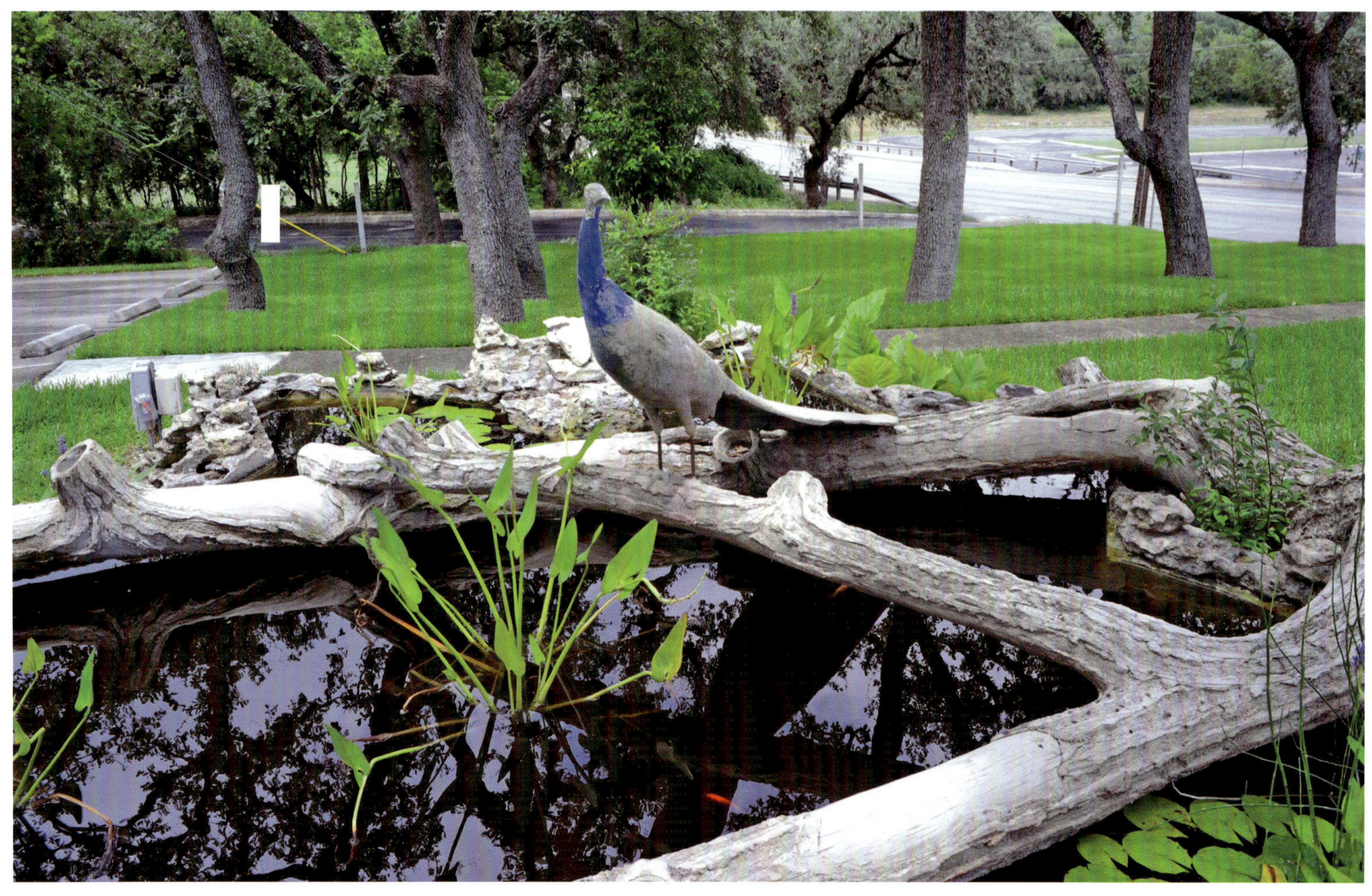

Antonio Lopez. San Antonio, TX. Pond with peacock. Private collection. Photo by Kent Rush.

By 1932 Lopez and W. C. Perez built a trabajo rústico replica of the First Hostyn Church, in Hostyn, Texas, which was erected in 1856. A cement plaque attached reads: "Dedicated to the Holy Infant of Prague in Commemoration of the Silver Jubilee of the Holy Rosary Society K.J.Z.T, No. 23, 1932."[46]

Very little information exists about Lopez's partner, William Cassiano Perez. He was born in 1885, and the census for 1942 lists his various occupations: cement worker, mason, cement plant, and working at home. His obituary lists Perez as a member of the Cassiano family, one of the original Canary Island immigrant families.[47]

During the years from 1932 to the 1950s, it is believed that Lopez worked on many trabajo rústico projects on property in San Antonio, including a fountain with a peacock in the center, a footbridge incorporating many different types of wood in concrete, a hollow treehouse, a small palapa, a large aviary, a birdbath, architectural

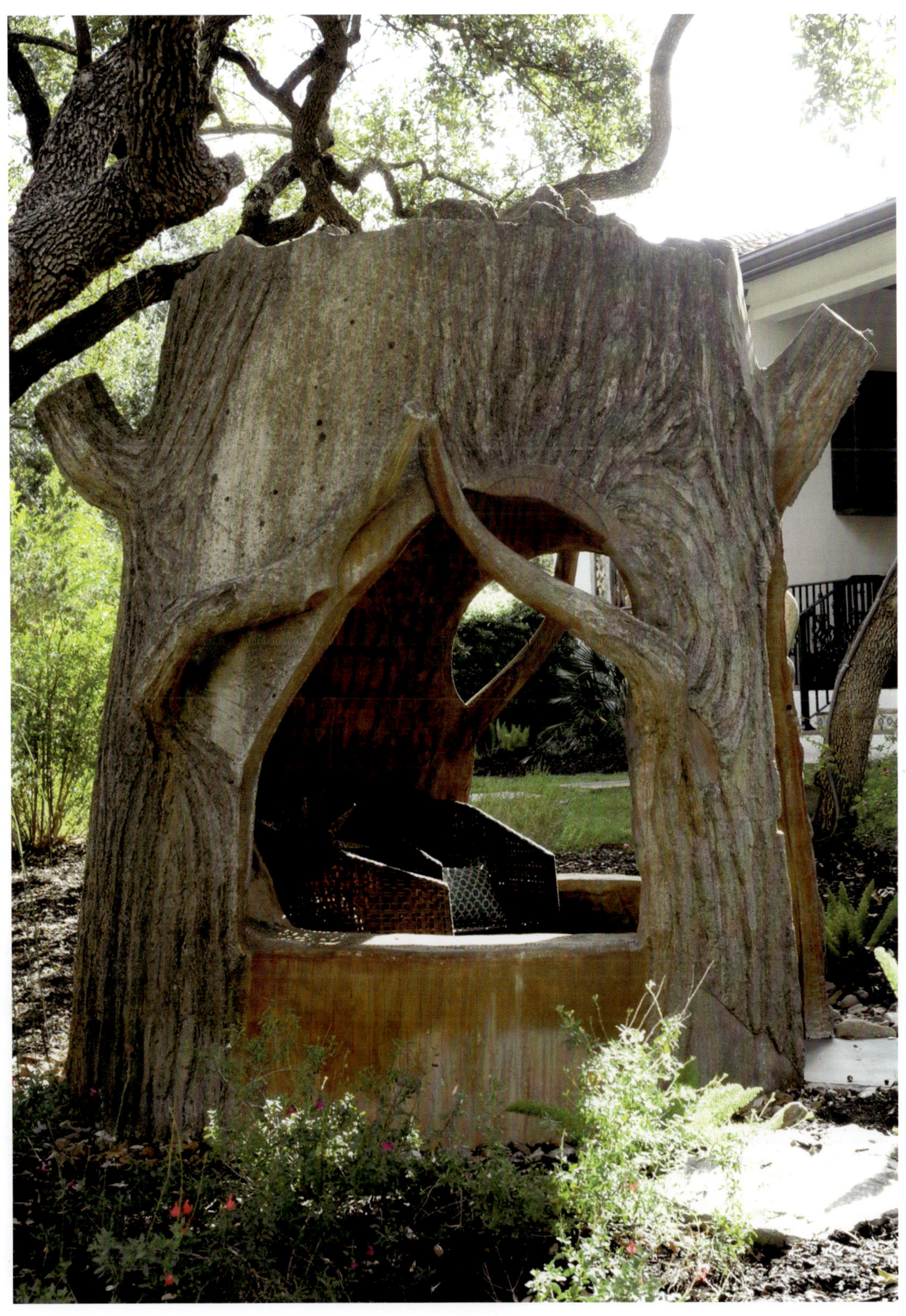

Antonio Lopez. San Antonio, TX. Hollow tree house. Collection of Carlos and Terri Solis. Photo by Kent Rush.

details on a rock residence, and an additional rock building. City directories for 1942 and 1951 list Lopez and his wife Berta as living at 333 Cecilia and give his occupation as carpenter, plasterer, and stonemason.[48] The date and place of Antonio's death are unknown.

Melinda Stump LoPresto and Megan Metheny Lashaway

MELINDA WAS born on a Michigan dairy farm, the youngest of twelve children. In 1996–97, she and her brother saw McCourtie Park in Somerset Center, Michigan, which was built in 1932–33 by two relatives of Dionicio Rodríguez, Ralph Corona and George Cardosa. Melinda and her brother took home a broken piece of a bridge and used it to copy a dozen pieces in hope of getting a contract to restore parts of the project. They did not get the contract, but Melinda continued making trabajo rústico in her spare time, while working as a full-time laborer.

Above: Megan Metheney Lashaway, L., Melinda Stump LoPresto, R. Hillsdale, MI. Photo by Steve LoPresto.

Right: Melinda LoPresto. Hillsdale, MI. LoPresto barbeque pavilion. Private collection of the artist. Photo courtesy of Melinda LoPresto.

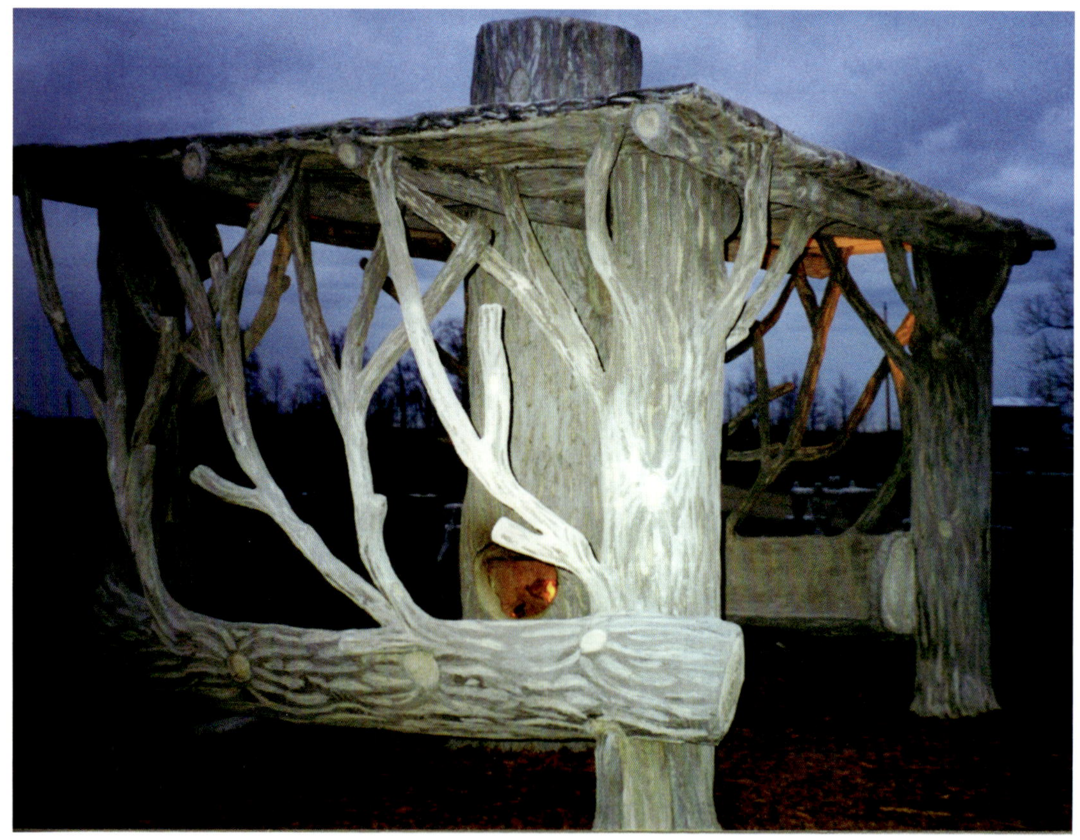

She visited St. Joseph Shrine in Irish Hills, Michigan (modeled in 1933 by Corona with the advice of Dionicio Rodríguez). It too needed restoration. She received a commission to work on the shrine, and she was able to quit her day job.

Melinda began working on her own and made a large gazebo with a fireplace, a bench to be used as a bus stop for her daughters, and more benches, trees, and railings. She perfected her skills and restored a bridge at McCourtie Park free of charge. Then she was commissioned to do more bridges with the help of her daughter, Megan Lashaway, and a friend, Troy Wasnich. Megan has assisted Melinda with the restoration of four bridges, and the two of them restored the Clearwater Beach Arch at Devil's Lake, Michigan. Megan now produces smaller works by commission, including garden planters, which she also exhibits at county fairs.

Melinda continues to work on projects, including a playhouse for her grandchildren. She has learned to weld and purchased a 1,000-pound lift for her truck. She says, "Sculpting is my passion and something that I will always love to do."[49]

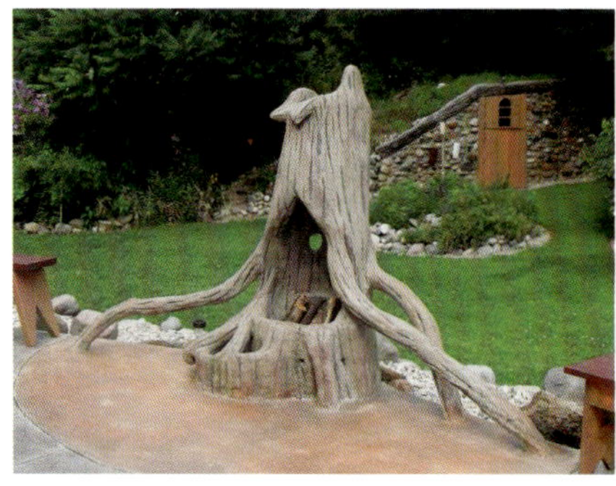

Melinda LoPresto. Hillsdale, MI. Private collection. Open fire pit. Photo courtesy of Melinda LoPresto.

Vidal Lozano

THE GAZEBO STRUCTURE, known as a *quiosco* in Spanish, in Hidalgo Park in the Mexican American community of Magnolia Park in Houston, Texas, was built by Vidal Lozano (1888–1936). A Mexican immigrant, he came to Texas in 1892 and lived in San Antonio and Houston. Although he signed the structure ("Houston Mexicans to Their City, V. Lozano"), there is no date. It can be assumed that Lozano completed the *quiosco* in the 1930s, as it was dedicated during a festival on September 16, 1934, celebrating both the opening of the park and the anniversary of Mexico's independence from Spain in 1821.[50]

The *quiosco*, designed and built in trabajo rústico style, is made of rebar covered with hand-textured concrete. Eight pillars supporting the roof resemble trunks of oak trees, and there are hand railings that mimic branches. The floor is textured with a concrete parquet wood pattern, and the ceiling resembles shingles, while the roof appears as thatch. Steps are textured to look like wooden planks, and a "tree branch" flagpole tops the structure.[51]

The style of the *quiosco* in Hidalgo Park resembles that of two rustic projects made by Dionicio Rodríguez in Houston: the aviary (now the flamingo habitat) at the Houston Zoo (1926) and the Woodlawn Garden of Memories cemetery (ca. 1931).[52] It is possible that Lozano, a contemporary of Rodríguez, might have learned

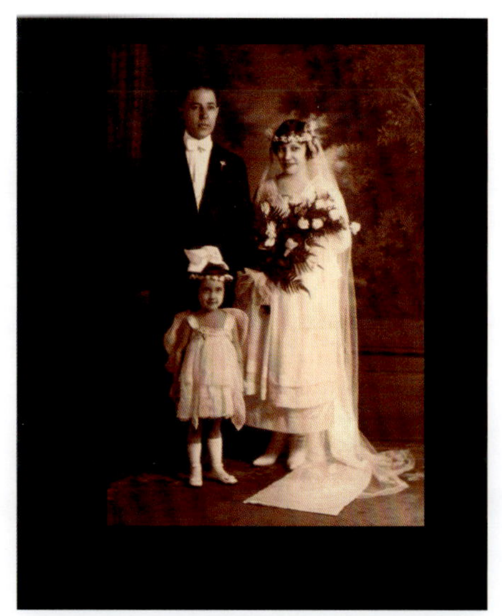

Vidal Lozano with his wife and wedding attendant. Photo courtesy of Patricia Blais.

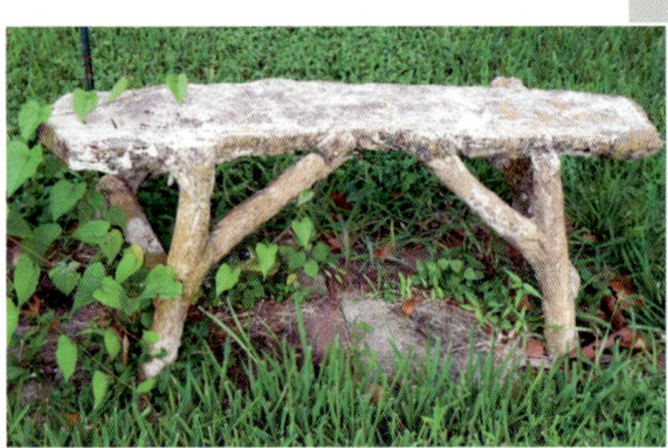

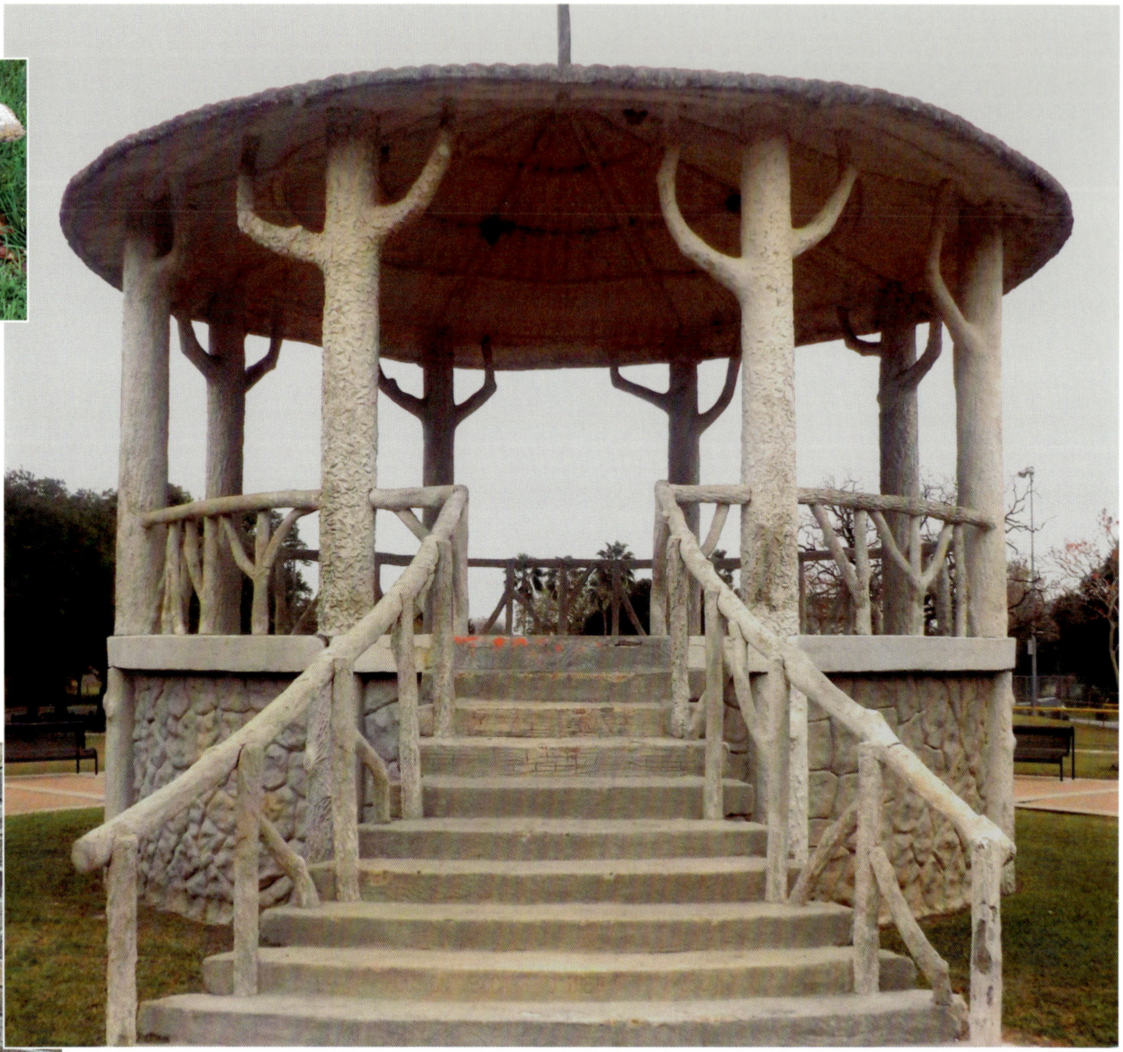

Above: *Vidal Lozano. Photo courtesy of Kathryn Meraz McElyea.*

Right *Vidal Lozano. Houston, TX. Kiosk or bandstand. Photo by Kent Rush.*

Below: *Vidal Lozano. Photo courtesy of Richard G. Meraz.*

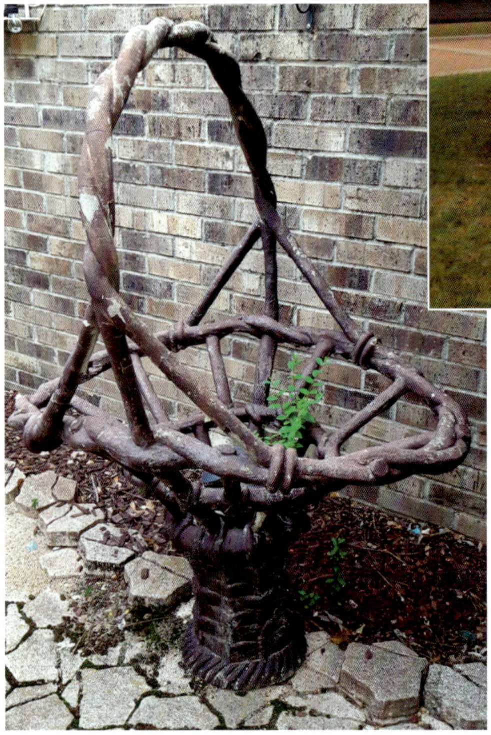

the technique in Mexico. Census records indicate that Lozano resided in San Antonio at Cementville, a community of cement workers employed by the Alamo Cement Company, where he was a "cement worker."[53] Rodríguez completed numerous projects for Alamo Cement Company and for its president, Charles Baumberger.[54] Lozano, an iron works molder and pipe fitter, knew the process for the framing for the *quiosco*, and he may have assisted Rodríguez with work in San Antonio and at the two sites in Houston. It is plausible that the two men crossed paths, and it is apparent that Rodríguez's work influenced Lozano. Lozano is credited with additional pieces, several of them made for family members.

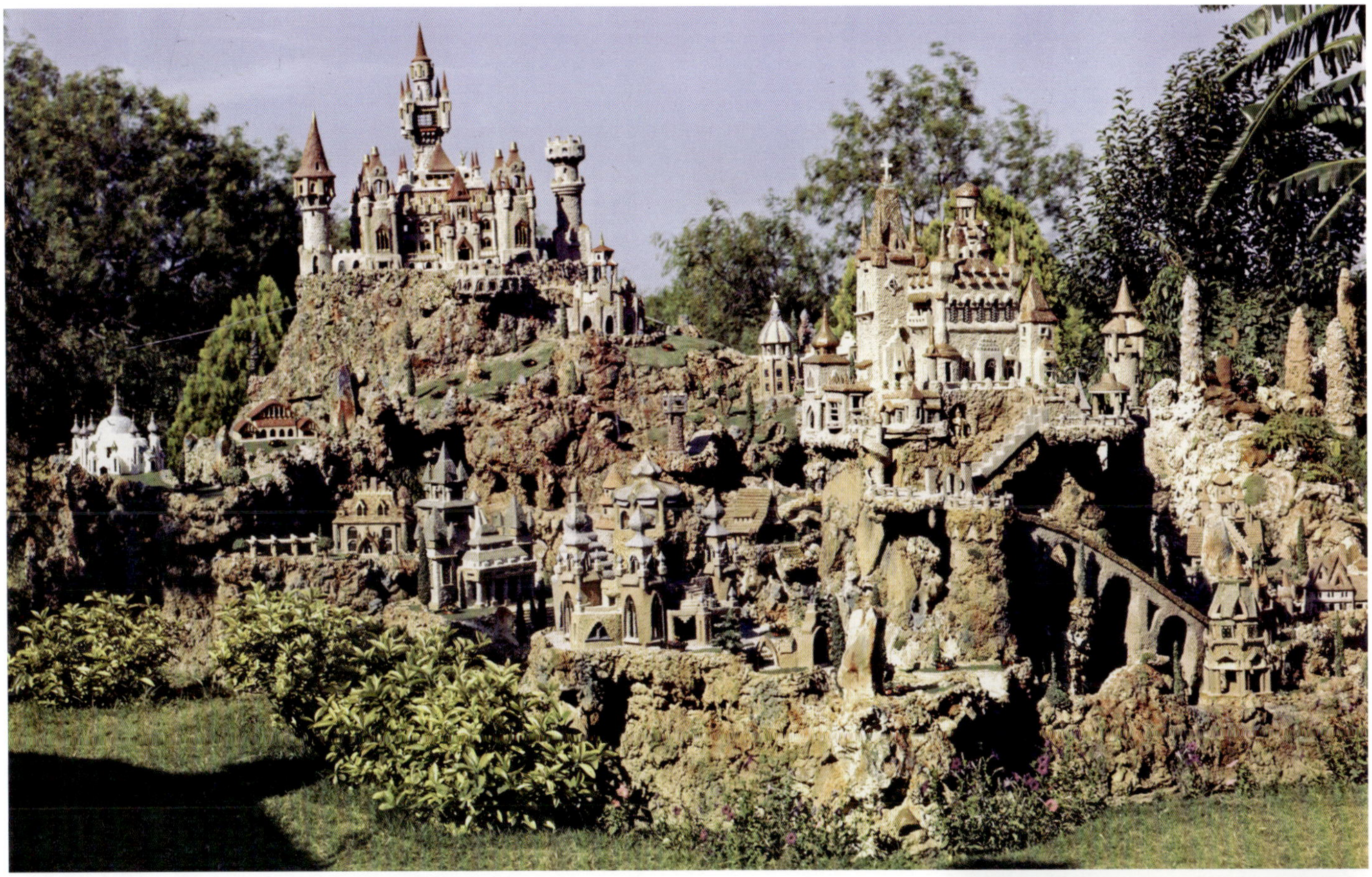

Leopold Michael Lux

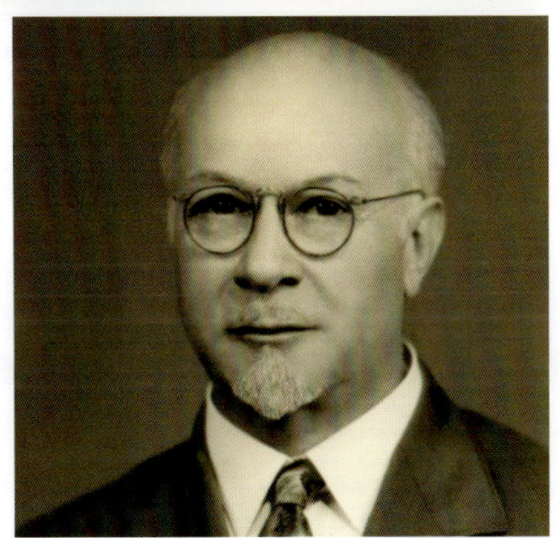

Above: *Leopold Michael Lux. Photo courtesy of A. de Arredondo.*

Top: *Leopold Michael Lux. San Antonio, TX. Archival photo of Lux Villages. Photo courtesy of A. de Arredondo.*

LEOPOLD LUX immigrated to the United States from Lindenthal, Germany, in his early twenties and began making surgical instruments in Minneapolis, Minnesota. He established his own company making artificial limbs in San Antonio in 1924, where he invented the first light-weight prosthetic leg.[55]

Although not considered a trabajo rústico artisan, Lux used his sculptural talents to make a tiny replica of his native German village out of concrete in his San Antonio backyard. The sculpture consists of 46 buildings, 200 trees, and bridges, roads, towers, cathedrals, and houses in a scene rising up over steep cliffs. After his retirement, Lux and helpers made the miniature components of "the town of memories" in his backyard studio, which was wired for electricity. Tiny hidden water faucets filled the streams and springs. The original blues, reds, greens, and browns have faded through the years.[56]

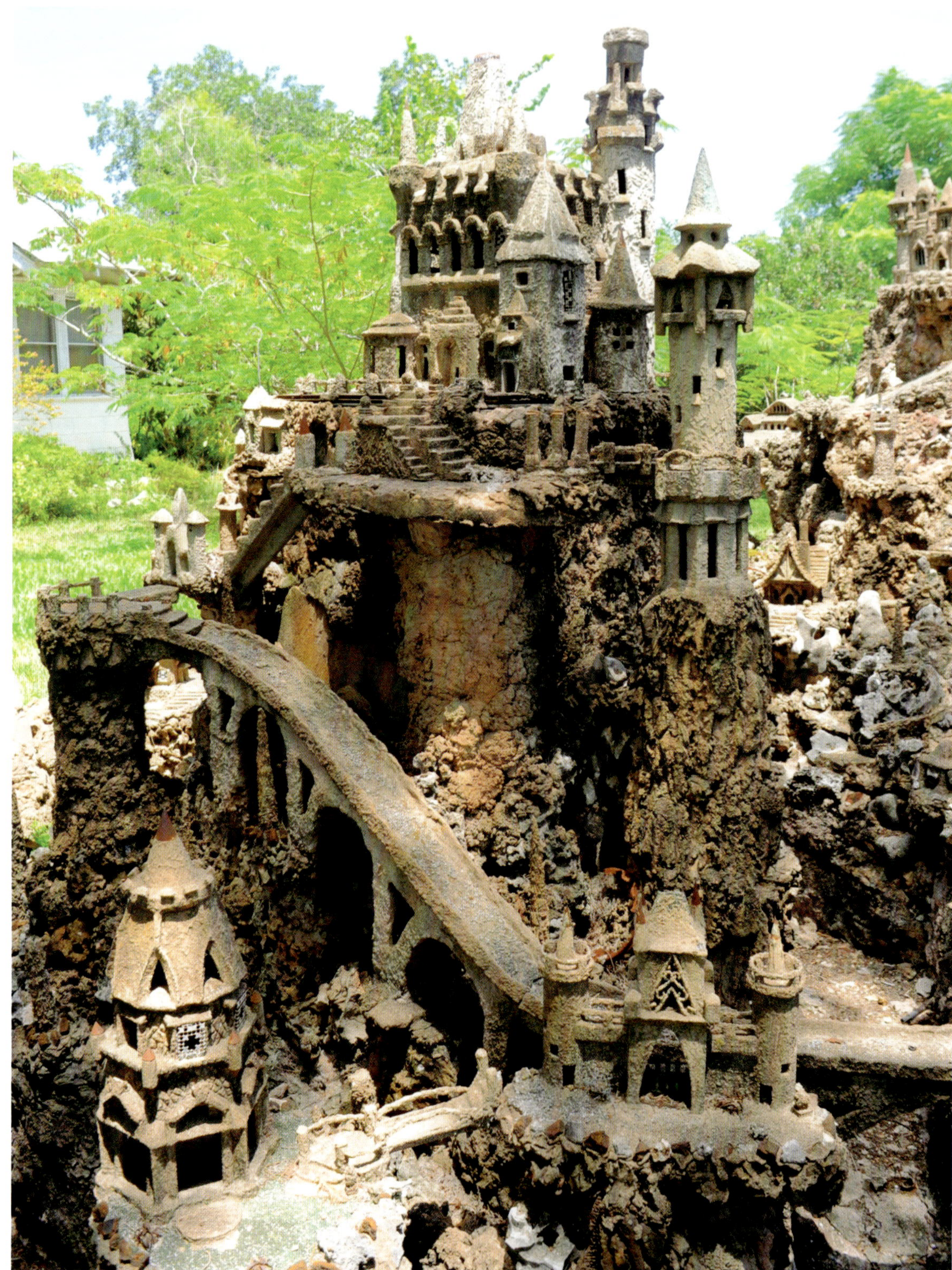

Leopold Lux. San Antonio, TX. Lux Village. Photo by Kent Rush.

A film of the miniature town was made by a film crew hired by Leopold, and, later, his family made a DVD copy. Begun in 1944 and completed in 1947, parts of the sculpture were deteriorating in 2021. It is optimistically hoped that it can be restored and remain as a unique project for many more years.

Sam Murray

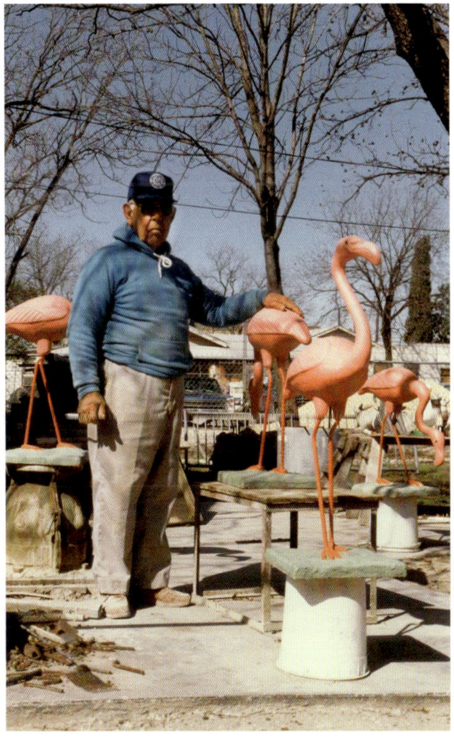

Sam Murray. Photo courtesy of Ron Bechtol.

Born in Skidmore, Texas, in 1908, a child of Hispanic and Irish parents, Sam Murray worked at Southern Cement Company in San Antonio creating pre-cast stone details for the Milam Building. When Southern Cement closed in 1929, Murray was out of work.[57] He described how he "ran into Rodríguez, and Rodríguez was working on that bridge there in Brackenridge Park. And I'd watch him. . . . I was surprised, you know, with what he was doing 'cause I had never seen that kind of work before. When you'd walk up to him, he'd stop the process. He was secretive in his kind of work."[58]

Although Rodríguez didn't give away any of his secrets, Murray perfected the trabajo rústico technique and the coloring process by working with him during the 1920s and 1930s, and together they worked on numerous commissions. Before World War II began, Sam started to work for the Quartermaster General at Fort Sam Houston, where he supervised German war prisoners. He retired from the Civil Service in 1943, applied to the ration board for supplies, and invested $4,500 in buying a lot across the street from his house, where he built a Quonset building for a workshop. He signed a contract for an advertisement in the *San Antonio Light*, but soon had so many customers that he wanted to cancel his ad. He never advertised again, relying on word-of-mouth business and special orders from customers.[59] His trabajo rústico techniques rivaled those of his peers. With his background in concrete casting, he continued to make cast objects: squirrels, flamingos, plus other species of birds and large animals, including deer and donkeys. Some of the smaller ones were used as decorations on his birdbaths, barbeques, wishing wells, and other projects. He also made cement objects covered with mosaic made of broken bits of china that he bought at yard sales.

After working for forty years in his workshop on Poplar Street in San Antonio, he moved his studio to Mico, Texas, on Medina Lake, where he worked into his late eighties. He said, "My clients won't let me retire. . . . I've done work for three generations of some families; it's tough to say no."[60] He died in 2005.

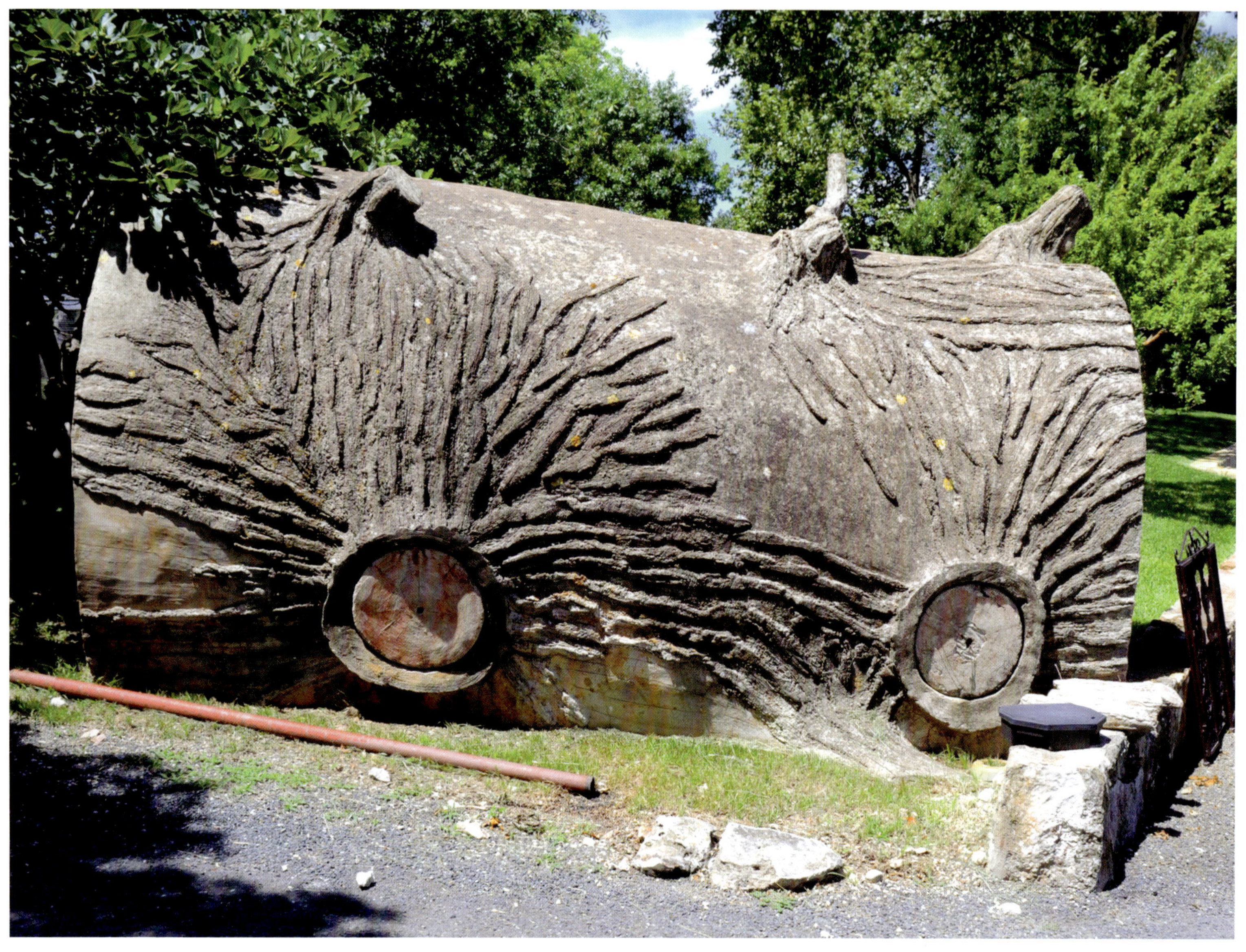

Above: Sam Murray. Hunt, TX. Pheasant coop. The Louis H. Stumberg Family Collection. Photo by Kent Rush.

Opposite: Sam Murray. San Antonio, TX. Collection of Cappy and Suzy Lawton. Photo by Kent Rush.

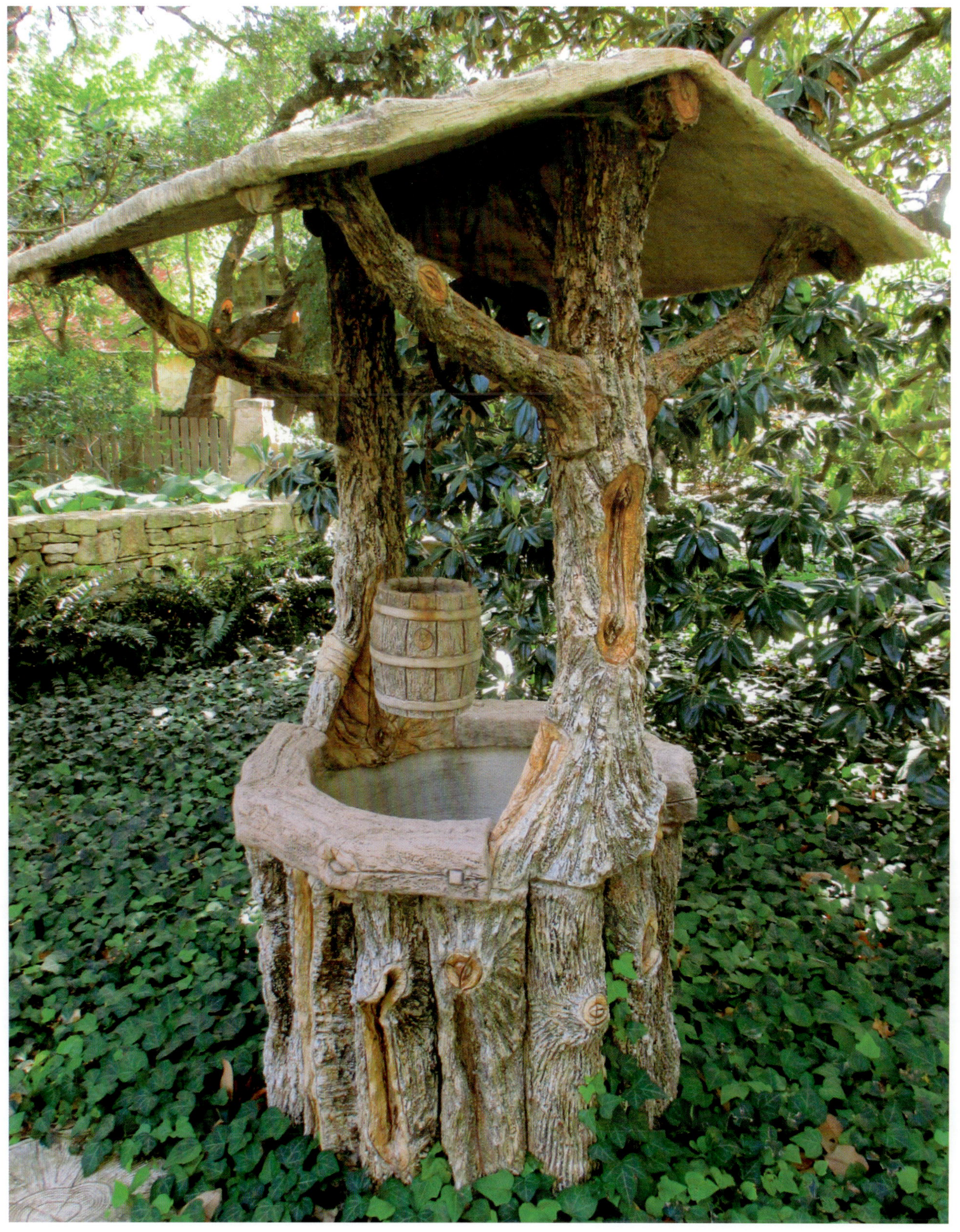

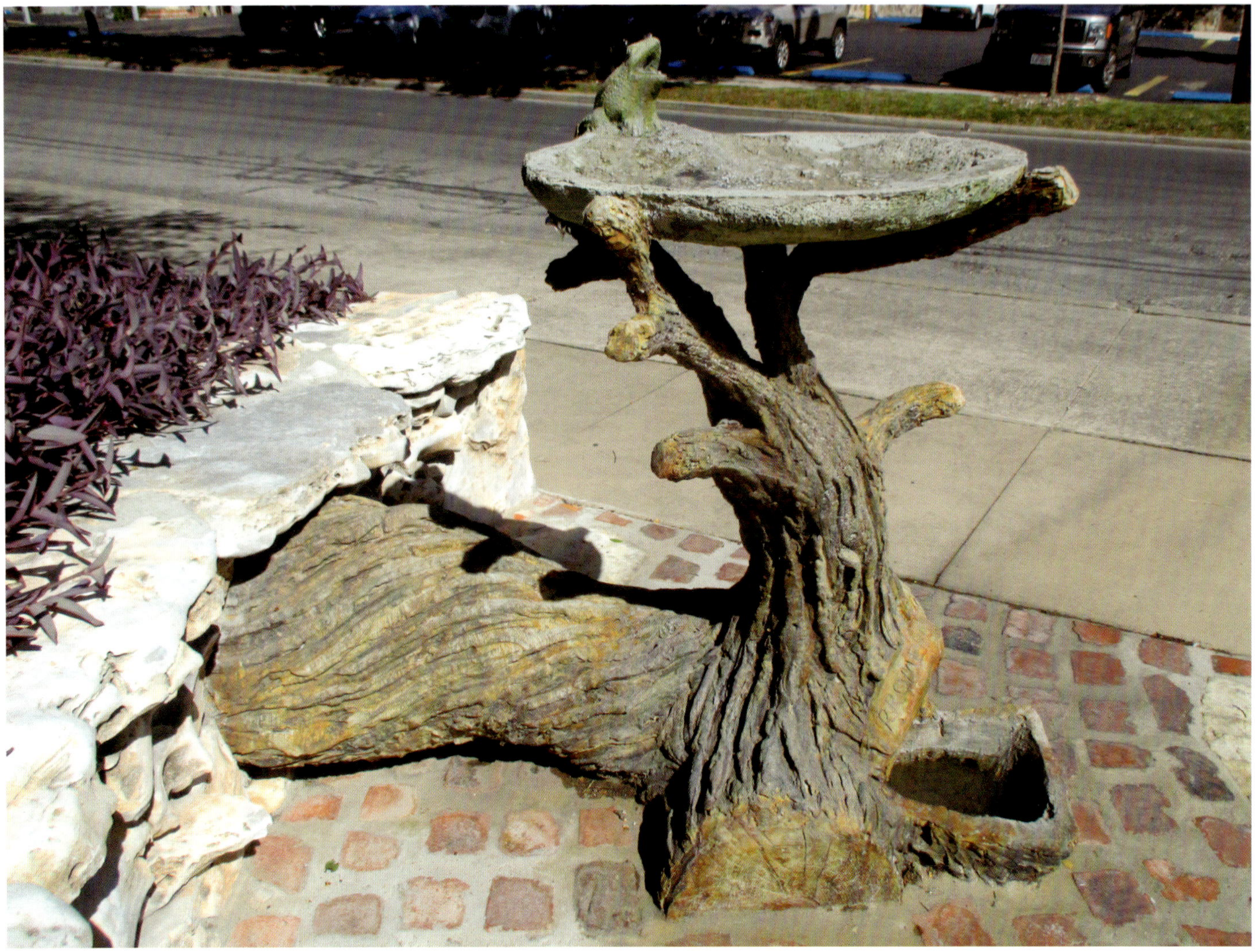

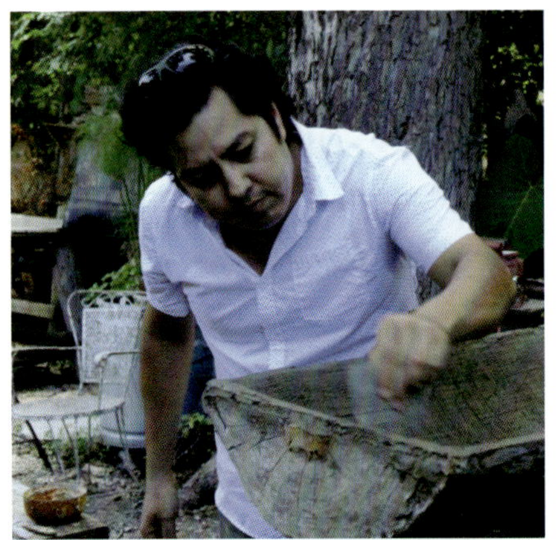

Rene Fabian Romero-Martínez

Rene Fabian Romero-Martínez was born in Mexico City in 1972. His mother was from Harlingen, Texas, and his father from Orizaba, Veracruz, Mexico. When Rene was four years old his family moved to Sumidero, Veracruz, where his father owned a coffee and sugar cane farm. Rene began drawing at an early age and got into trouble at school for drawing caricatures of his fellow students and his teachers. He attended high school in Mexico until he acquired a green card through his mother's American citizenship and moved to St. Paul, Minnesota. While working as a caricature artist in the Mall of America in Bloomfield, Minnesota, he ob-

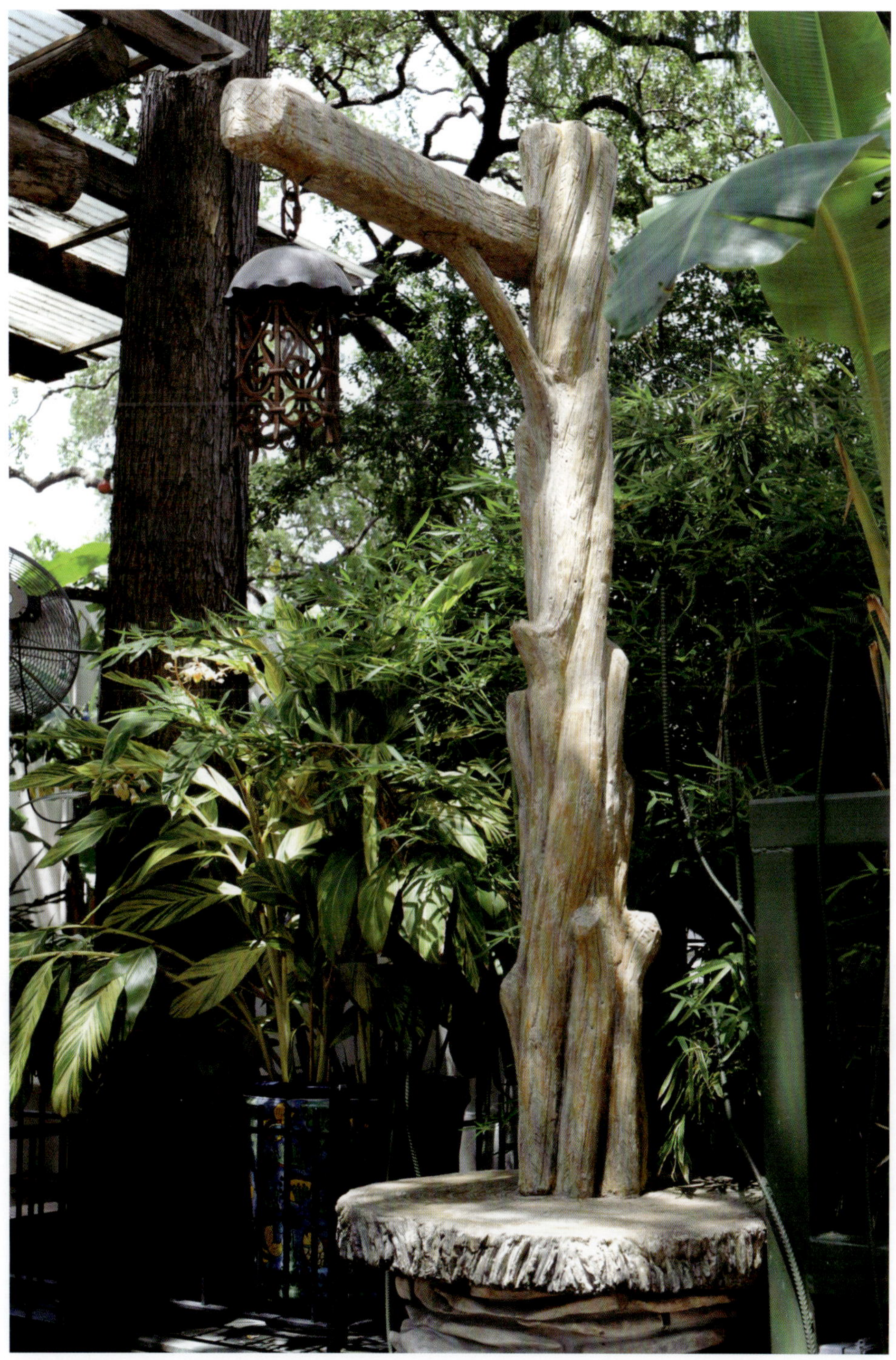

Opposite top: *Rene Romero. San Antonio, TX. Birdbath. Donated to the City of Monte Vista by Cappy and Suzy Lawton. Photo by Kent Rush.*

Opposite below: *Rene Romero. San Antonio, TX. The artist at work.*

Left: *Rene Romero. San Antonio, TX. La Fonda on Main. Lamppost. Collection of Cappy and Suzy Lawson. Photo by Kent Rush.*

tained his GED at Normandale Community College. He moved to San Antonio in 1998 and became an American citizen.[61]

According to Rene, he "found the passion for faux bois while working for Toxey/McMillan Designs in 2007."[62] He worked on projects for the design company in six locations around Texas, and during this period he began taking fine art, ceramic, and painting classes at Our Lady of the Lake University. From 2008 to 2012 he worked for Carlos Cortés. For a ten-month contract job of building a trabajo rústico fence around the mill at Mission San José for Los Compadres (the former name for the support group of the San Antonio Missions National Historical Park, a group now known as Heritage Partners of the San Antonio Missions), he enlisted the aid of his father, Samuel Ramirez, to whom he taught the technique and who has continued to produce work in Mexico.[63]

In 2017 Rene was invited to show his trabajo rústico work in a joint exhibit with Mexican painter Carlos Sens at the Casa de la Cultura de Tampico in Tampico, Mexico. As an independent artisan, Rene has received many private and public commissions, including for construction of benches, water fountains, birdbaths, bridges, planters, and stepping-stones. He has been commissioned by the City of San Antonio Parks Department to repair several works by Dionicio Rodríguez. He received advice from preservationist Shane Winter, who works on restoration of cement projects for the Koehler Foundation throughout the United States.

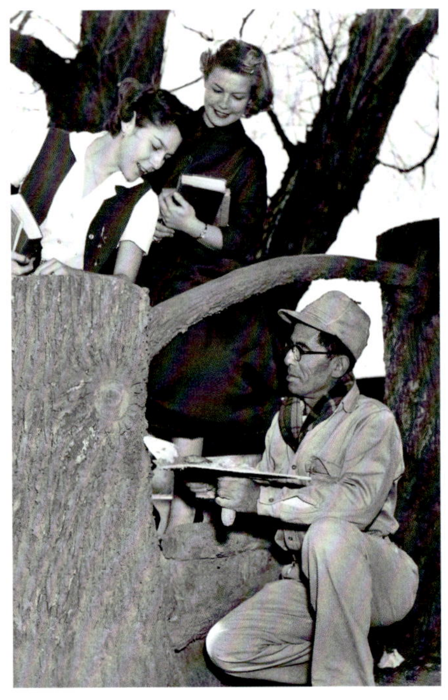

Dionicio Rosales. San Antonio, TX. Rosales with Our Lady of the Lake students at Elmendorf Lake Park. Photo from The University of Texas at San Antonio, Special Collections, San Antonio Light. ZUMA Press.

Dionicio Rosales

In 1949, the City of San Antonio began work on the Elmendorf Lake Beautification Project. A portion of the project was a boat dock and stage with a bandstand, mostly constructed in trabajo rústico style. Dionicio Rosales, who was born in Ciudad Guerrero, Mexico, worked on the project.[64]

He had fled to the United States in 1919 with his father, Nastacio, during the unrest resulting from the Revolution in Mexico. When he was twelve years old, Rosales learned trabajo rústico from his father, who taught him to sculpt the texture of tree bark from concrete.

During the period when he worked on the Elmendorf Lake project, he must have known Dionicio Rodríguez, as it was later learned (in 2007) that Rodríguez built the concrete bench for the stage.[65] Both Rosales's and Rodríguez's works at

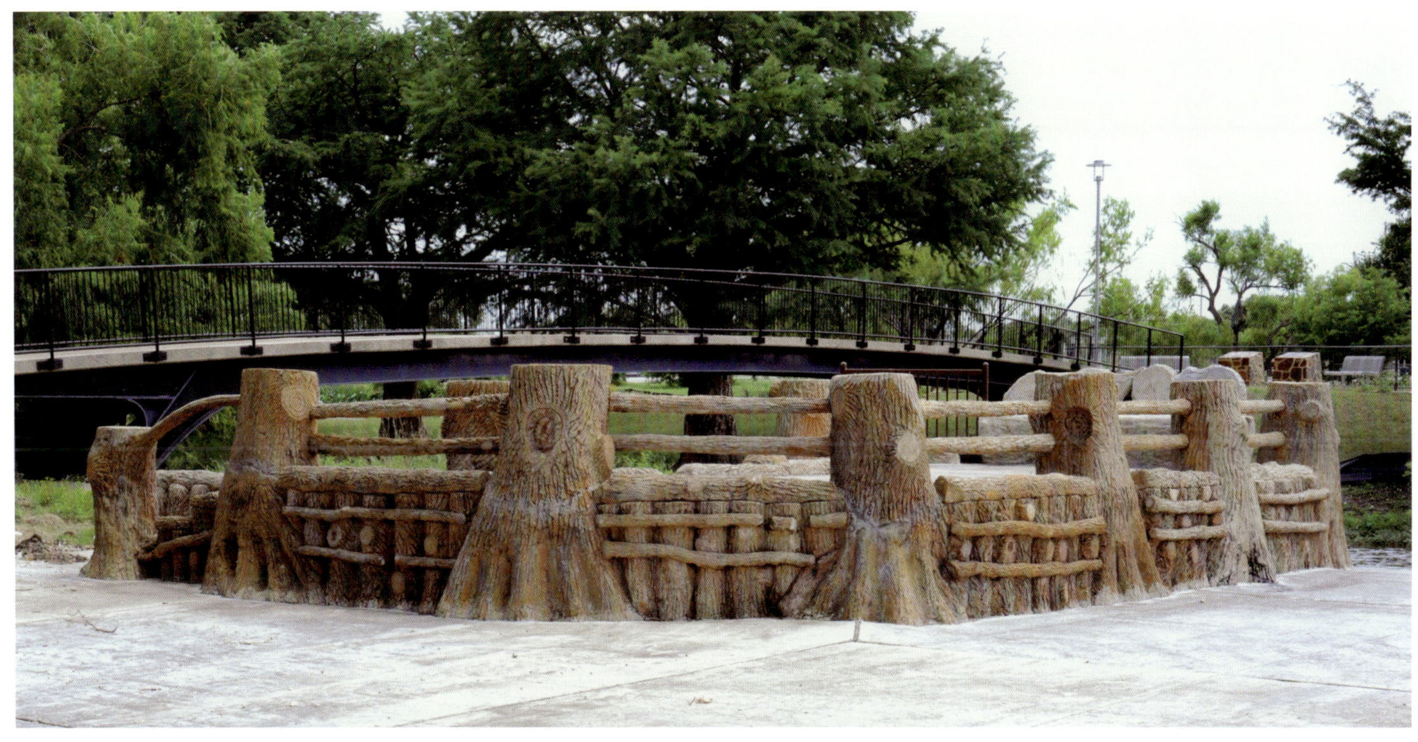

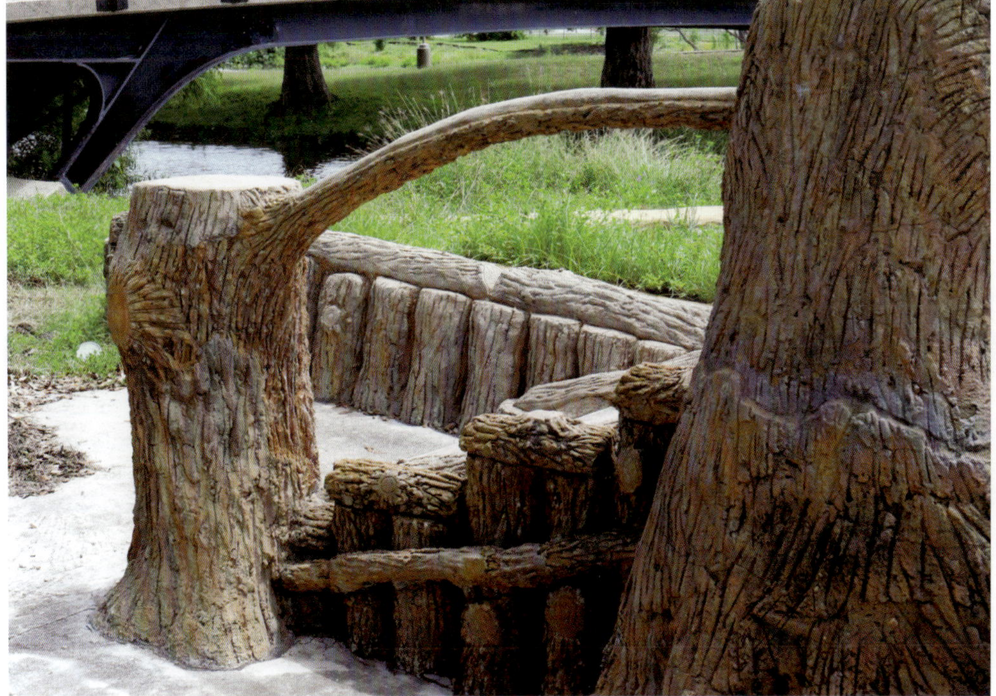

Above: *Dionicio Rosales. San Antonio, TX. Elmendorf Lake Park stage. Photo by Kent Rush.*

Left: *Dionicio Rosales. San Antonio, TX. Elmendorf Lake Park. Detail of stage. Photo by Kent Rush.*

Below: *Donald R. Tucker. Houston, TX. Photo by William (Billy) Ralston.*

Bottom: *Donald R. Tucker. Houston, TX. Detail. Photo courtesy of Donald Tucker.*

Bottom right: *Donald Tucker. Houston, TX. Private collection. Photo courtesy of Donald Tucker.*

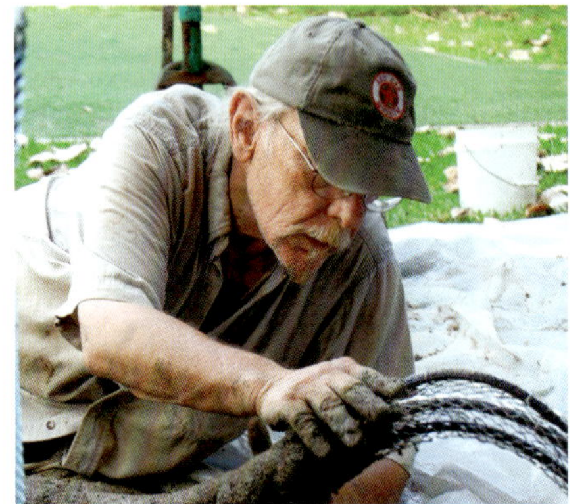

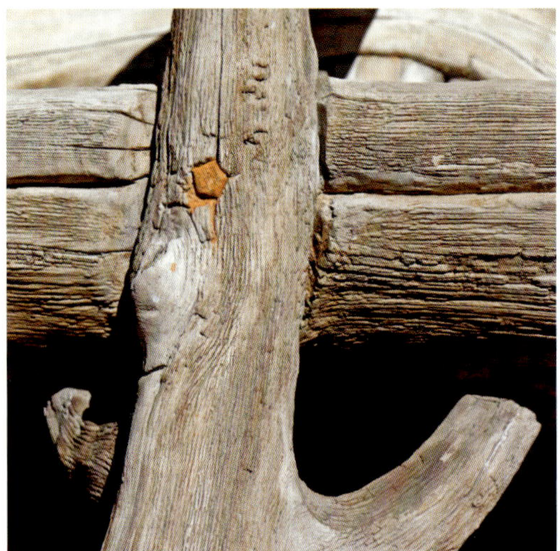

the project were in dire need of repair and were included for restoration in a City of San Antonio bond issue in 2007.

The bench is made to appear as crosscut wood slabs joined together, and large, heavily textured tree trunks surround the stage. The trunks hold railings of branches, and the base is formed with vertical cut branches joined together by horizontal branches.

According to a newspaper article, Rosales started working for the Parks Department in 1949 and completed several projects for the department. He lived at 3335 West Salinas Street, which was at the rear of Hermino Peña's store and residence.[66] As of 2021 no known additional works by Rosales exist.

Donald R. Tucker

B ORN IN Houston in 1945, Donald Tucker began his art career as a teenager, painting t-shirts and race cars. After serving three tours in Vietnam, he enrolled in the Houston Academy of Art. Discovering he was an idea man, he began working in design and layout for large advertising agencies and helped to launch the Compaq Computer.[67] When he retired, he became interested in trabajo rústico but discovered that the early cement artisans left no written records and most of the surviving practitioners were very secretive. When he was unable to find information on the tech-

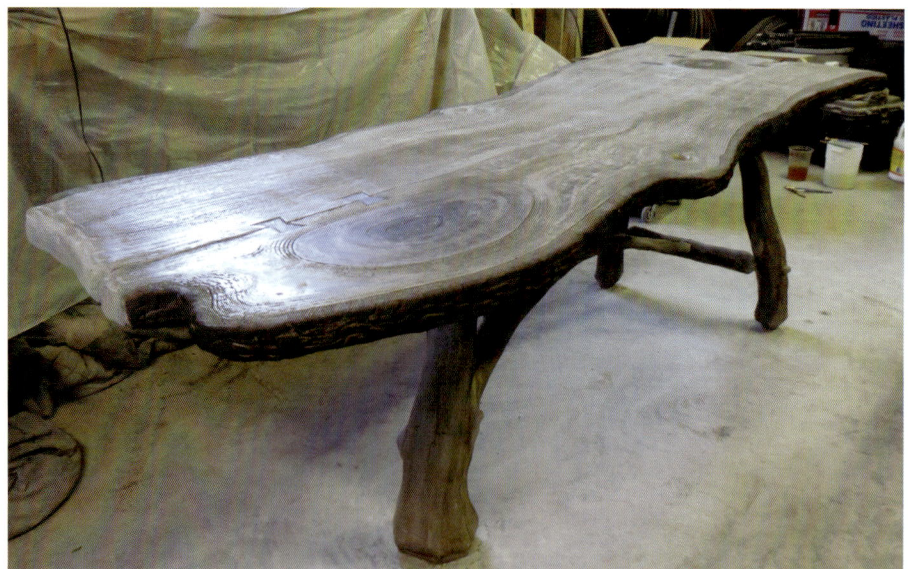

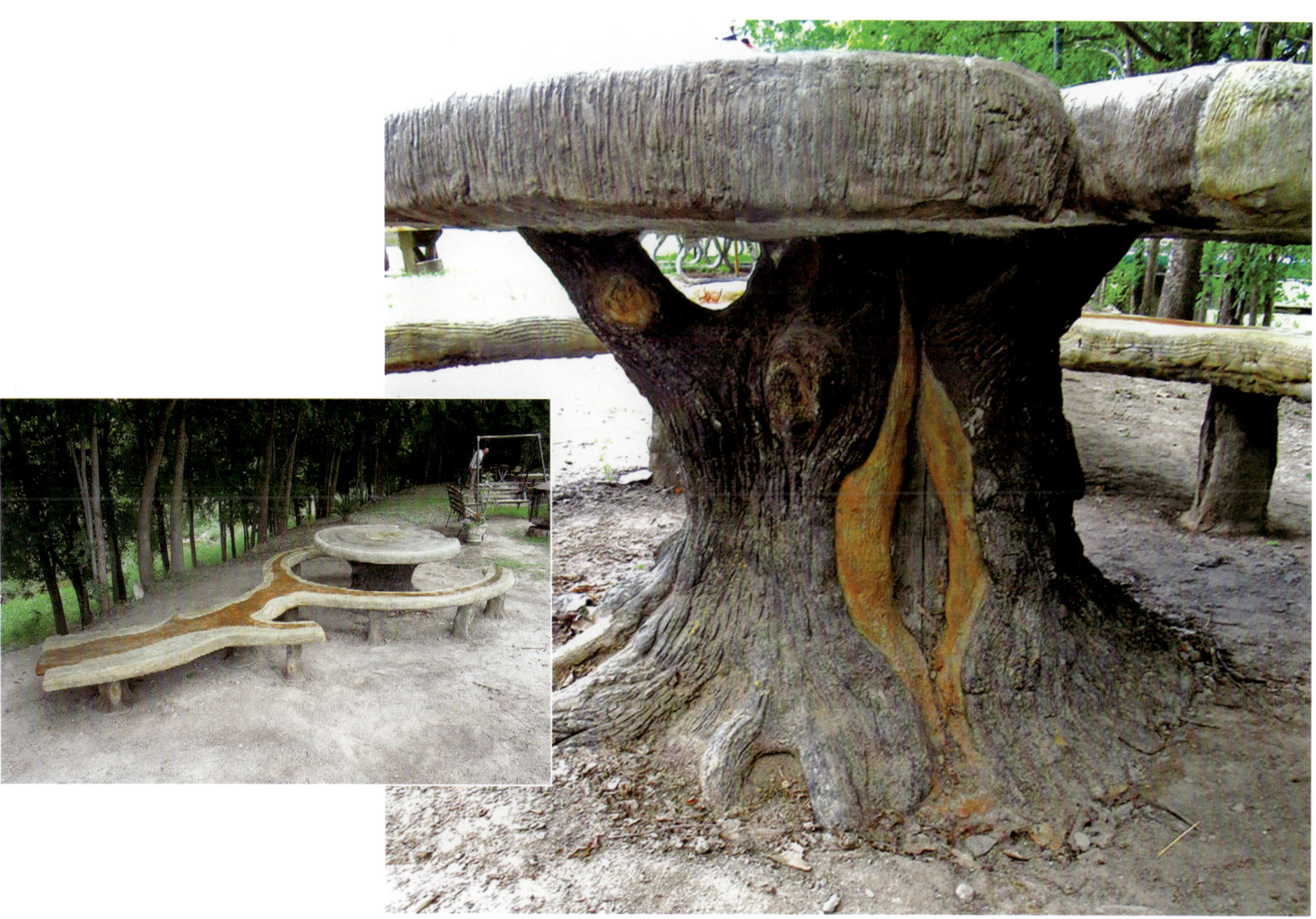

nique from the Library of Congress, he spent many years researching "historical works as well as the artistic techniques, and chemistry." He even photographed the Japanese Tea Garden gate from the top, standing on it.[68]

His research enabled him to apply modern technology and the information he had gathered to his own work, which consisted of commissioned projects for private and public spaces. He was the only *trabajo rústico* artisan in the "history of this unique craft [to make his] knowledge available to anyone" who wanted to learn it. Tucker conducted classes throughout the United States, authored a book on the subject, and operated "a free informational website and discussion forum (thegardenartforum.com) for over 10 years."[69] In contrast to other artisans, his work most often exhibited the surface of bare wood with no bark. At the time of his death in 2019, he was involved in "the development of standards for restoration and conservation" and had been invited to assist in restoration work at Parc des Buttes-Chaumont in Paris.[70]

Above left: *Donald Tucker. Houston, TX. Private collection. Photo courtesy of Donald Tucker.*

Above: *Donald Tucker. Houston, TX. Wound at base of tree table. Private collection. Photo courtesy of Donald Tucker.*

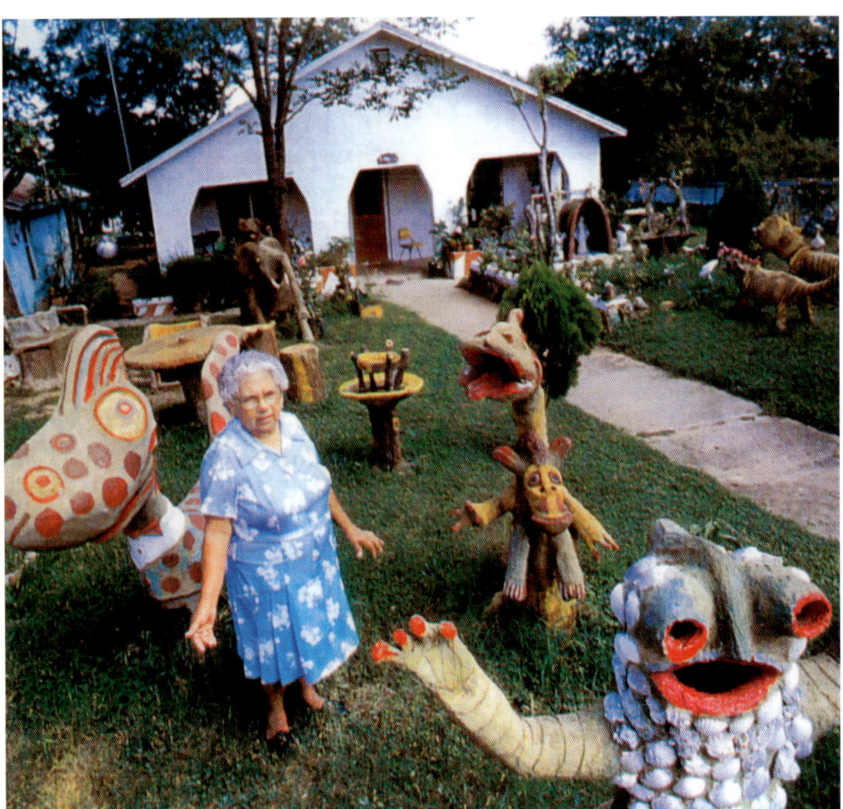

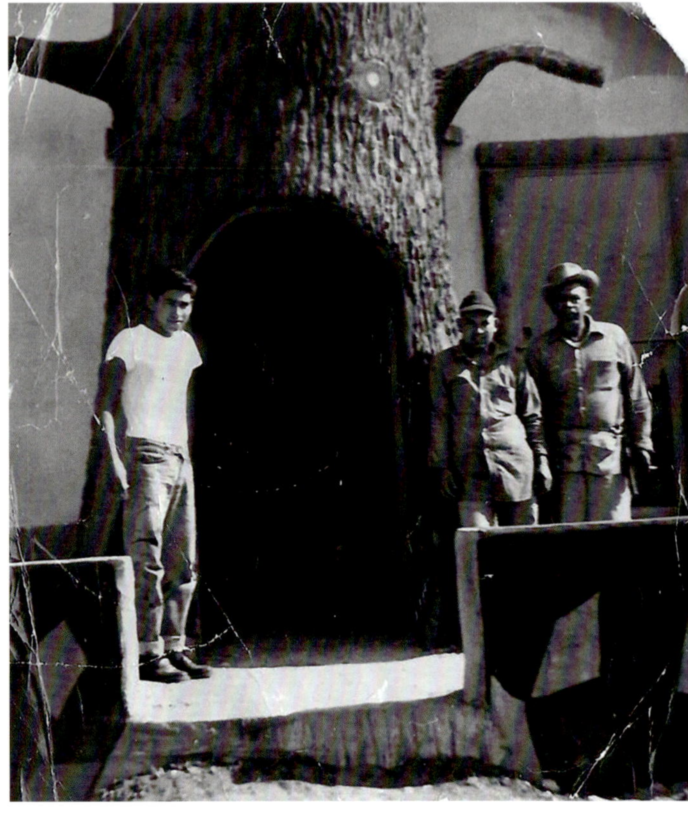

Beatrice and Pedro Ximénez

Above: Beatrice Ximénez. Floresville, TX. The artist in her yard. Photo by Julie Newton.

Above right: Arthur Ximénez Sr. Floresville, TX. L. to R., Jose "Chico" Ximénez, Pedro Ximénez, and Arthur V. Ximénez Sr. Photo courtesy of Mary Jane Ximénez.

BORN IN 1904 in Graytown, Texas, Beatrice grew up in San Antonio. For a woman who received no formal education, she left her mark with her creation of fantasy animals made in the trabajo rústico technique.

After she and Pedro Ximénez were married in 1923, they moved to Floresville, where they had seven children: a daughter and six sons.[71] Sam Murray, who learned the technique from Dionicio Rodríguez, taught Pedro: Murray had a commission to make furniture for a client in Floresville, and Pedro worked as his assistant.[72] Ximénez later taught his wife and family, and they not only made and sold cement furniture but also created trabajo rústico projects: "a store, a gas station, a dance hall, cottages, and a barbeque pit on their Floresville property."[73]

According to his granddaughter, Mary Jane Ximénez, Pedro's execution of the technique was very detailed.[74] Pedro died in 1956, and eleven years later Beatrice

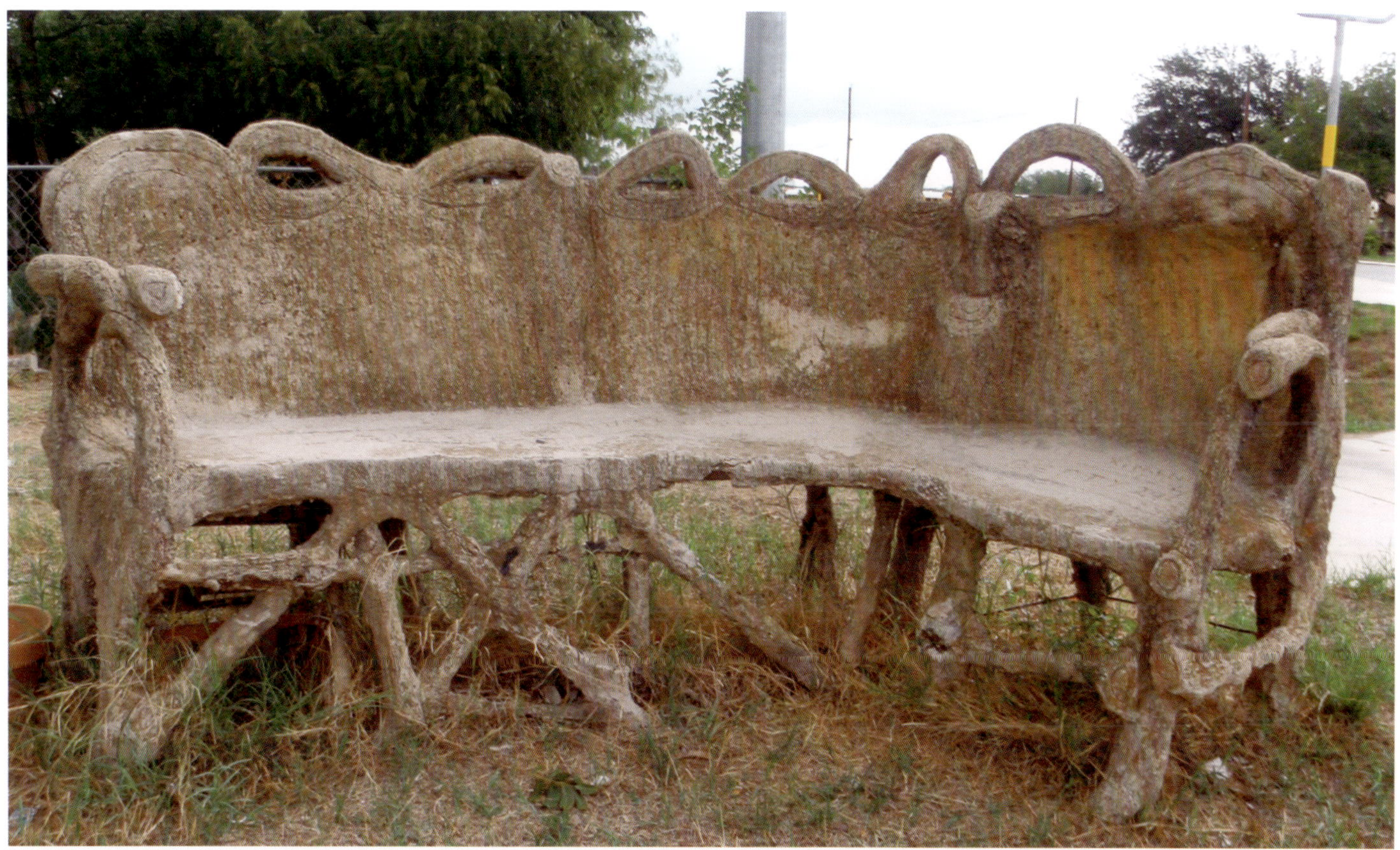

Beatrice and Pedro Ximénez. San Antonio, TX. Private collection. Photo by Kent Rush.

began making her *"animales feos"* ("ugly animals") in the same technique, gleaning subjects from "children's books, science fiction movies, television nature programs."[75] Her grandson, Johnny Verduzo, helped her with some of the heavier projects. Her brightly colored creatures, including a zebra, a monkey, a giraffe, a tiger, an elephant, and an alligator, were decorated with PVC pipe, shiny marbles, scallop shells, and real teeth. Her son, Arturo, bought a basketball hoop for his children. When he couldn't find it, he discovered that Beatrice had used it in one of her projects.[76]

She created more than fifty full-scale animals over a twenty-two-year period, transforming her front yard into a concrete menagerie, which was a tourist attraction for many years. Many of her projects are in private collections, and some of her figures were in a traveling exhibit sponsored by Texas Folklife Resources in

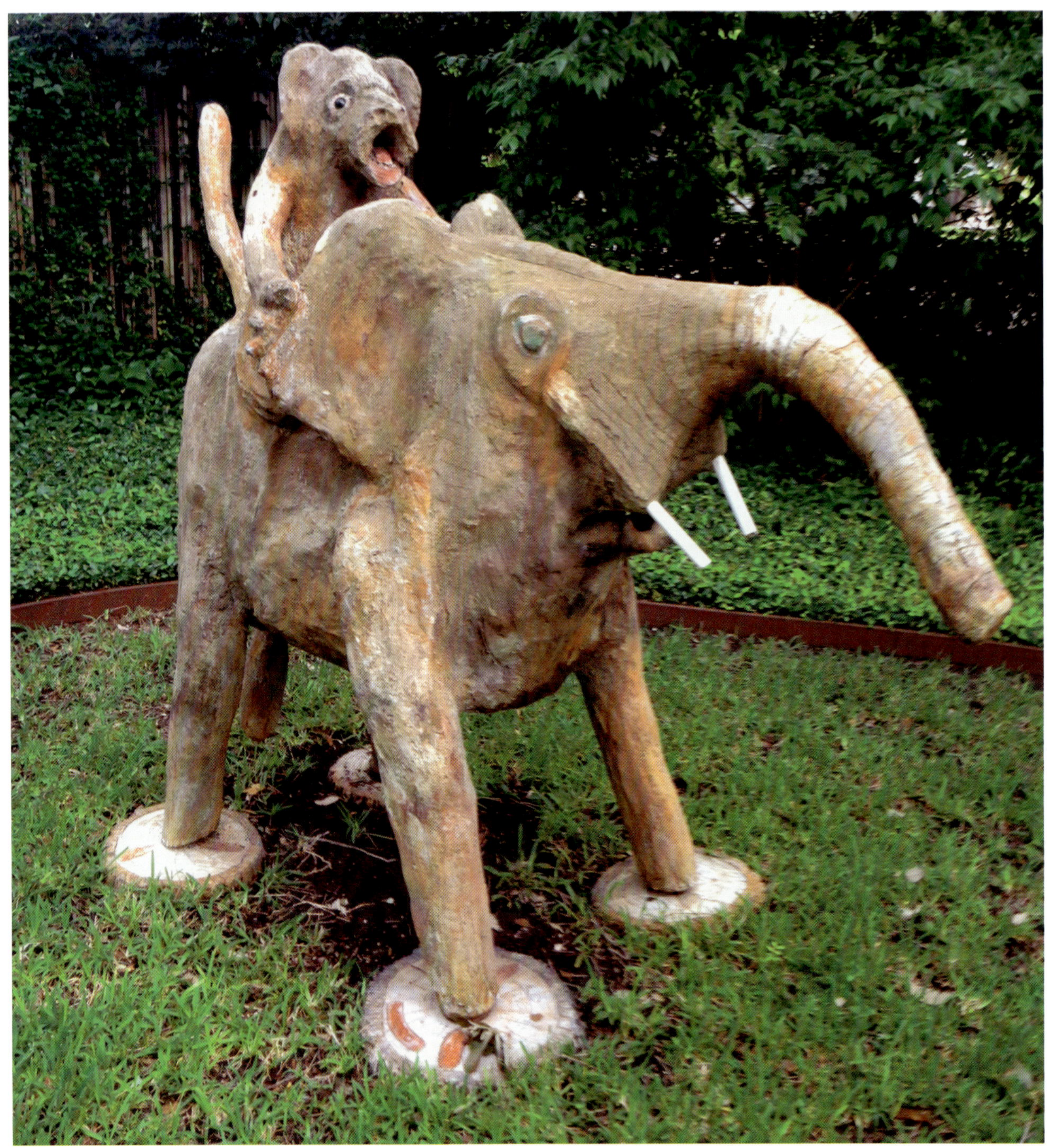

Beatrice Ximénez. San Antonio, TX. Private collection. Photo by Kent Rush.

1986.[77] In 1987, at the age of eighty-three, Mrs. Ximénez was invited to participate in the Guadalupe Cultural Arts Center's Popular Arts/Artes Populares II exhibit, where she taught a workshop in cement sculpture.[78] She died in 1989, leaving a rare legacy of a Texas Hispanic woman of her time involved in a family-based folk-art tradition.

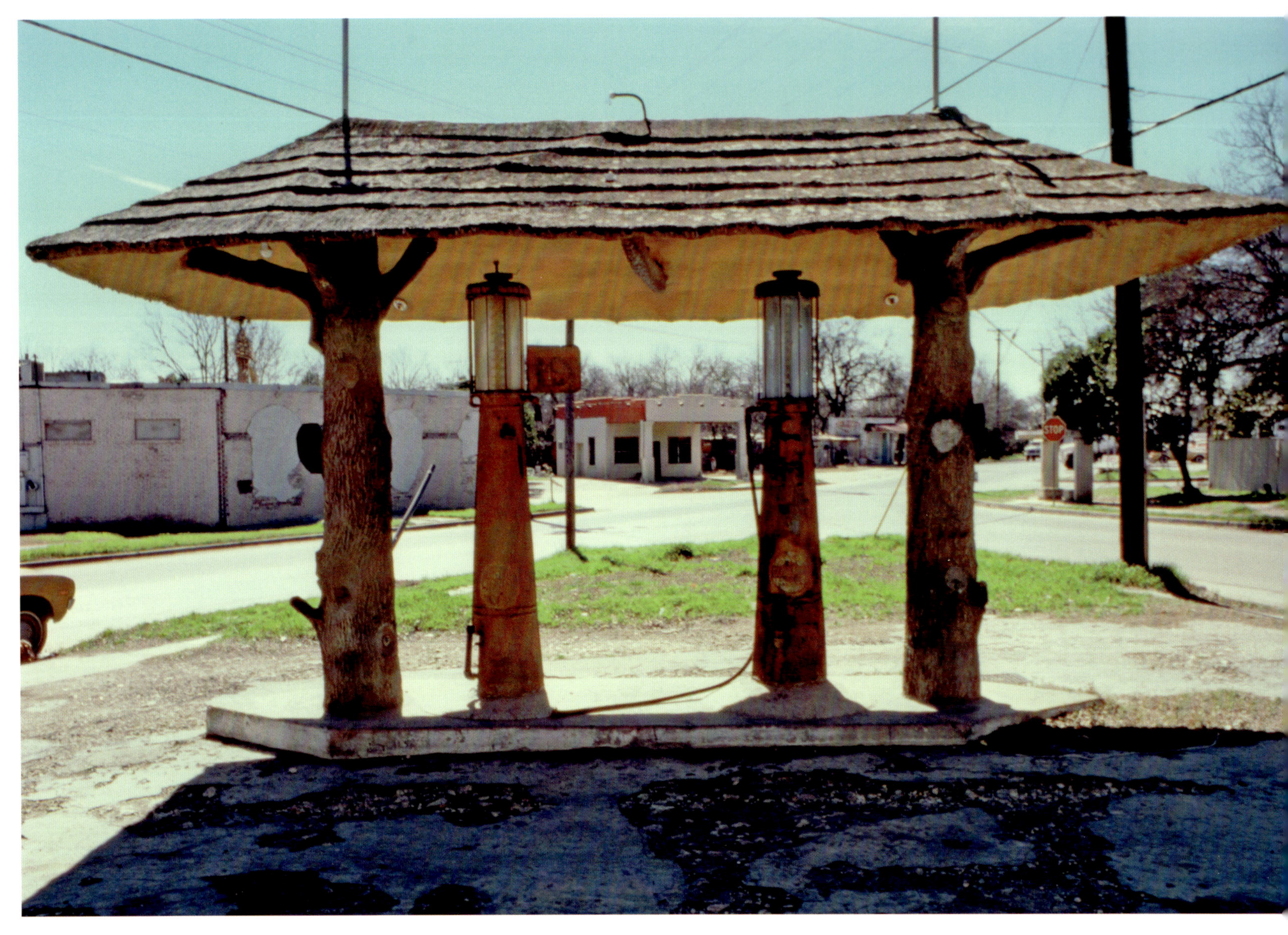

Bacilio Aguilar. San Antonio, TX. Private collection. Gas pump shelter. Photo by Kent Rush.

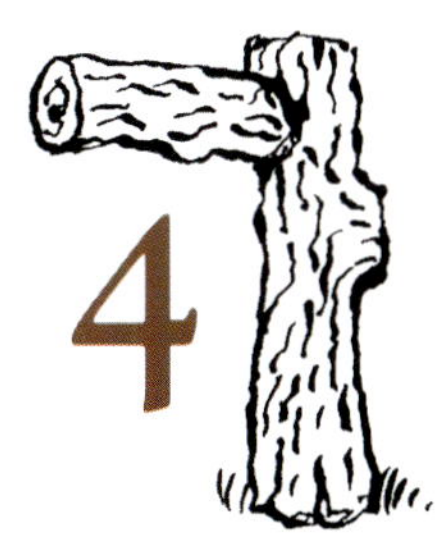

Gallery of
Trabajo Rústico Artisans

THE PHOTOGRAPHS in this section demonstrate the talent and resourcefulness of many trabajo rústico artisans in the US. They are meant to provide a sampling of a wide variety of objects, configurations, styles, textures, and coloration in the works of artisans who were trained as assistants by Dionicio Rodríguez, or directly or indirectly influenced by him. In addition to the artisans who worked during the era of Rodríguez, the section includes works by contemporary practitioners. As many early artisans did not sign their names to their creations nor is there any remaining documentation, their works need to be shown and appreciated even if we do not know, or are uncertain, who made them.

We hope to convey a sense of the sheer quantity of objects made in trabajo rústico (especially in San Antonio and the region). In researching this book, the authors visited more than 100 sites in South Texas and photographed at least 300 individual pieces, primarily vintage works from the 1920s through the 1950s. Unlike many of the Rodríguez works which, for the most part, are situated in public places, many pieces illustrated here are in private locations and may never be seen and appreciated by the public except in these reproductions.

Many works are owned by families, appreciative collectors, or agencies such as civic parks; some were handed down through inheritance or through the purchase of property; some were moved from their original locations; others were commissioned for a specific location. Places of creation and names of the artisans are added when known. Still others are nonextant.

The photographs often reveal well-kept landscapes. Other backgrounds show that some historic pieces are not cared for and simply exist in less than ideal or even abandoned environments, their futures insecure. We hope that through this book an awareness and appreciation for this genre will grow, and, as a result, more pieces will be protected.

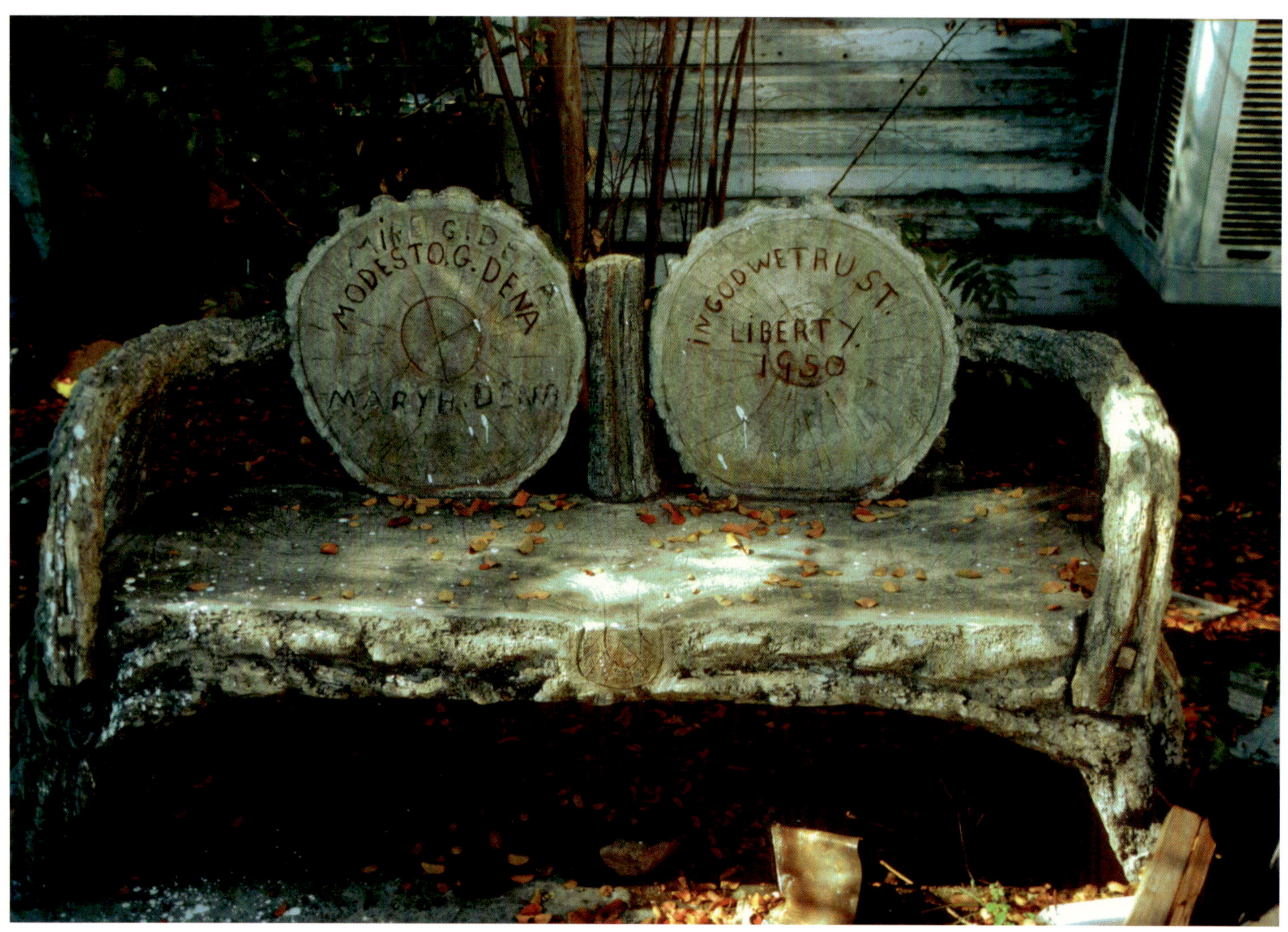

Modesto Dena. San Antonio, TX. Current location unknown. Photo by Ron Bechtol.

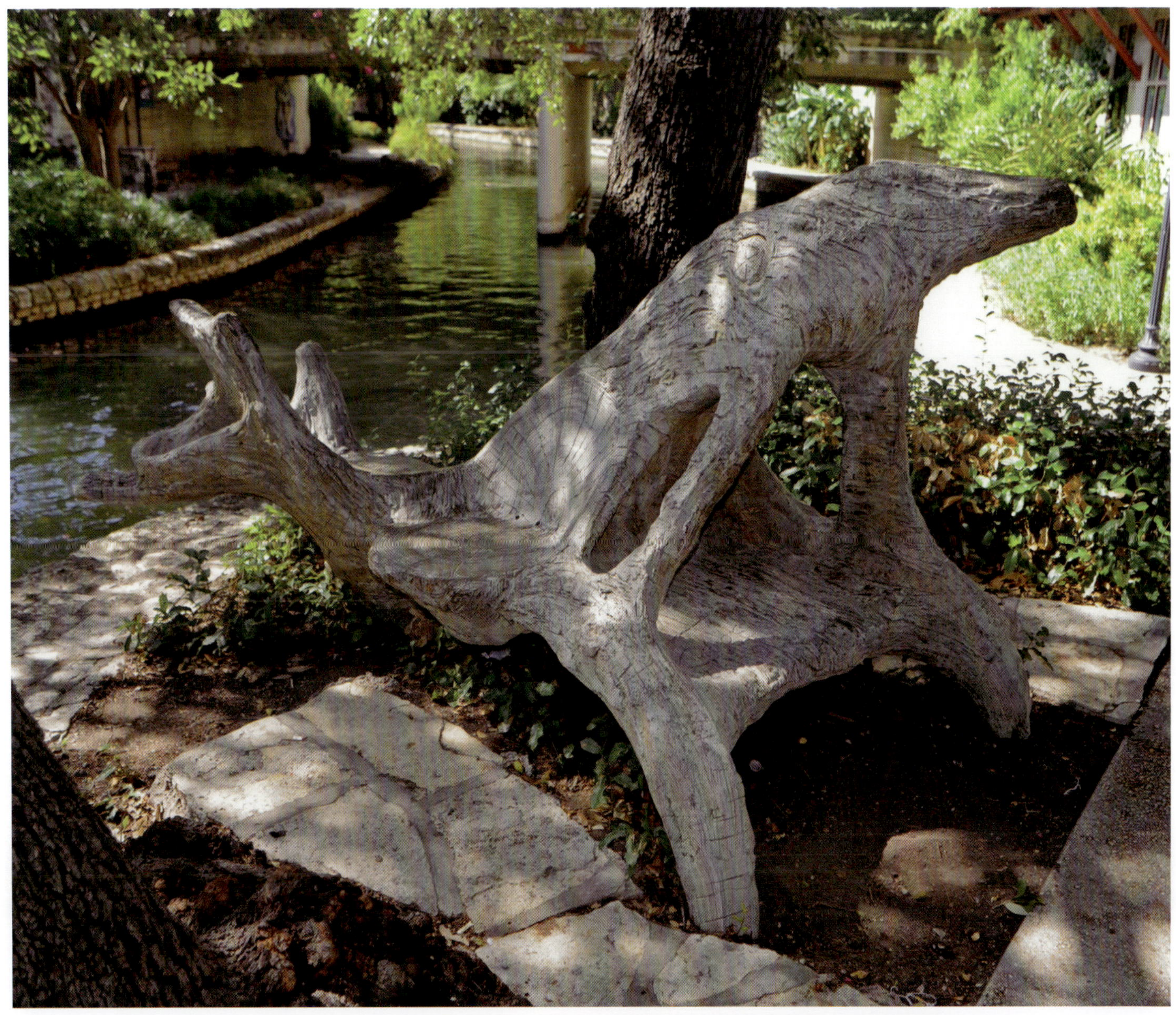

Carlos Cortés. San Antonio, TX. San Antonio River Walk. Fantasy chair. Photo by Kent Rush.

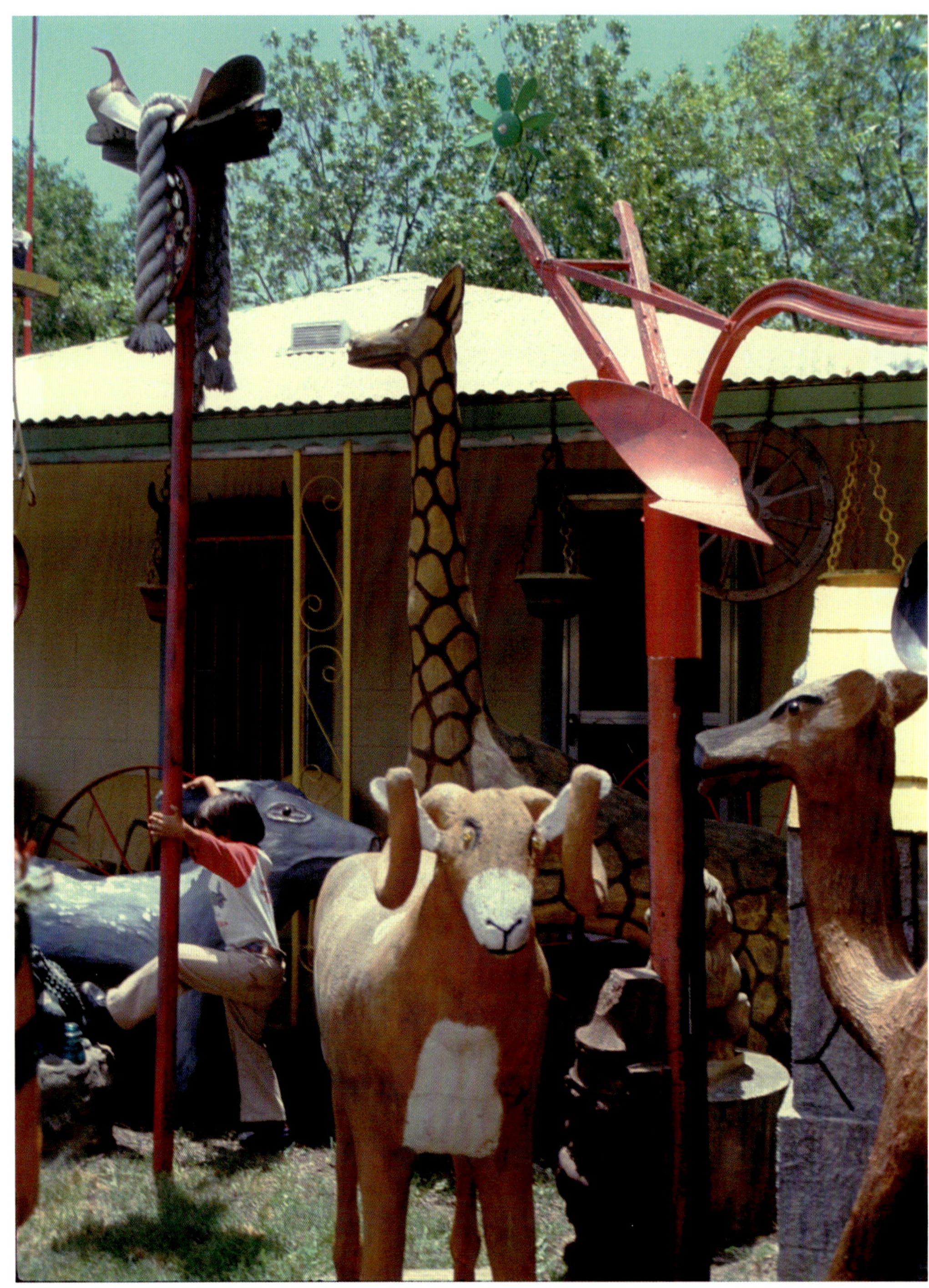

Eliseo Alvarado. San Antonio, TX. The artisan's yard (another view). Photo by Larry Harris.

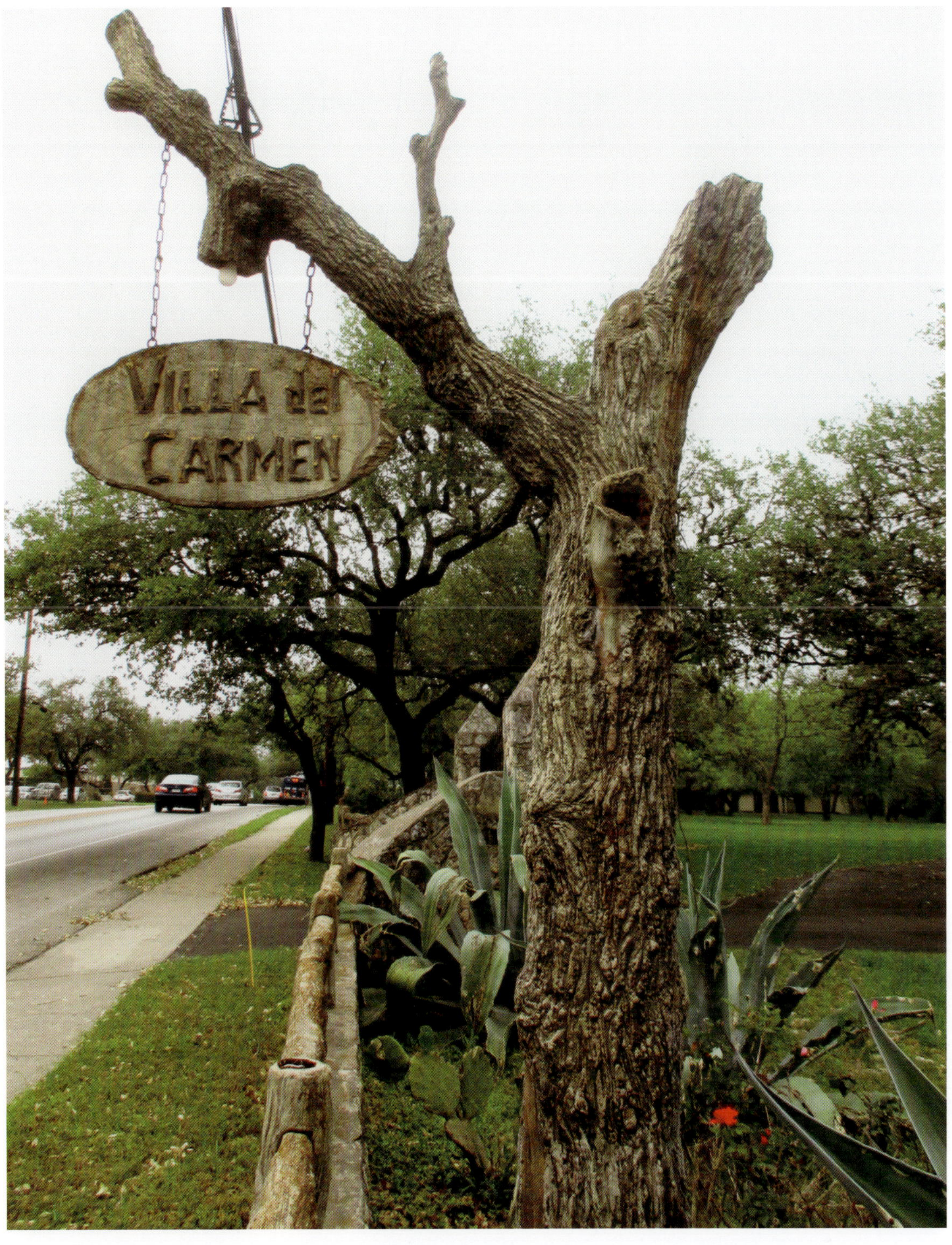

Máximo Cortés. San Antonio, TX. Signpost of Villa del Carmen. Collection of Carmen and Roy Barrera Sr.
Photo by Kent Rush.

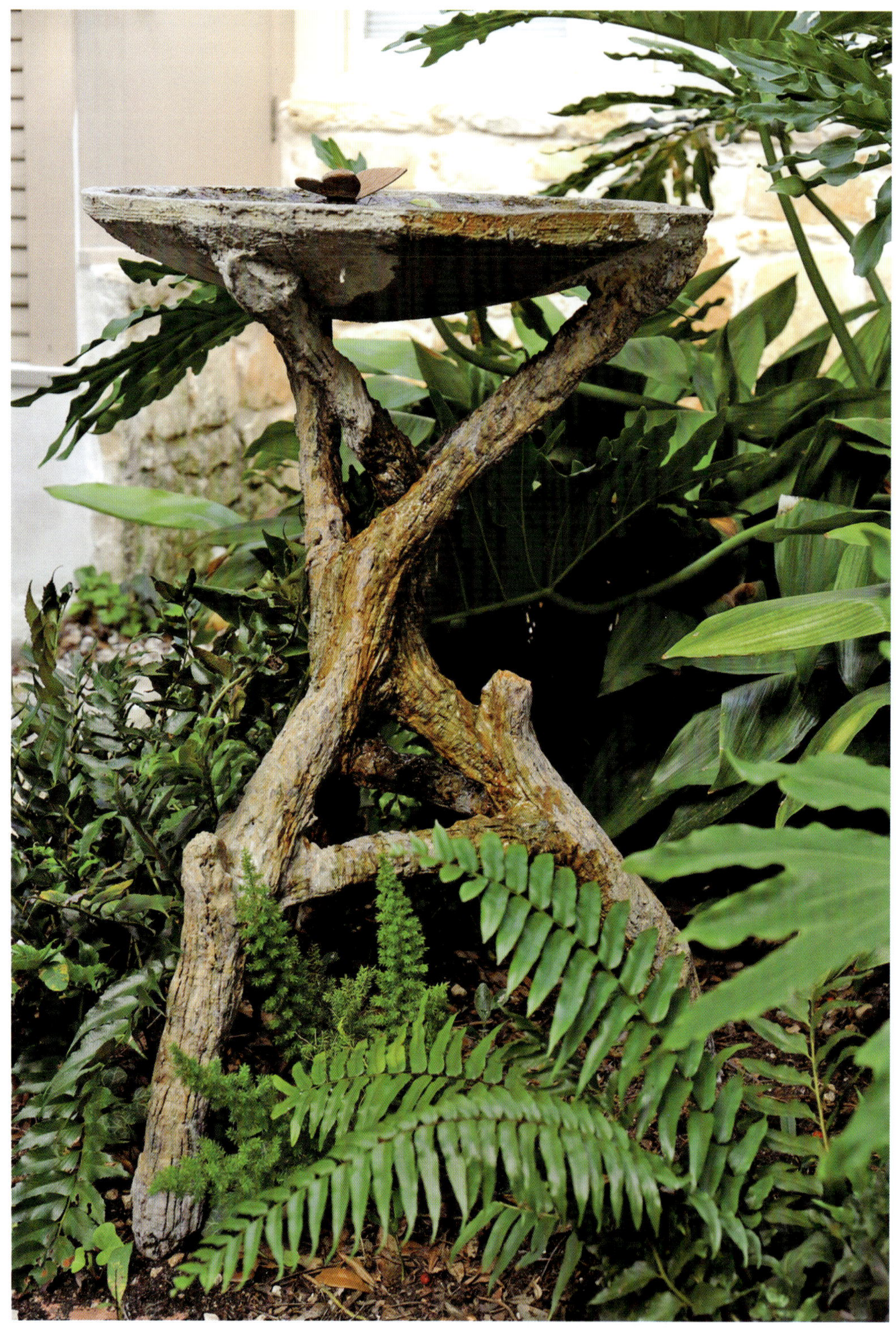

Rene Romero. San Antonio, TX. Birdbath. Collection of Cappy and Suzy Lawton. Photo by Kent Rush.

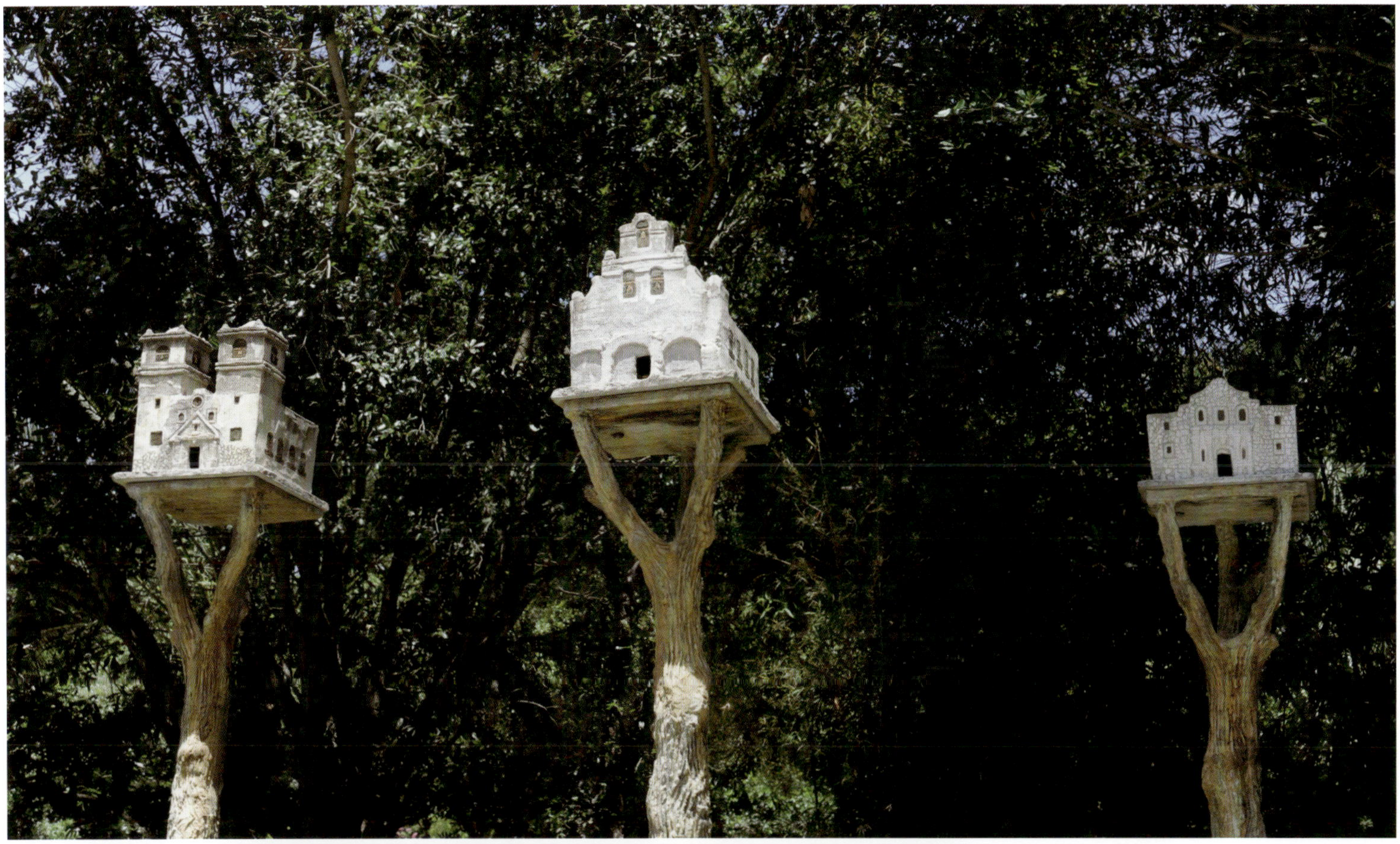

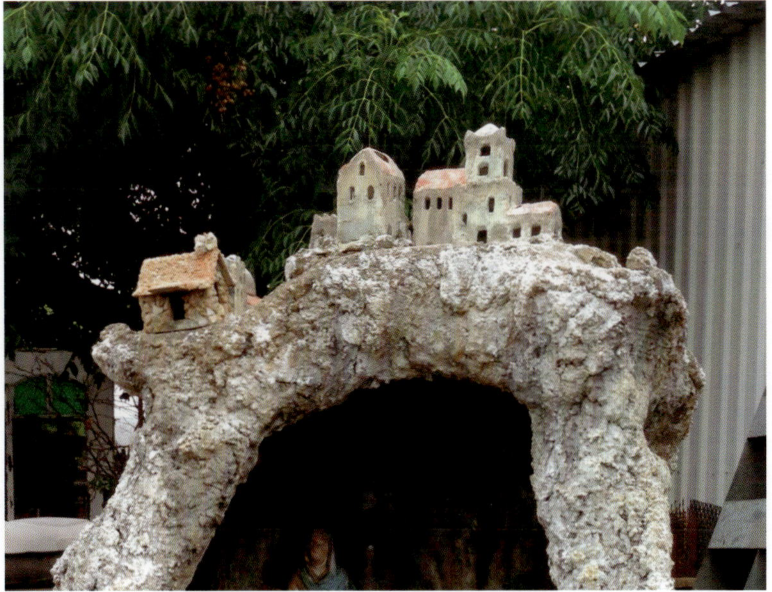

Above: *Carlos Cortés. San Antonio, TX. Collection of Karen and Ronald J. Herrmann. Photo by Kent Rush.*

Left: *Artisan unknown. San Antonio, TX. Village on grotto. Private collection. Photo by Kent Rush.*

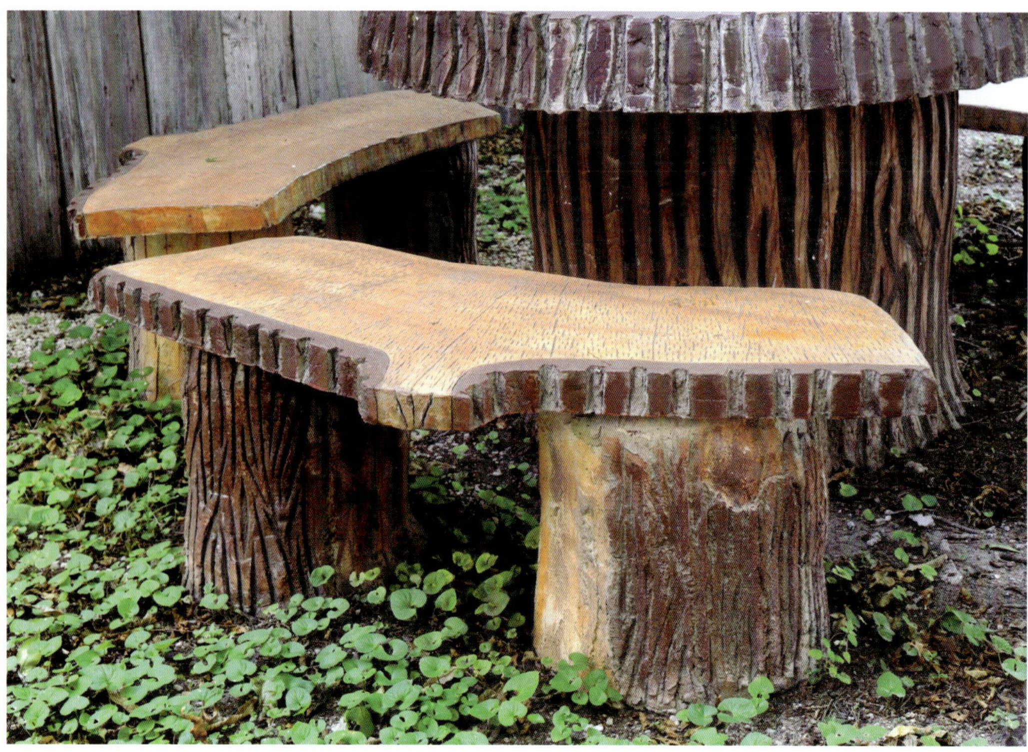

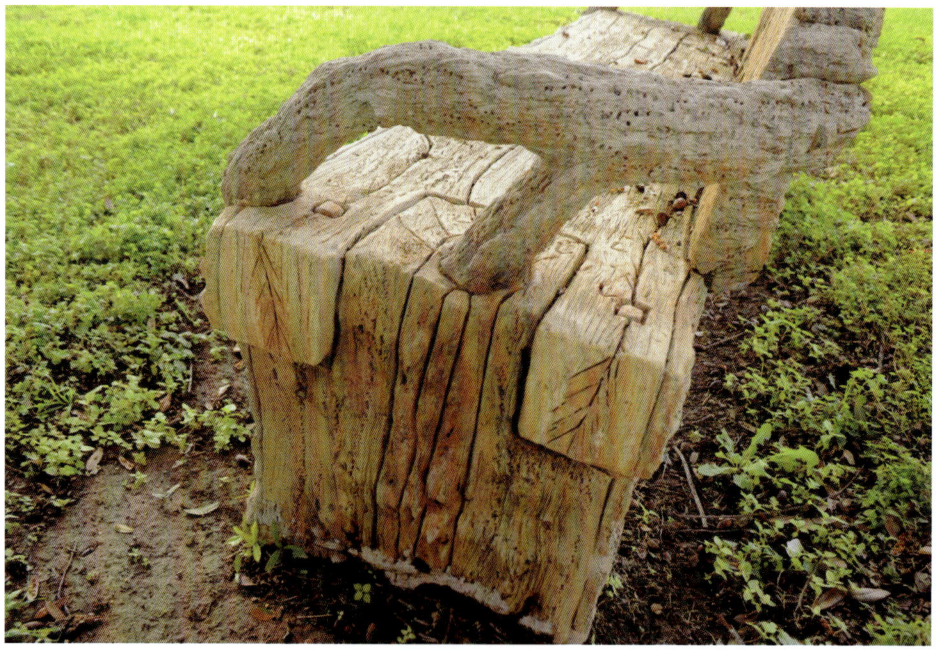

Above: *Frank Ramos. Boerne, TX. A Little Nature Store, Patti Roetman, owner. Benches and table. Photo by Kent Rush.*

Right: *Sam Murray. Uvalde, TX. City of Uvalde Collection. Photo by Kent Rush.*

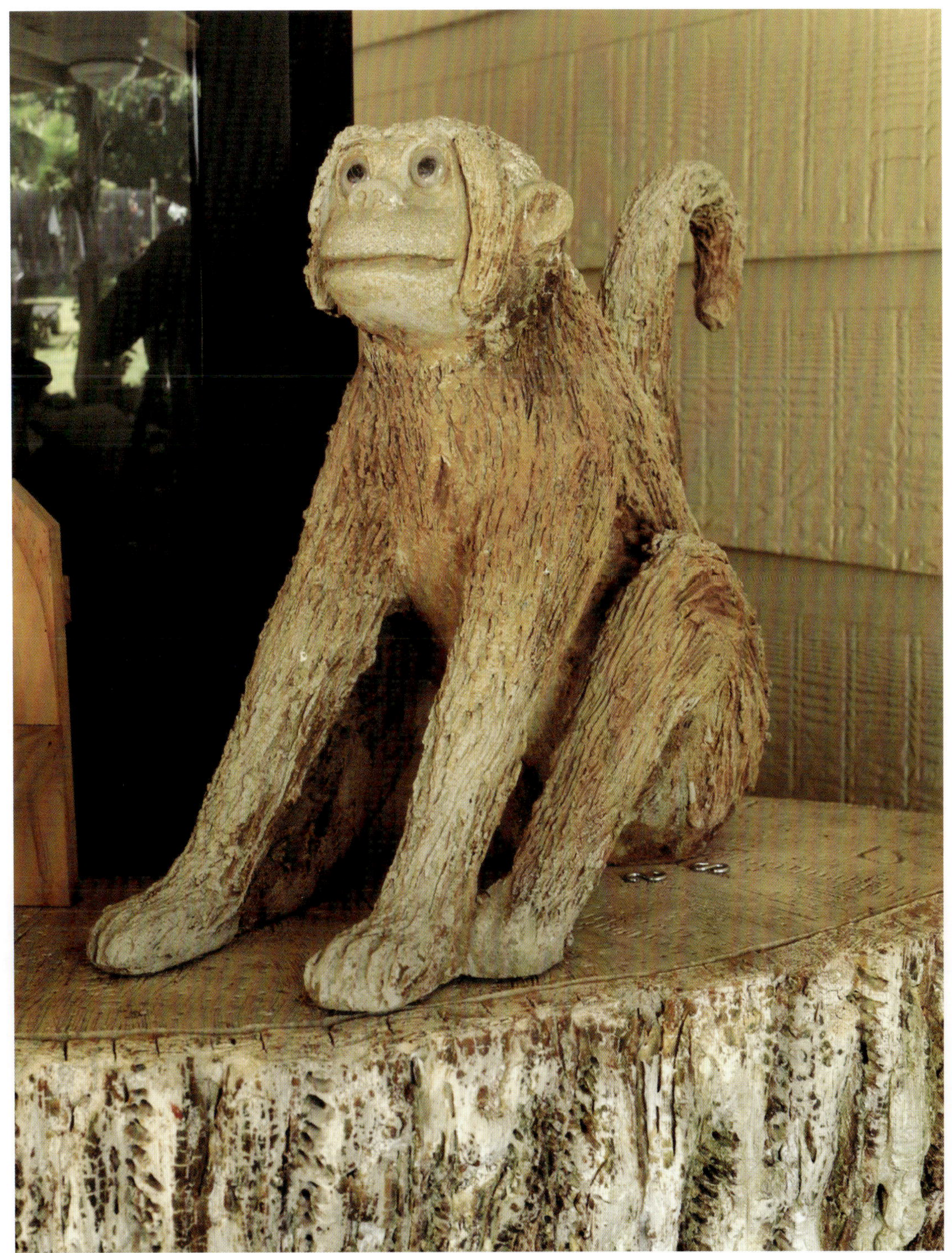

Sam Murray. San Antonio, TX. Private collection. Photo by Kent Rush.

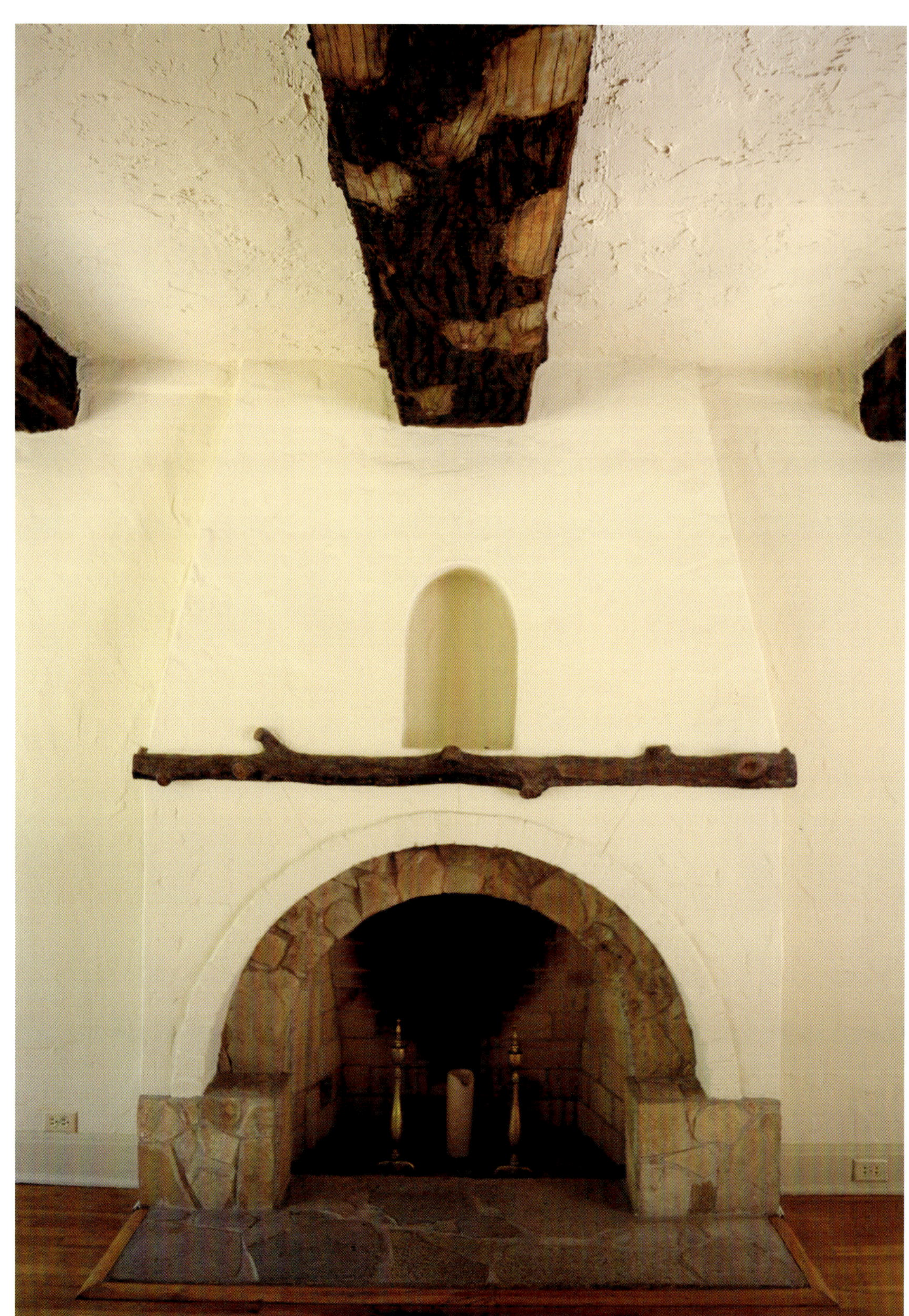

*Artisan unknown.
San Antonio, TX.
Fireplace and
beams. The Emily
Lemberg Family
Collection.
Photo by Kent Rush.*

102

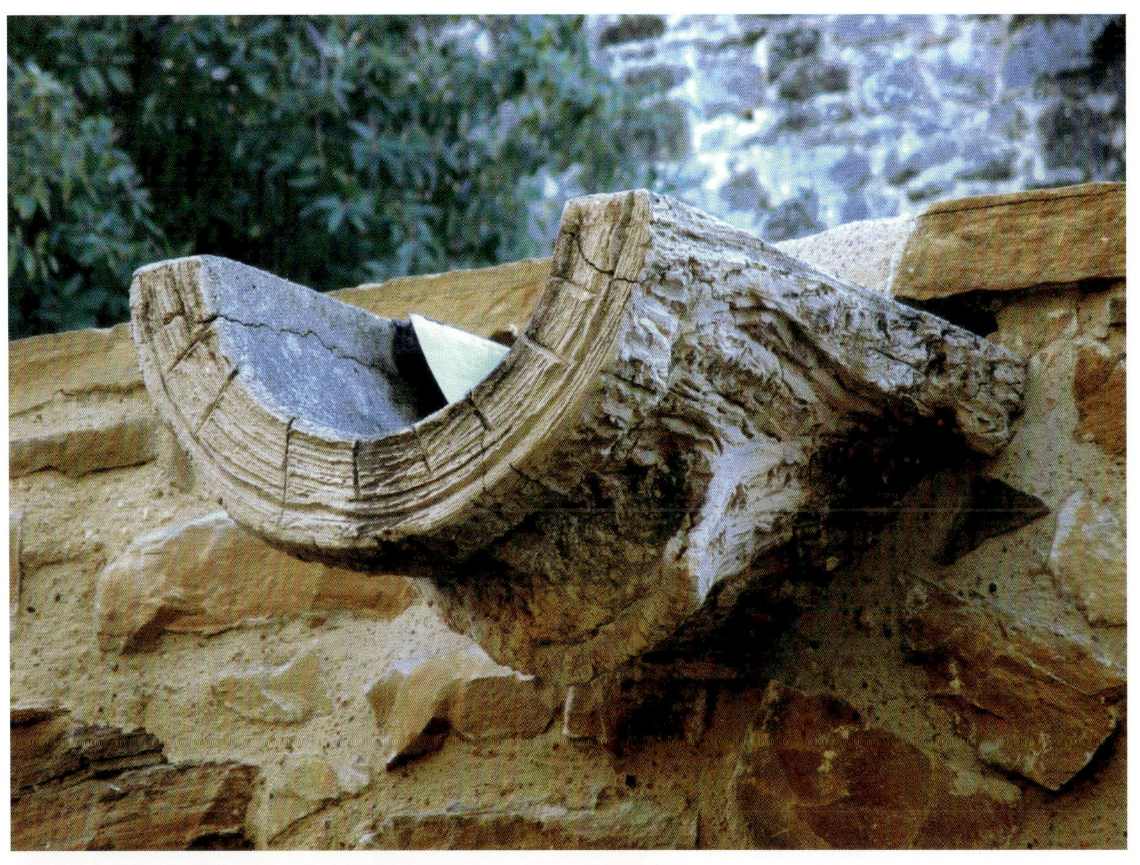

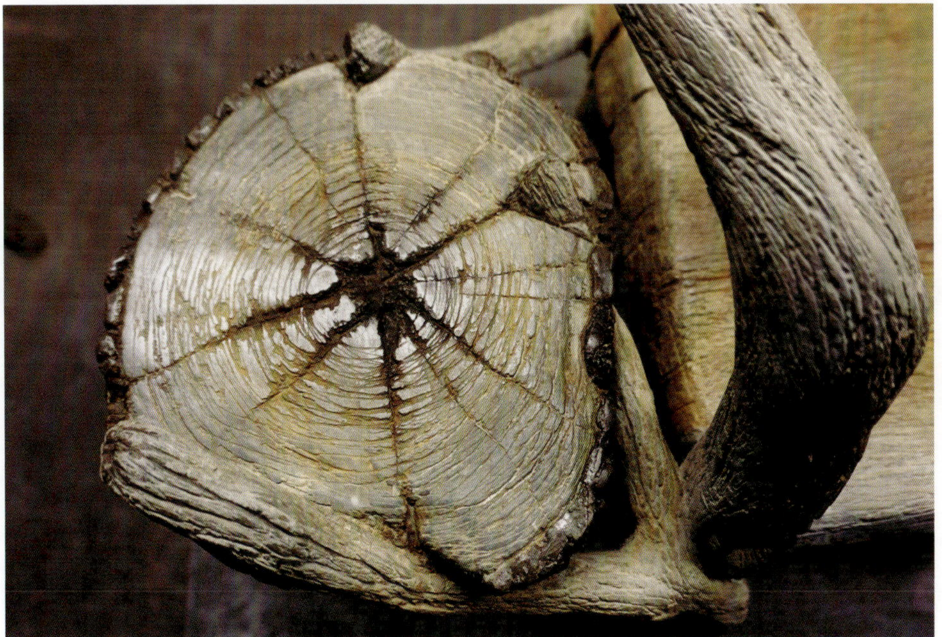

Above: Artisan unknown. San Antonio, TX.
Mission San Jose y San Miguel Aguayo.
Downspout. Photo by Kent Rush.

Left: Marcella Marie. St. Louis, MO. Detail,
bench. Private collection. Photo by Marcella
Marie.

103

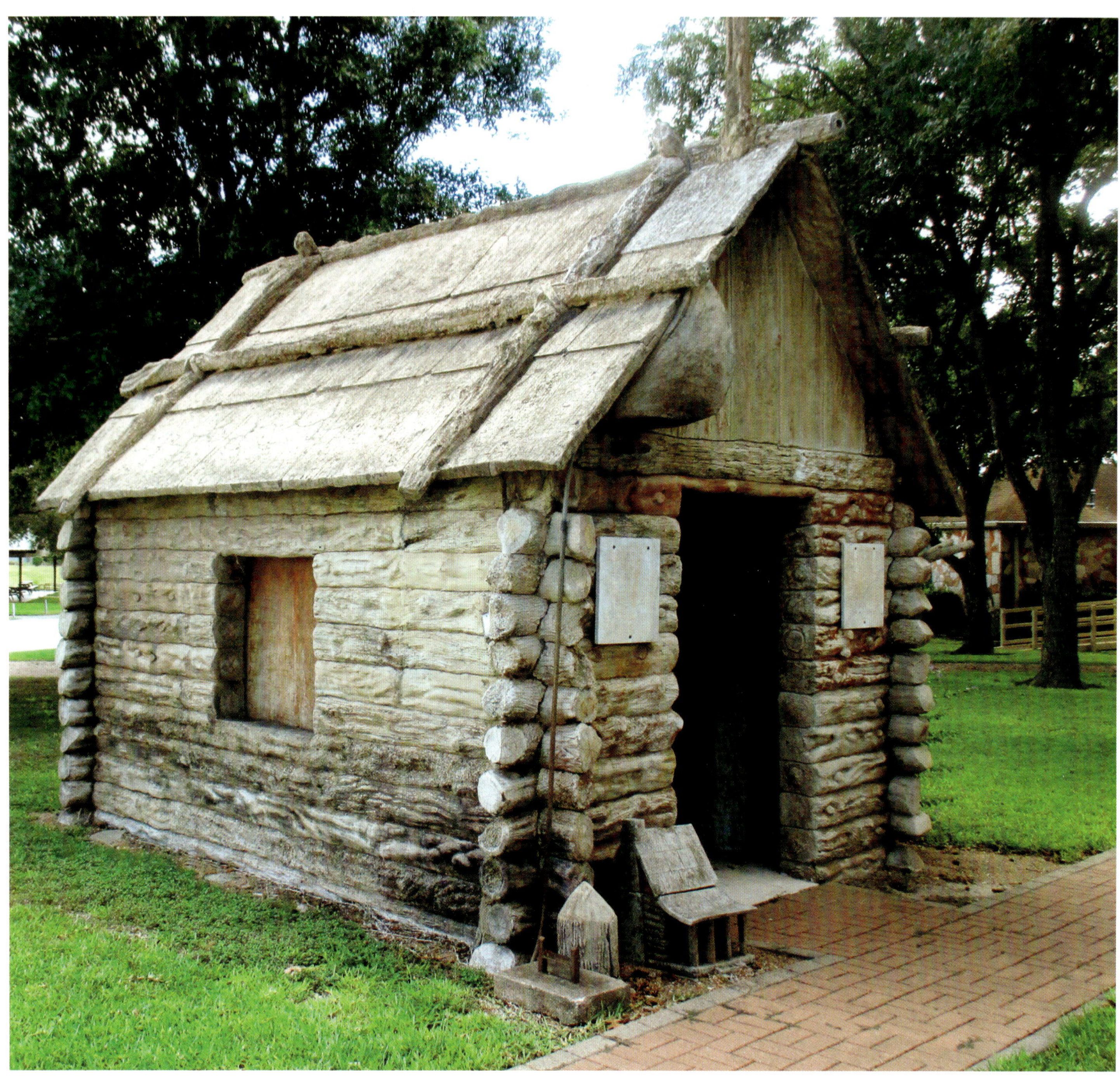

Antonio Lopez and W. C. Perez. Hostyn, TX. Queen of the Holy Rosary Church. Trabajo rústico concrete log replica of Holy Trinity Church. Photo by Kent Rush.

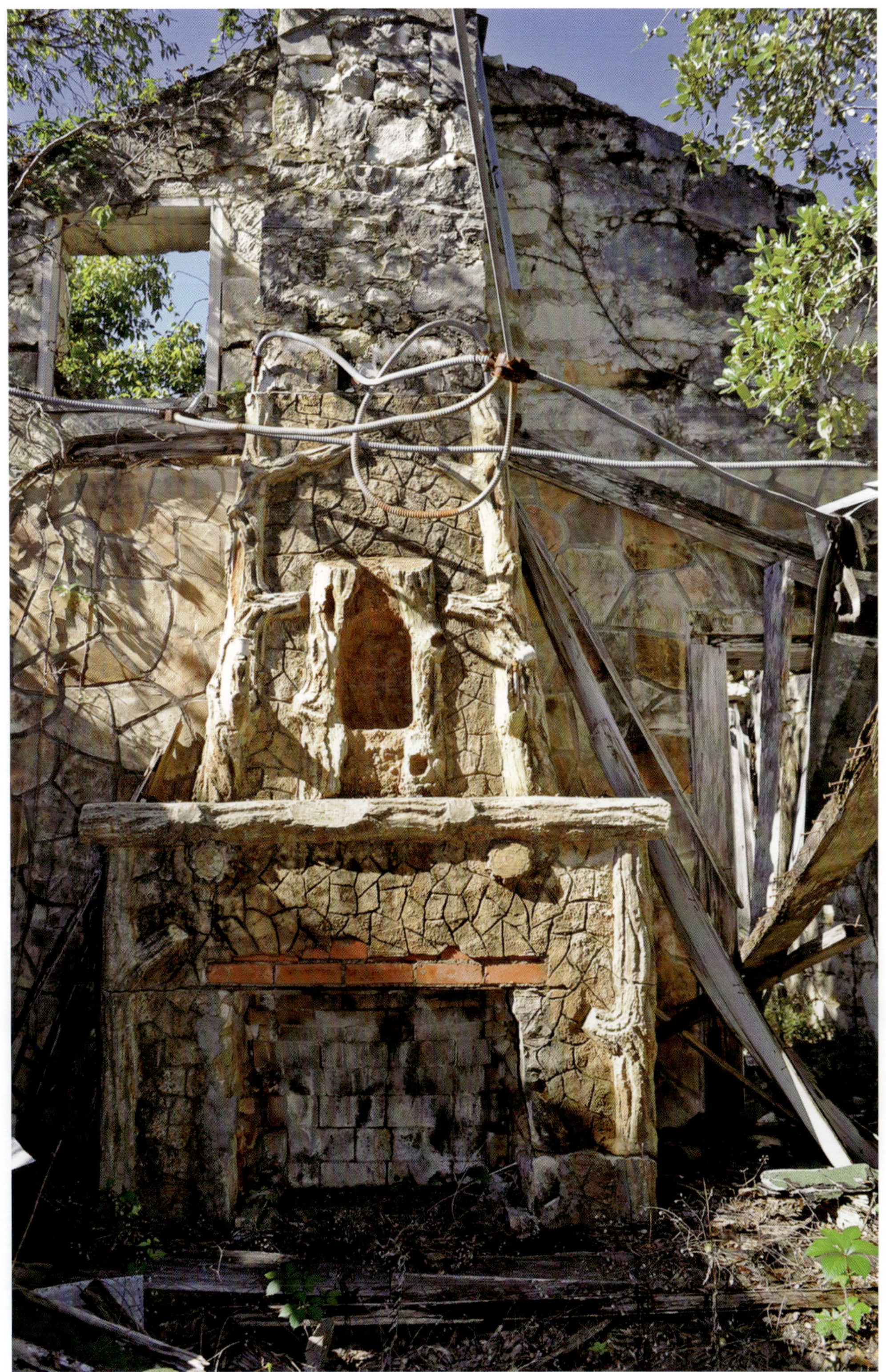

Artisan unknown. Bexar County, TX. Camp Bullis Military Training Reservation. Photo by Kent Rush.

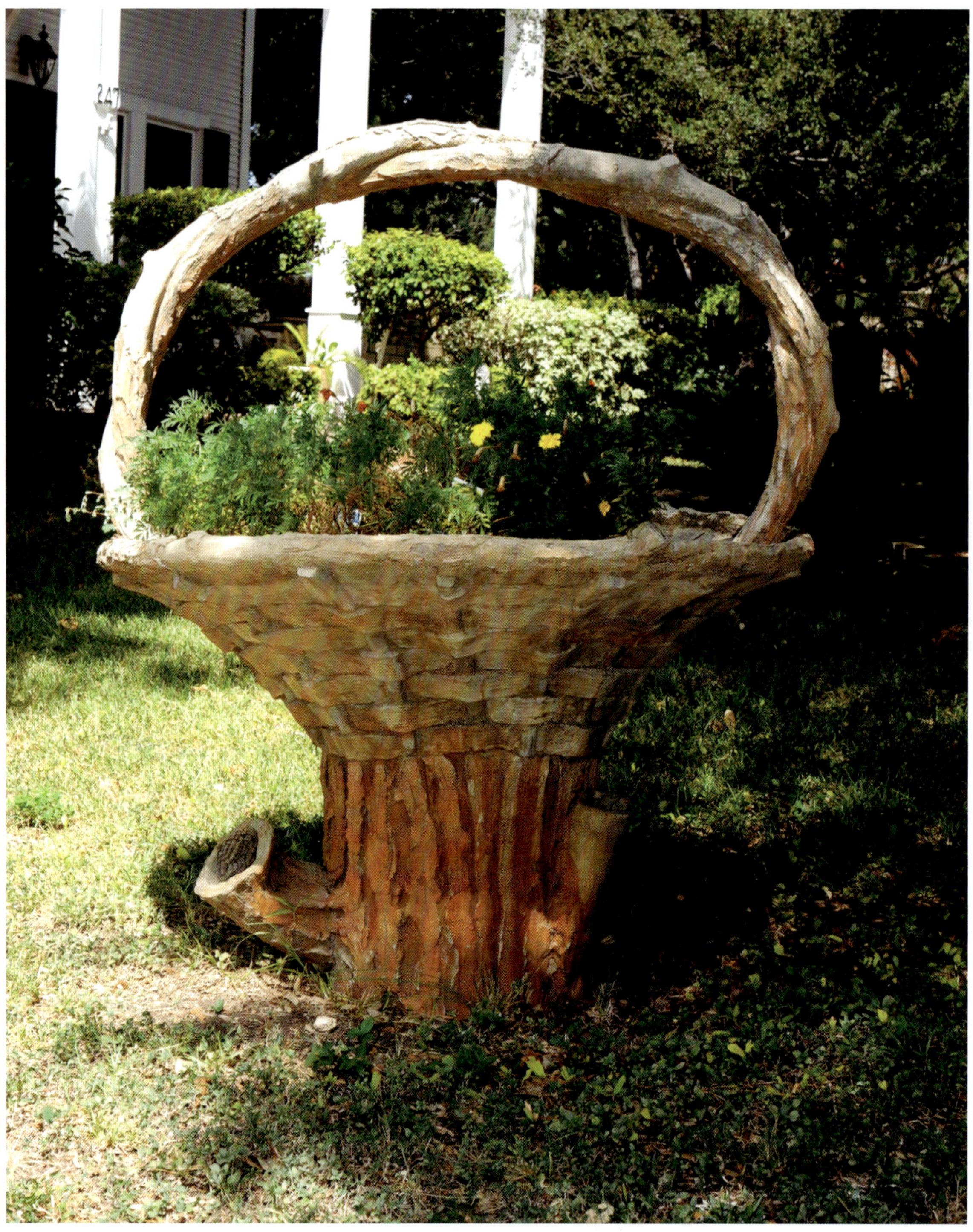

Margarito Del Castillo. San Antonio, TX. Courtesy of Mrs. Helen Davila and Family. Photo by Kent Rush.

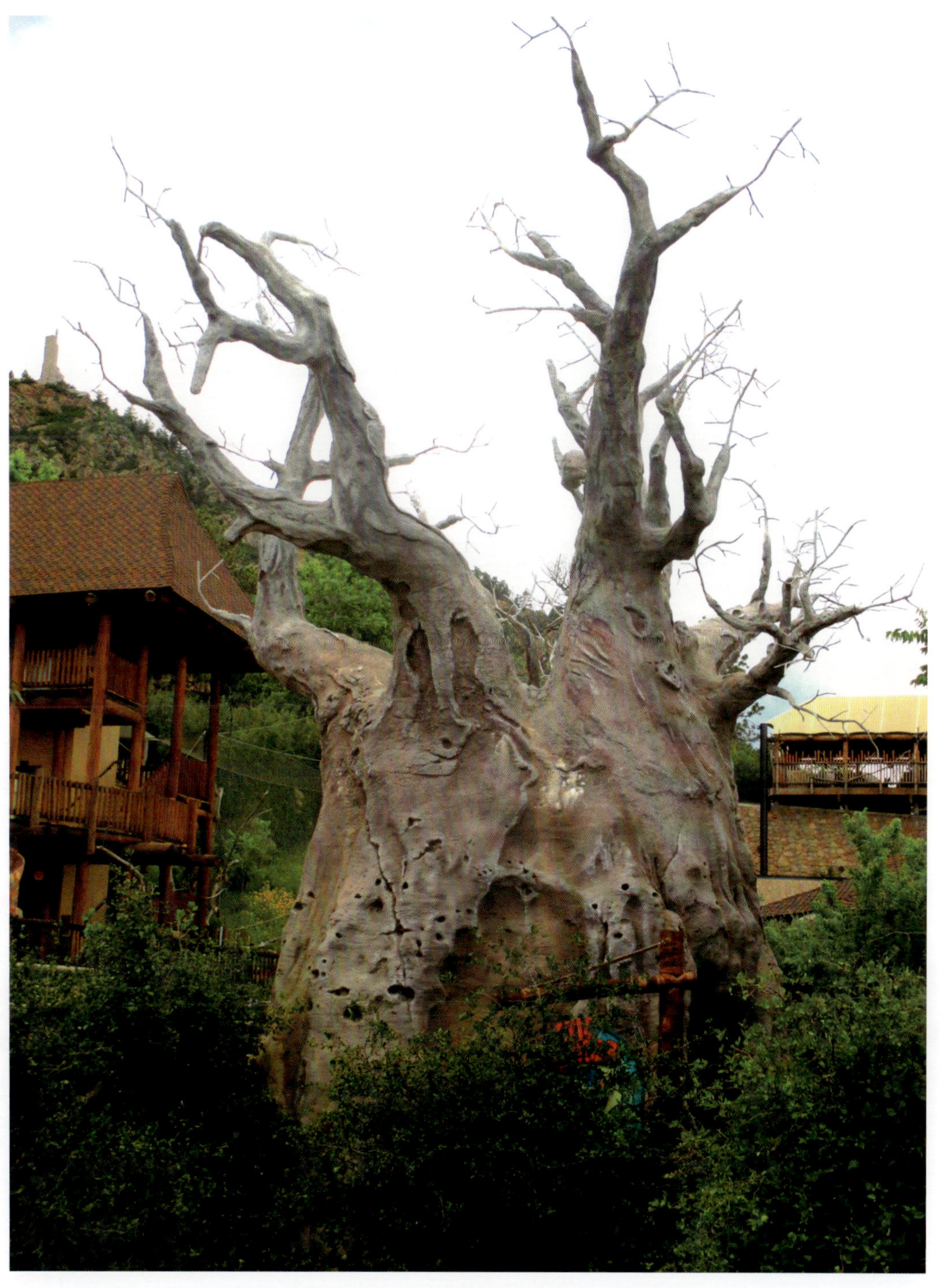

CLR Design, Inc., under direction of Gary Lee. Fabrication by Cemrock Landscape. Colorado Springs, CO. Boabab. Cheyenne Mountain Zoo. Photo by Kent Rush.

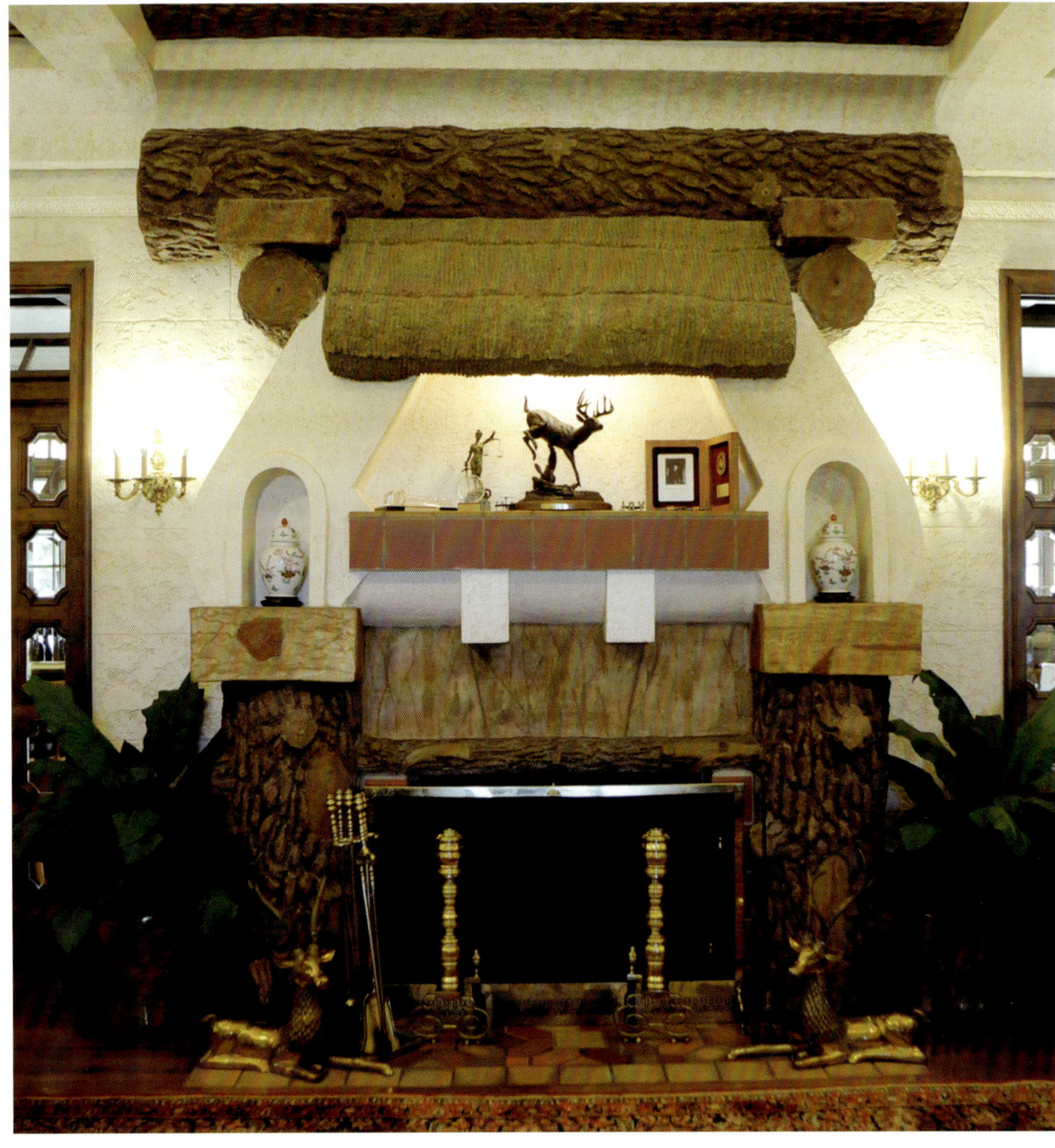

Máximo Cortés and Dionicio Rodríguez. San Antonio, TX. Fireplace, mantel trim, and beams. Private collection. Photo by Kent Rush.

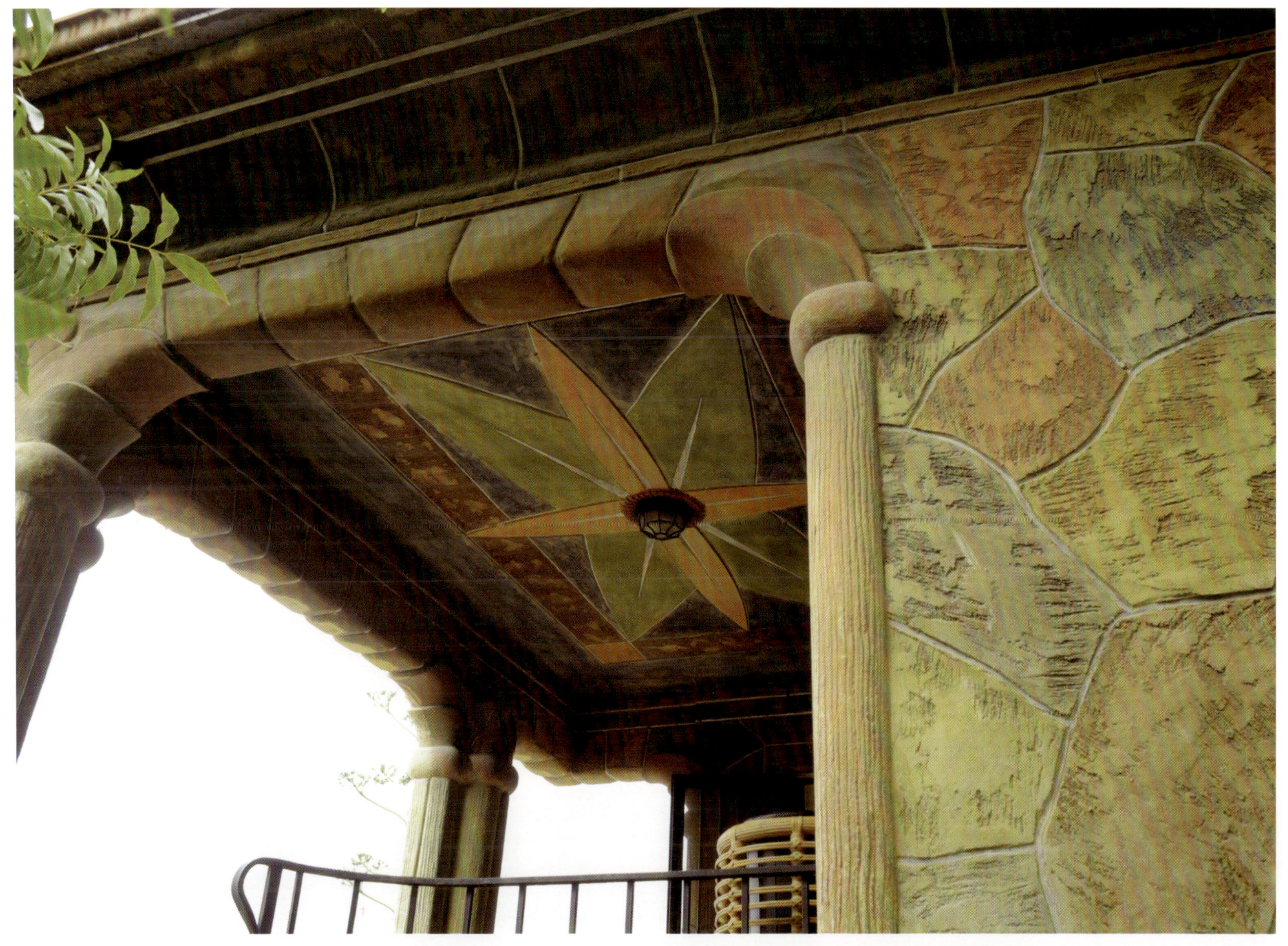

Genaro Briones. Austin, TX. House porch detail. Laurie D. Marchant and Robert L. Marchant, owners. Photo by Kent Rush.

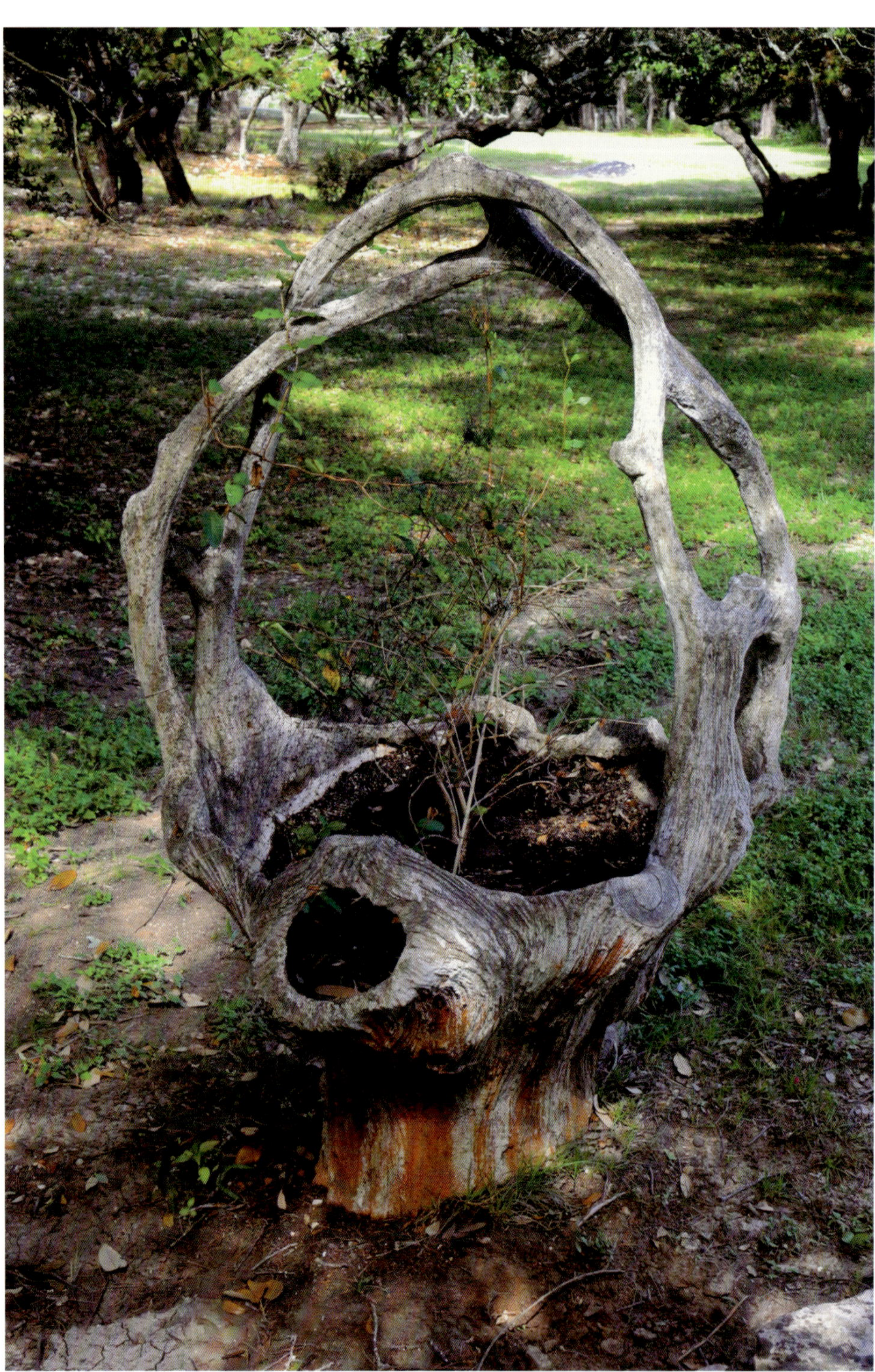

Máximo Cortés. Leon Springs, TX. Basket. Collection of Wanda Palmer. Photo by Kent Rush.

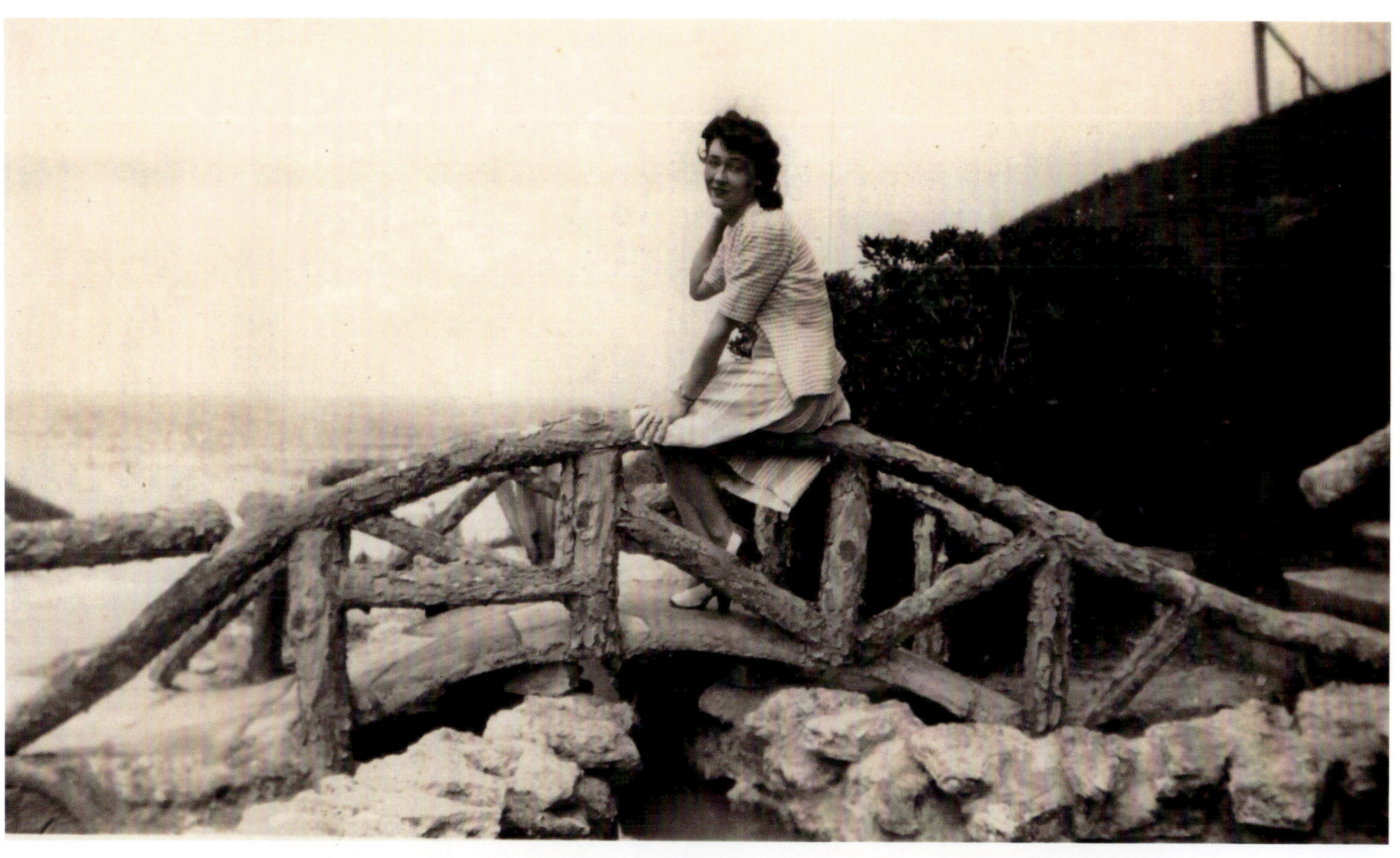

Artisan unknown. Corpus Christi, TX. Cole Park non-extant railings. Photo courtesy of Robert Parks.

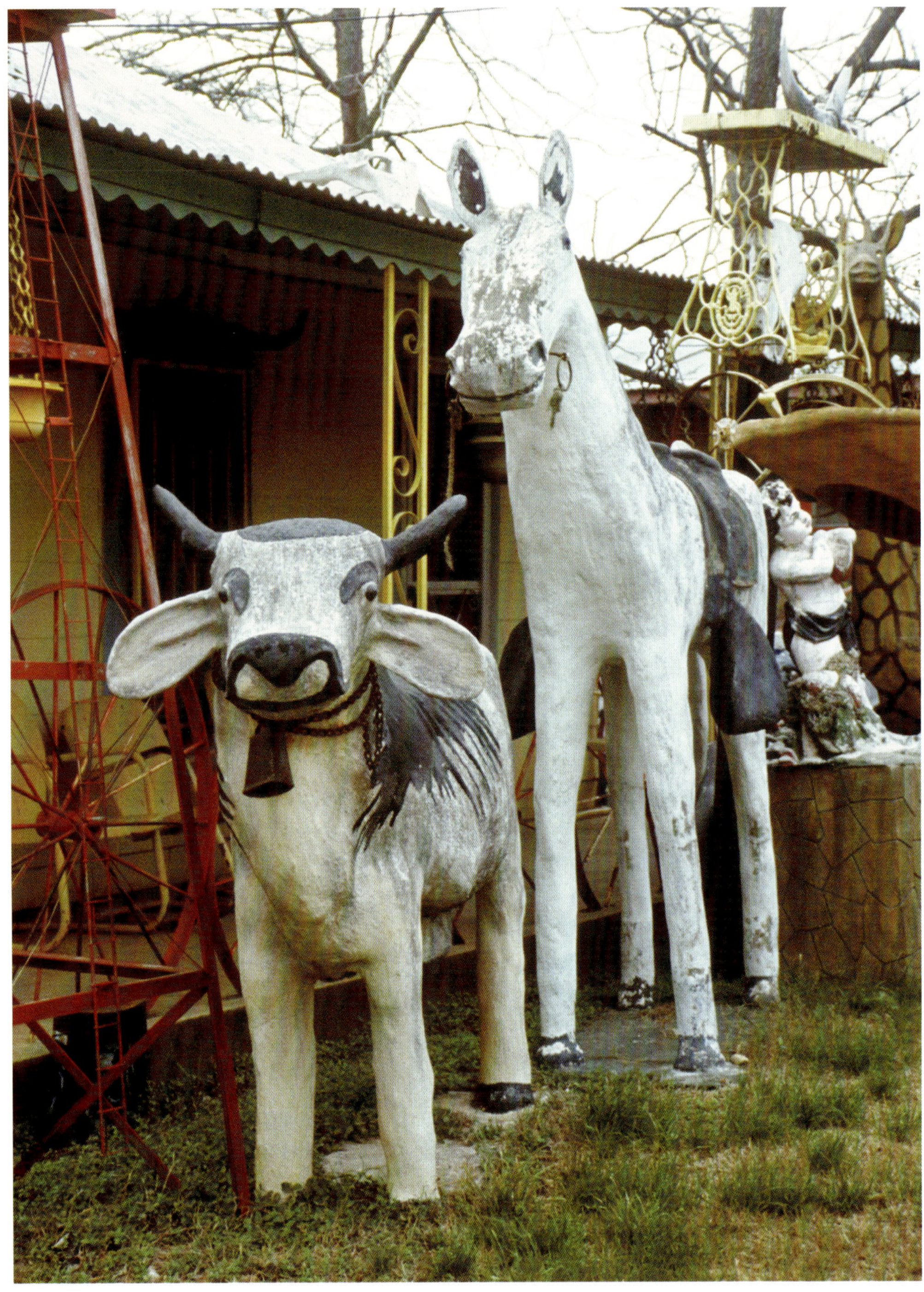

Eliseo Alvarado. San Antonio, TX. Alvarado yard (another view). Photo by Larry Harris.

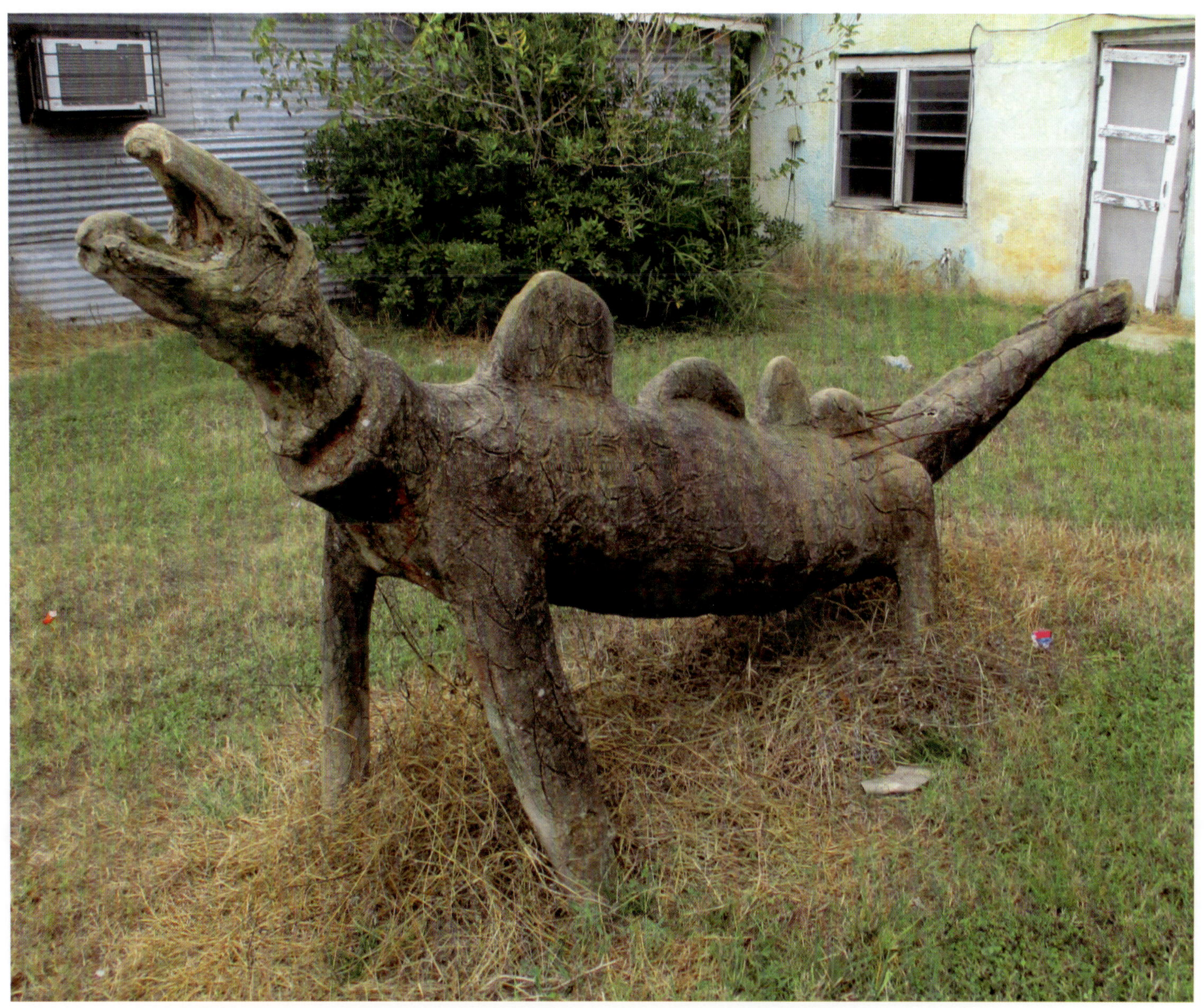

Beatrice Ximénez. Location unknown. Dinosaur. Photo by Kent Rush.

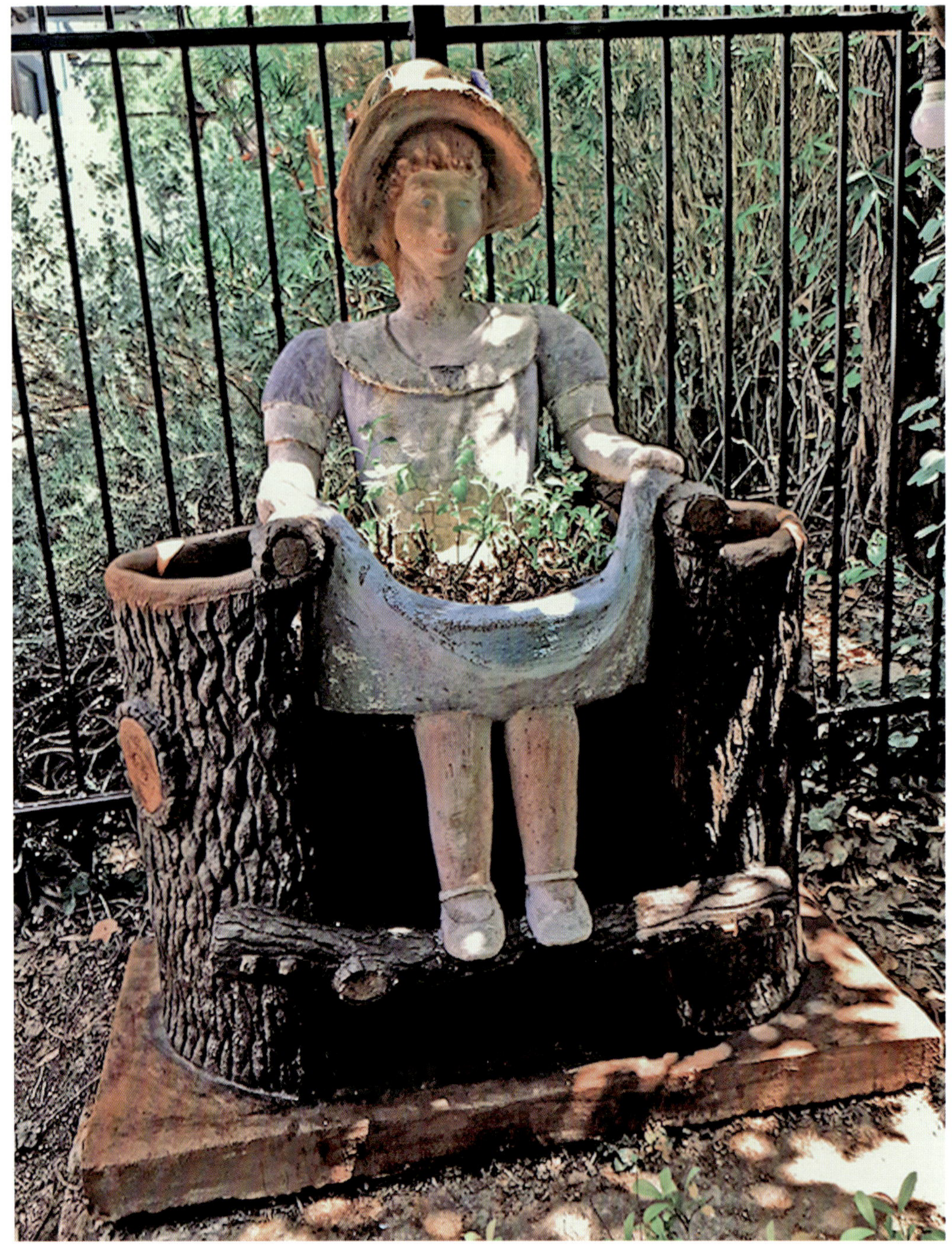

Artisan unknown. San Antonio, TX. Girl with trabajo rústico flower pots. Private collection.
Photo by Rene Romero.

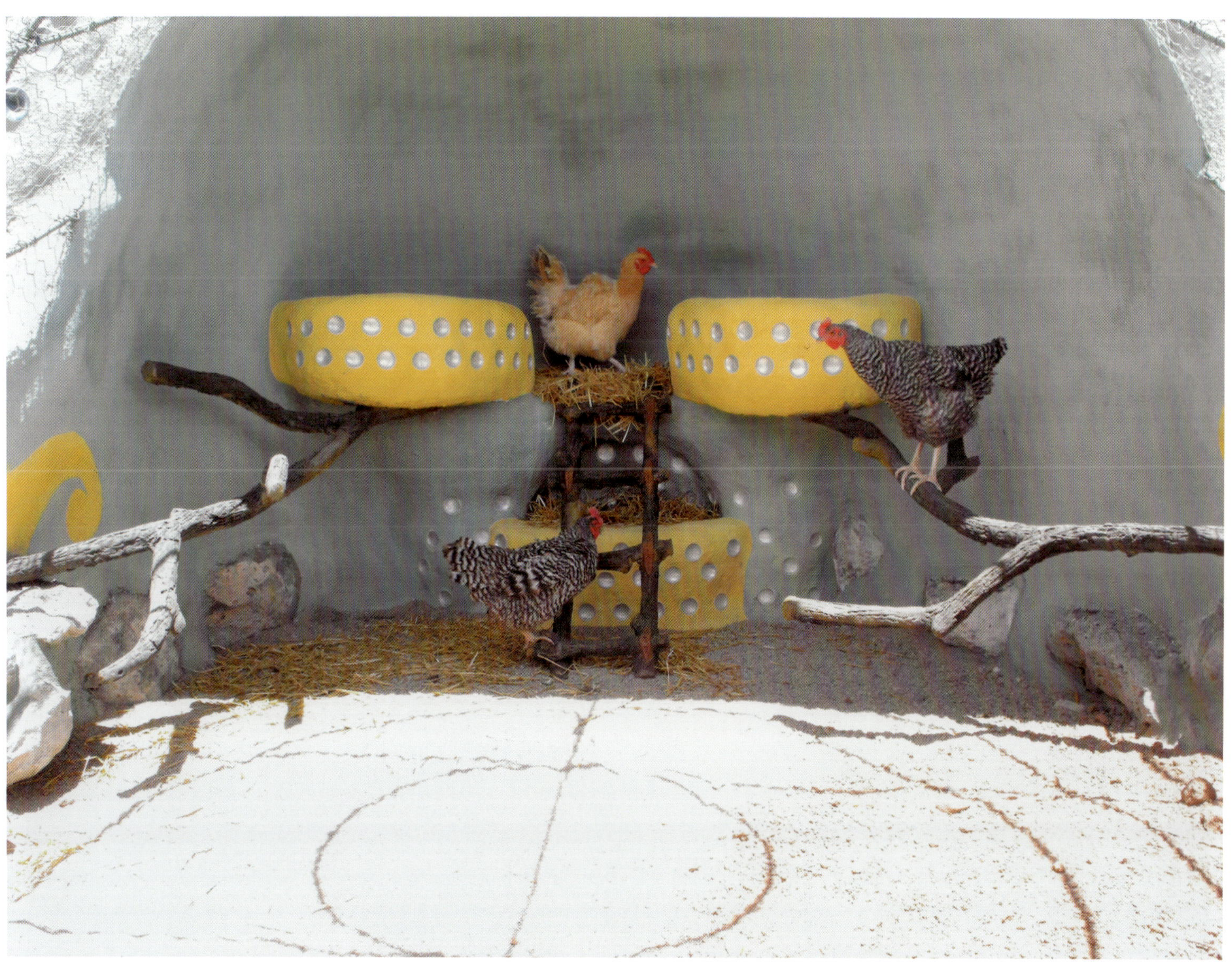

Jacob Tobar. Taos, NM. Private collection. Photo courtesy of Jacob Tobar.

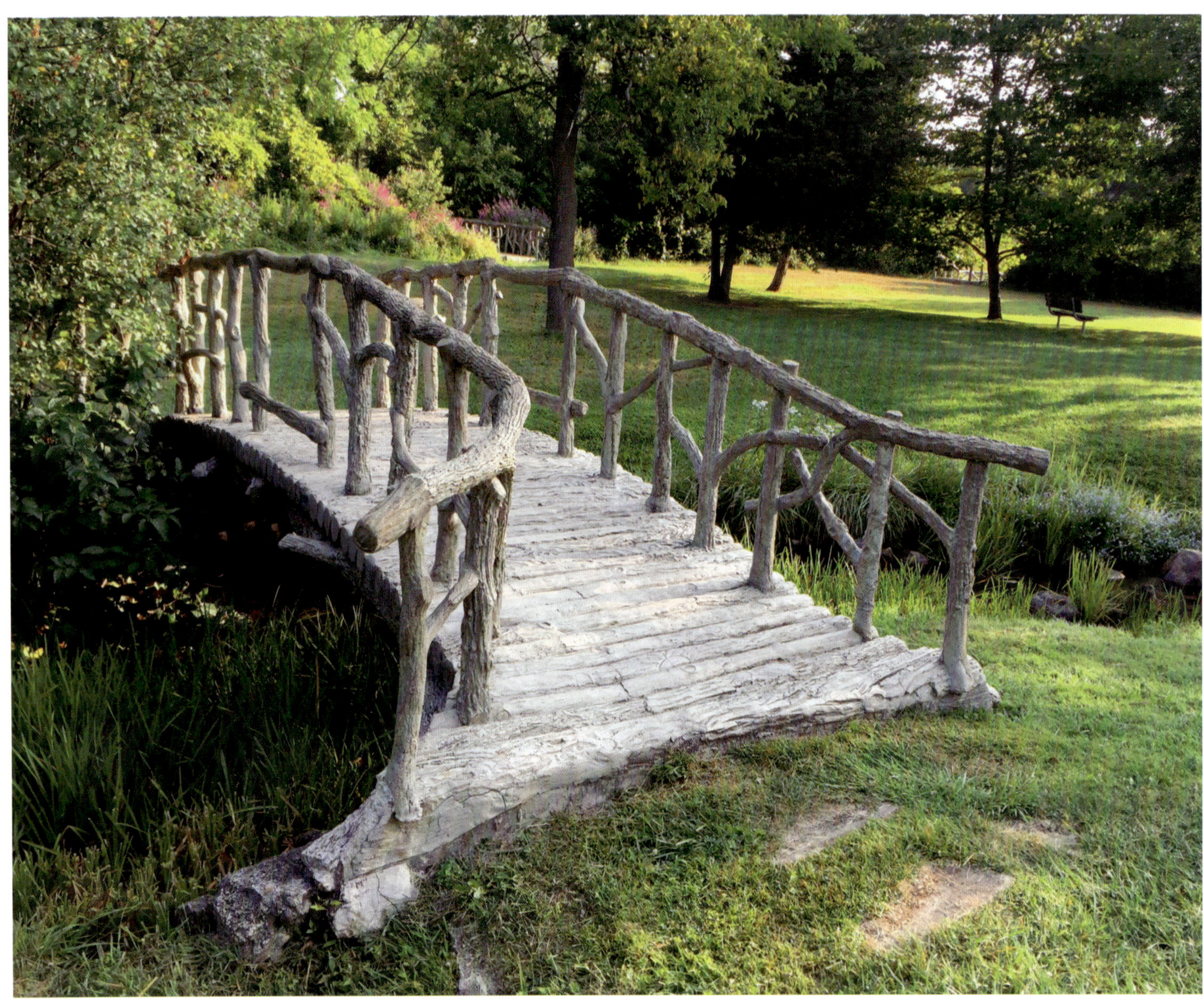

George Cardosa and Ralph Corona. Cement City, MI. McCourtie Park, Somerset Center, MI. Photo by Diane Husson.

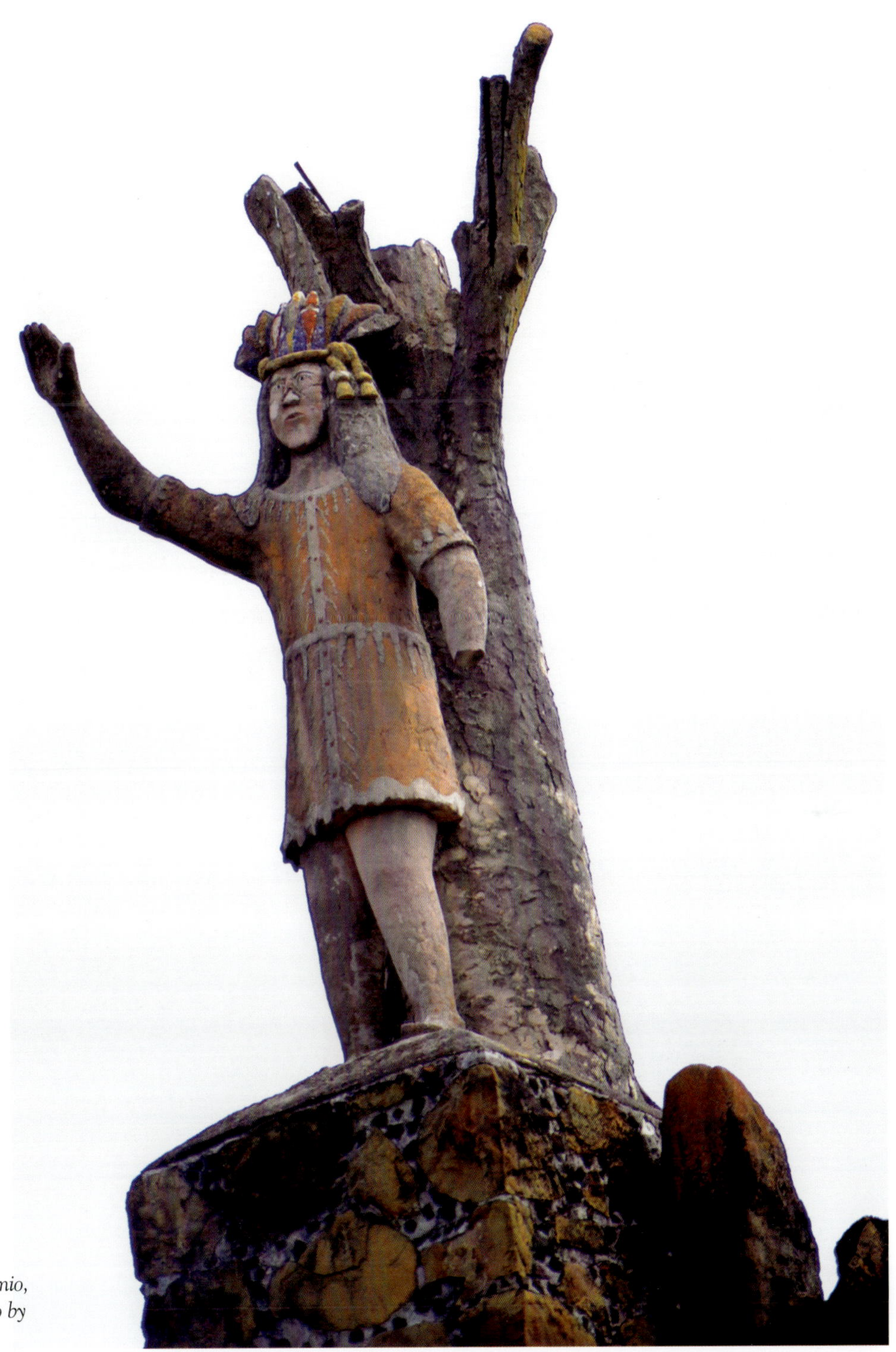

Artisan unknown. San Antonio, TX. Private collection. Photo by Kent Rush.

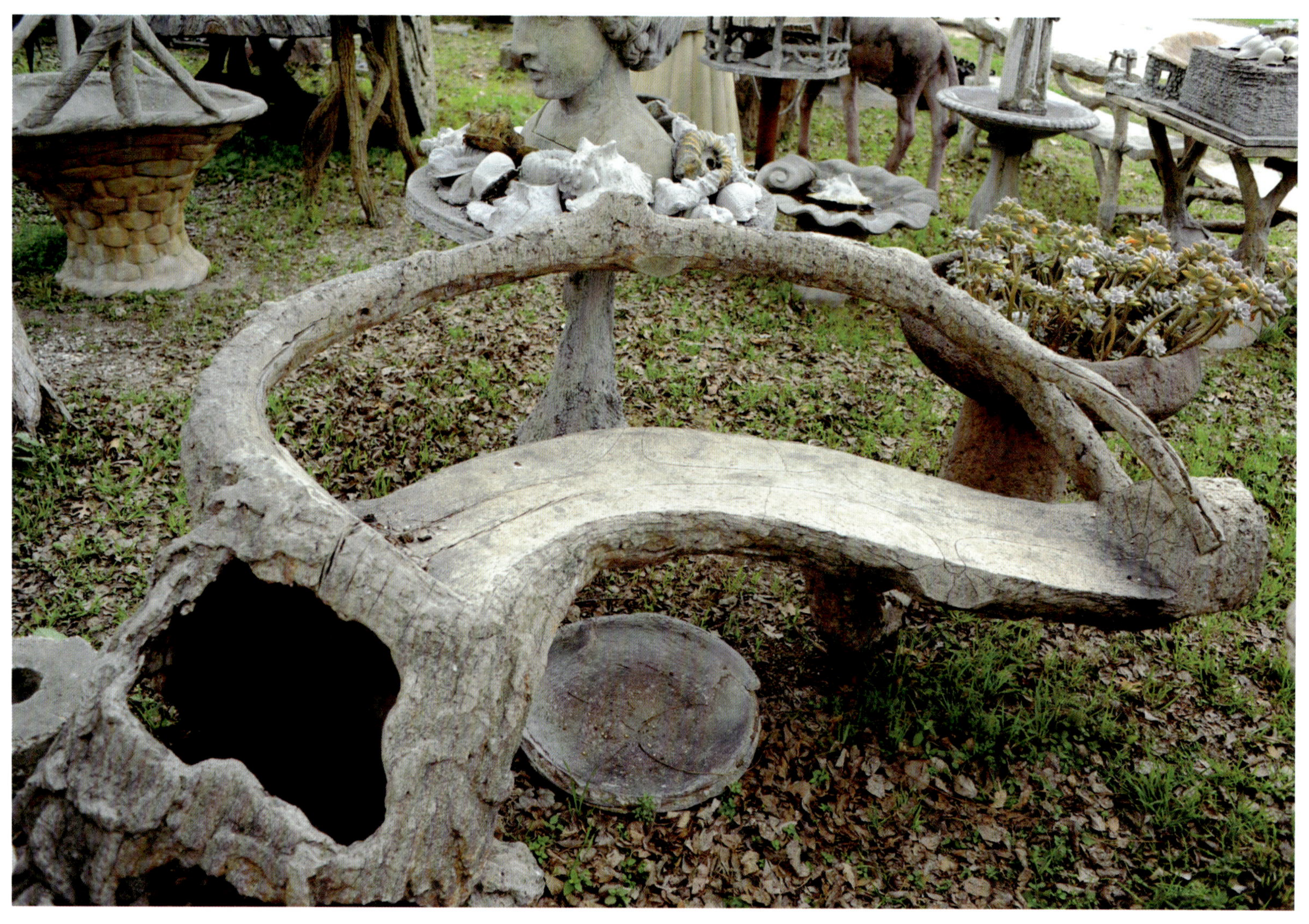

Dionicio Rodríguez. San Antonio, TX. Collection of Carlos Cortés. Photo by Kent Rush.

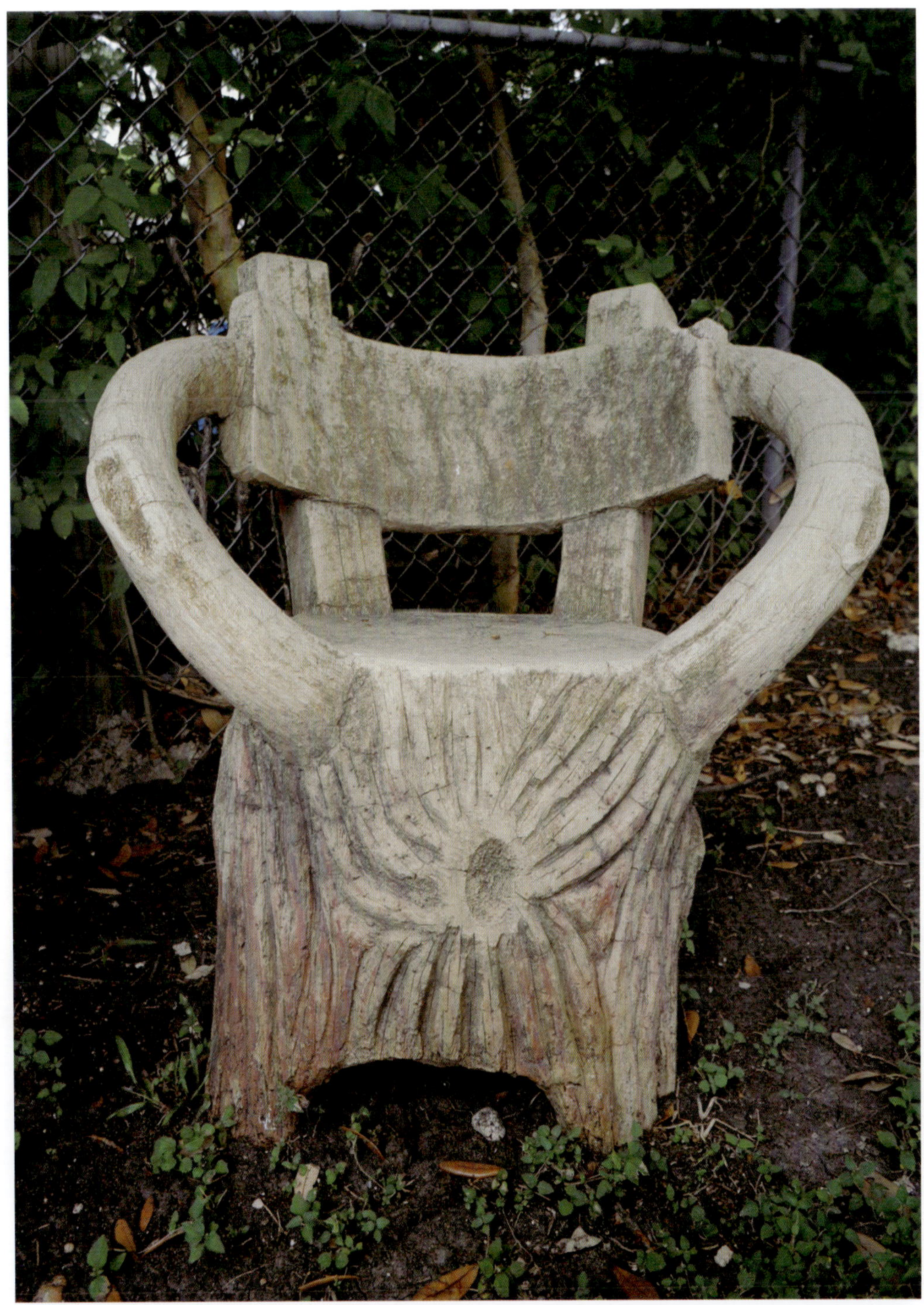

Artisan unknown. San Antonio, TX. Collection of Ms. Kathy Hoermann. Photo by Kent Rush.

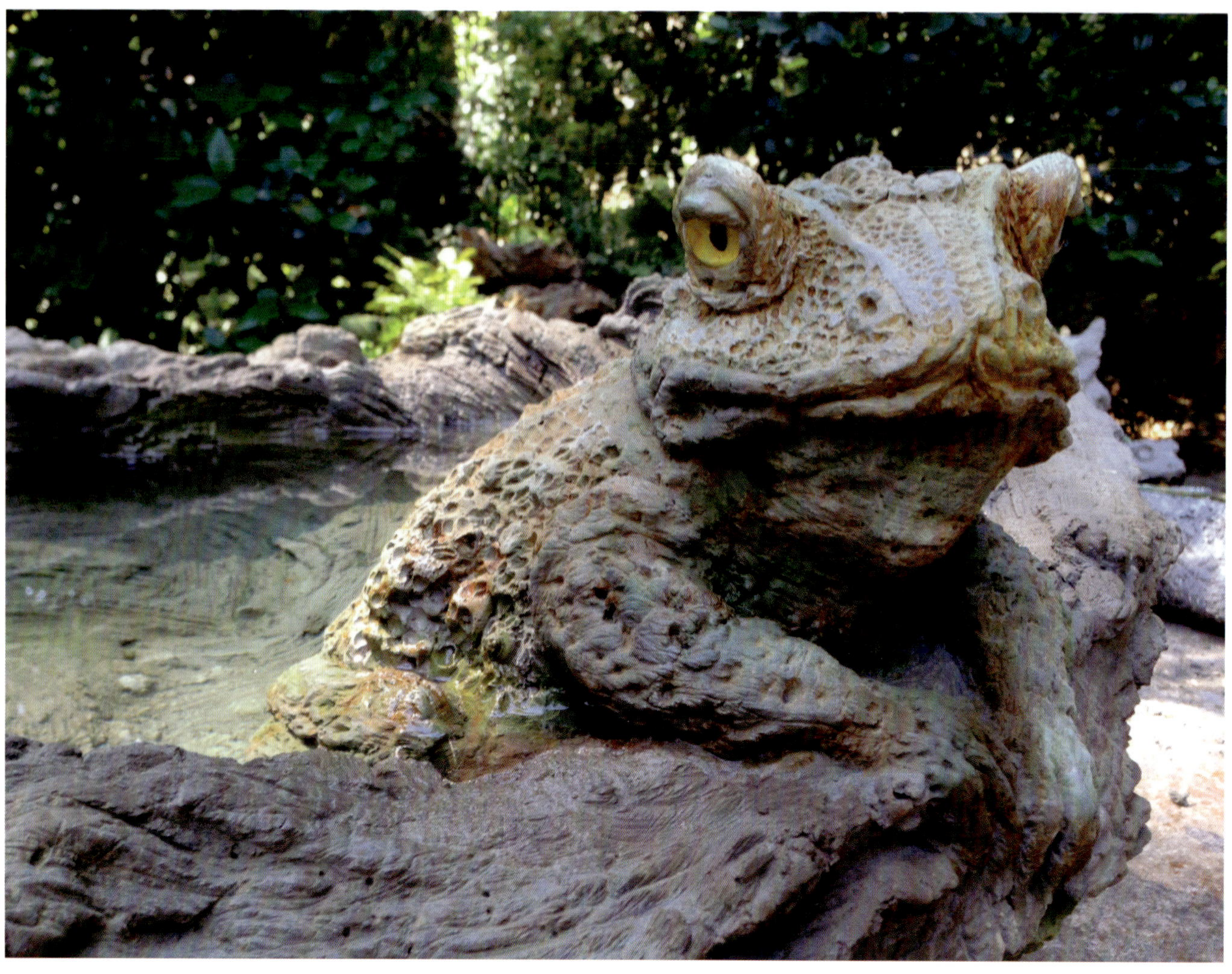

Gregory Everingham. France. Villeneuve-lès-Avignon. Private collection. Photo by Gregory Everingham.

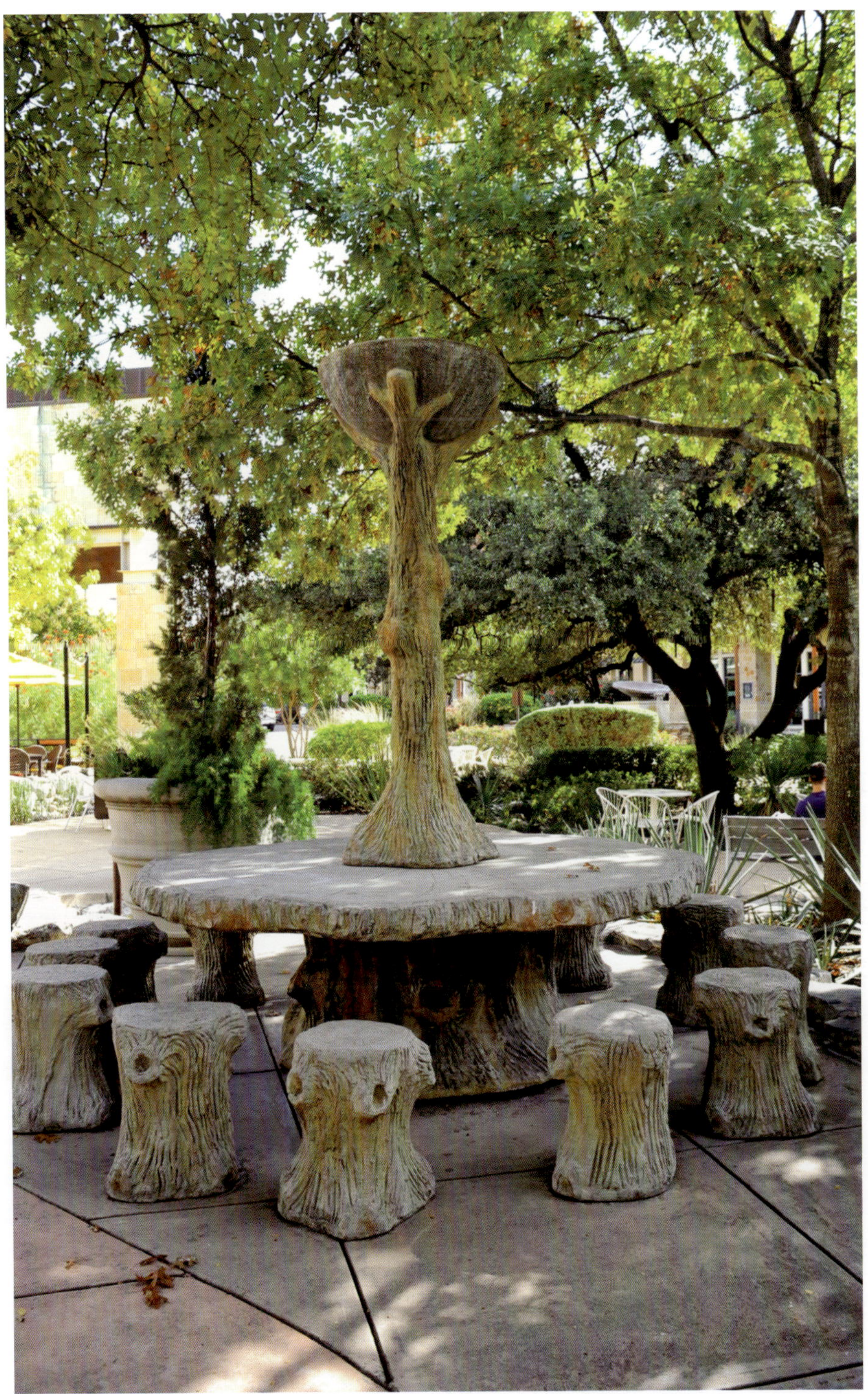

Carlos Cortés. San Antonio, TX.
The Shops at La Cantera.
Photo by Kent Rush.

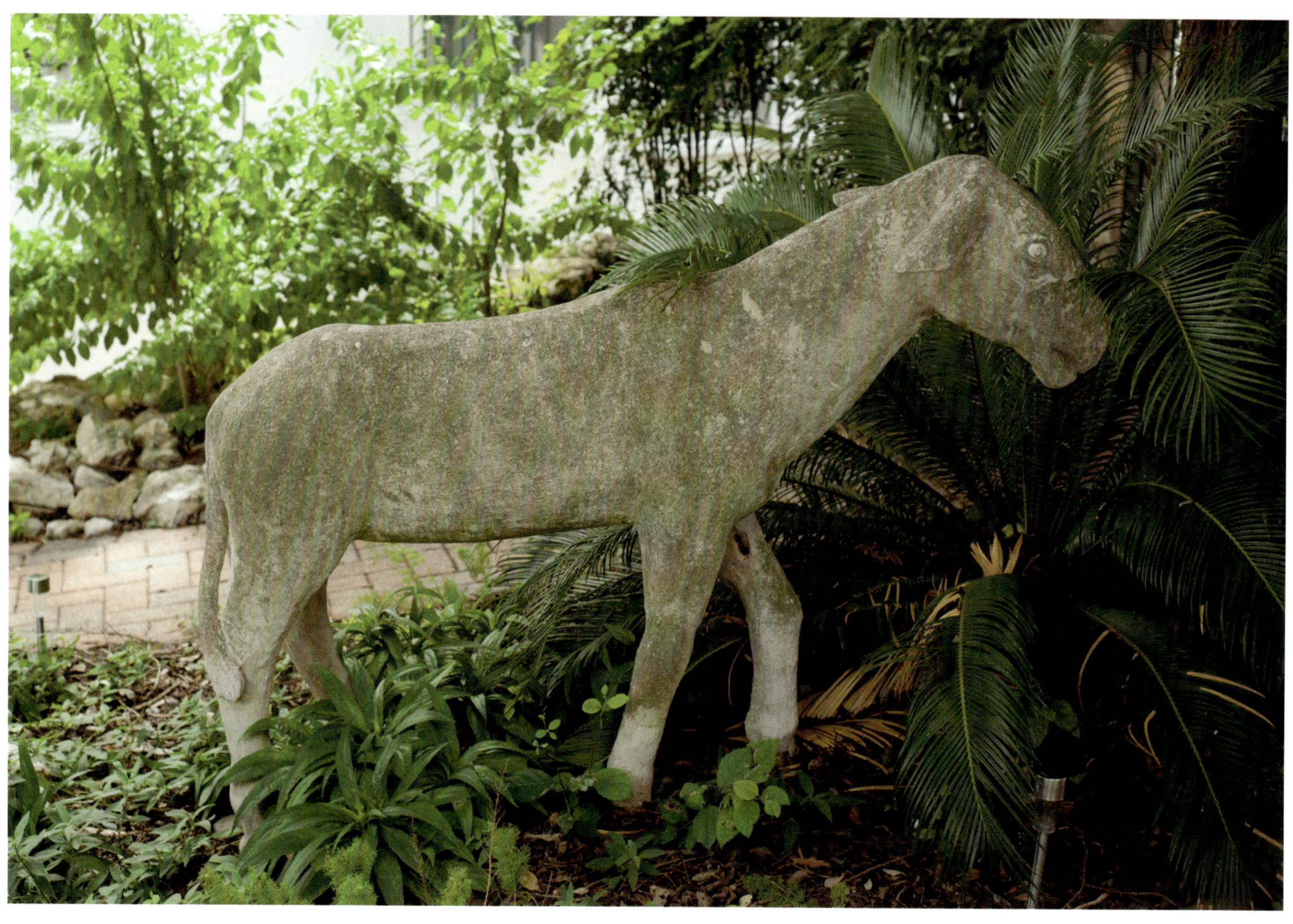

Máximo Cortés. San Antonio, TX. Private collection. Photo by Kent Rush.

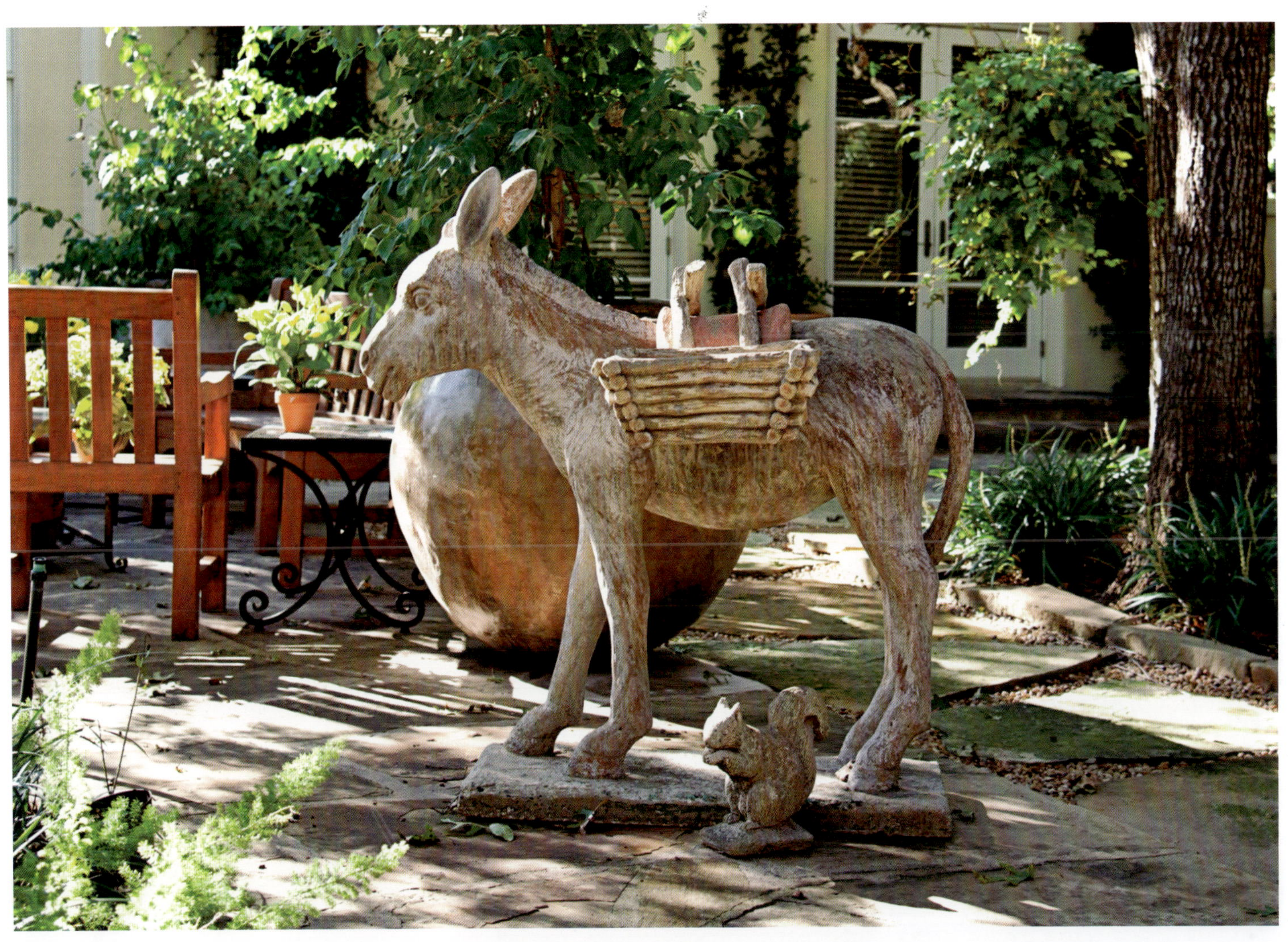

Artisan unknown. San Antonio, TX. Collection of Linda and Harry S. Affleck Jr. Photo by Harry Affleck III.

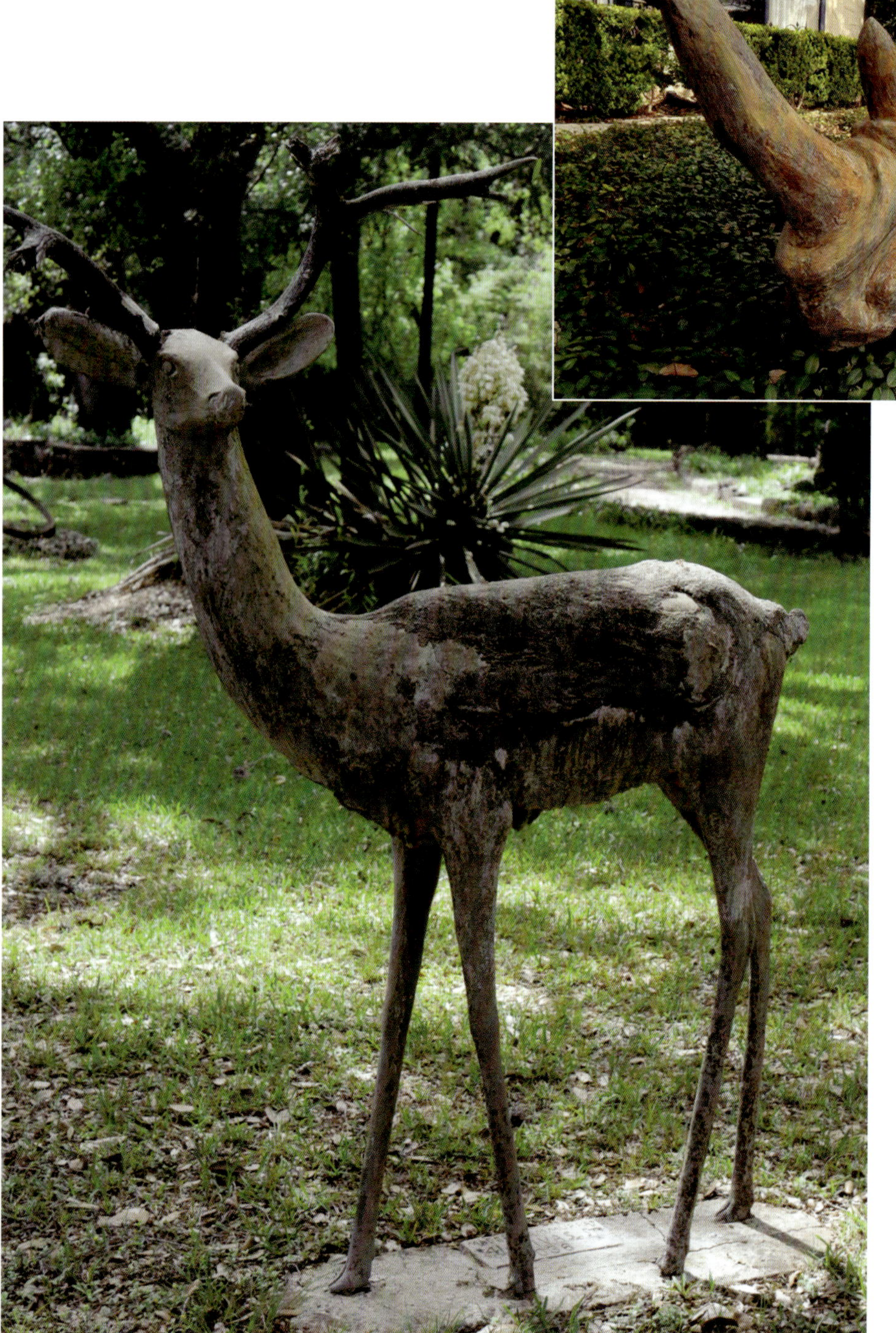

Above: *Rene Romero. San Antonio, TX. Rhinoceros. Private collection. Photo by Rene Romero.*

Left: *Sam Murray. San Antonio, TX. Private collection. Photo by Kent Rush.*

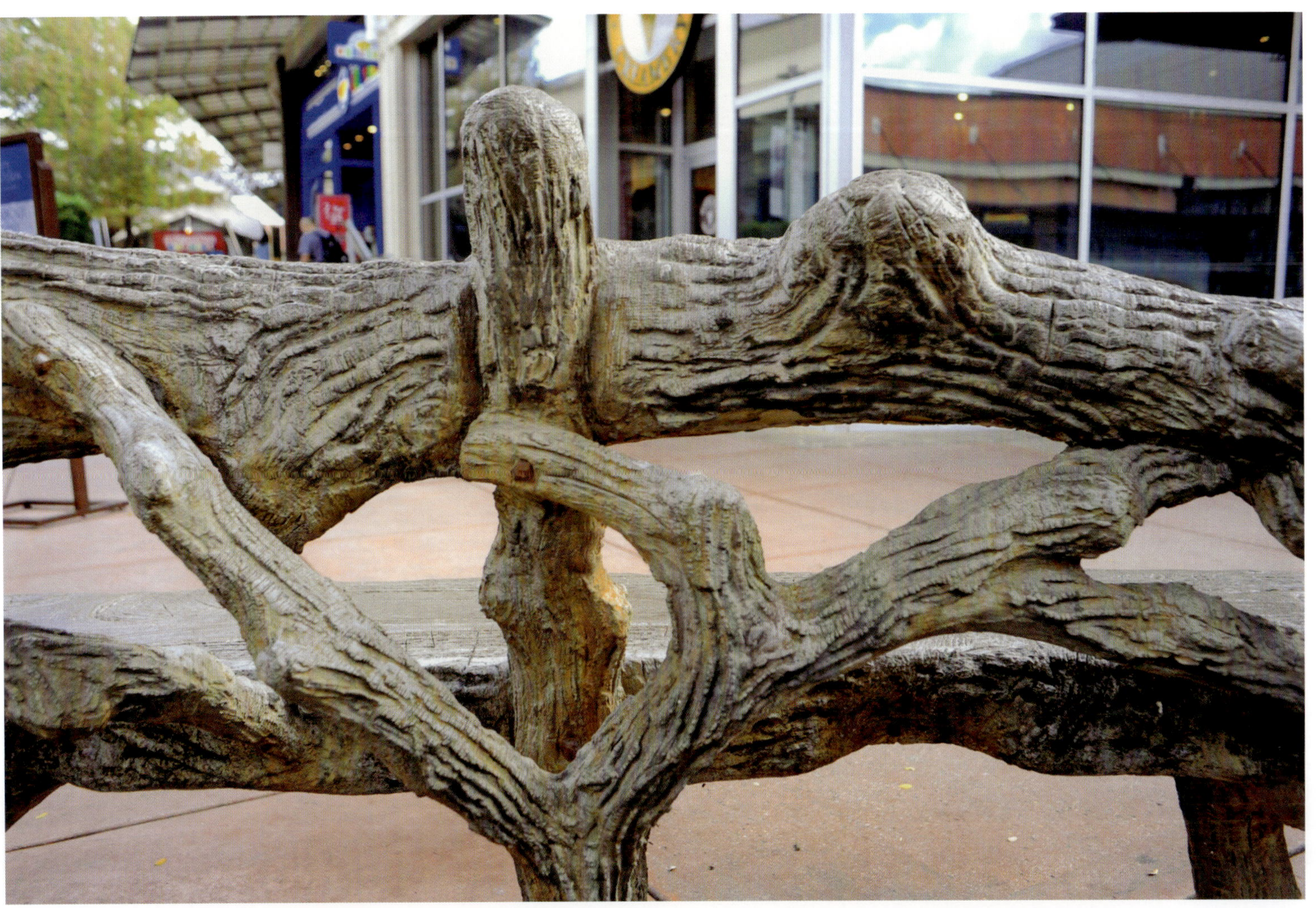

Carlos Cortés. San Antonio, TX. The Shops at La Cantera. Bench detail. Photo by Kent Rush.

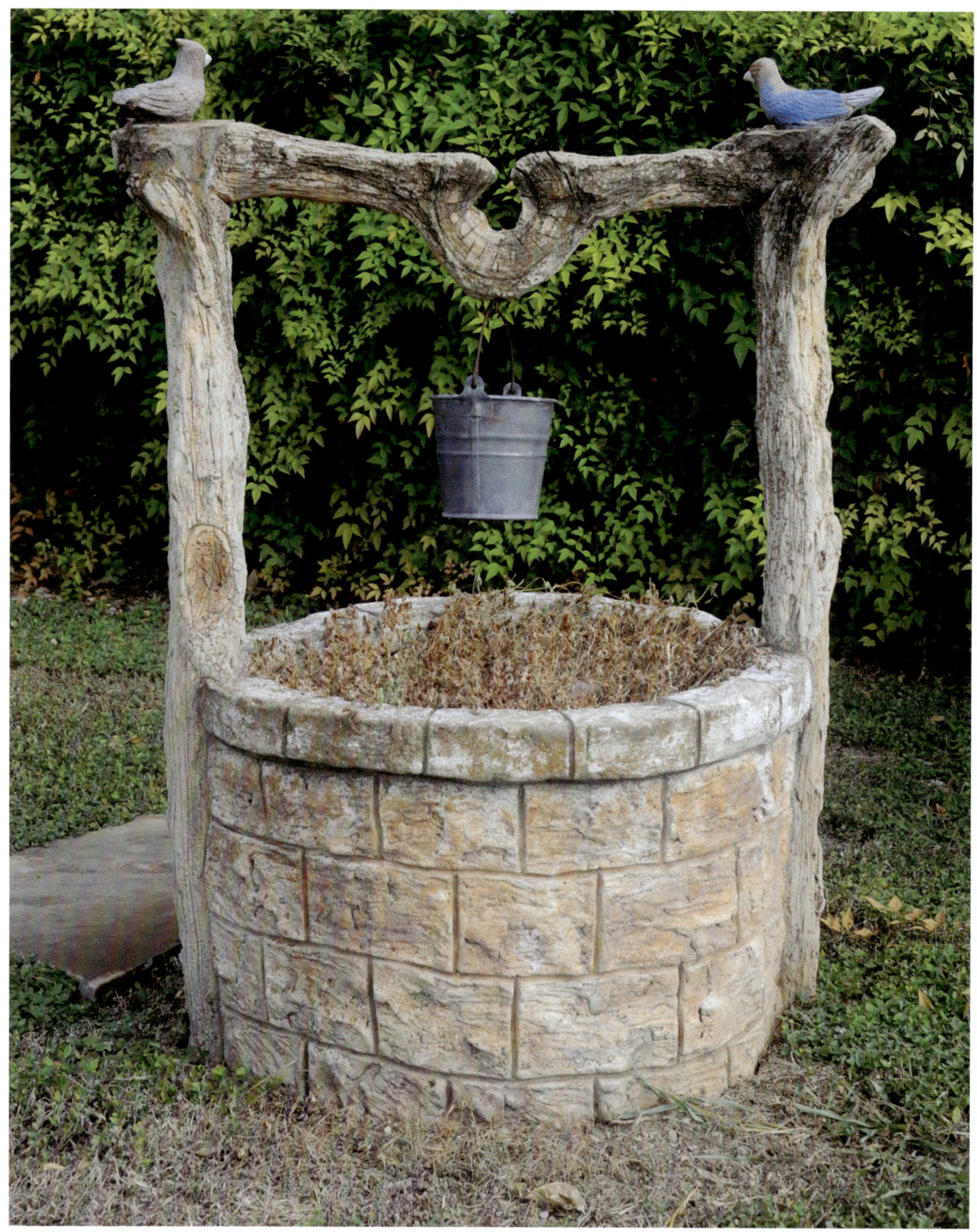

Artisan unknown. San Antonio, TX. Private collection. Photo by Kent Rush.

Right: *Artisan unknown. Randolph Air Force Base, TX. Vintage photo. Randolph gas station.*

Below: *Artisan unknown. Randolph Air Force Base, TX. Photo by Kent Rush.*

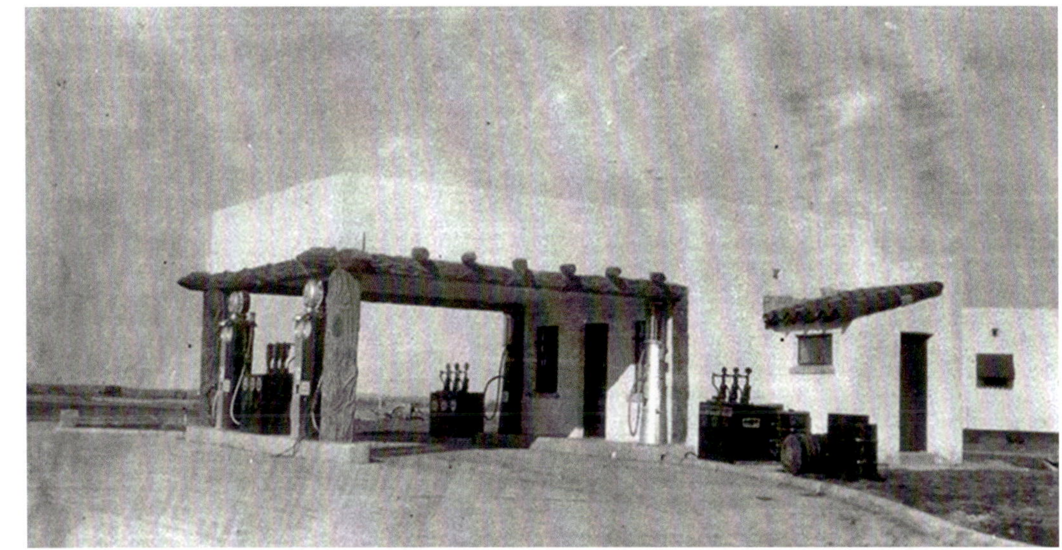

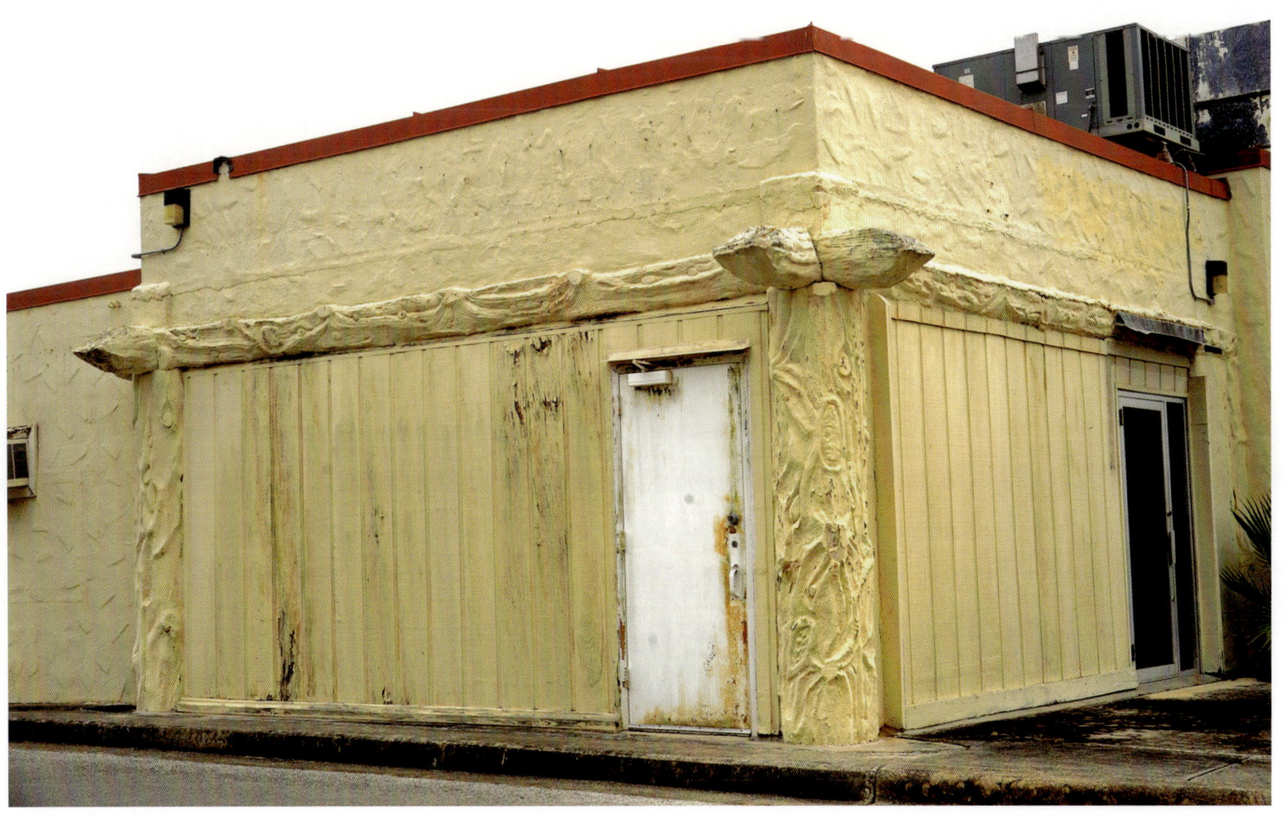

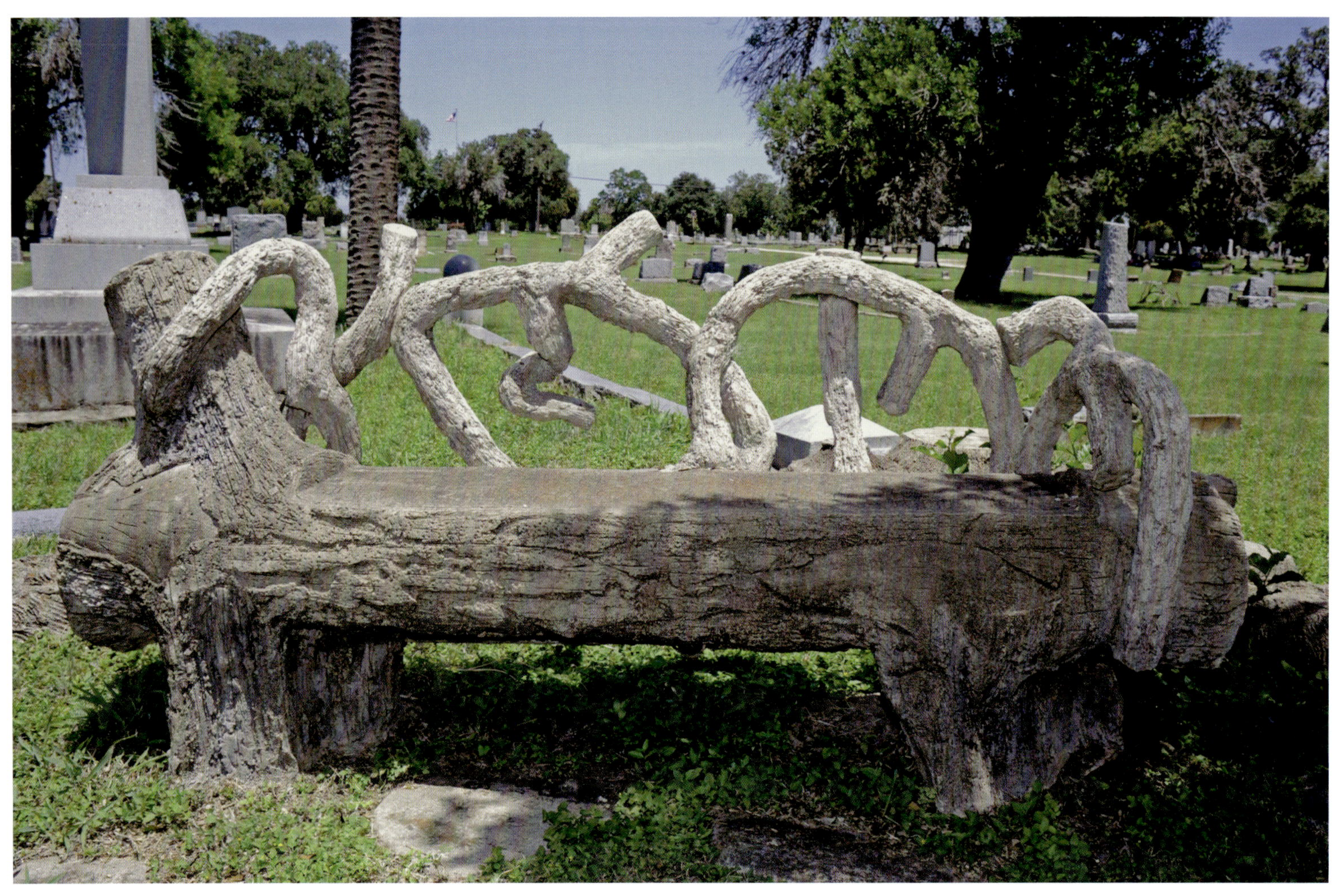

Artisan unknown. San Antonio, TX. Friedrich Plot, Cemetery No. 1. Photo by Kent Rush.

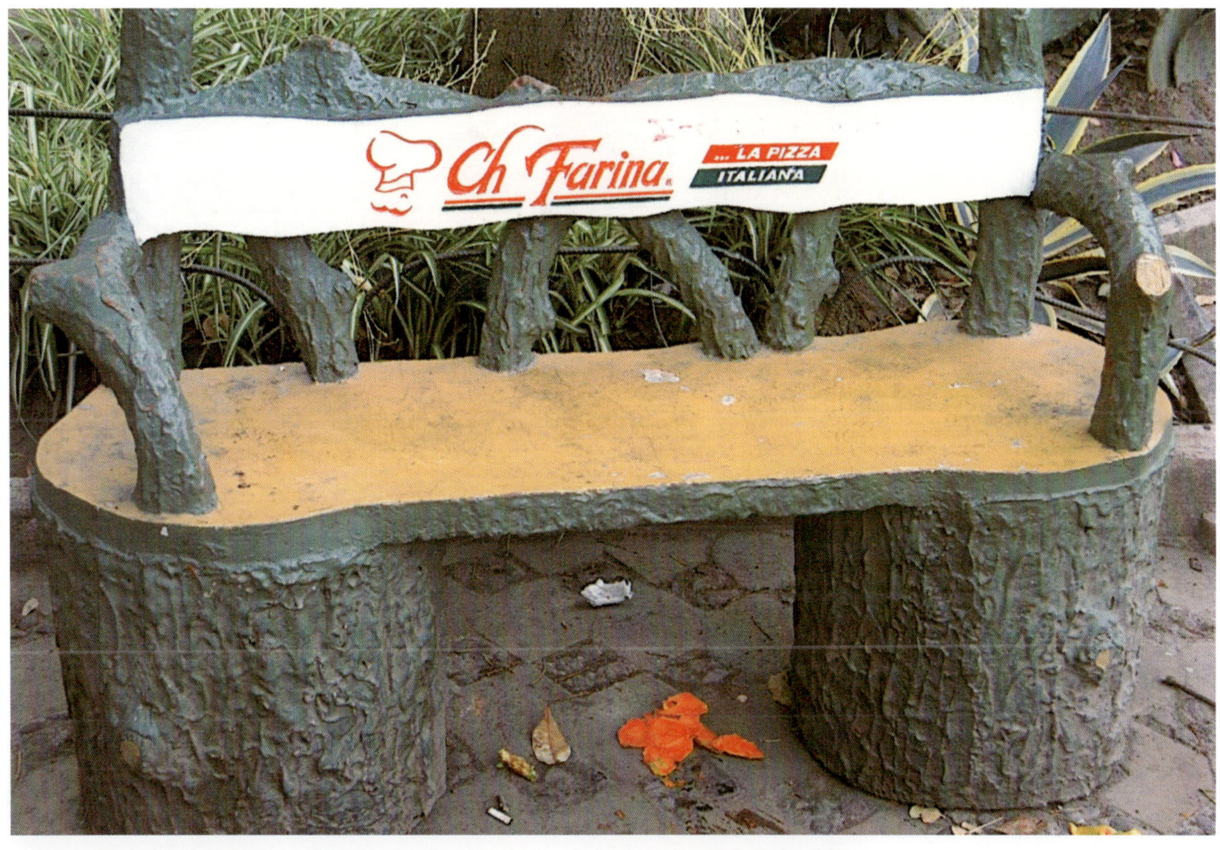

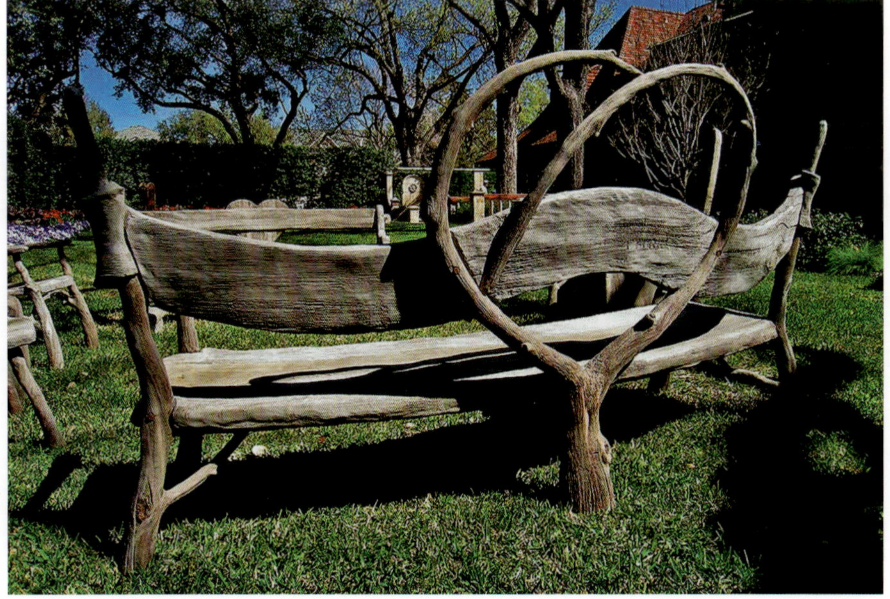

Above: *Artisan unknown. Quito, Ecuador. Bench with advertisement. Photo by Patsy Pittman Light.*

Left: *Donald Tucker. Houston, TX. Private collection. Photo courtesy of Donald Tucker.*

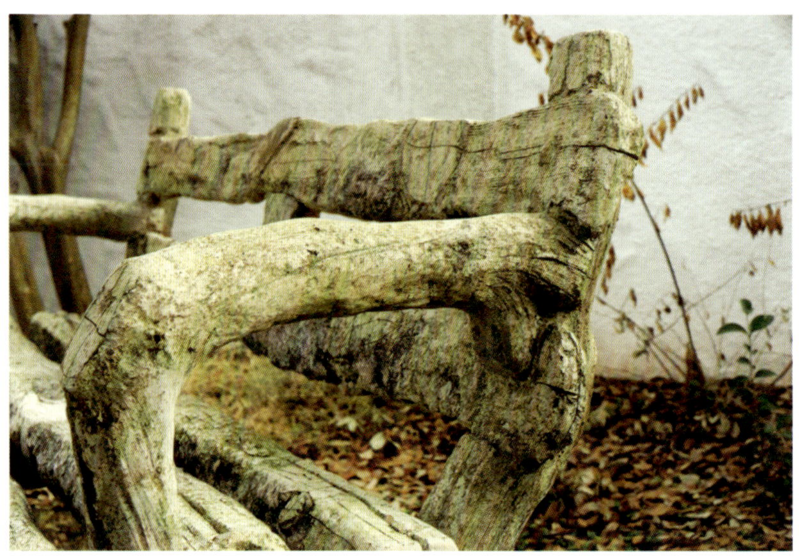

Right: Artisan unknown. Randolph Air Force Base, TX. Bench detail. Photo by Kent Rush.

Below: Carlos Cortés. San Antonio, TX. Collection of Claire N. Golden. Chair and table. Photo by Kent Rush.

Below right: Bacilio Aguilar. San Antonio, TX. Bench detail. Collection of H. H. Batchelder III. Photo by Kent Rush.

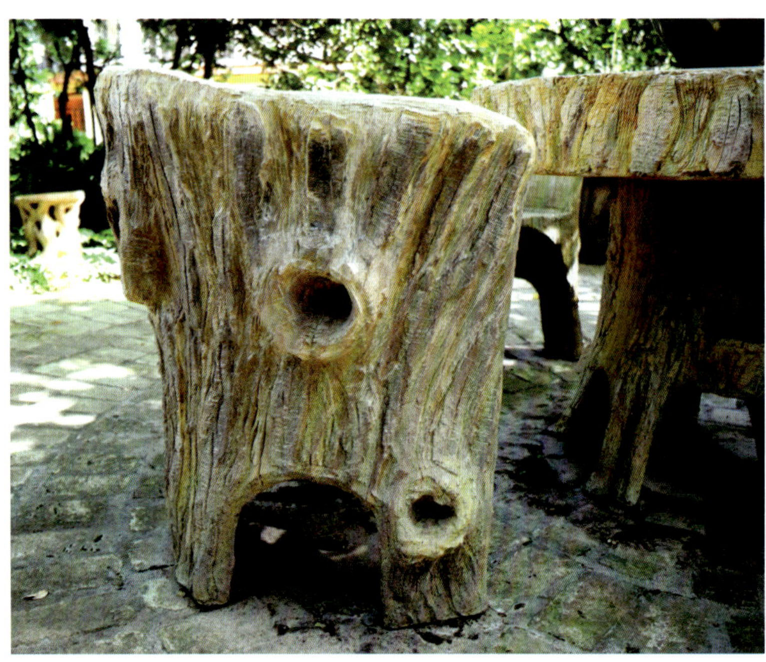

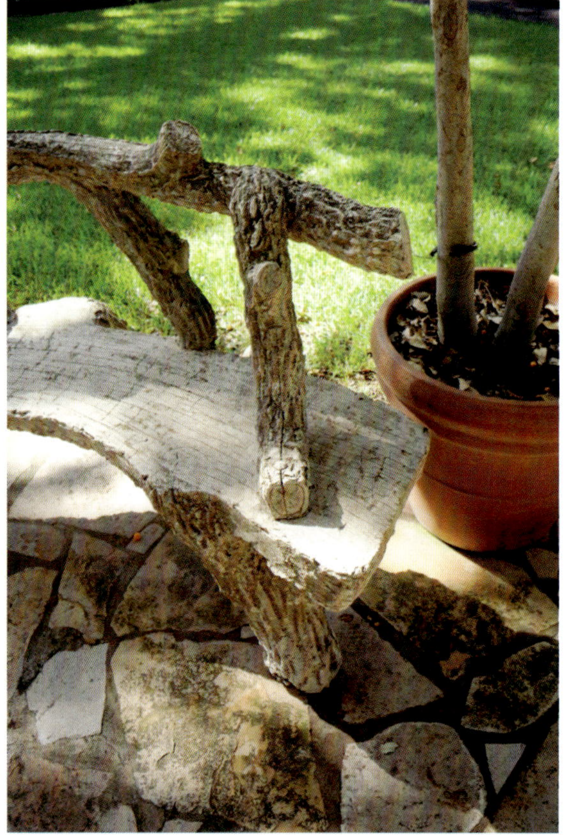

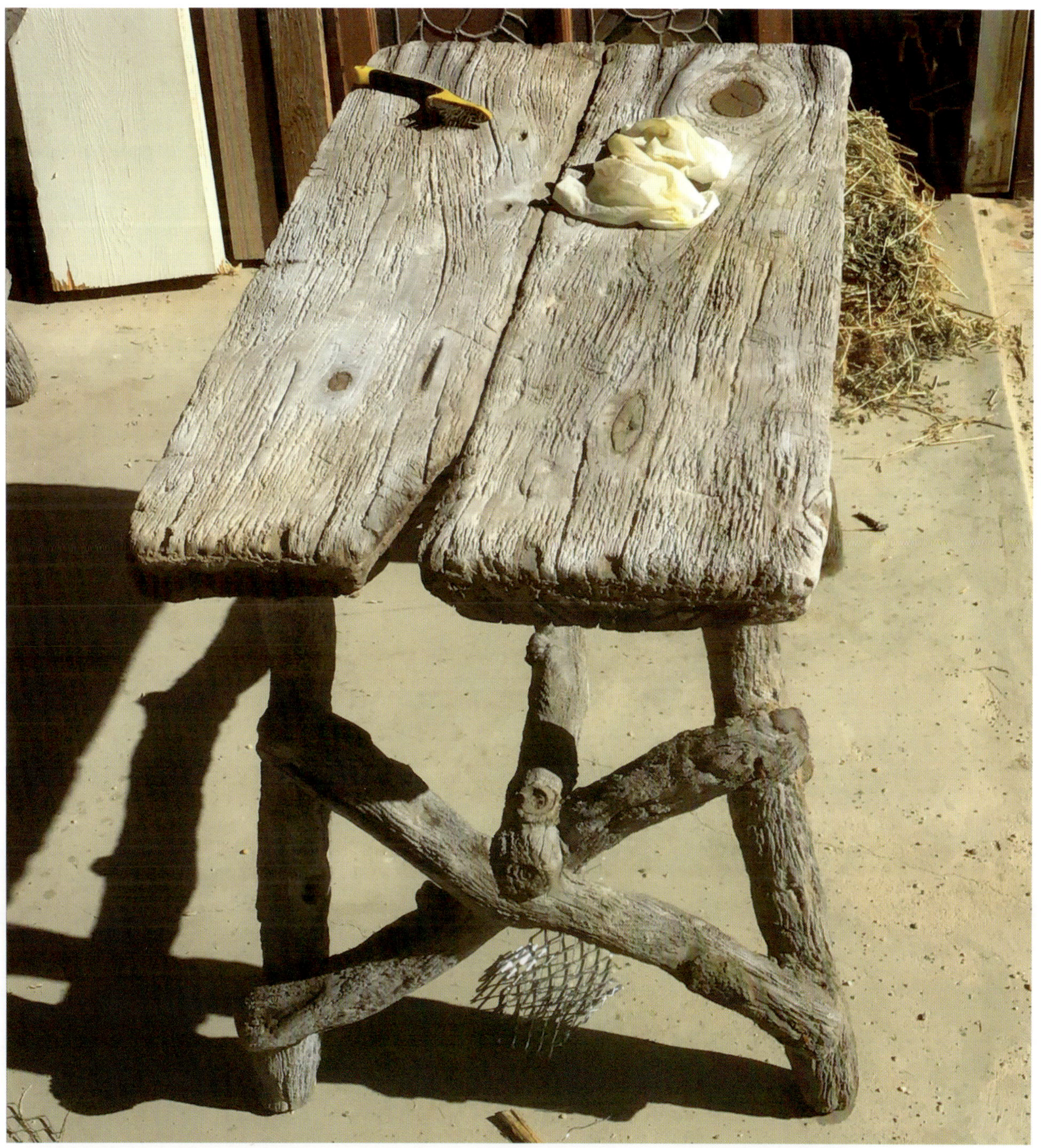

Beau Johnstone. Deniliquin, New South Wales. Australia. Private collection. Photo by Beau Johnstone.

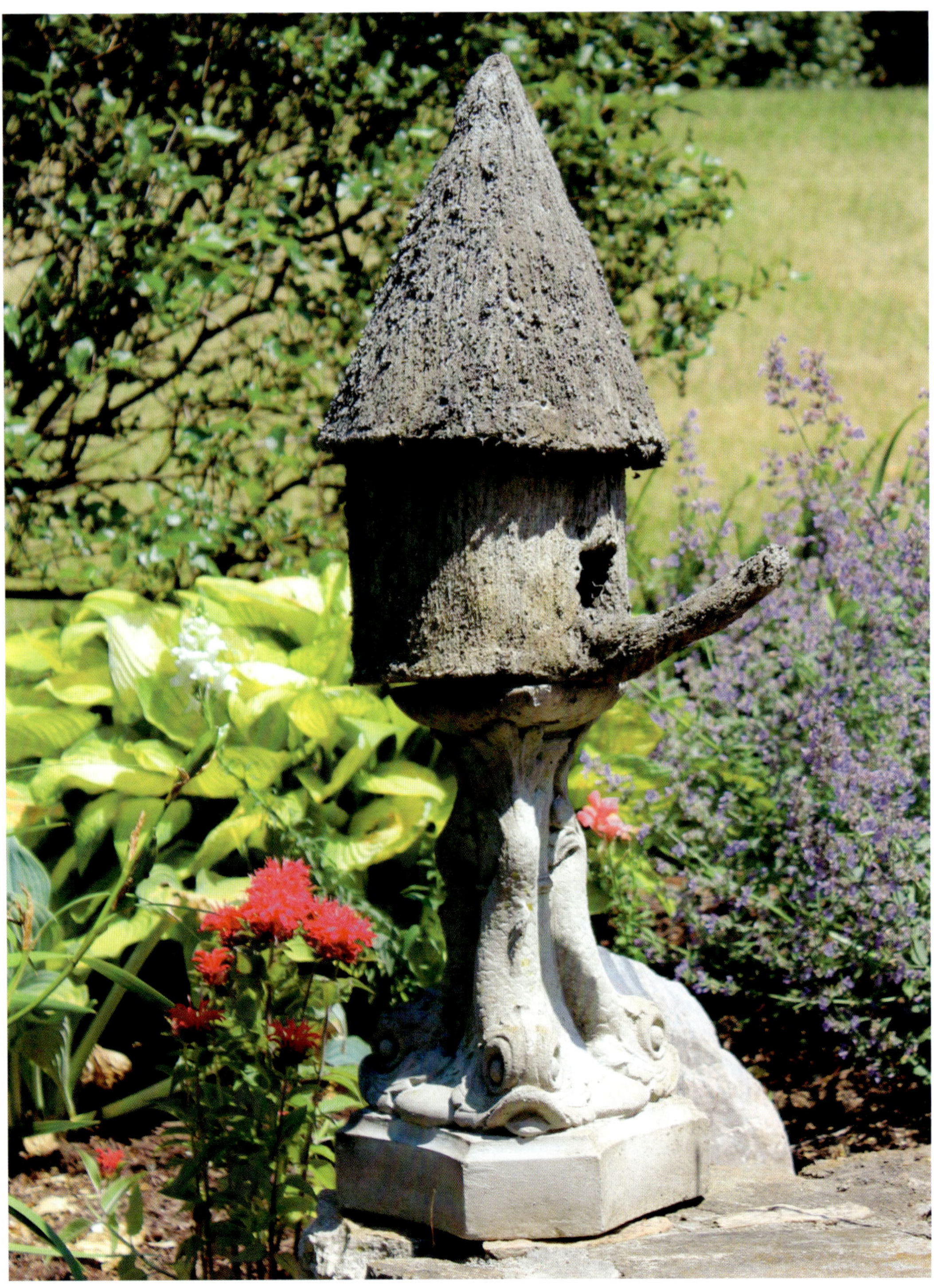

Michael Palella. New Preston, CT. Private collection. Photo by Helene Palella.

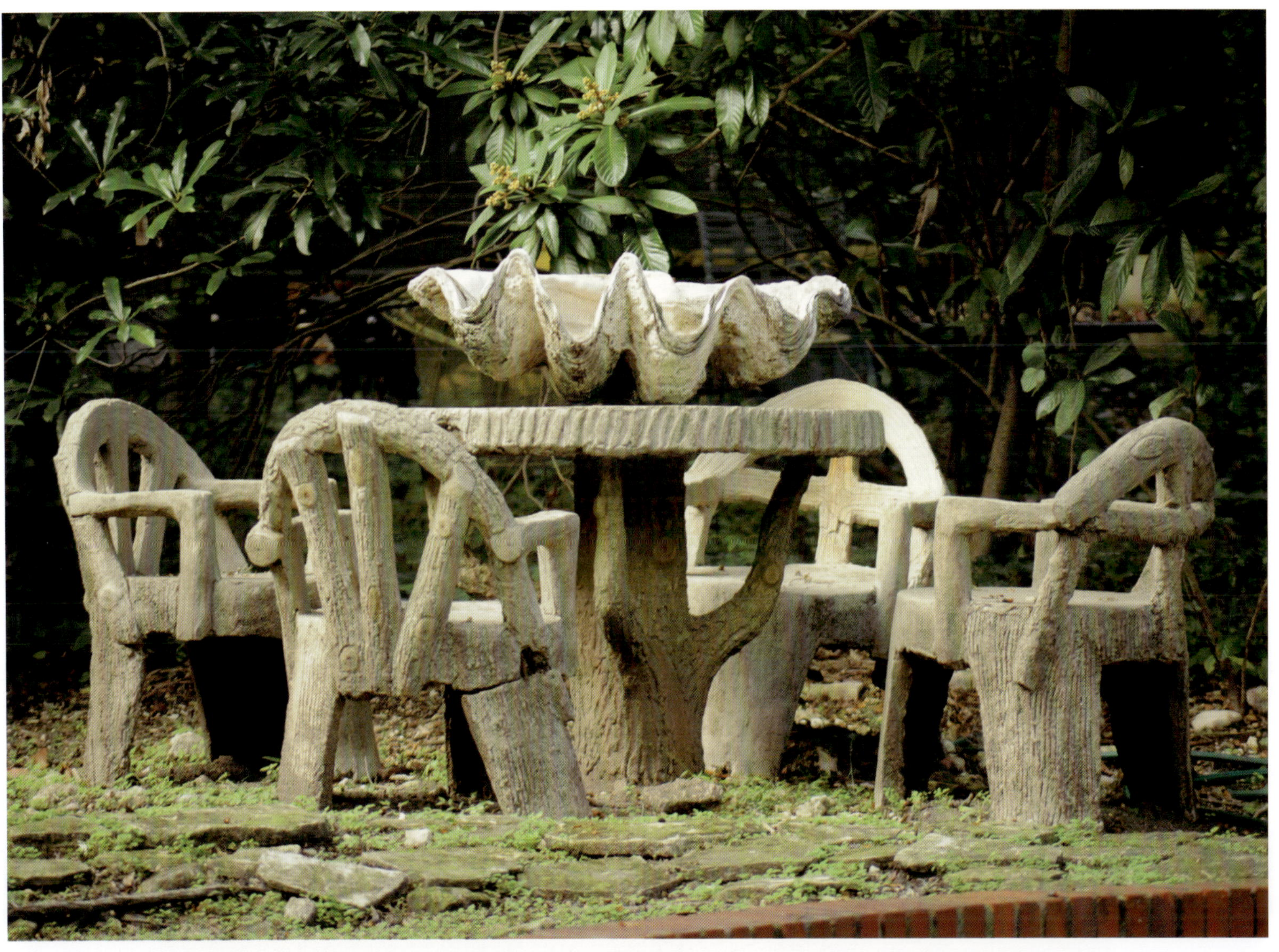

Artisan unknown. San Antonio, TX. Private collection. Photo by Kent Rush.

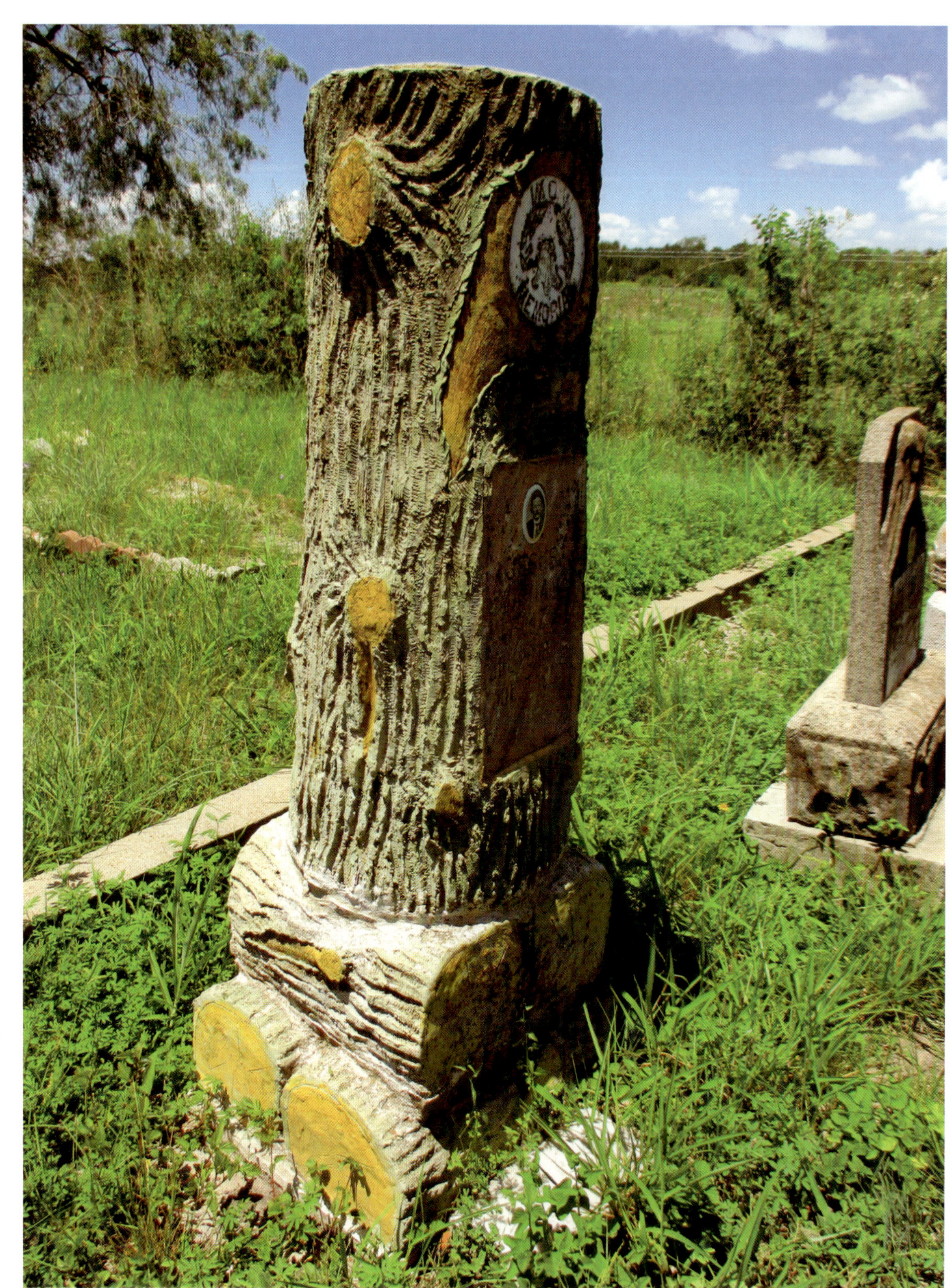

Artisan unknown. Kenedy, TX. Sacred Heart Cemetery. Woodmen of the World grave marker. Photo by Kent Rush.

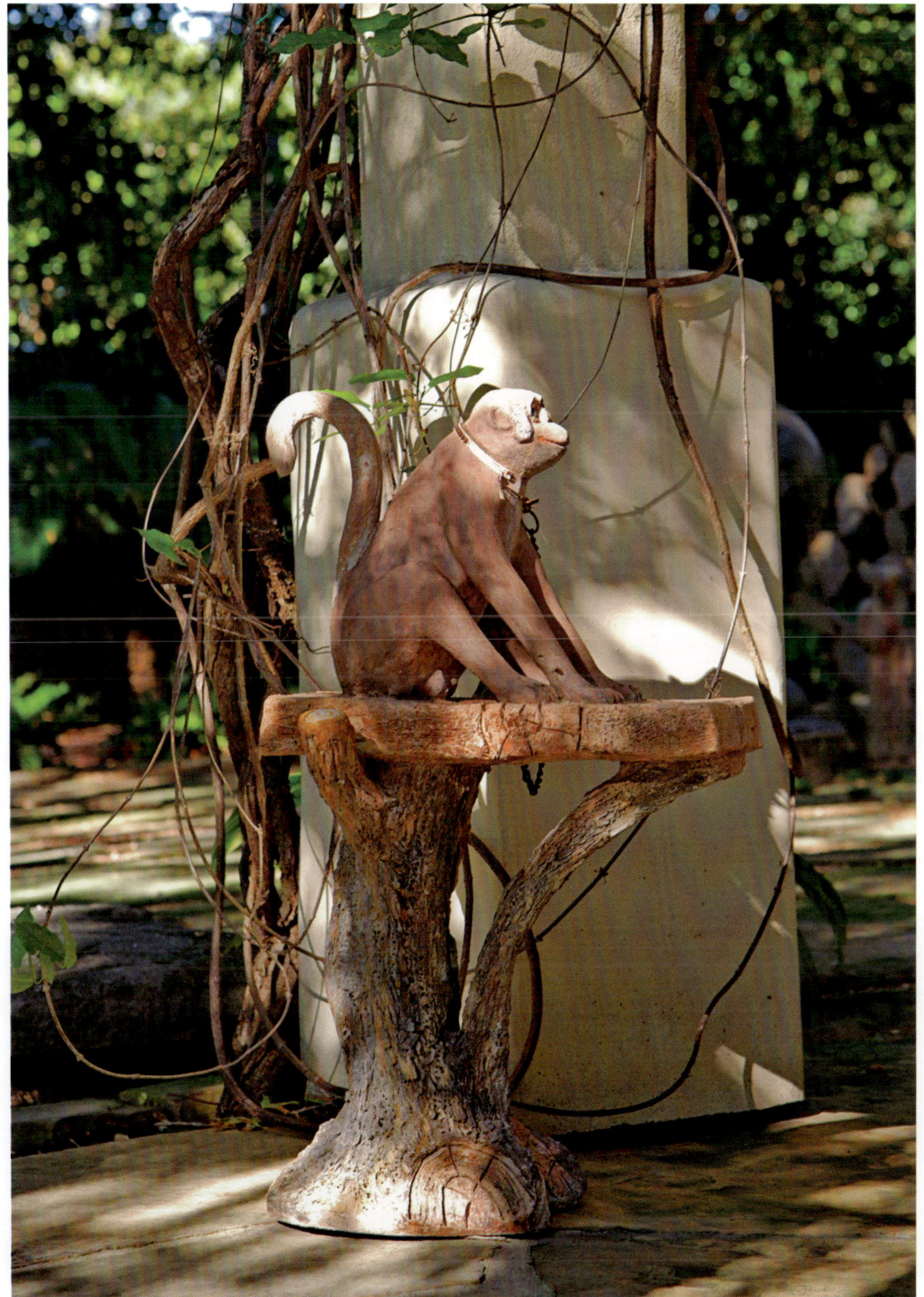

Sam Murray. San Antonio, TX. Collection of Linda and Harry S. Affleck Jr.
Photo by Harry S. Affleck III.

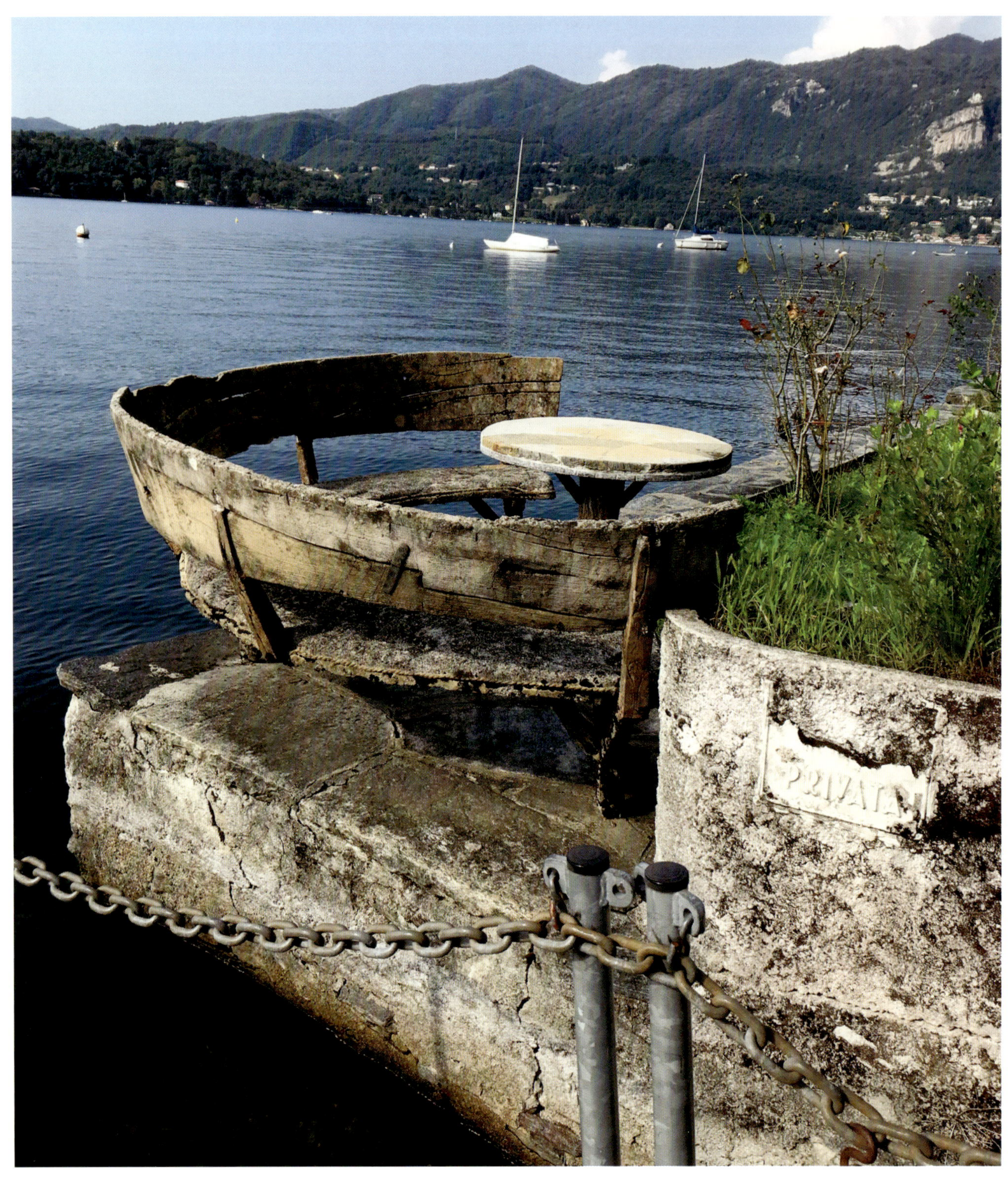

Artisan unknown. Orta San Giulio, Novara, Italy. Bench. Private collection. Photo by Kelly Williamson.

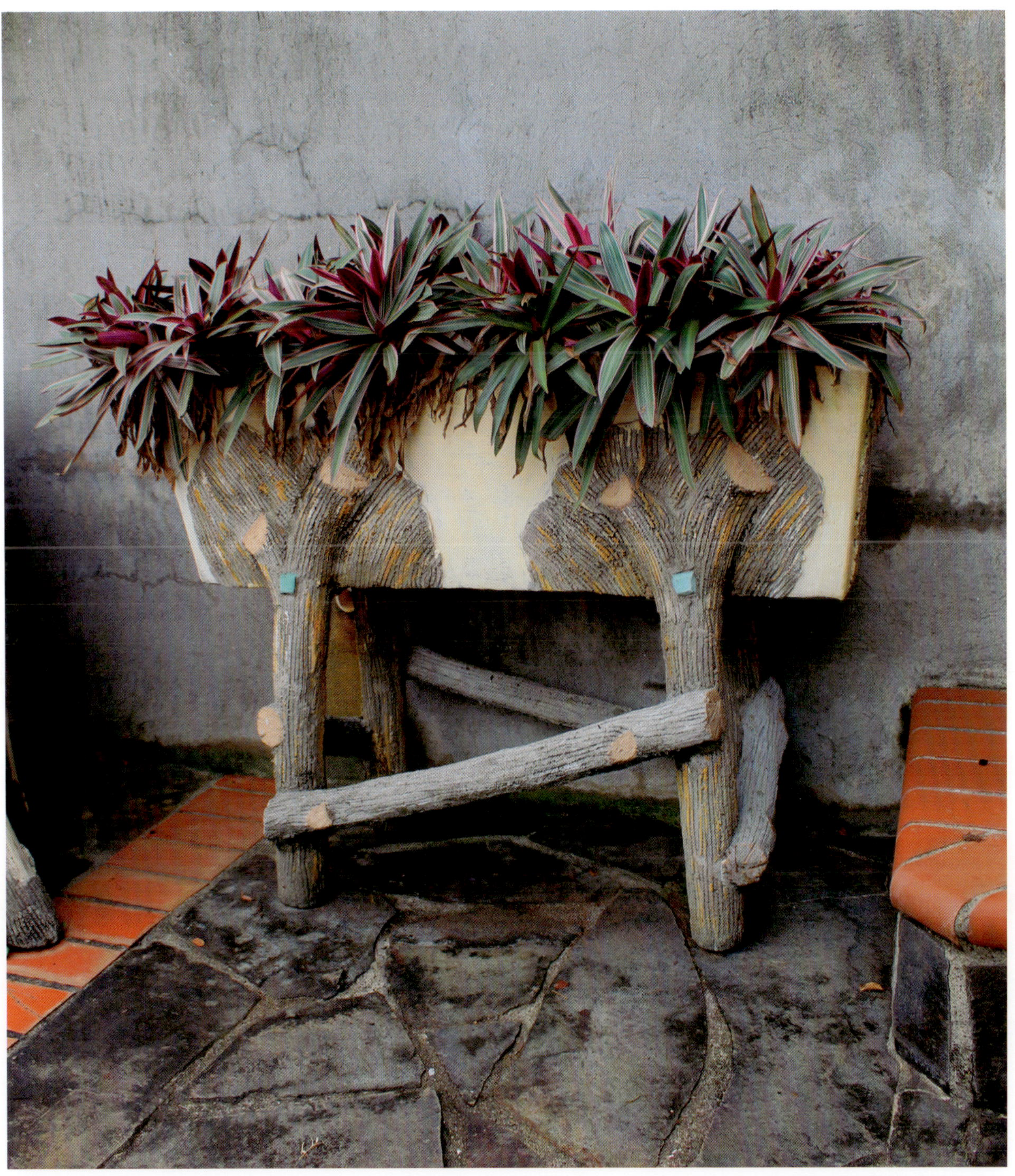

Artisan unknown. Las Cumbres, Panama. Collection of Alfredo De Souza. Photo by Alfredo De Souza Jr.

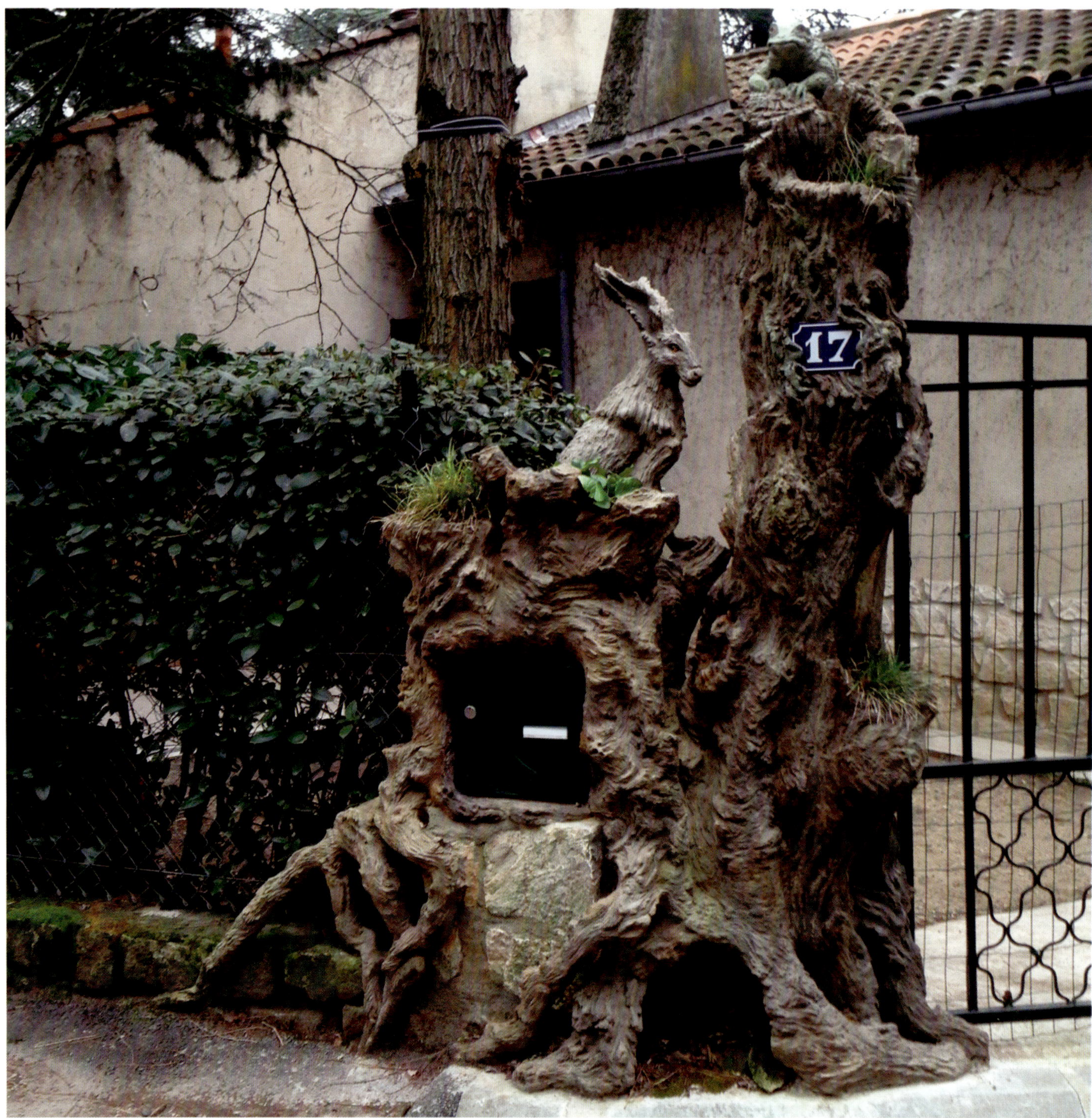

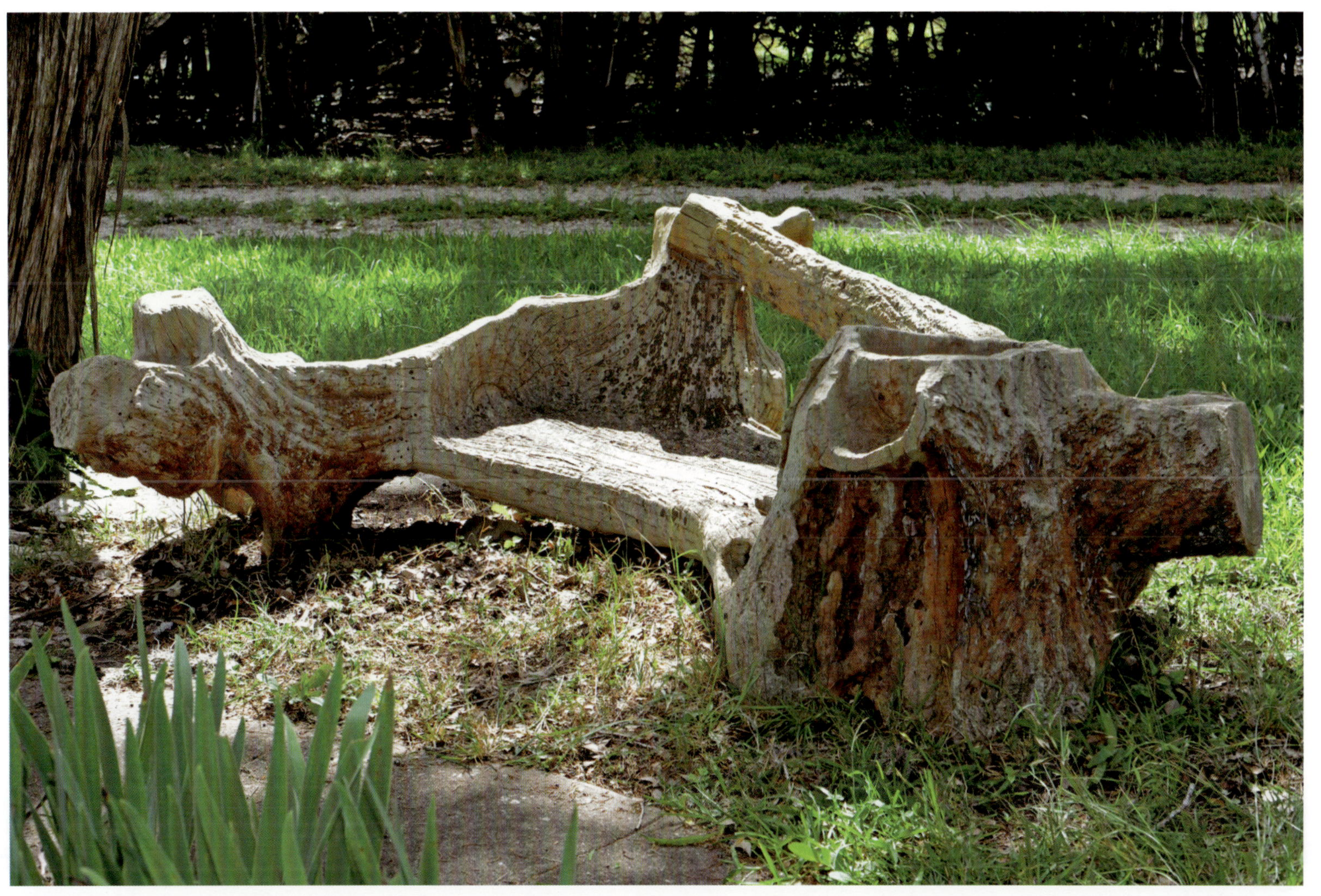

Above: *Dionicio Rodríguez. Boerne, TX. Private collection. Photo by Kent Rush.*

Opposite: *Gregory Everingham. Villeneuve-lès-Avignon, France. Private collection. Photo by Gregory Everingham.*

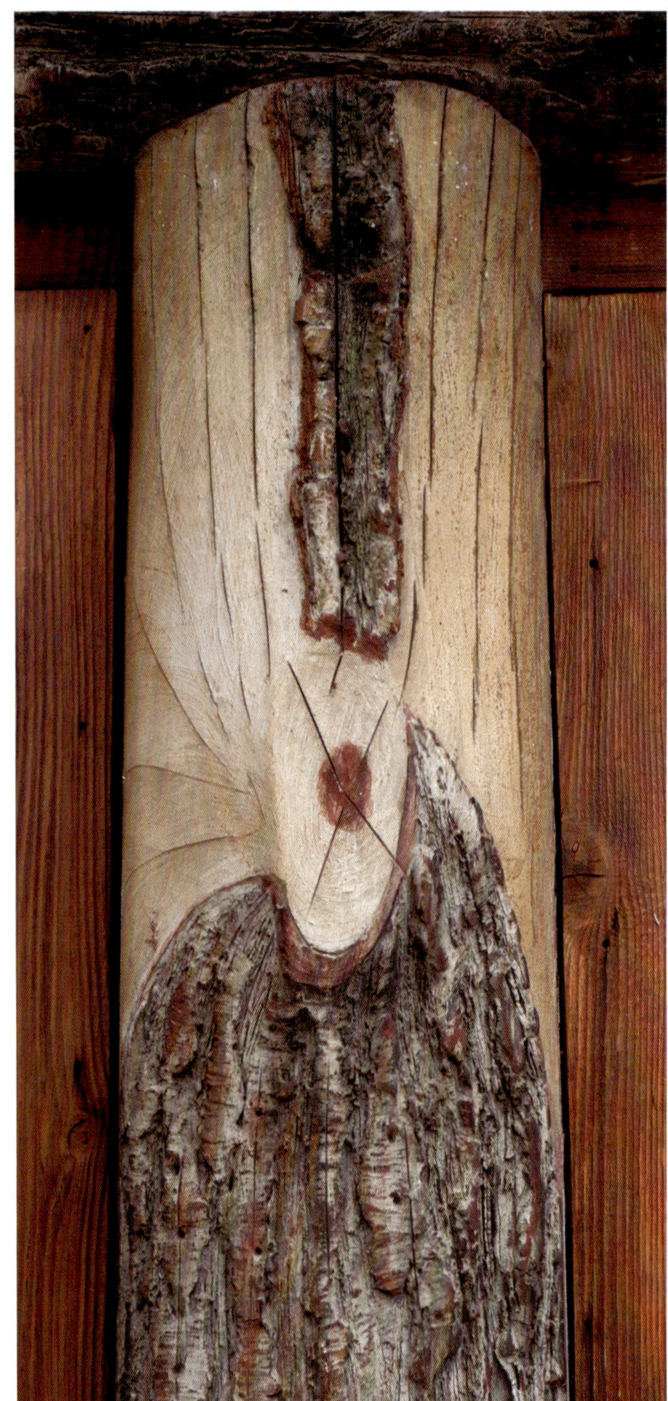

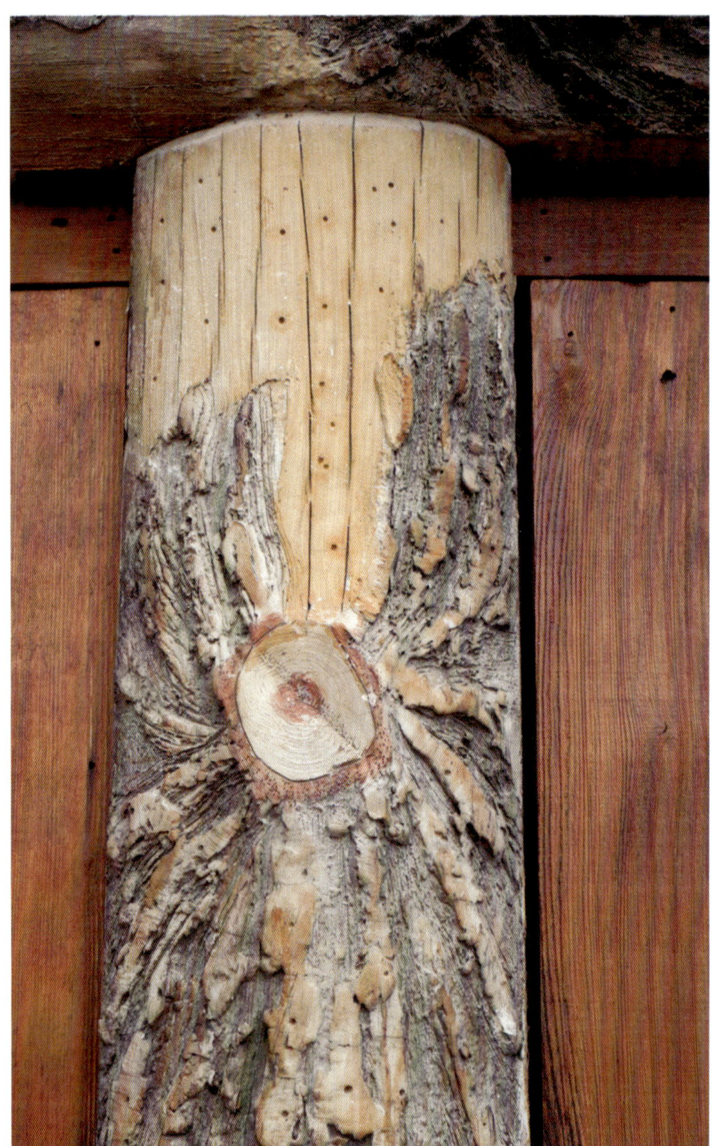

Antonio Lopez. San Antonio, TX.
Façade trim. Private collection. Photo by
Kent Rush.

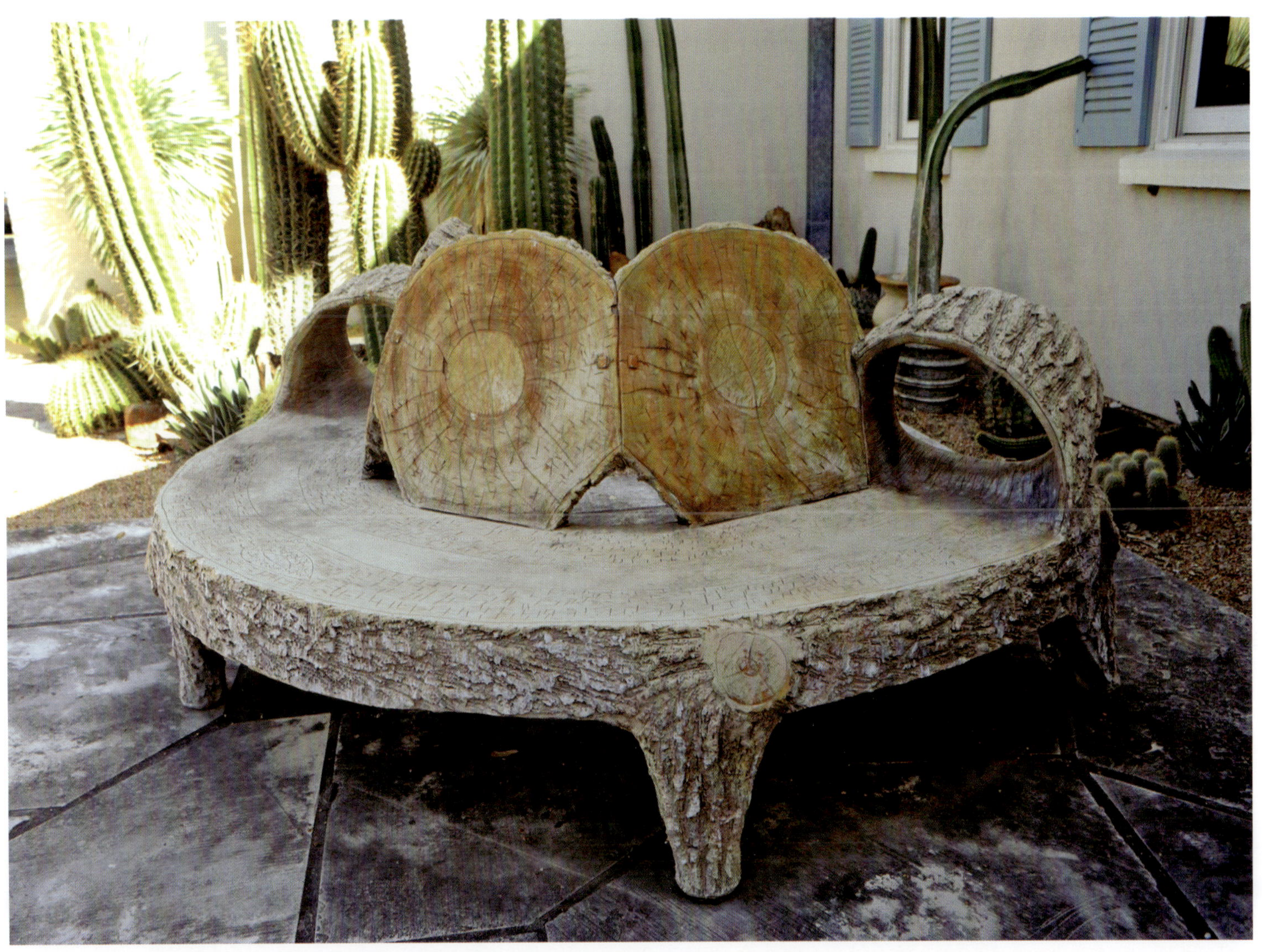

Artisan unknown. Gillet, TX. Collection of Amy Stieren Smiley. Photo by Kent Rush.

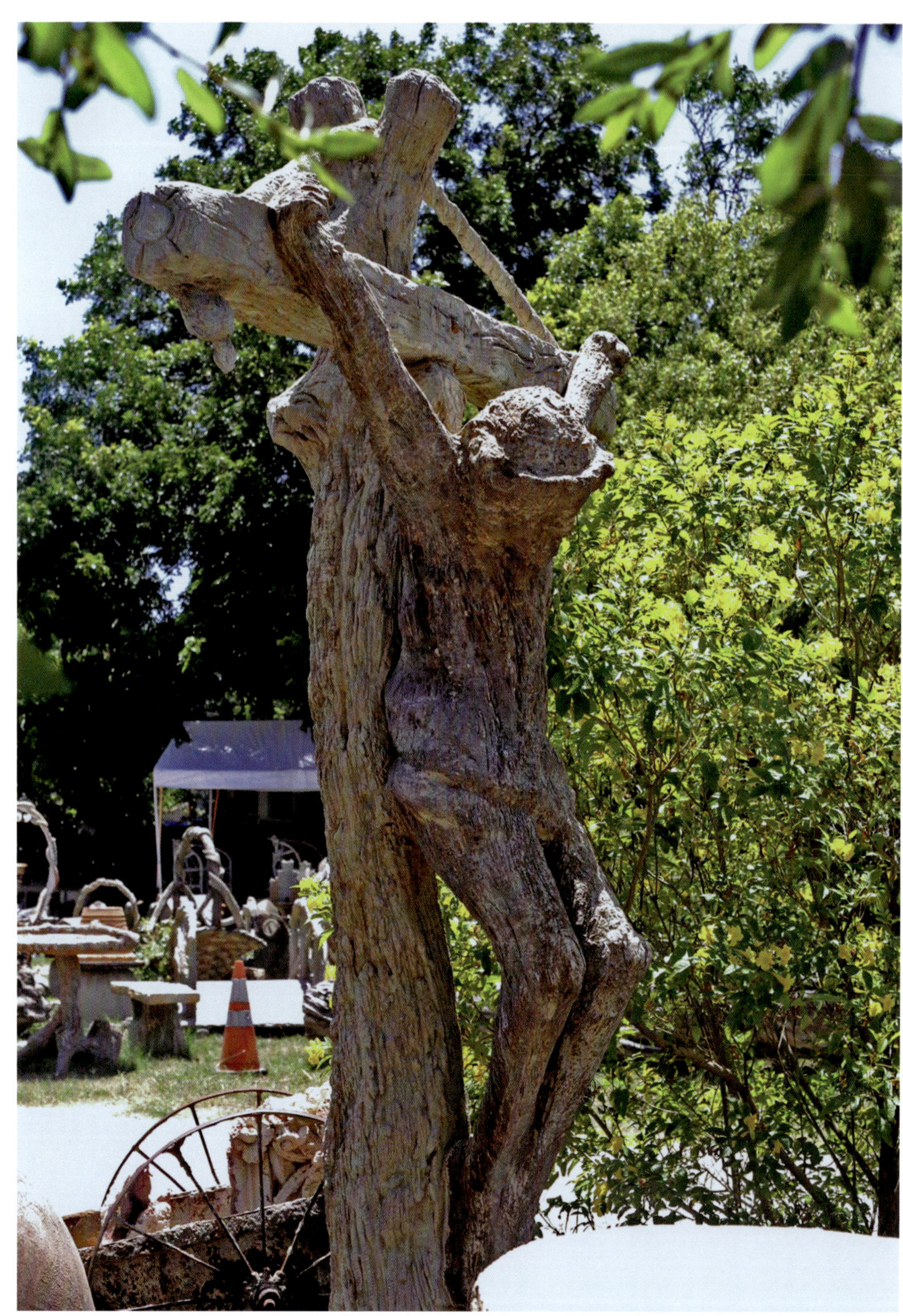

Carlos Cortés. San Antonio, TX. Crucifix. Collection of Carlos Cortés. Photo by Kent Rush.

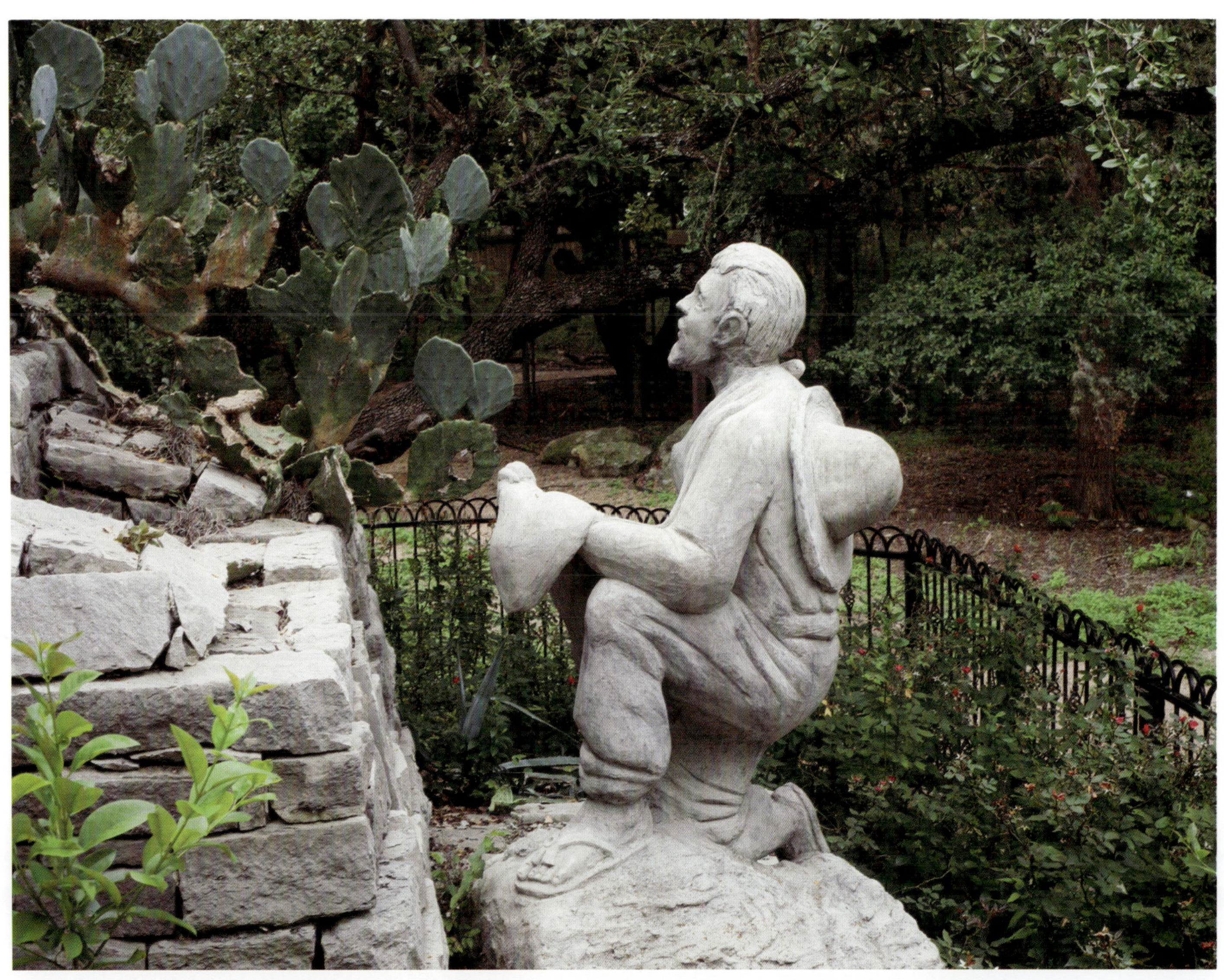

Carlos Cortés. San Antonio, TX. St. Matthew Sports Complex. Juan Diego figure. Photo by Kent Rush.

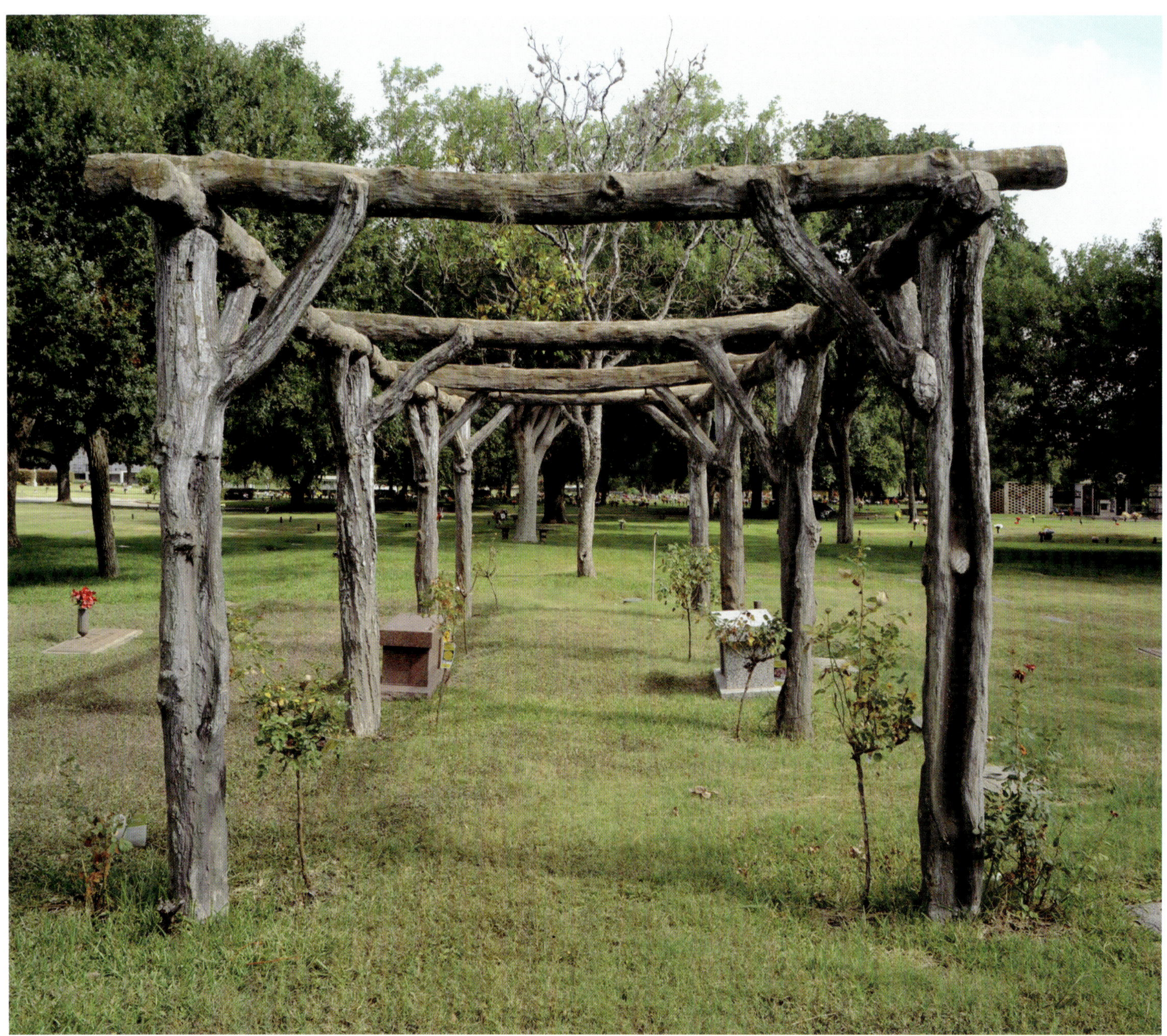

Artisan unknown. San Antonio, TX. Sunset Memorial Park Cemetery. Arbor. Photo by Kent Rush.

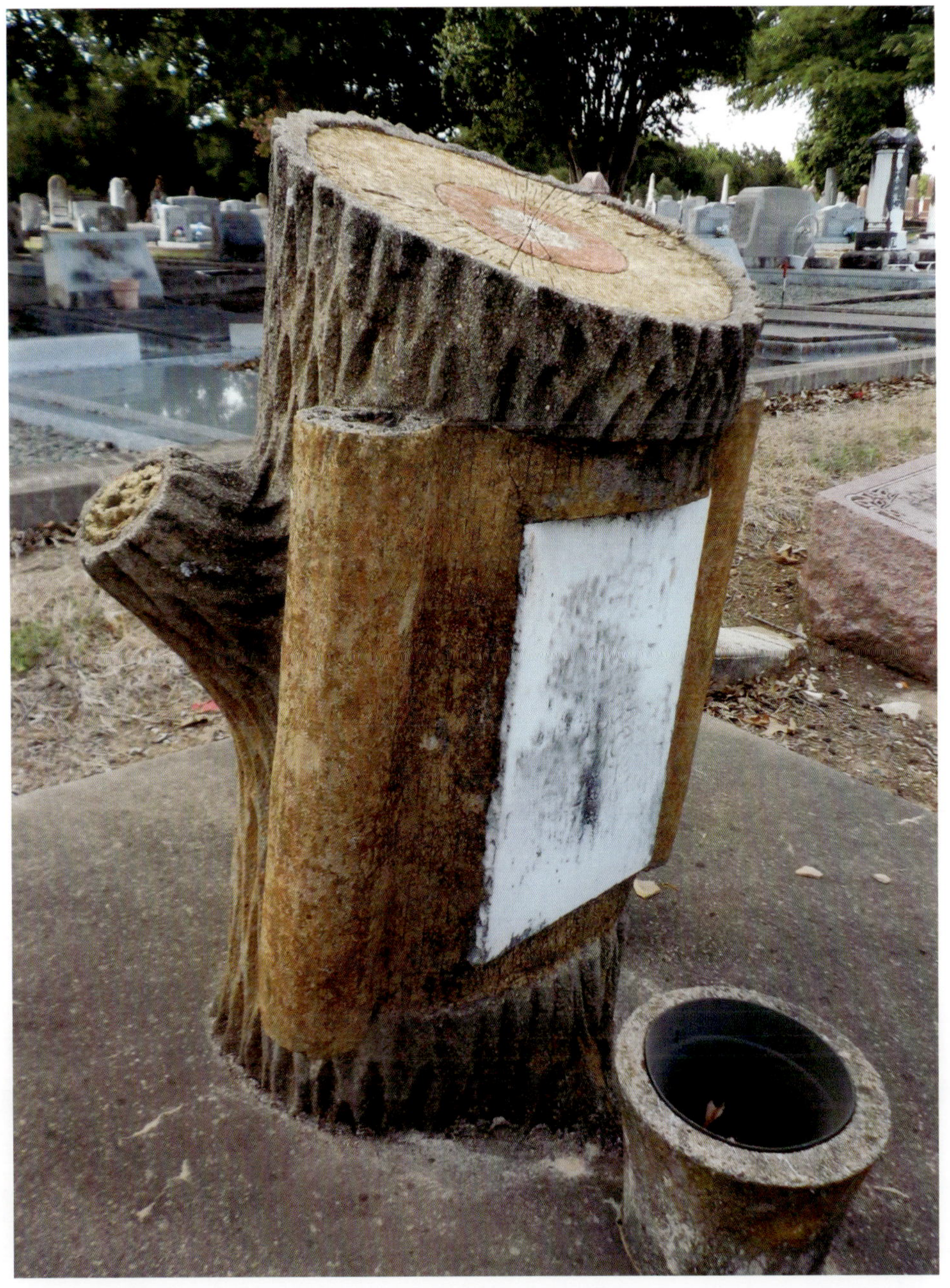

Artisan unknown. Comfort, TX. Comfort Cemetery. Grave marker. Photo by Kent Rush.

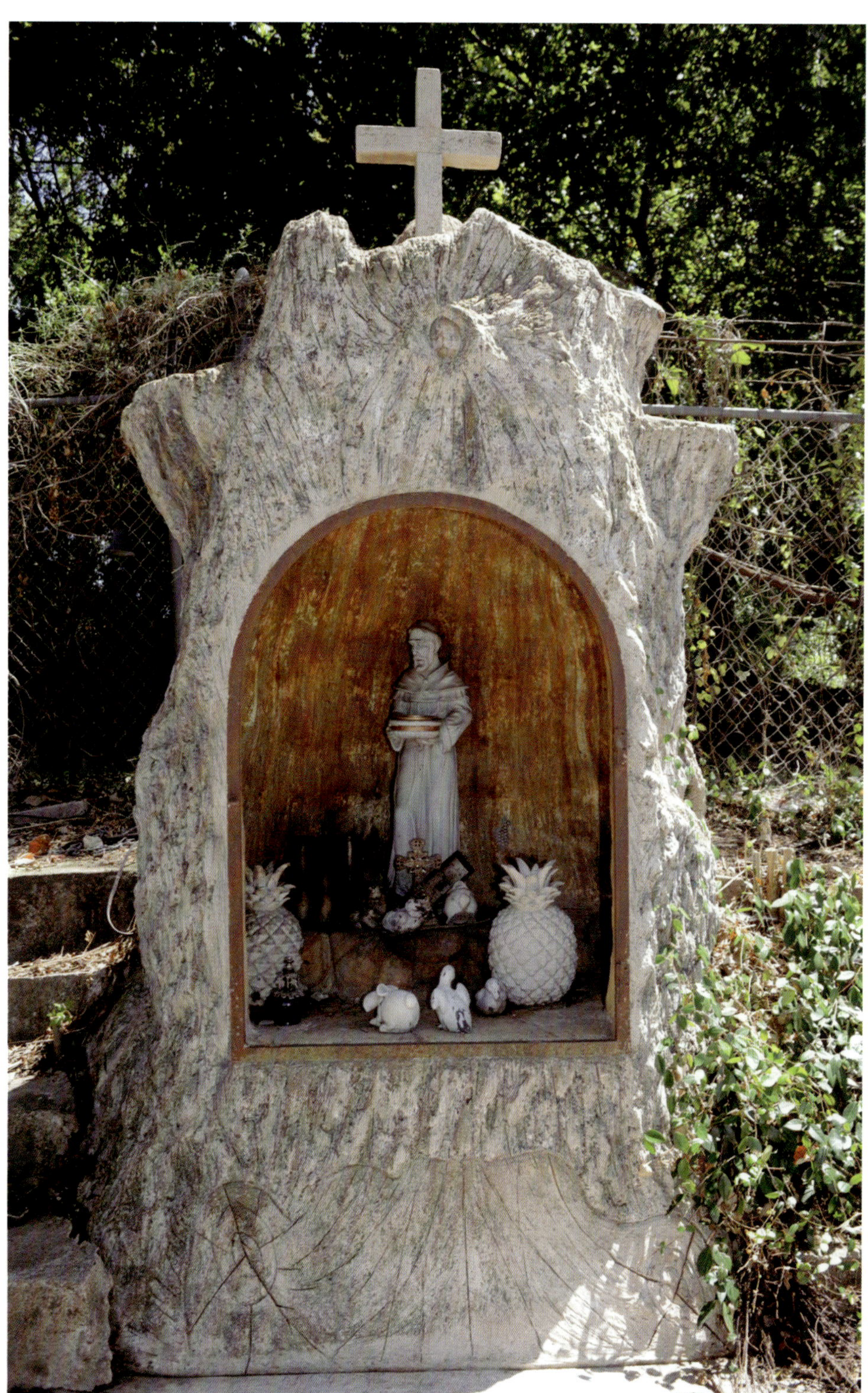

Artisan unknown. San Antonio, TX. Grotto. Private collection. Photo by Kent Rush.

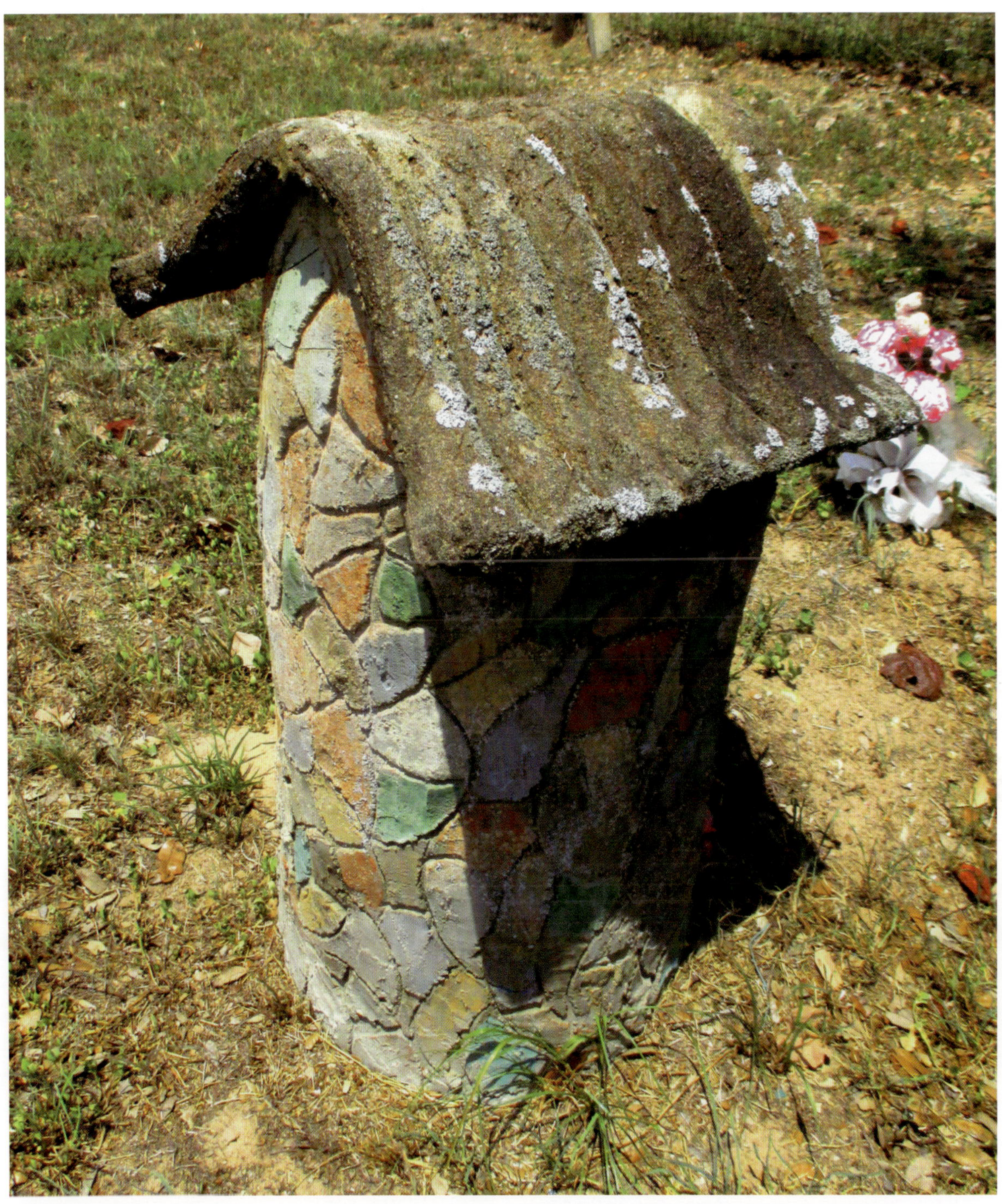

Artisan unknown. Pleasanton, TX. Saint Andrew's Cemetery. Relicarito (small shrine filled with icons). Photo by Kent Rush.

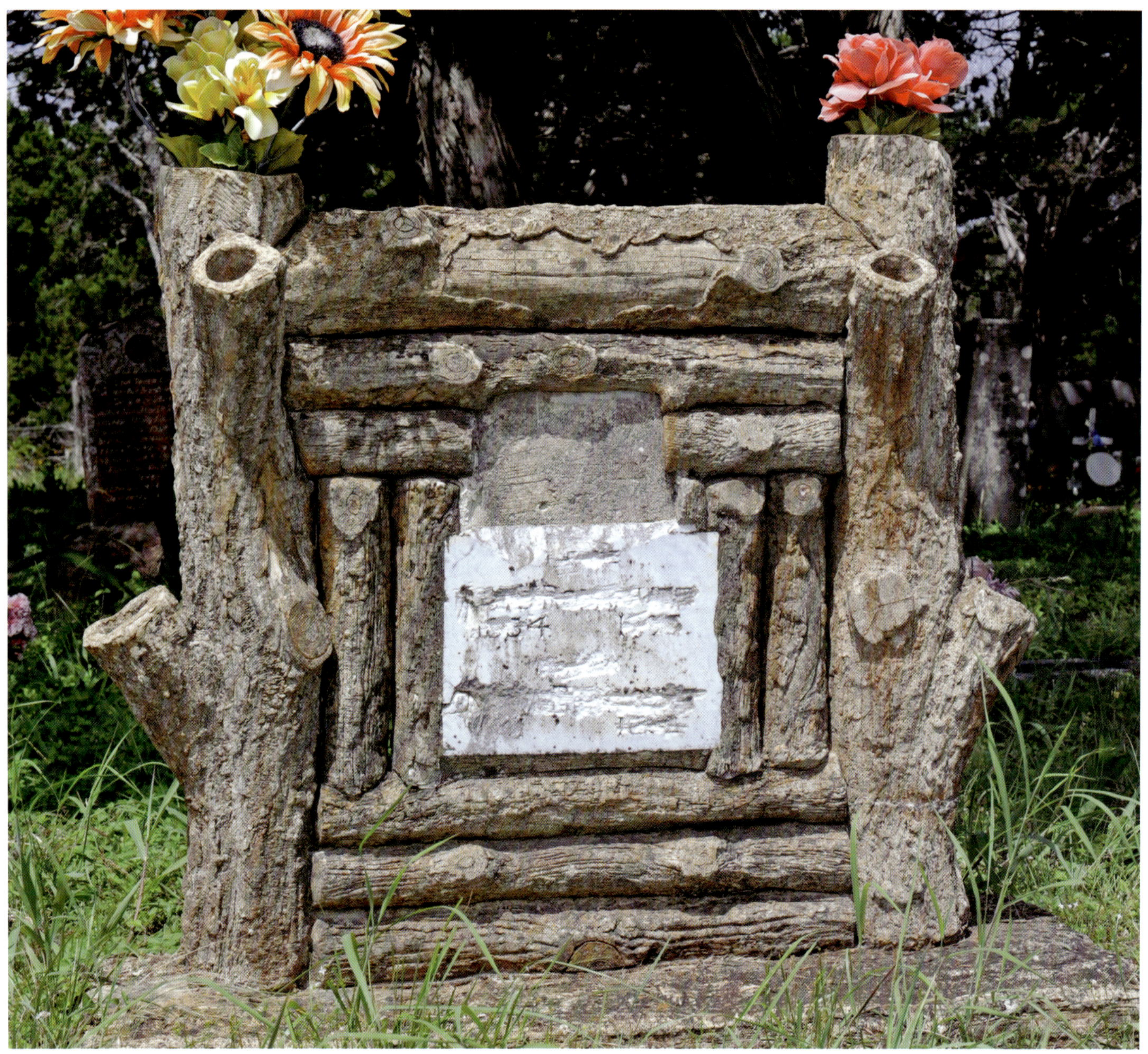

Artisan unknown. Bandera County, TX. Polly's Cemetery. Grave marker. Photo by Kent Rush.

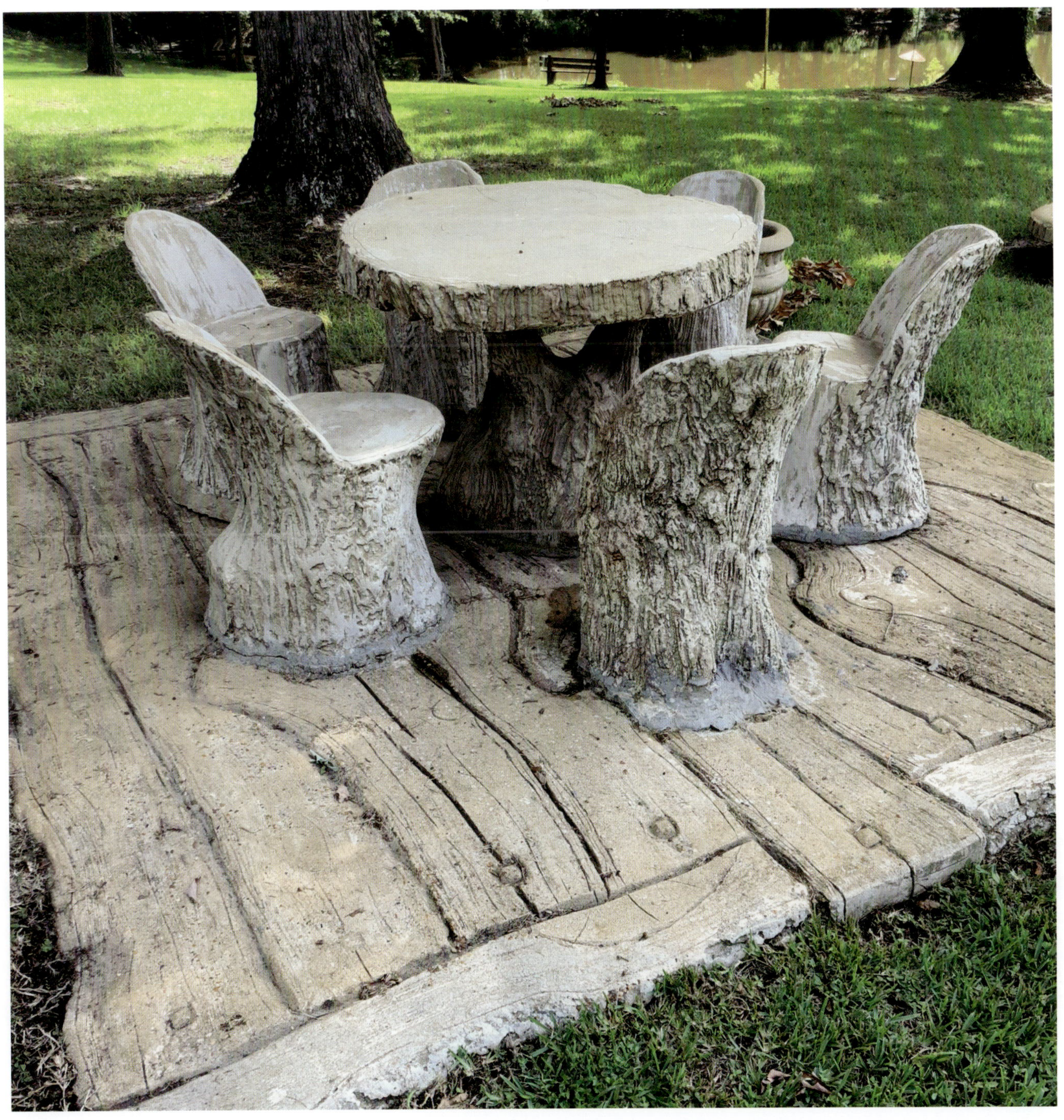

Máximo Cortés. Monroe, LA. Photo courtesy of Carlos Cortés.

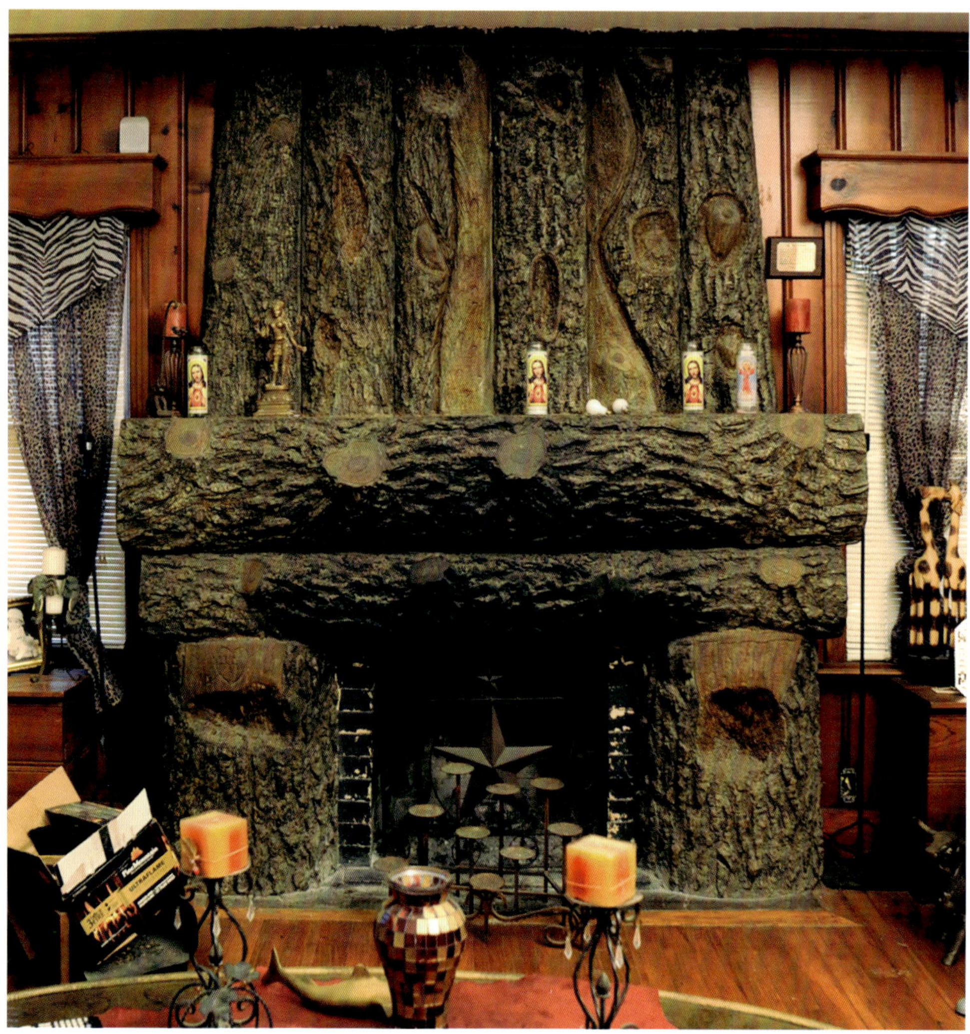

Artisan unknown. San Antonio, TX. Fireplace. Mark Rhodis, owner. Photo by Kent Rush.

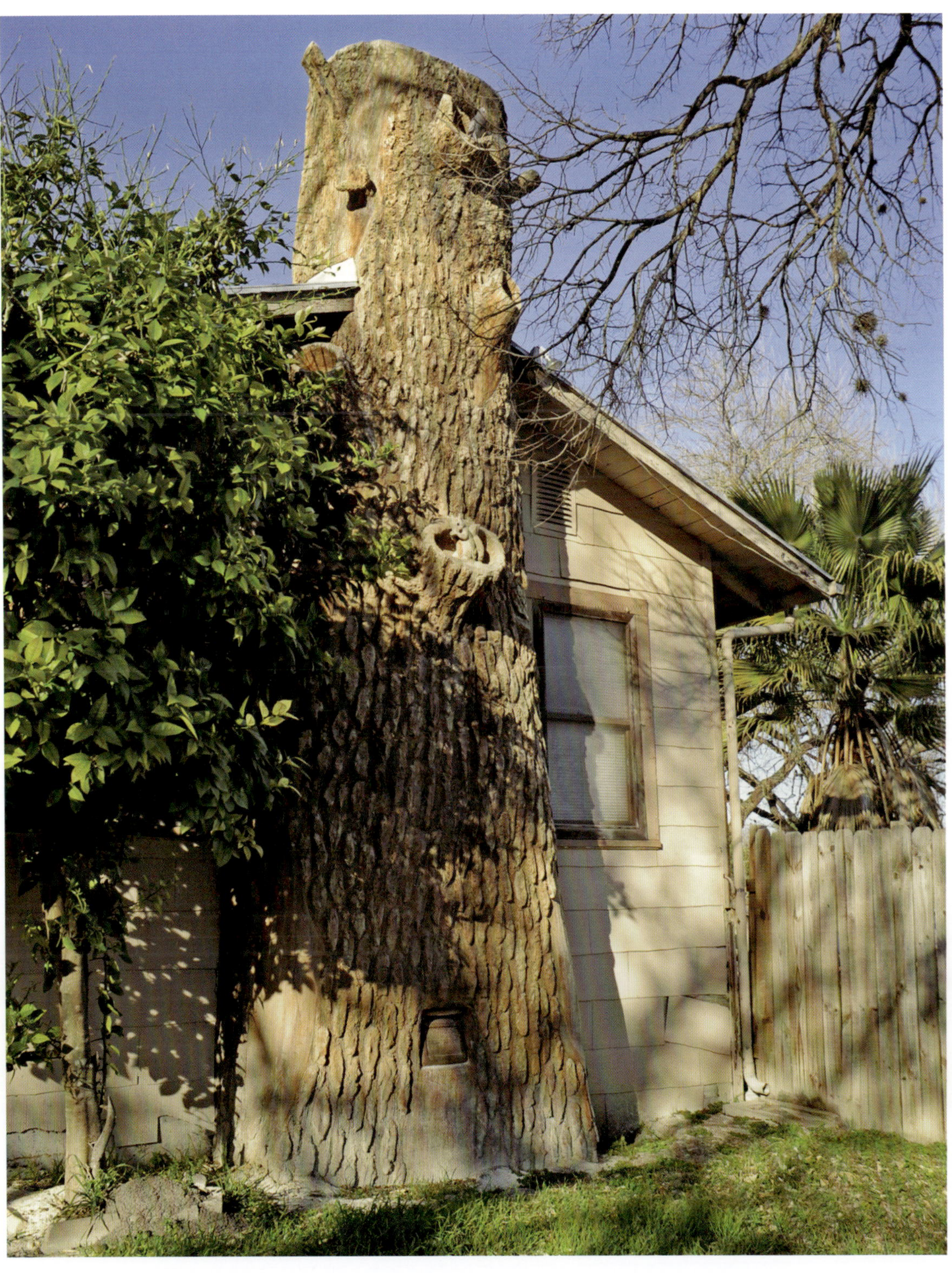

Artisan unknown. San Antonio, TX. Mark Rhodis, owner. Photo by Kent Rush.

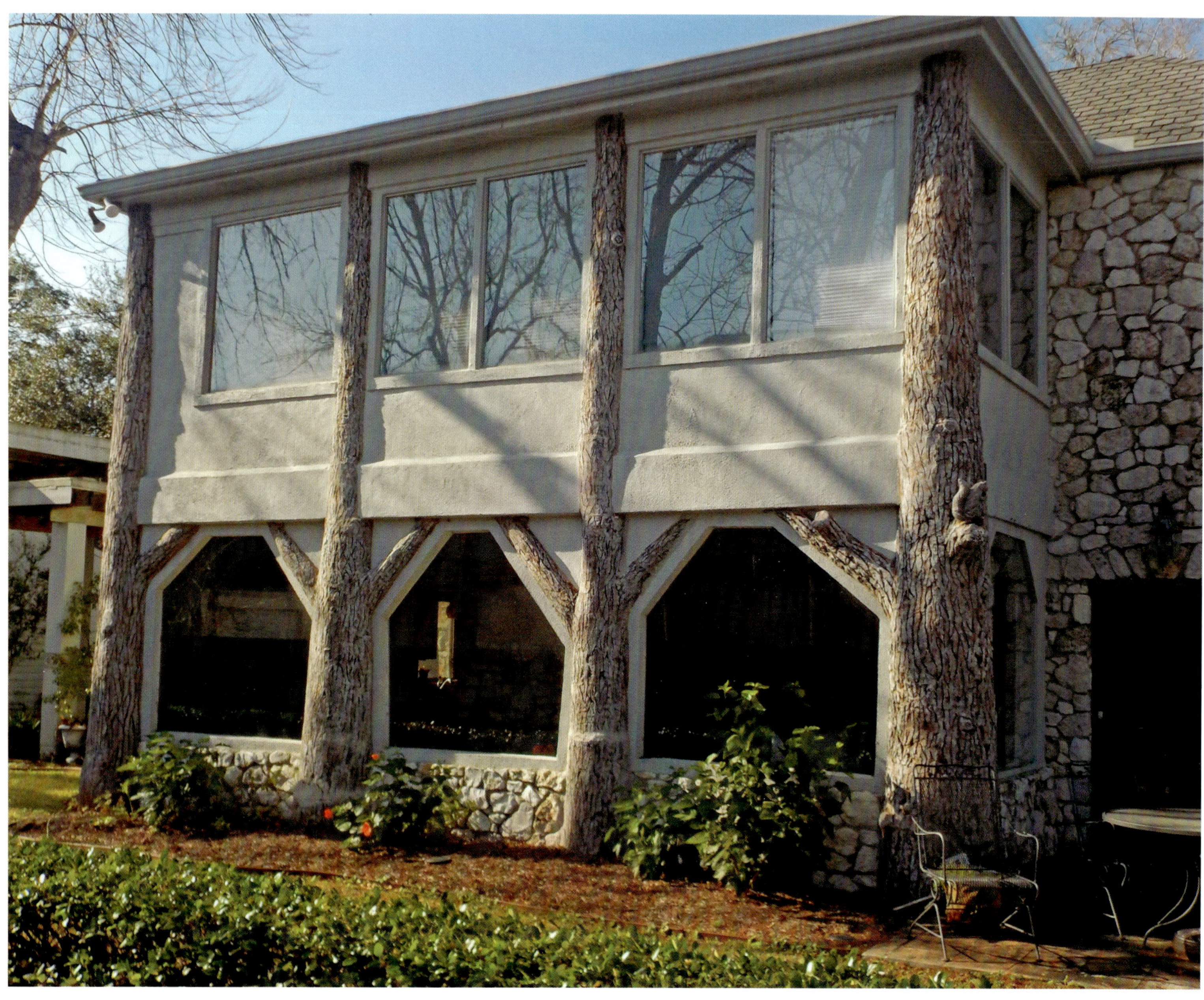

Artisan unknown. La Porte, TX. Walker house. Joan and Bill Ravenswaay, owners. Photo by Kent Rush.

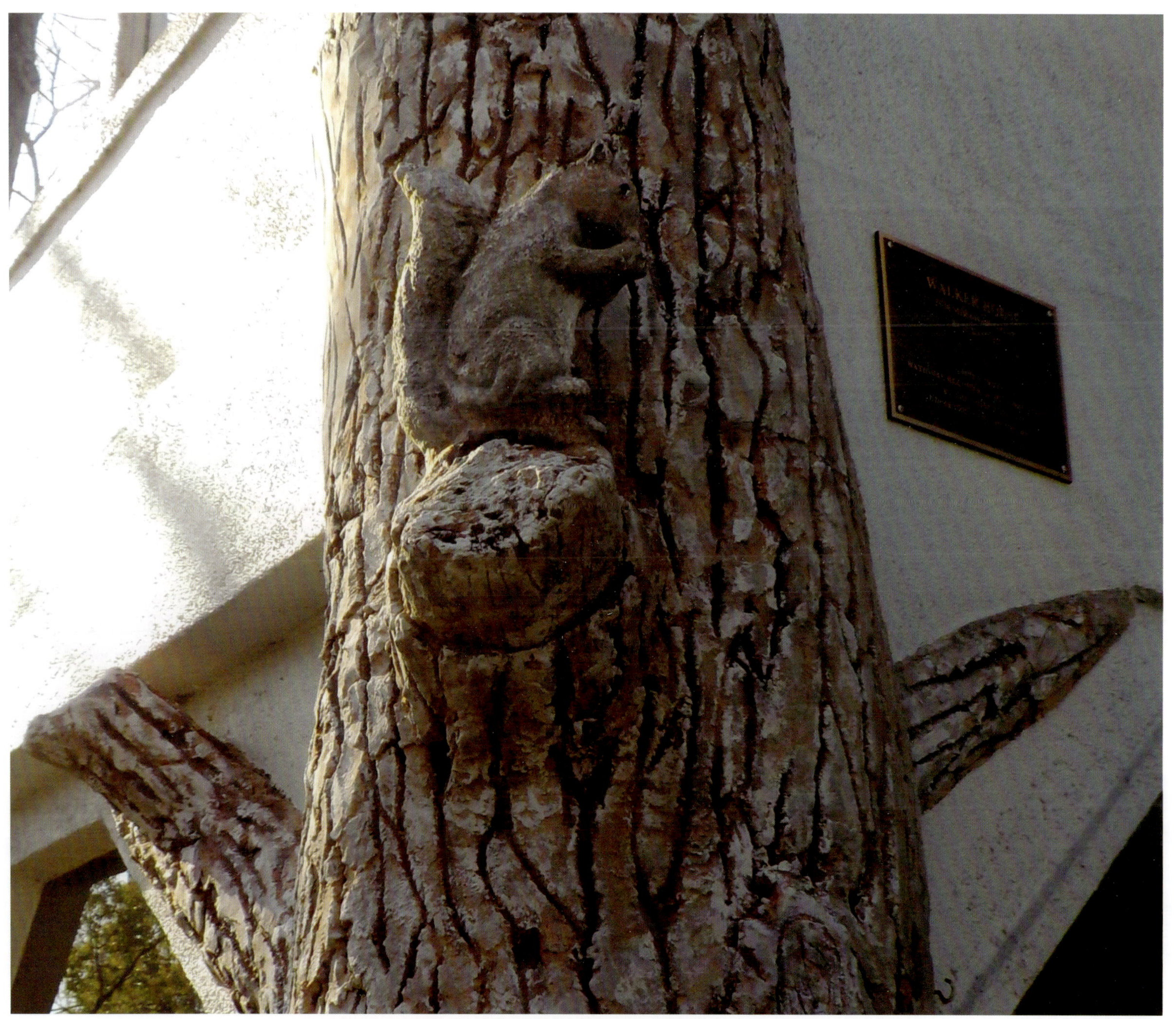

Artisan unknown. La Porte, TX. Walker house squirrel. Joan and Bill Ravenswaay, owners. Photo by Kent Rush.

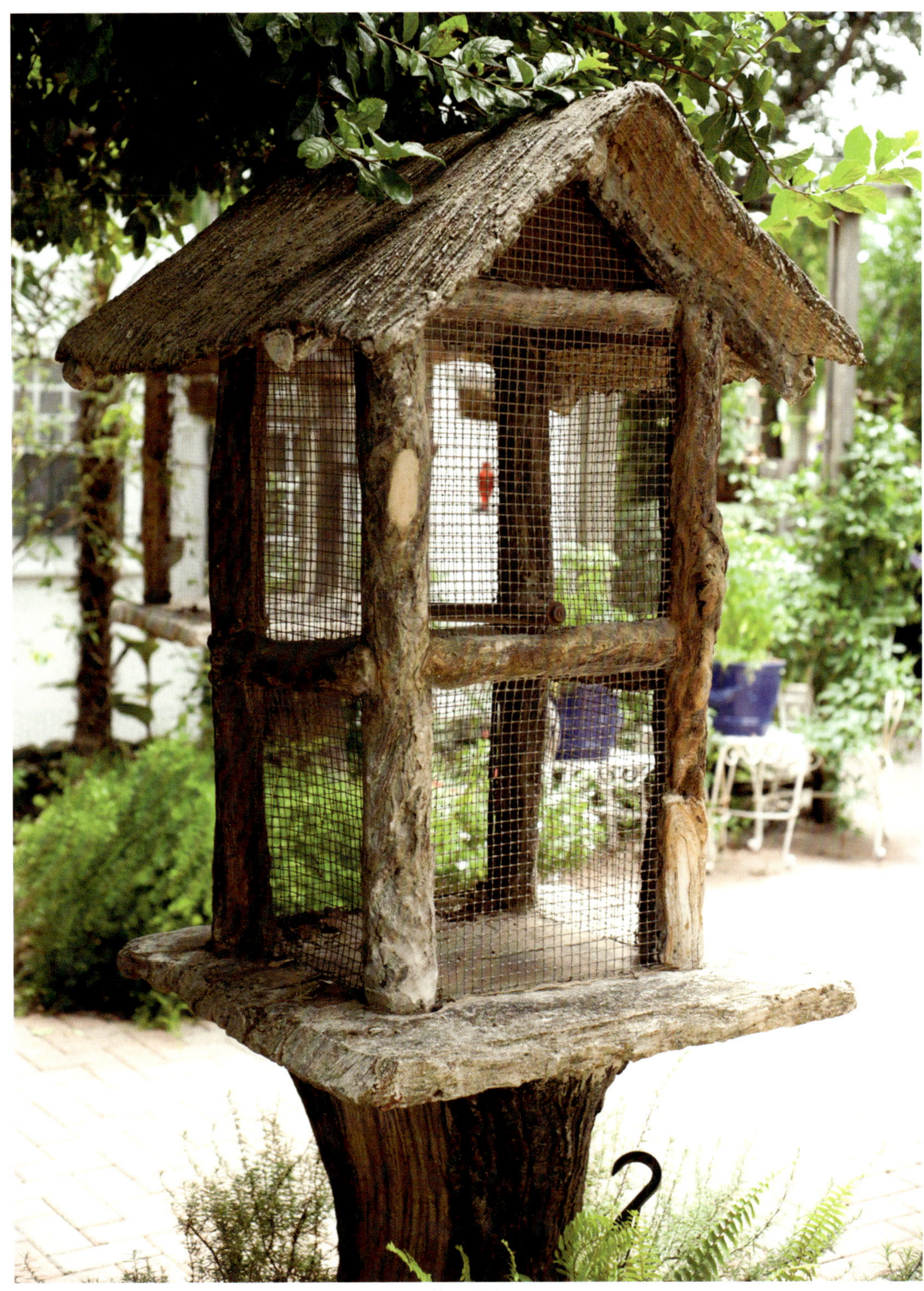

Máximo Cortés. San Antonio, TX. Private collection. Photo by Kent Rush.

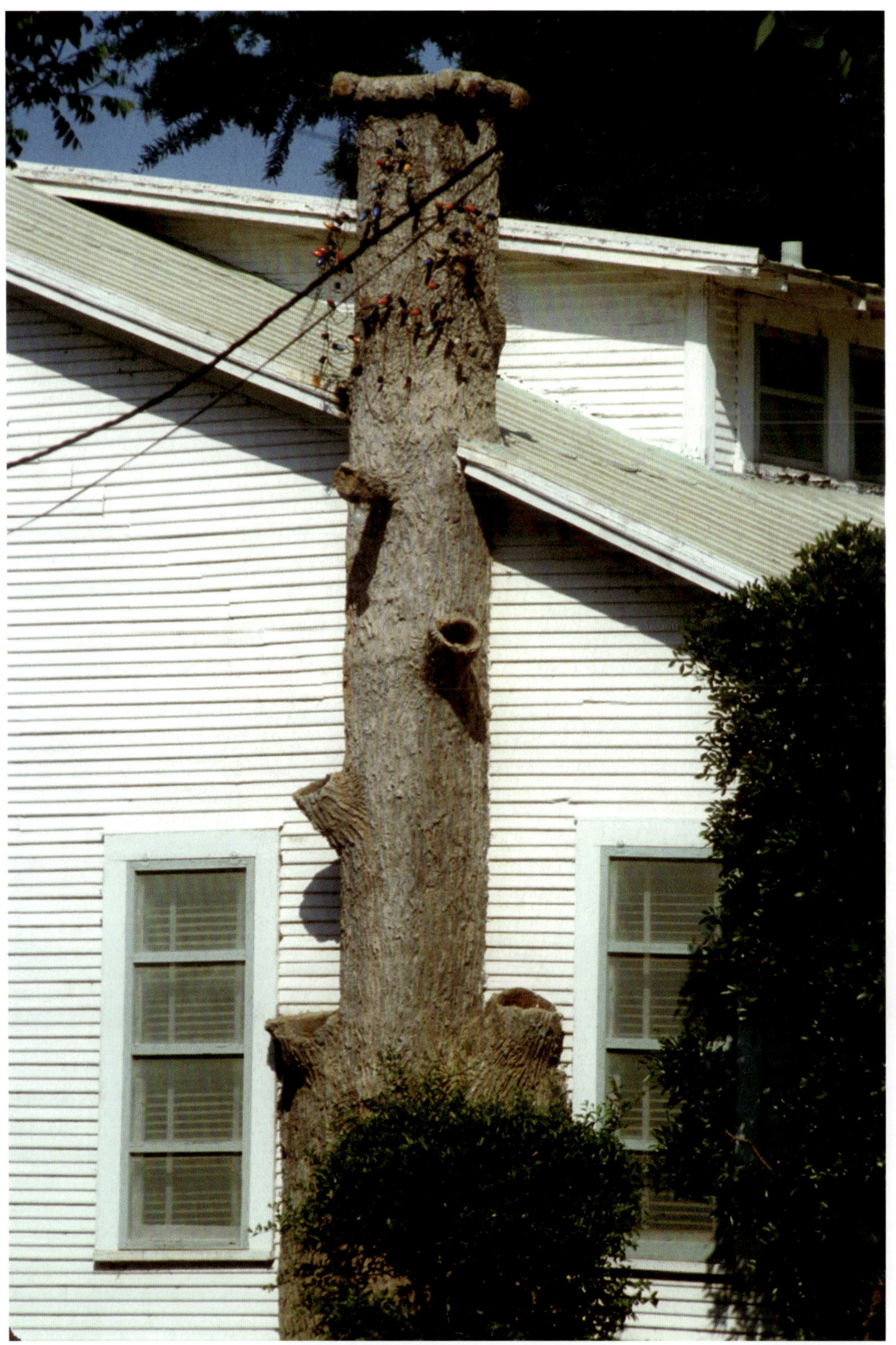

Artisan unknown. San Antonio, TX. Private collection. Photo by Ron Bechtol.

155

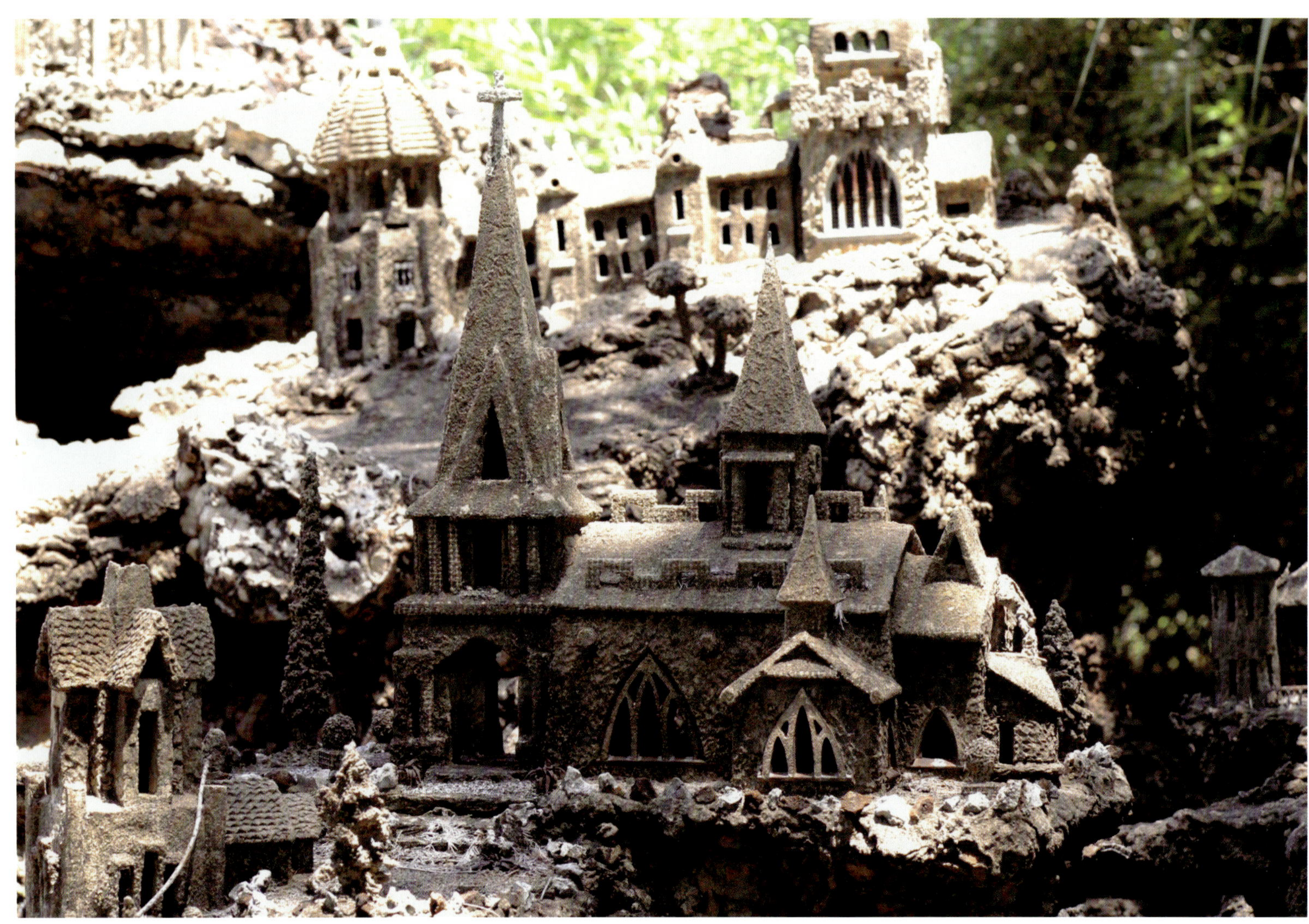

Leopold Lux. San Antonio, TX. Lux Village church. Collection of A. de Arredondo. Photo by Kent Rush.

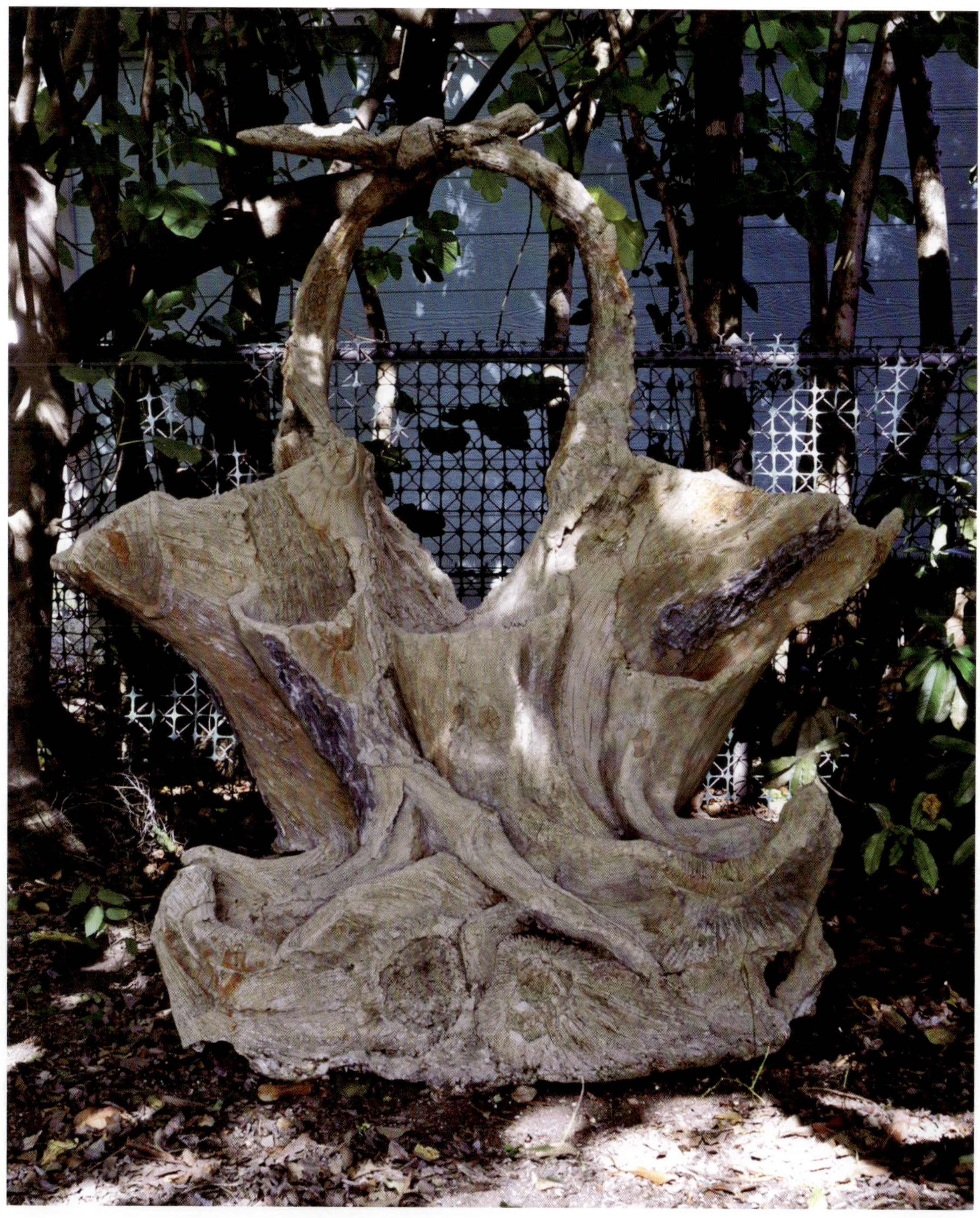

Artisan unknown. San Antonio, TX. Planter. Private collection. Photo by Kent Rush.

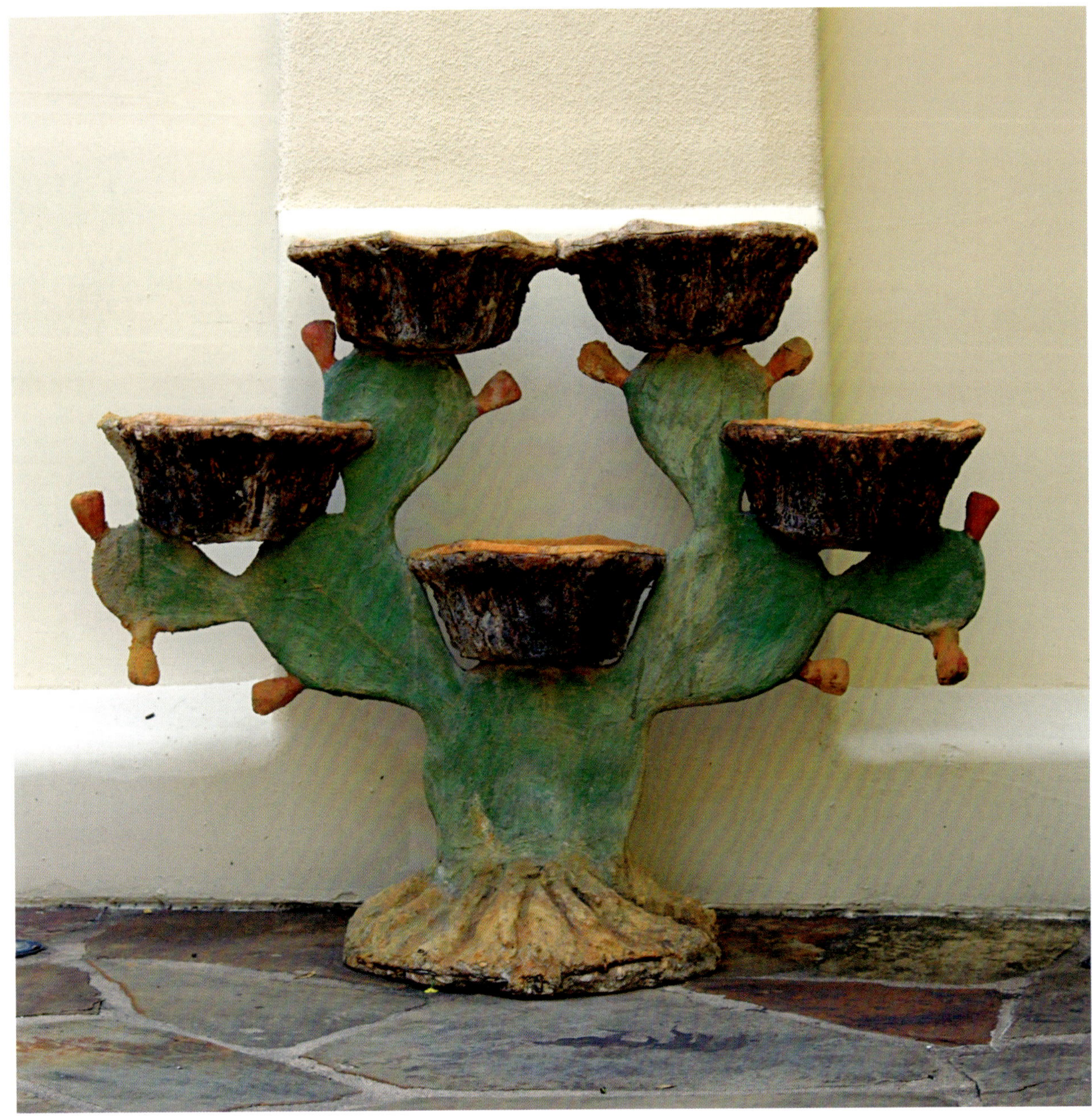

Artisan unknown. San Antonio, TX. Cactus planter. Collection of Linda and Harry S. Affleck Jr. Photo by Harry Affleck III.

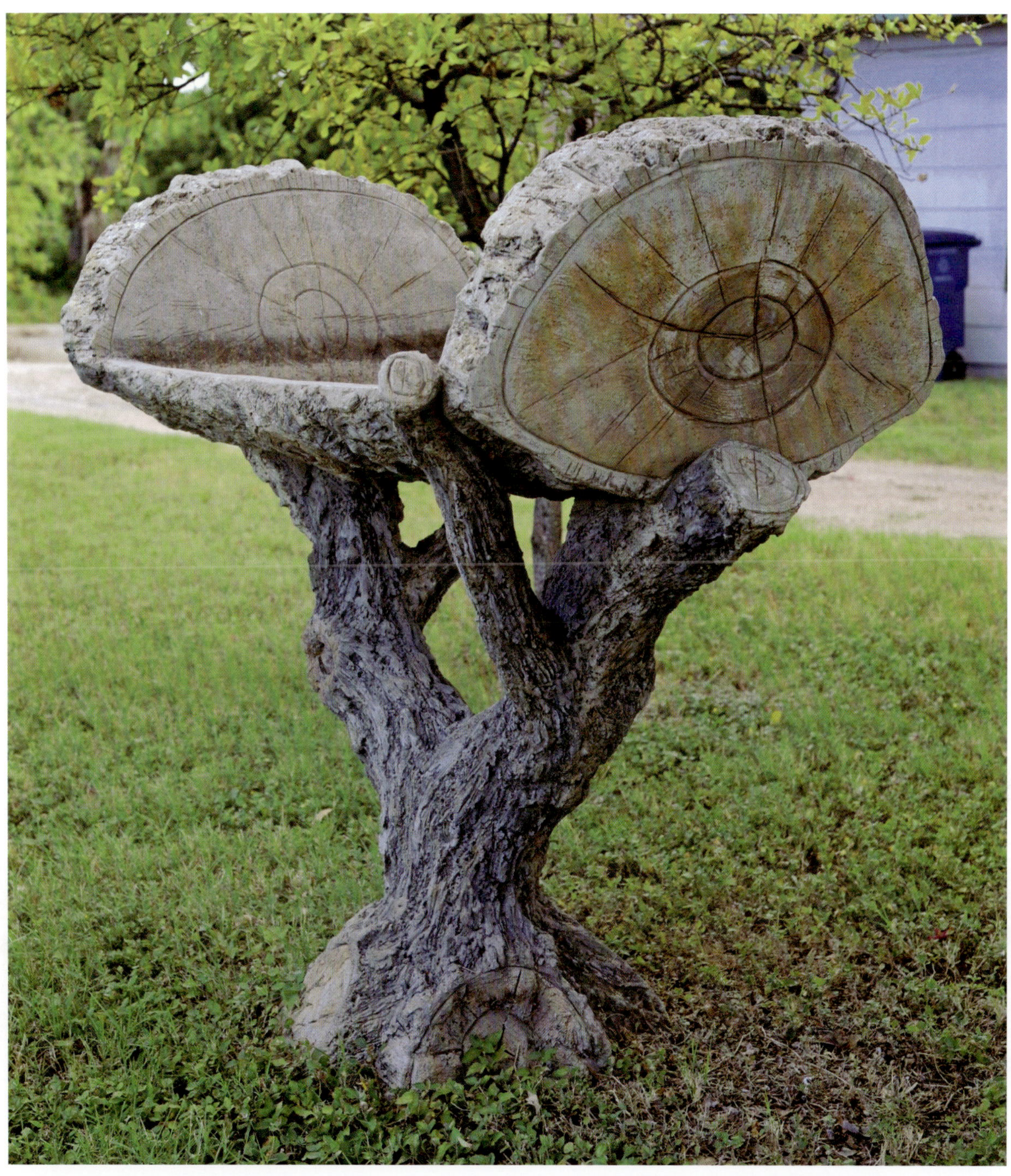

Artisan unknown. San Antonio, TX. Birdbath/feeder. Private collection. Photo by Kent Rush.

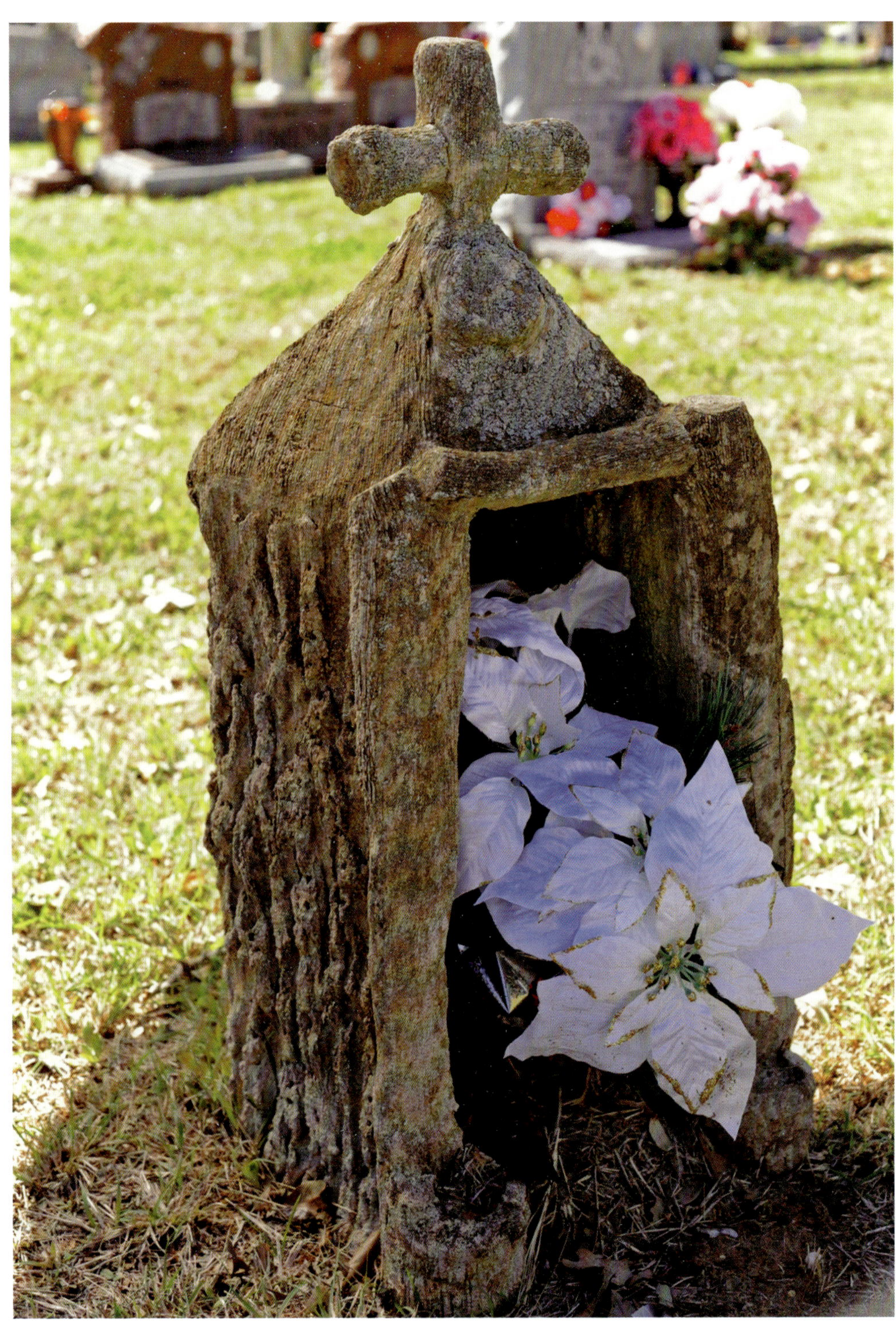

Artisan unknown. Floresville, TX. Sacred Heart Cemetery. Relicarito. Photo by Kent Rush.

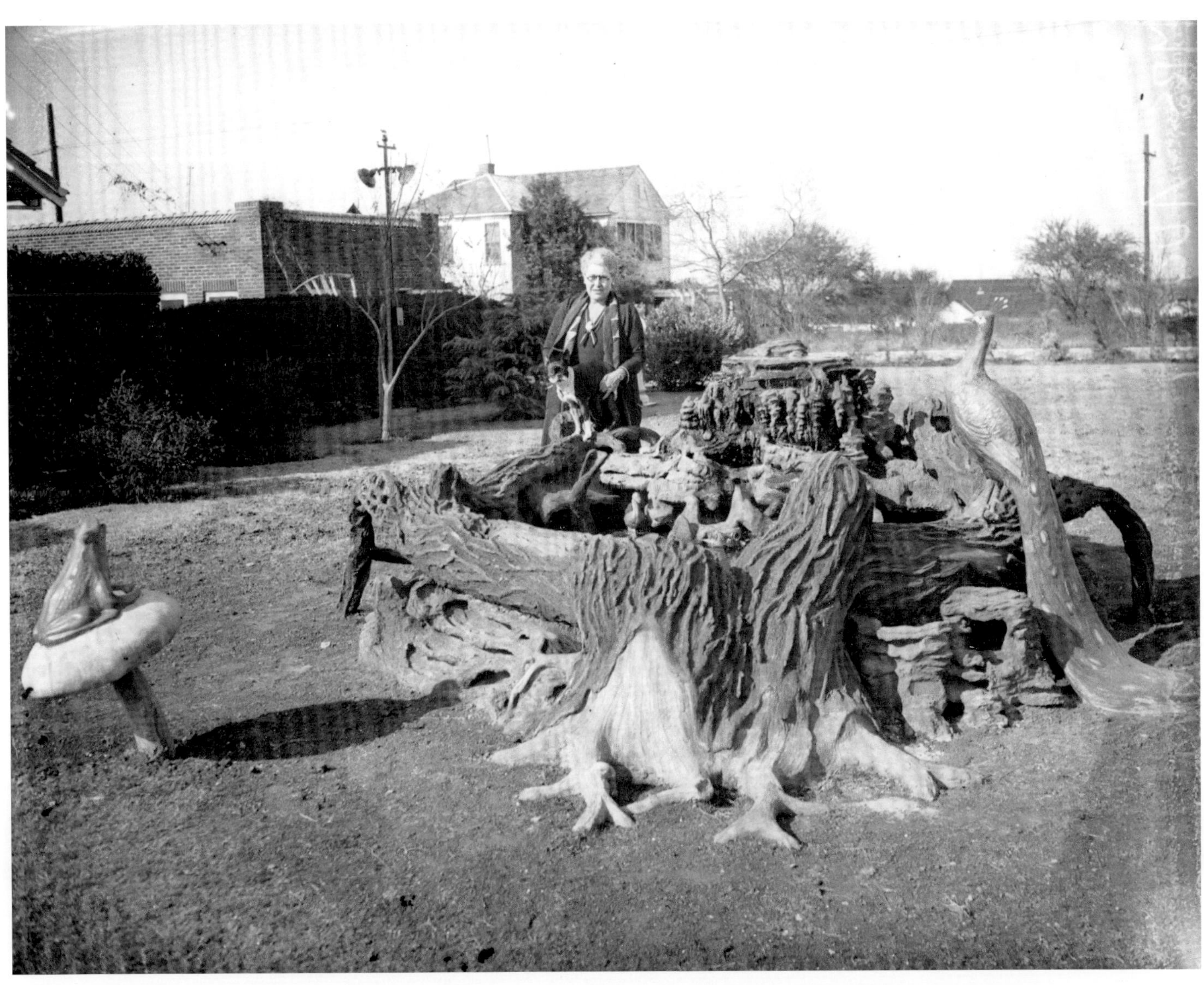

Máximo Cortés. San Antonio, TX. Bertha Schramm and the fountain she designed about 1932.
Photo from The University of Texas at San Antonio Special Collections. San Antonio Light Collection. ZUMA Press.

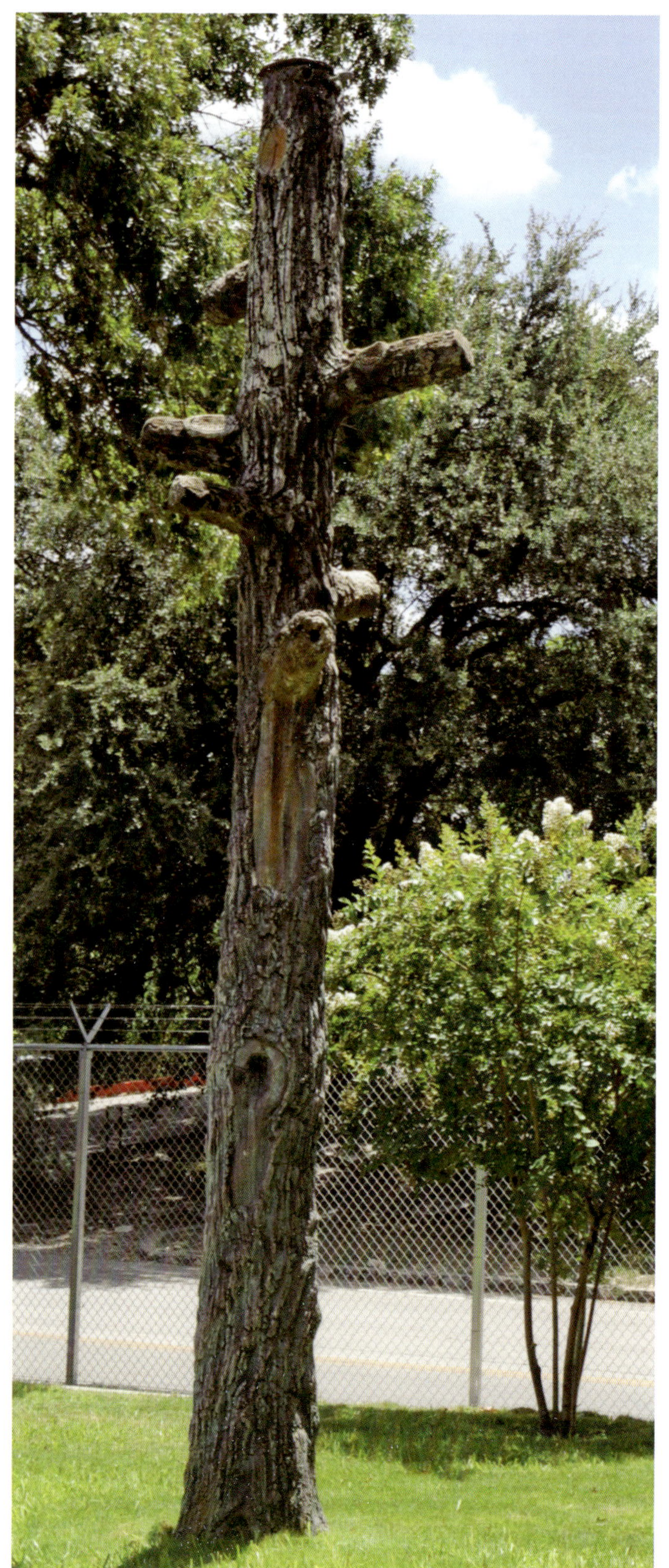

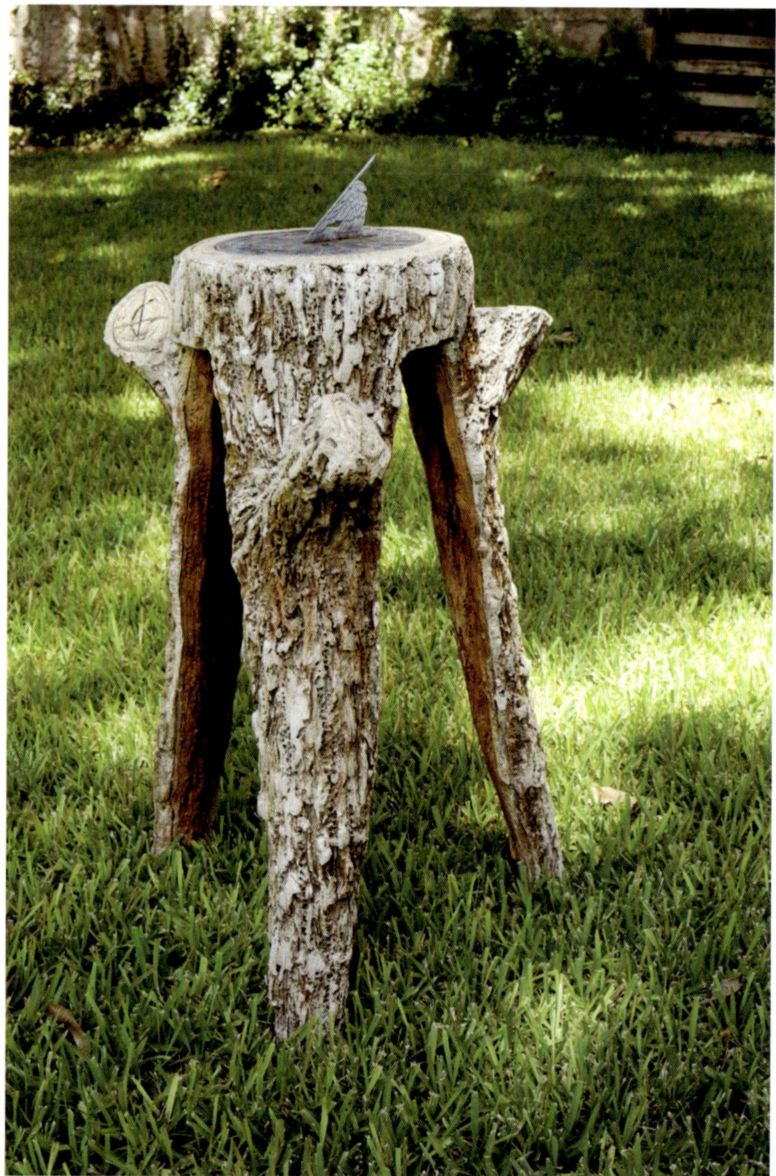

Left: *Artisan unknown. San Antonio, TX. San Antonio Zoo. Tree trunk. Photo by Kent Rush.*

Above: *Sam Murray. San Antonio, TX. Sundial. Collection of Maria and Fred Pfeiffer. Photo by Kent Rush.*

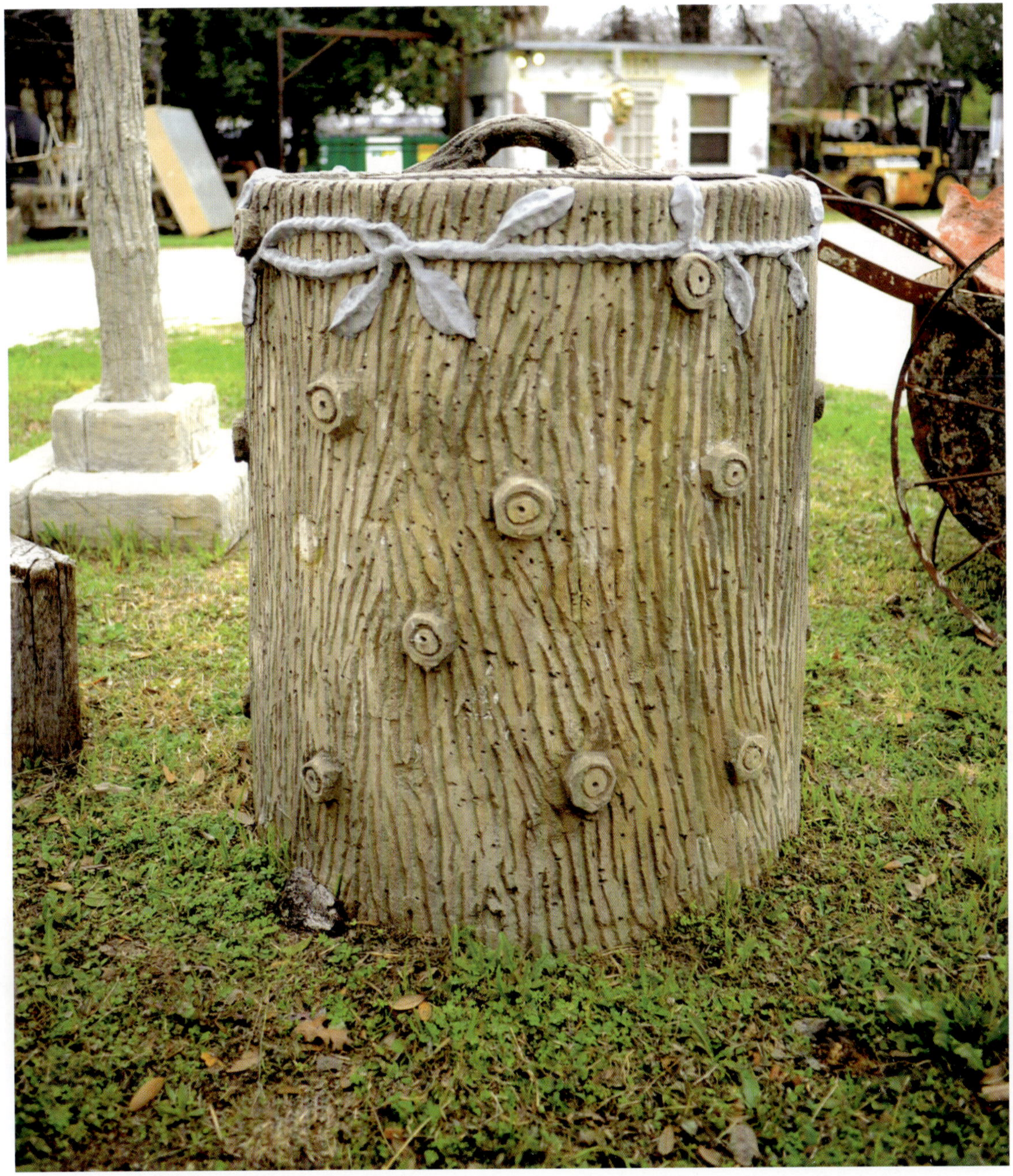

Artisan unknown. San Antonio, TX. Trash container. Collection of Carlos Cortés. Photo by Kent Rush.

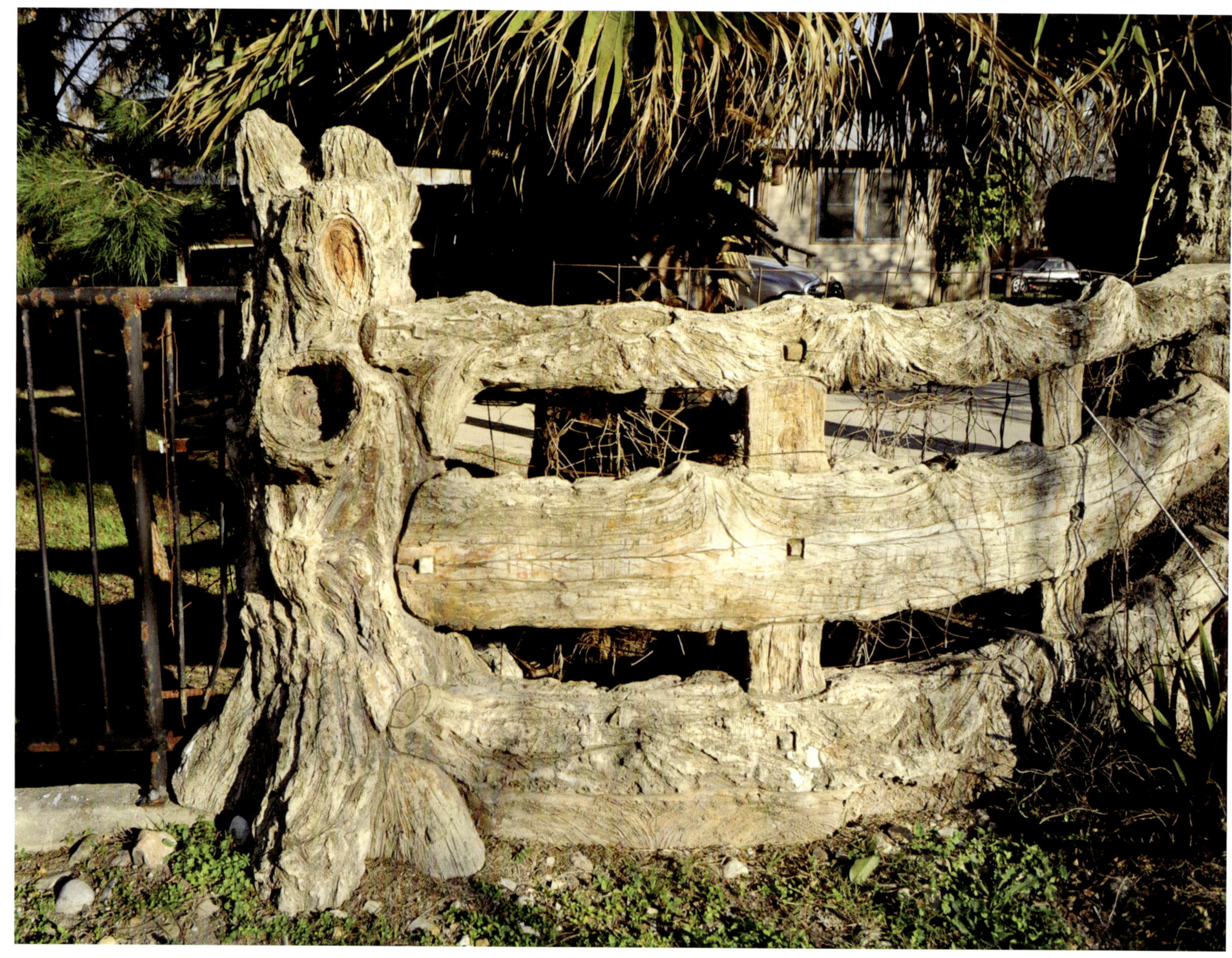

Artisan unknown. San Antonio, TX. Gate section. Mark Rhodis, owner. Photo by Kent Rush.

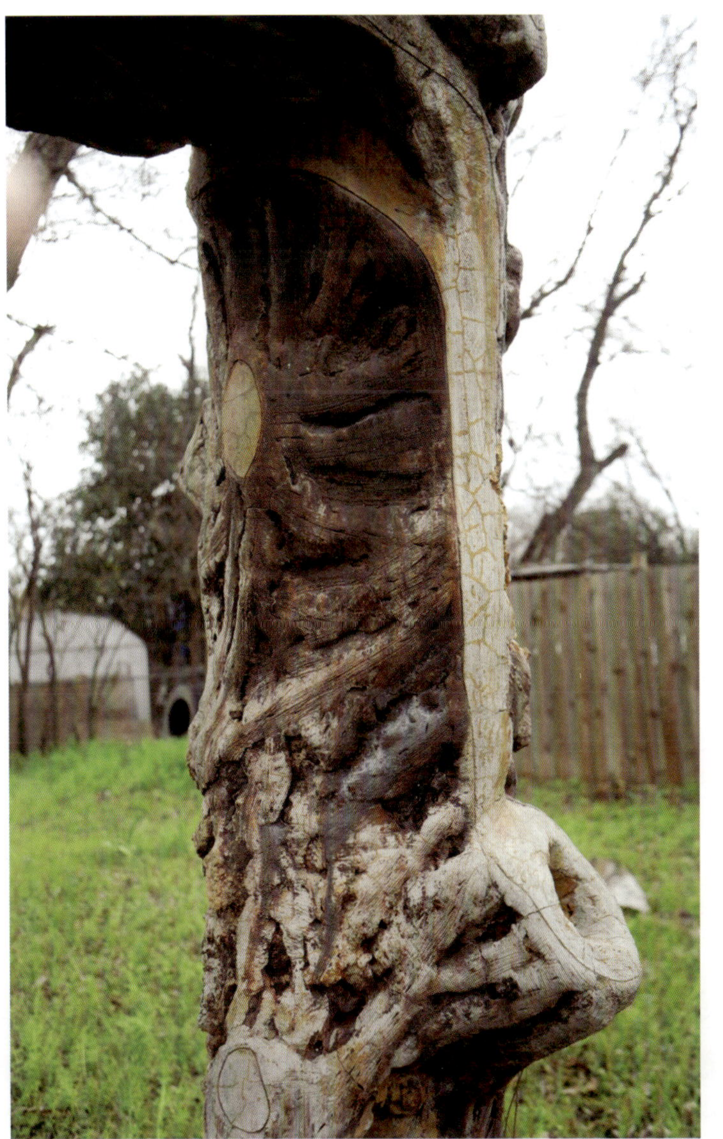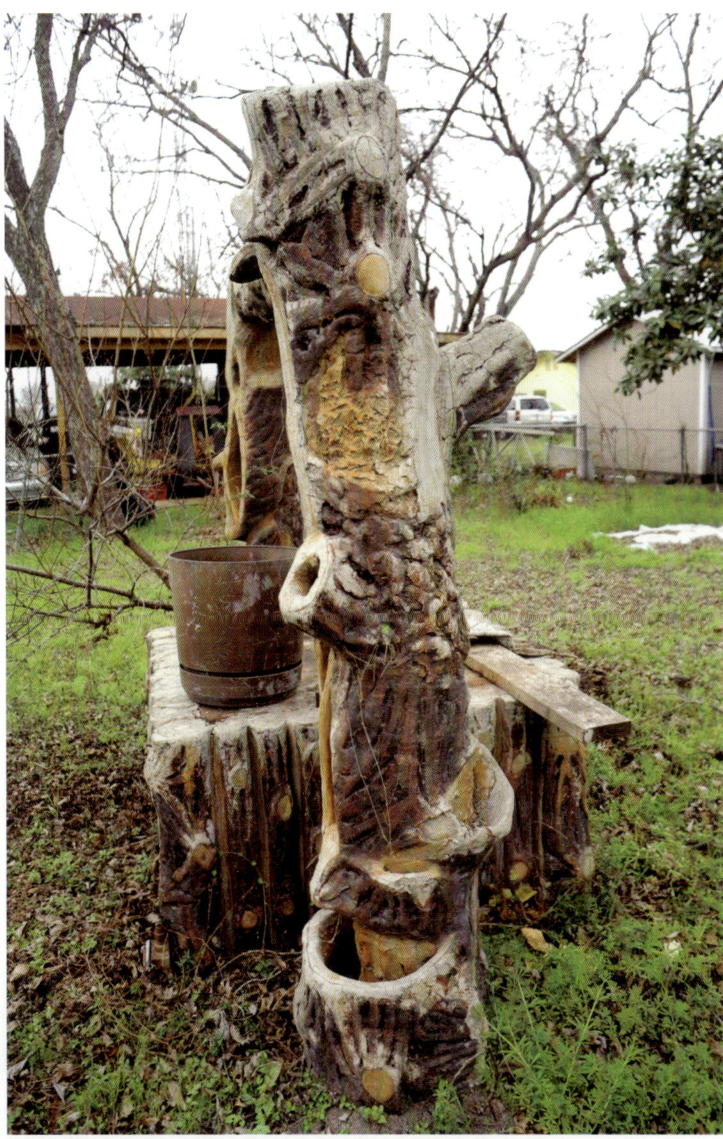

Mauro Del Toro. San Antonio, TX. Left: Well detail. Right: Side view of well. Collection of Del Toro Family. Photos by Kent Rush.

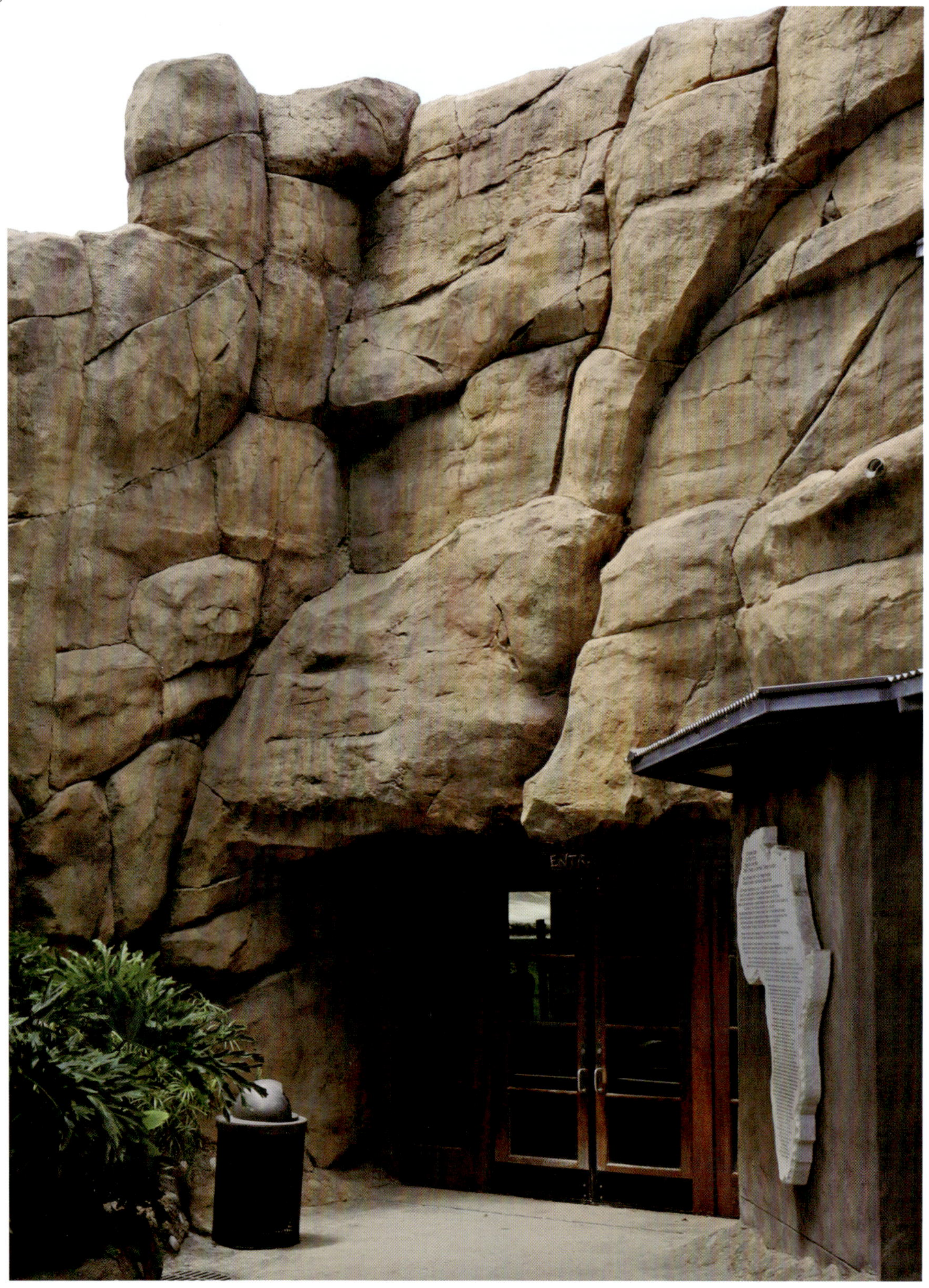

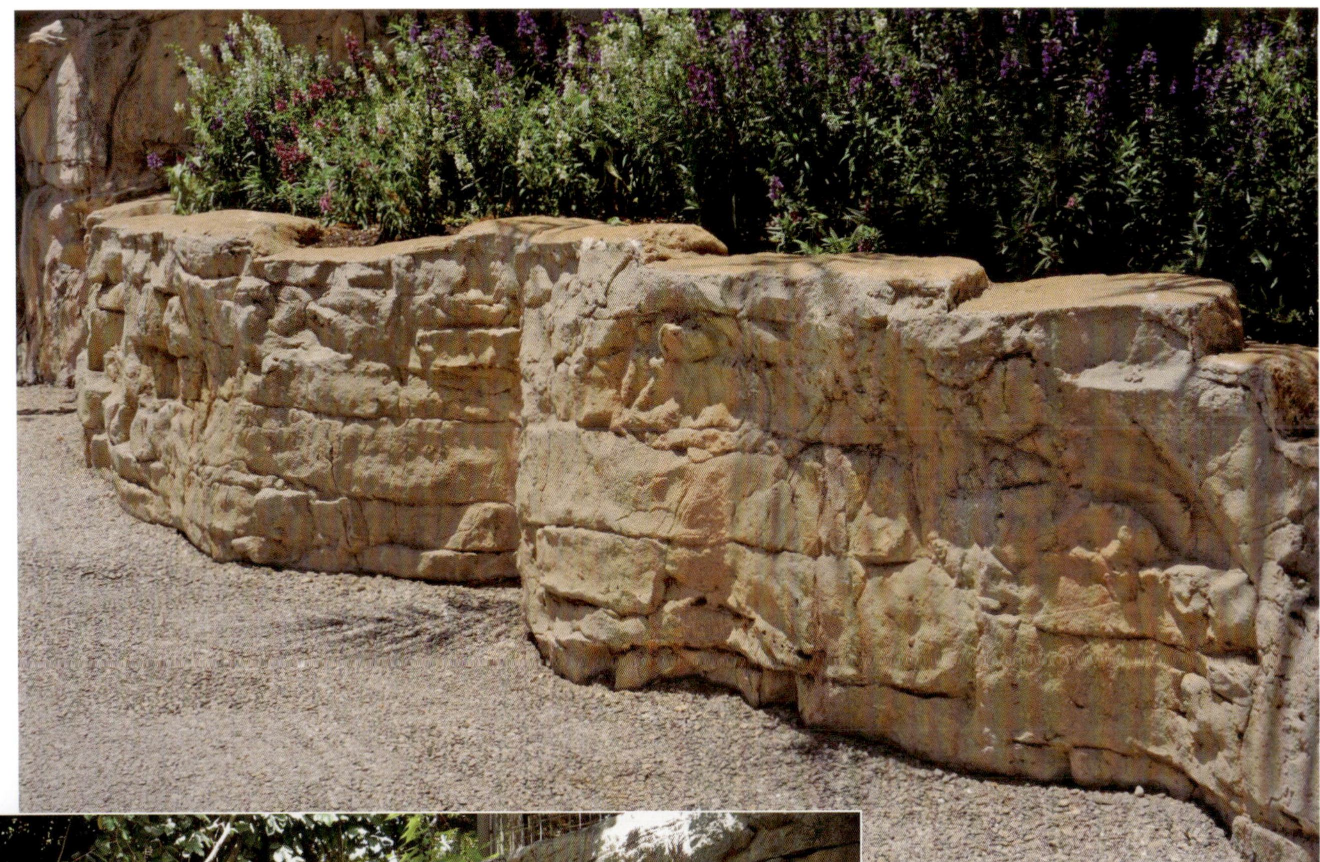

Opposite: *Artisan unknown. San Antonio, TX. San Antonio Zoo. Wall rock detail. Photo by Kent Rush.*

Above and left: *Artisan unknown. San Antonio, TX. San Antonio Zoo. Planter wall. Photo by Kent Rush.*

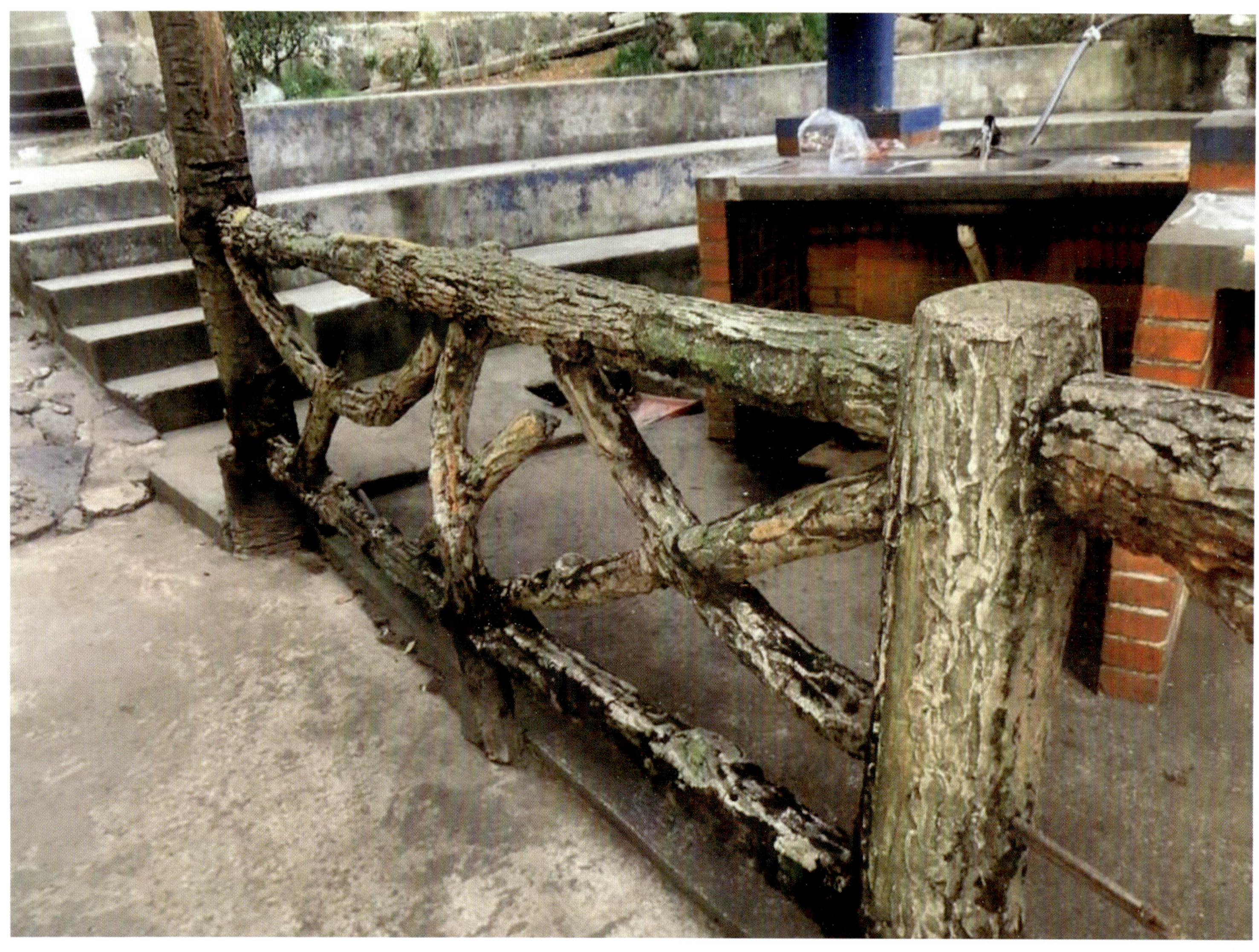

Attributed to Dionicio Rodríguez. Toluca de Lerdo, Mexico. Park railing. Photo by Rene Romero.

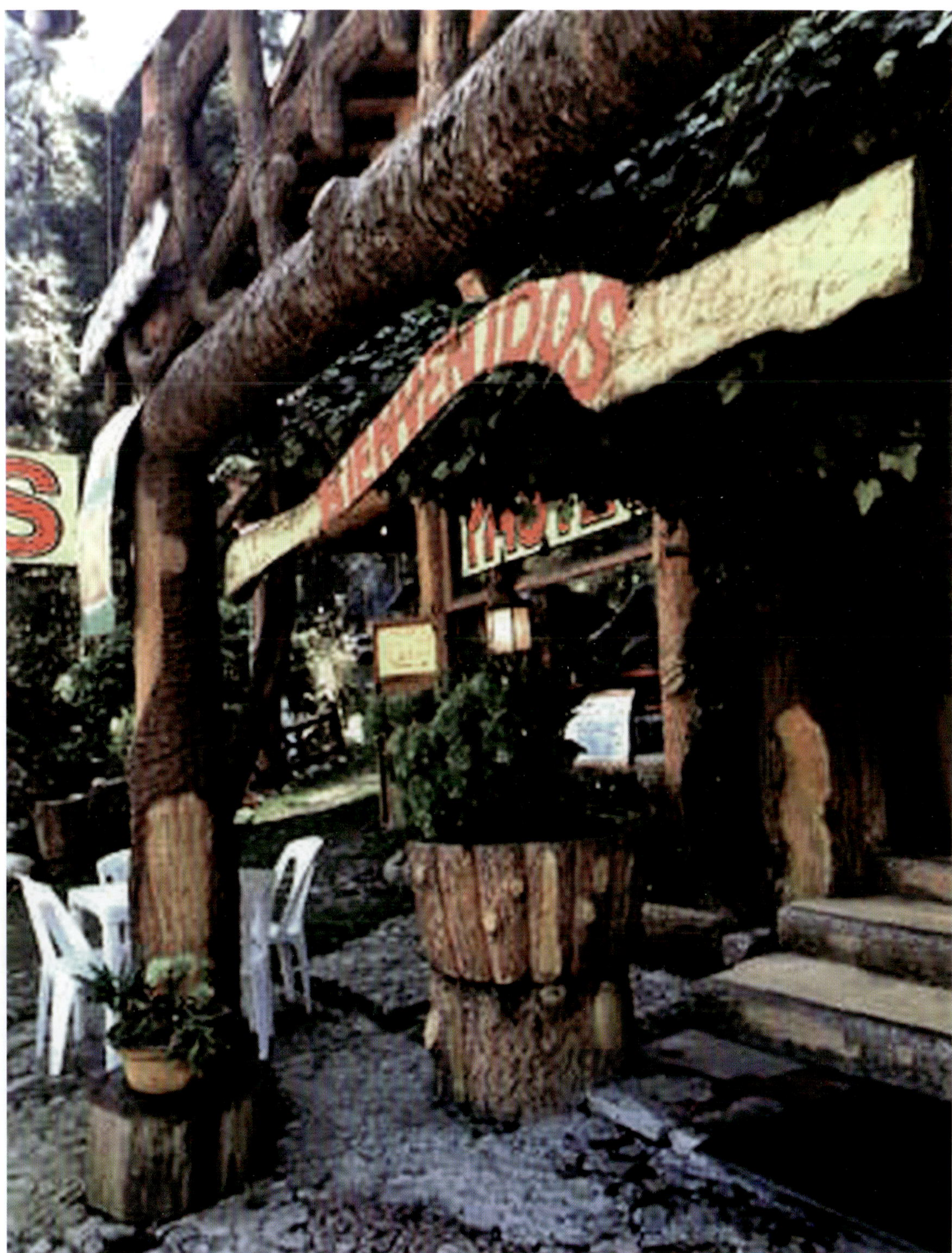

Attributed to Dionicio Rodríguez. Toluca de Lerdo, Mexico. Exterior of El Chinaco. Photo by Rene Romero.

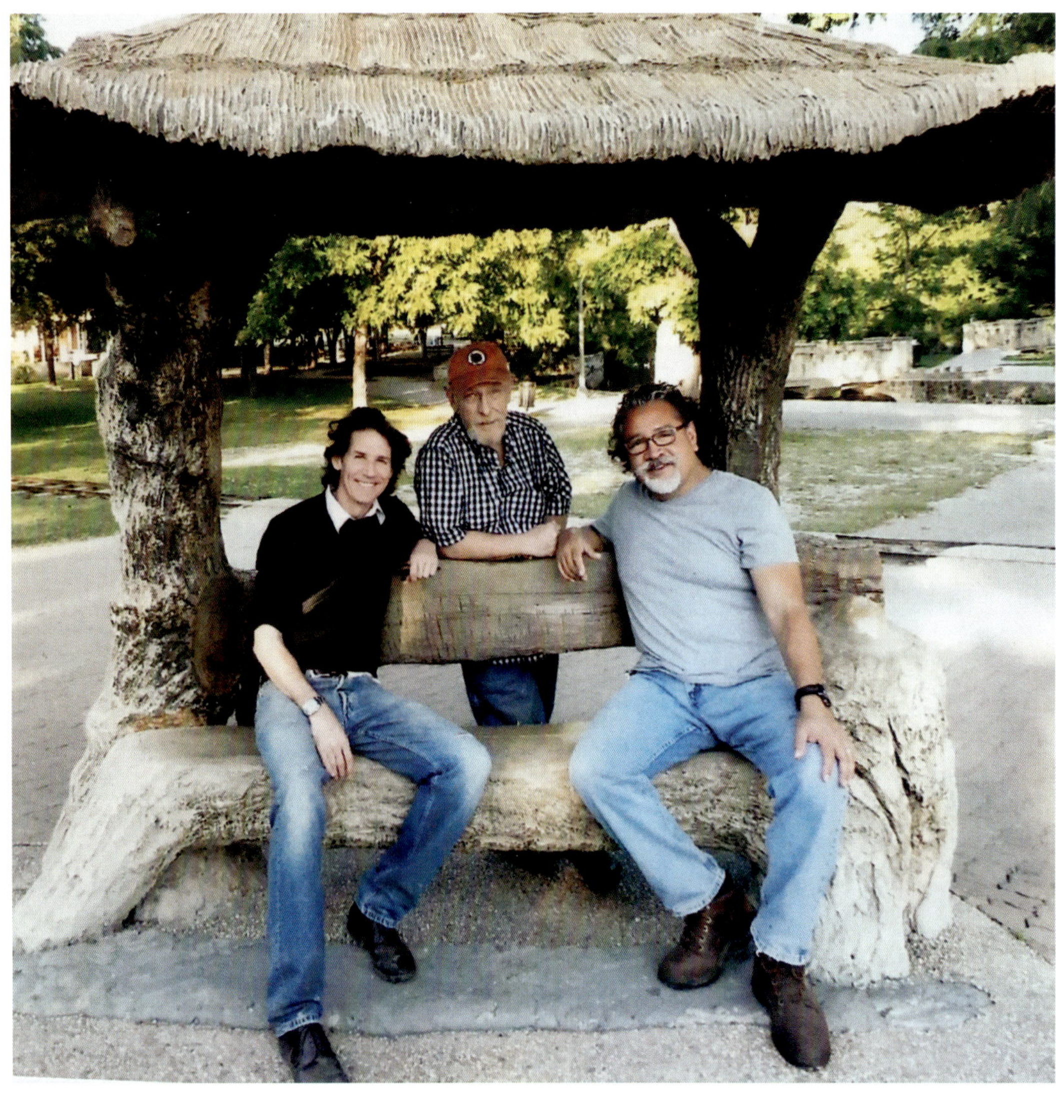

Dionicio Rodríguez, San Antonio, TX. Palapa in San Antonio Zoo.
Artisans (left to right) Gregory Everingham, Donald Tucker, and Carlos Cortés. Photo by Hope Garza-Cortés.

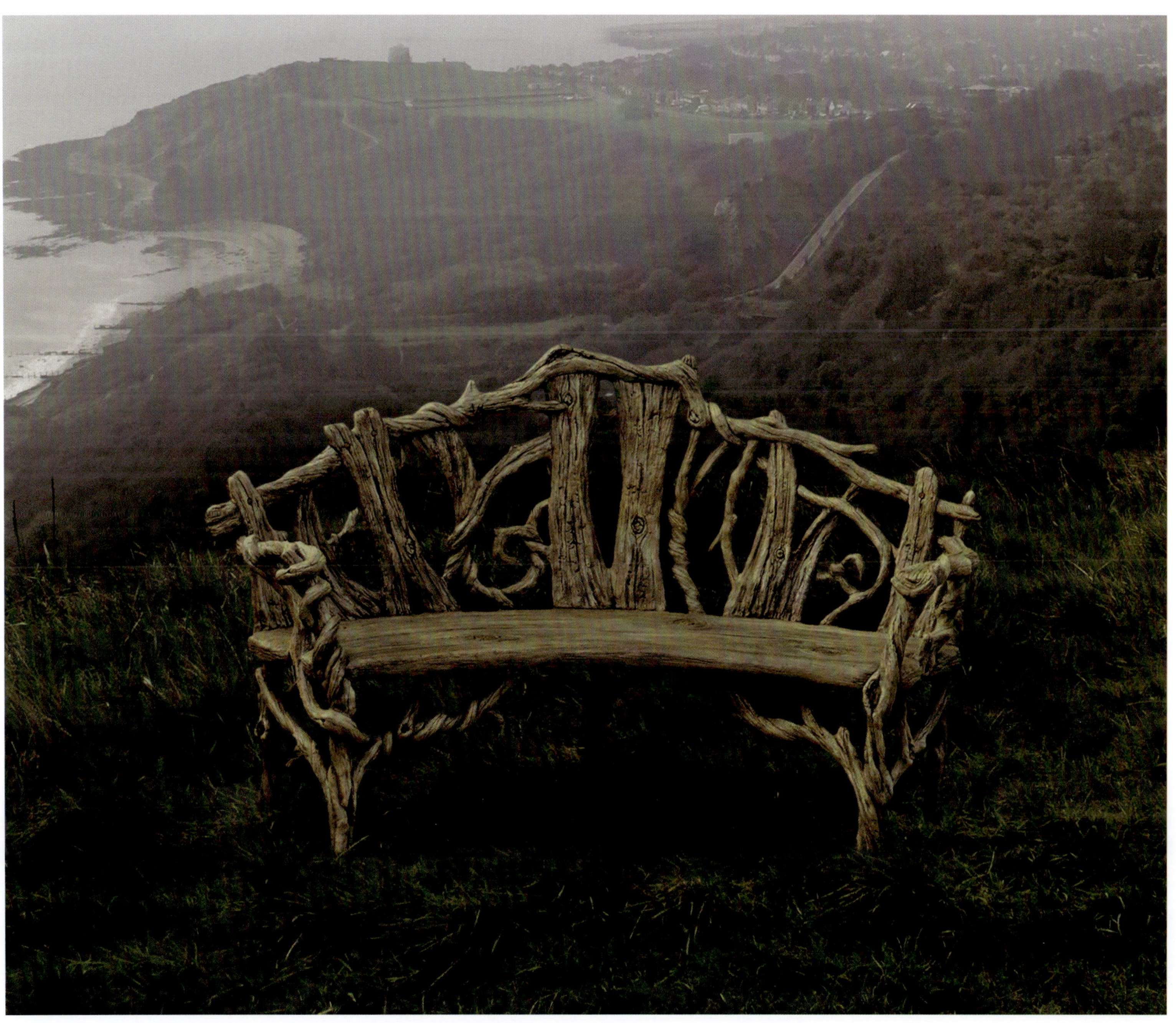

Diane Husson, Norfolk, VA. Private collection. Photo Emile Husson.

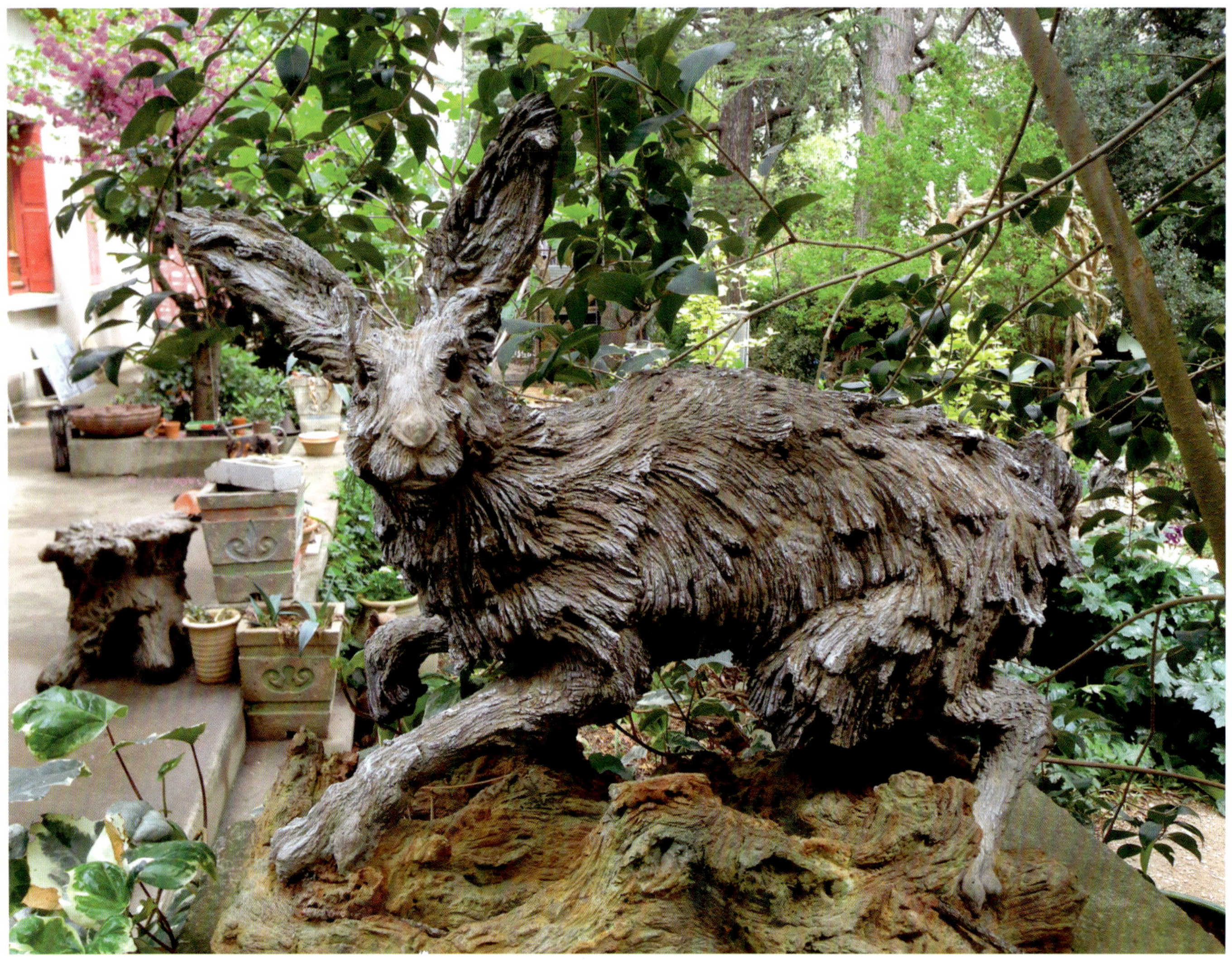

Gregory Everingham. Villeneuve-lès-Avignon, France. Hare. Private collection. Photo by Gregory Everingham.

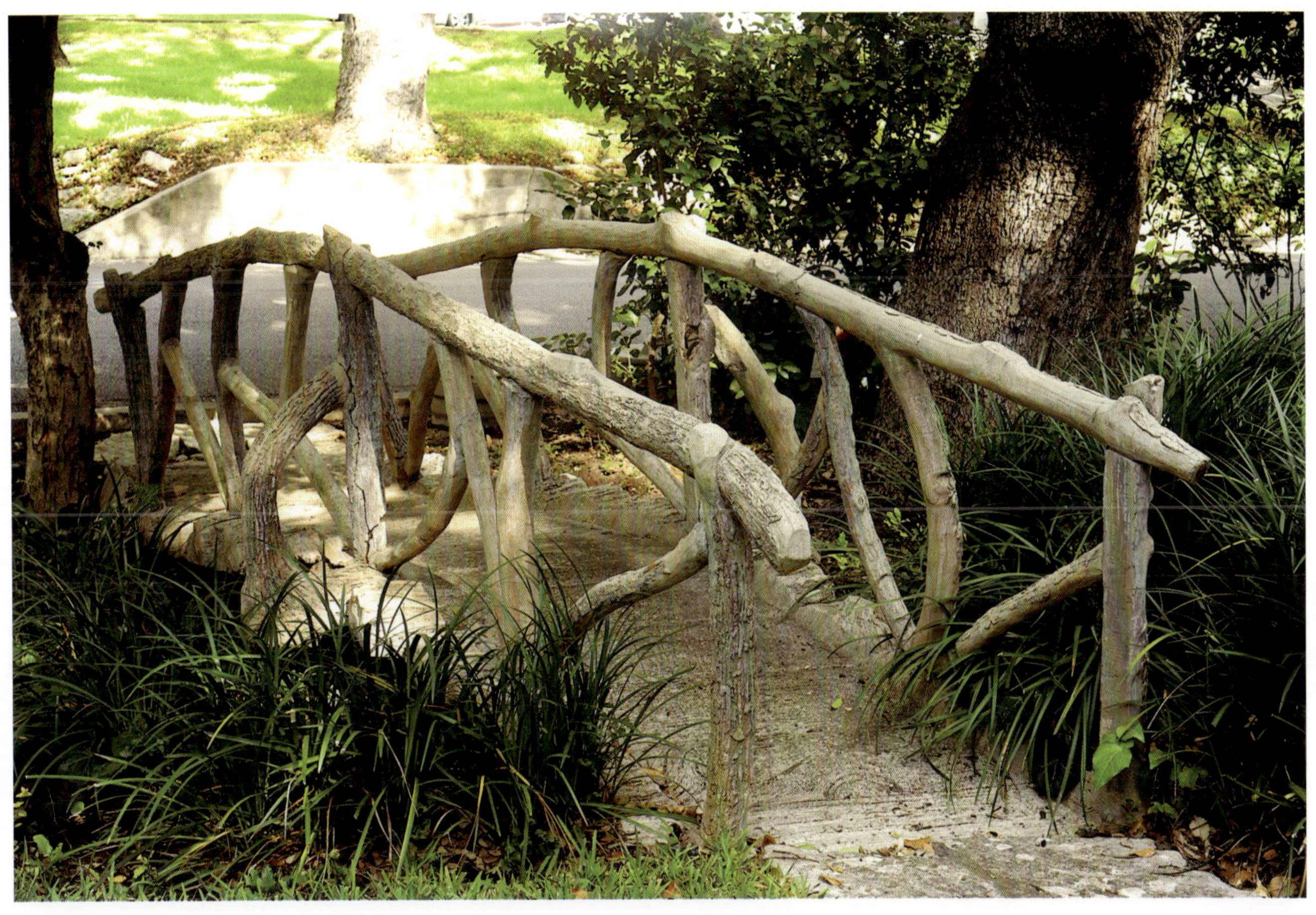

Artisan unknown, San Antonio, TX. Private collection. Photo by Kent Rush.

Notes

Chapter 1

1. "What Is Folk Art?," Museum of International Folk Art, accessed May 24, 2018, http://www.in-ternationalfolkart.org/learn/what-is-folk-art.html.

2. "Tangible Cultural Heritage," UNESCO, accessed January 13, 2018, http://www.unesco.org/new/en/cairo/culture/tangible-cultural-heritage.

3. *Merriam-Webster Learner's Dictionary*, s.v. "concrete (noun)," http://www.learnersdictionary.com/definition/concrete.

4. *Merriam-Webster*, s.v. "cement (noun)," https://www.merriam-webster.com/dictionary/cement.

5. Donald Tucker, *An Introduction to Sculpting Ferro-cement Faux Bois* (Scotts Valley, CA: Create-Space Independent Publishing Platform, 2011), 4.

6. Nick Gromicko and Kenton Shepard, "The History of Concrete," International Association of Certified Home Inspectors, accessed December 24, 2016, https://www.nachi.org/history-of-con-crete.htm.

7. Ibid., "Early Use of Concrete."

8. Ibid.

9. Ibid.

10. Ibid.

11. Ibid., "Rome."

12. Elizabeth P. Benson, *The Maya World* (New York: Thames & Hudson, 2015), 38.

13. Michael D. Coe and Stephen Houston, *The Maya* 9th ed., (New York: Thames & Hudson, 2015), 81.

14. Encyclopedia Britannica s.v. "Chicanel-culture," accessed July 30, 2020, Encyclopedia Britannica s.v. "Chicanel culture" accessed July 30, 2020, https://www.britannica.com/topic/Chicanel-culture

15. Benson, *Maya World*, 43.

16. *Encyclopedia Britannica*, s.v. "pozzolana, hydraulic cement," accessed October 17, 2017, http://www.britannica.com/technology/pozzolana

17. Sarah Pruitt, "The Secrets of Ancient Roman Concrete," History Stories, accessed May 3, 2017, http://history.com/news/the-secrets-of-ancient-roman-concrete

18. Gromicko and Shepard, "History of Concrete."

19. Marco Merola, "Romans on the Bay of Naples," *Archaeology* 69, no. 5 (Sept.–Oct. 2016), 26–27.

20. Maureen Carroll, *Earthly Paradises: Ancient Gardens in History and Archeology* (Los Angeles: Getty Publications, 2003), 6.

21. Ibid., 42.

22. *Encyclopedia Britannica*, s.v. "Agora, ancient Greek meeting place," accessed September 1, 2017, http://www.britannica.com/topic/agora.

23. Carroll, *Earthly Paradises*, 30.

24. "History Timeline," accessed February 18, 2017, http://www.auburn.edu/academic/architecture/bsc/classes/

25. Gromicko and Shepard, "History of Concrete," "Technological Milestones."

26. Sarah Rutherford, *Capability Brown and His Landscape Gardens* (London, UK: National Trust Books, 2016), 20, 21.

27. Jamie Doward, "England's Pastoral Symphony—A Celebration of the Country Garden," *Guardian*, UK edition, accessed January 20, 2016,
https://www.theguardian.com /lifeandstyle/2016/jan/10/year-of-english-garden-capability-brown-bake-off

28. Vanessa Bezemer Sellers, "From Geometric to Informal Gardens in the Eighteenth Century," The Met, accessed November 25, 2016, https://www.metmuseum.org/toah/hd/gard_3/hd_gard_3.htm.

29. Rutherford, *Capability Brown*, 9.

30. Ibid., 110.

31. Ibid., 104.

32. Martha Alexander, "Crystal Grotto at Painshill Is Restored," *Britain Magazine*, accessed September 15, 2017, http://www.britain-magazine.com/news/crystal-grotto-at-painshill-is-restored/.

33. Stephanie Mahon, "Design Styles: Rococo Gardens," *The English Garden*, July 3, 2015, accessed February 16, 2017, http://www.theenglishgarden.co.uk/top-picks/inspiration/design-styles-rococo-gardens/.

34. Michael Symes, introduction to Thomas Whately, *Observations on Modern Gardening: An Eighteenth-Century Study of the English Landscape Garden* (1770; Rochester, NY: Boydell Press, 2016), 2.

35. Bernd H. Dams and Andrew Zega, *Pleasure Pavilions and Follies: In the Gardens of the Ancien Régime* (Paris: Flammarion, 1995), 124, 147.

36. Elizabeth Barlow Rogers, *Landscape Design: A Cultural and Architectural History* (New York: Harry N. Abrams, 2001), 261.

37. John Beardsley, *Gardens of Revelation: Environments by Visionary Artists* (New York: Abbeville Press, 1995), 130.

38. "The History of Concrete," *Concrete Contractor*, accessed September 10, 2017, http://concretecontractor.com/concrete-history/.

39. "Louis Vicat, Inventor of Artificial Cement," Vicat, accessed November 25, 2016, https://www.vicat.com/about-us/vision/history-of-louis-vicat

40. Gromicko and Shepard, "History of Concrete," "Technological Milestones."

41. R. E. Shaeffer, *Reinforced Concrete: Preliminary Design for Architects and Builders* (New York: McGraw-Hill, 1992).

42. Ibid.

43. Graham McKay, "Assorted Architecture Myths," Misfits' Architecture, accessed May 24, 2018, https://misfitsarchitecture.com/2011/10/29/the-things-architects-believe-1/.

44. N. de Tedesco, "Reinforced Concrete in France: The Historical Evolution," *Concrete and Constructional Engineering* 1, nos. 1–6 (1906–1907), 159–60.

45. Joseph Monier, "Reinforced Concrete: Famous Inventors," accessed April 3, 2002, http://www.edubilla.com/invention/reinforced-concrete/

46. Ibid.

47. Ibid.

48. *Encyclopedia Britannica*, s.v. "Francois Hennebique," accessed January 2, 2018, https://www.britannica.com/biography/Francois-Hennebique

49. Laetitia Barbier, "Francois Hennebique's Concrete Manor," Atlas Obscura, accessed January 2, 2018, https://atlasobscura.com/places/francois-hennebique-concrete-manor

50. See Frank Newby, ed., *Early Reinforced Concrete*, Studies in the History of Civil Engineering 11 (Burlington, VT: Ashgate Publishing, 2001), 126–28.

51. Joseph S. Spoerl, *A Brief History of Iron and Steel Production* (PDF), accessed February 23, 2020, https://www.academia.edu/31060927/A_Brief_History_of_Iron_and_Steel_Production

52. William E. Ward House, Rye, NY. Listed on National Register of Historic Places, #76001294. Also known as Ward's Castle. https://catalog.archives.gov/id/75323289.

53. Gromicko and Shepard, "History of Concrete," "Building Milestones."

54. Michel Racine, *Jardins au naturel: Rocailles, grotesques et art rustique* (Arles, France: Actes Sud, 2001), 94–95.

55. Suki Gershenhorn, "History and Materiality of Rustic Cement Sculptures," (MS in Historic Preservation, Columbia University, 2015), 17. https://doi.org/10.7916/D89G5M91

56. Ann Komara, "Concrete and the Engineered Picturesque: The Parc des Butte Chaumont (Paris, 1867)," *Journal of Architectural Education* 58, no. 1 (September 2004), 5–12. doi 10.1162/1046488041578158

57. Ibid., 9.

58. William Robinson, *The Parks, Promenades, and Gardens of Paris* (London, UK: Macmillan, 1878), 66.

59. Rogers, *Landscape Design*, 261, 262.

60. Arturo Almandoz, ed., *Planning Latin America's Capital Cities 1850–1950* (New York: Routledge, Taylor and Francis Group, 2002), 52.

61. Daniel Schávelzon and Francisco Girelli, "Grutas, rocallas y arboles de cemento: Otra arquitectura desaparecida de Buenos Aires 1880–1910," *Anales del Instituto de Arte Americano e Investigaciones Estéticas* 44, no. 2 (2014), accessed January 26, 2019, http://ref.scielo.org/wx4v8c.

62. Daniel Schávelzon, *El Árbol de cemento: Arquitecturas de rocallas, Argentina y América Latina* (Buenos Aires, Centro de Arqueología Urbana, 2019).

63. Beatrice M. Ursh, "Julio Carlos Thays," Los arboles de Buenos Aires—Trees of Buenos Aires (blog), accessed August 2, 2017, https://losarbolesdebuenosaires.blogspot.com/search?q=thays.

64. Cristiane Maria Magalhães, "Rustic Works and Ornaments: The Technique of Rockery and Its Craftsmen in the Gardens and Urban Parks of Brazil at the Turn of the Twentieth Century" trans. David Yann Chaigne, 4, accessed June 15, 2018 (original Portuguese, http://www.academia.edu), abstract, http://www.scielo.br/scielo.php?pid=S0101-47142017000300019&script=sci_abstract.

65. Ibid., 4.

66. Cristiane Maria Magalhães, email to Patsy Light, July 30, 2018, regarding work of Francisco da Silva Reis in Parque das Águas, Caxambu.

67. For background see Raimon Díaz Mariño, "Sobre mi," accessed February 13, 2019, https://www.raimondiaz.com

68. George E. Woodward and F. W. Woodward, *Woodward's Architecture and Rural Art: Landscape Gardening, and Rural Art*, two vols (New York, NY: Geo. E. and F. W. Woodward, 1867), 1:1, 68.

69. Daniel Mack, *Making Rustic Furniture* (Asheville, NC: Lark Books, 1992), 100.

70. Ibid., 100.

71. Gary W. Clark, *Nineteenth Century Card Photos: KwikGuide* (n.p.: PhotoTree, 2013), 64–65, www.PhotoTree.com.

72. "A Look at Our Past," Old Hickory Furniture Co., accessed September 2, 2019, https://www.oldhickory.com/history.

73. "Alamo Cement Company," *Pit and Quarry* Magazine (Chicago), December 1982.

74. Ibid.

75. Ibid.

76. Carlos Cortés, who worked on the restoration of Rodríguez's drawings and notes, shared them with conservator Michael Haynes and Patsy Light. Personal communication with Patsy Light, January 26, 2018.

77. Maneula Vargas Theall, taped interviews with Patsy Light, Arlington, Texas, 2000–2005.

78. Luis Robles Gil, letter of recommendation for Dionicio Rodríguez, March 14, 1924. When Rodríguez left Mexico City to come to the United States, Gil wrote this letter for him, stating that Rodríguez had worked on "obras de cemento rústico" (works of rustic cement). Hence the genre became known as "trabajo rústico." Courtesy of Carlos Cortés.

79. Oral history stating that Rodríguez learned from Gil, who learned the techniques in Spain, could have credence in that dates of work in Argentina, Brazil, and Cuba predate the 1924 date of Gil's letter. It is possible that the work of European artisans who worked in these countries influenced the work in Mexico. Patsy Light, *Capturing Nature: The Cement Sculpture of Dionicio Rodríguez* (College Station: Texas A&M University Press, 2008), 19.

80. Daniel D. Paul, email to Patsy Light, August 12, 2008; Paul was inquiring for information about Benjamin Dominguez, a cement artisan who attended Academia de Artes Plásticas, worked on faux details in the Mexico City zoo in Chapultepec Park, and later worked in California.

81. For Zacatecas see Light, *Capturing Nature*, 7, 16.

82. Jorge Eduardo Sanchez Martinez, title unknown, *Hora Cero Tamaulipas* magazine (Tamaulipas, Mexico), *segunda quincena* (second fortnight), May 2014; see also "Orizatlán: La historia en concreto," La Prensa.MX, http://www.laprensa.mx/notas.asp?id=27332

83. Elise Urrutia, Dr. Urrutia's granddaughter wrote, "Urrutia was intercepted and escorted into exile under the armed guard of Funston's army," email to Patsy Light, March 5, 2018.

84. Funston served as the US military governor of Vera Cruz during the unrest in Mexico. Frederick Funston Papers, Collection 33, Kansas Historical Society, accessed May 23, 2018, https://www.kshs.org/index.php?url=p/frederick-funston-papers/14027.

85. Light, *Capturing Nature*, 27.

86. Aureliano Urrutia, M.D., letter to Ray Lambert, San Antonio Park Commissioner, recommending Rodríguez, date unknown, courtesy of Carlos Cortés.

87. Manuela Theall, interviews with Patsy Light.

88. Gladys Saborio, "Creating Art; Michigan's Trabajo Rústico," *Michigan History Magazine* 92, no. 4 (July–Aug. 2008), 32–44.

89. William E. Rutter, Bureau of History, Michigan Department of State, Inventory Form for St. Joseph Church and Shrine, Apr. 19, 1990.

90. Saborio, "Creating Art," 36. *See also* Gladys Saborio and Susan Kosky, *Michigan's US 12 Heritage Trail, America's Second Federal Highway* (Traverse City, MI: Arbutus Press, 2015).

91. Gene Fowler, "*Trabajo Rústico*: Preserving the Lost Art of Faux Bois Cement Sculptors," accessed October 2017, https://texashighways.com/culture/trabajo-rustico/.

92. Donald Tucker, *An Introduction to Sculpting Ferrocement Faux Bois* (Scotts Valley, CA: CreateSpace Independent Publishing Platform, 2011).

93. Terry G. Jordan, *Texas Graveyards: A Cultural Legacy* (Austin: University of Texas Press, 1982), 76.

94. Daniel D. Paul, email to Patsy Light, July 1, 2008. Paul related that Dominguez graduated from UNAM in 1925 and worked in the Chapultepec Zoo designing the enclosures for the lions and tigers. In El Paso and Los Angeles he created children's playgrounds.

95. Ronald J. Beckwith, "Landscape Gardens and Gardeners at Manzanar Relocation Center," *Discover Nekkei*, January 25, 2008, accessed January 24, 2010, http://www.discovernikkei.org/en/journal/2008/1/25/landscape-manzanar/.

96. Terrance Eagan, telephone interview with Patsy Light, February 24, 2018. After a trip to Paris in 1915, Huntington commissioned the wooden arbor supports to be replaced with trabajo rústico. Eagan works under a tent and fulfills the educational purpose of the museum by providing answers to visitors about the technique. Formerly an artisan in several media, he says he is using the original work as an armature to "create new work within the footprint of the original work."

97. Shane Winter, telephone interview with Patsy Light, May 16, 2018.

98. Ibid., Phelan mansion detail.

99. Ibid.

100. Gershenhorn, "History and Materiality," 55.

101. Fowler, "Trabajo Rústico," 4.

Chapter 2

1. Merriam-Webster, s.v. armature (noun, 2d), https://www.merriam-webster.com/dictionary/armature.

2. Tucker, *An Introduction*.

3. Ibid., 5.

4. Light, *Capturing Nature*, 23.

5. Ibid., 36.

6. W. E. Barker, "Beauty in Concrete Wood," Popular Mechanics, October 1927, 585–87.

Chapter 3

1. Pat Jasper and Kay Turner, eds., *Art among Us: Mexican American Folk Art of San Antonio*, with photographs by Kathy Vargas (San Antonio, TX: San Antonio Museum Association, 1986). This catalog was produced for an exhibit at the San Antonio Museum of Art that ran from April 27 to June 15, 1986.

2. Michael Ennis, "Art of the People," *Texas Monthly*, January 1987, 134–35. The exhibit *Con Cariño* ("With Apprieciation") was organized from two major collections of Nelson Rockefeller and Robert K. Winn. Rockefeller was assisted in his collecting by muralist Diego Rivera, and Winn was also a collector who owned a store of Mexican American folk art in San Antonio. Both began collecting in the 1930s.

3. Jasper and Turner, *Art among Us*, 13.

4. Jill Vexler, personal communication with Patsy Light, March 3, 2019. A pre-Columbian codex illustrates an adult woman weaving with a child at her side. Later, villagers of Mexico continued to be known as producers of family-made products. In Tenanchingo, Tlaxcala, backstrap and upright looms are used to weave *rebozos*, a type of shawl, and in Tzintzuntzán, Michoacán, utilitarian glazed ceramics are made.

5. Maribel Alvarez, "Made in Mexico: Souvenirs, Artisans, Shoppers and the Meanings of Other 'Border-Type Things,'" PhD diss., University of Arizona, 2003.

6. Bacilio Capetillo Aguilar, "All Mexico, Select Baptisms, 1560–1950," www.ancestry.com.

7. US Census Bureau, Bexar County, Texas, San Antonio Ward 2, ED37, 1920.

8. Aurora Rocha (daughter of Bacilio Aguilar), interview with Patsy Light and Kent Rush, September 15, 2016.

9. On Guadalupe Pozos see Fannie B. Campbell, "Mexican Mother Is Park Nightingale, Modesty Keeps Her from Singing in Public," *San Antonio Light*, February 12, 1937.

10. US Census Bureau, Bexar County, Texas, San Antonio, Texas, 1940. The census records indicate that Bacilio had a fourth-grade education.

11. Jo Farb Hernández, "About the Artist," Spaces, accessed June 7, 2016, http://spacesarchives.org (URL inactive).

12. Ibid.

13. Ihosvani Rodríguez, "Wild Kingdom; Retiree's Animal Pieces Cause Quite a Stir," *San Antonio Express-News*, October 19, 1999, 1E–3E.

14. Marion Oettinger, personal communication with Patsy Light, October 1999.

15. Rodríguez, "Wild Kingdom," 3E.

16. Hernández, "About the Artist."

17. Greg Smith, "Genaro P. and Carolina Briones House," National Register of Historic Places nomination (Austin: Texas Historical Commission, 1997), Section 8, 14–15.

18. Ibid., 14.

19. Ibid., 16.

20. Tom Foster, "Made in the South: Keeping a Rustic Furniture Tradition Alive in Texas," *Garden and Gun*, August–September 2018, accessed August 18, 2018, https://gardenandgun.com/?s=Keeping+a+Rustic+Furniture+Tradition+Alive+in+Texas

21. Molly Glentzer, "Concrete Realism: Faux Bois, Sculpture Contributed by Mexican Immigrants," *Houston Chronicle*, June 27, 2004, accessed June 28, 2014, https://www.chron.com/news/article/Concrete-Realism-Faux-Bois-sculpture-1627903.php.

22. David Uhler, "Concrete Artist Creates Illusions: Trabajo Rustico Carries on Style of Dionisio [sic] Rodríguez," San Antonio Express-News, June 24, 2004, Section F, 3F.

23. Cary Clack, "Sculptor Cortés Dies at Age 93," *San Antonio Express-News*, January 18, 1997, n.p.

24. Bill Minutaglio, "Sylvan Concrete that Could Fool a Termite," *San Antonio Express-News*, January 18, 1981, 3-m.

25. Ibid.

26. Clack, "Sculptor Cortés.

27. Marcella Marie, "A Little about Myself," Marcella Marie Faux Bois, accessed July 15, 2016, http://www.marcellamariefauxbois.com/about/.

28. Marcella Davis, written statement, email to Patsy Light, May 11, 2018.

29. Davis, "A Little about Myself"; Donald Tucker, *An Introduction to Sculpting Ferrocement Faux Bois* (Scotts Valley, CA: CreateSpace Independent Publishing Platform, 2011).

30. Davis, "A Little about Myself."

31. "Who Said It's a Dog's Life?" *San Antonio Light*, February 12, 1932, B1.

32. Ibid.

33. Antonio Lopez, City of San Antonio death certificate, Office of the City Clerk's central Vital Records Division.

34. Emma Bailey, telephone interview with Patsy Light, November 5, 2016.

35. Ibid.

36. Guadalupe Del Toro, interview with Patsy Light and Maria Pfeiffer, December 21, 1998.

37. Yvonne Perez, conversation with Patsy Light, April 3, 2018.

38. Michael Fogg, email to Patsy Light, October 28, 2017.

39. Judith H. Dobrzynski, "Artisan: Michael Fogg," accessed July 23, 2016, http://www.traditionalhome.com/design/artisan-michael-fogg (URL inactive).

40. Ibid.

41. Ibid.

42. Draft Registration Card, Antonio Acebedo Lopez, 1942.

43. Esperanza Flores, interview with Patsy Light, February 7, 1987.

44. *San Antonio City Directory*, 1931.

45. "Who Said It's a Dog's Life?" *San Antonio Light*, February 12, 1932, Section B1.

46. Gina Kozelsky supplied a photograph and information, July 15, 2016.

47. Obituary, William Cassiano Perez, *San Antonio Express-News*, December 12, 1945, 141, https://newspaperarchive.com/sanantonioexpress-news/.

48. *San Antonio City Directory*, 1940 and 1951.

49. Melinda LoPresto, selections from autobiography, emailed to Patsy Light, 2016.

50. Christopher Varela, "Hidalgo Park Quiosco," Application for an Official Texas Historical Marker, rev. March 17, 2011, https://texashistory.unt.edu/ark:/67531/metapth491877/m2/1/high_res_d/Harris-Co_Hidalgo-Park-Quiosco.pdf.

51. Ibid.

52. Light, *Capturing Nature*, 58–59, 61–62, 69–71.

53. Christopher Varela, "Hidalgo Park Quiosco, Addendum: The Vidal Lozano/Dionicio Rodriguez Connection," Application for an Official Texas Historical Commission Marker, n.d., https://texashistory.unt.edu/ark:/67531/metapth491877/m2/1/high_res_d/Harris-Co_Hidalgo-Park-Quiosco.pdf, p. 32

54. Light, *Capturing Nature*, 34–40.

55. "Childhood Village Rebuilt in Backyard," *San Antonio Sunday Light*, October 7, 1945, section 2.

56. Ibid.

57. Ashley Blaker, "Chain Saws Are No Threat to Sam Murray's Stone Forest," *San Antonio Business Journal*, November 29, 1987, 28.

58. Jasper and Turner, *Art among Us*.

59. Blaker, "Chain Saws," 28.

60. Ron Bechtol, "Home Is Where the Art Is: A Tribute to San Antonio's Unheralded Artists," *San Antonio Light*, April 1, 1984, 30.

61. Rene Romero, email to Patsy Light, June 17, 2016.

62. Ibid.

63. Ibid. After completing the Mission San José fencing project, Samuel Ramirez returned to his farm in Veracruz, where neighboring farmers were cutting his fences. According to Rene, once his father constructed trabajo rústico fence posts, his troubles were over.

64. "Sculpture in Concrete," *San Antonio Light*, February 13, 1951.

65. Carlos Cortés, personal communication with Patsy Light, 2007.

66. *San Antonio Light*, February 13, 1951.

67. Donald Tucker, personal communication with Patsy Light, July 11, 2006.

68. Donald Tucker, "Faux Bois: Reviving a Lost Art" (blog), June 24, 2007, accessed November 21, 2016, https://fauxboisinconcrete.blogspot.com.

69. Tucker, *An Introduction*.

70. Tucker, "*Faux Bois*."

71. Kendall Curlee, "Ximénez, Beatrice Valdez," *Handbook of Texas Online*, accessed October 17, 2017, https://www.tshaonline.org/handbook/entries/ximenez-beatrice-valdez

72. Beatrice Ximénez, workshop offered, listed in *Popular Art/Artes Populares II*, catalog of folk art workshops held at Guadalupe Theatre Gallery, November 13–December 23, 1987.

73. Curlee, "Ximénez."

74. Mary Jane Ximénez, conversation with Patsy Light, April 29, 2018.

75. Curlee, "Ximénez."

76. Ann Gallaway, "Last Menagerie? No Cement!" *Texas Highways*, July 13, 2012, http://texas-highways.com.

77. Ibid.

78. Ibid.; Ximénez workshop, *Popular Art* catalog.

Selected Bibliography

Alvarez, Maribel. "Made in Mexico: Souvenirs, Artisans, Shoppers and the Meanings of Other 'Border-Type Things.'" PhD diss., University of Arizona, 2003.

Andrews, Evan. "10 Innovations That Built Ancient Rome," November 20, 2012. Accessed April 9, 2017, https://www.history.com/news/10-innovations-that-built-ancient-rome

Beardsley, John. *Gardens of Revelation: Environments by Visionary Artists*. New York: Abbeville Press, 1995.

Bechtol, Ron. ""Home is Where the Art Is: A Tribute to San Antonio's Unheralded Artists." *San Antonio Light,* April 1, 1984, 30.

Benson, Elizabeth P. *The Maya World*. New York: Thames & Hudson, 2015.

Bosc, Jean-Louis, Jean-Michel Chauveau, Jacques Clément, Jacques Degenne, Bernard Marrey, and Michel Paulin. *Joseph Monier et la naissance du ciment armé,* 1st ed. Paris, France: Editions du Linteau, 2001.

Britannica Online Encyclopedia, s.v. "Folk art," accessed June 6, 2018. https://www.britannica.com/art/folk-art-visual-arts

Carroll, Maureen. *Earthly Paradises: Ancient Gardens in History and Archaeology*. Los Angeles: Getty Publications, 2003.

Clark, Gary W. *19th Century Card Photos KwikGuide: A Step-by-Step Guide to Identifying and Dating Cartes de Visite and Cabinet Cards*. PhotoTree.com, 2013.

Coe, Michael D., and Stephen Houston. *The Maya* 9th ed. New York: Thames & Hudson, 2015.

Dams, Bernd H., and Andrew Zega. *Pleasure Pavilions and Follies: In the Gardens of the Ancien Regime*. Paris, France: Flammarion, 1995.

de Tedesco, N. "Reinforced Concrete in France: The Historical Evolution." *Concrete and Constructional Engineering,* 1(1–6), 1906–1907, 159–60.

Encyclopedia Britannica s.v. "Agora, Ancient Greek Meeting Place." Accessed September 1, 2017, https://www.britannica.com/topic/agora

Encyclopedia Britannica s.v. "Pozzolana." Accessed July 11, 2017, https://www.britannica.com /technology/pozzolana

Ennis, Michael. "Art of the People. A new exhibition in San Antonio demonstrates the purity and persistence of Mexican folk art," *Texas Monthly,* January 1987.

Farrar, Linda. *Ancient Roman Gardens*. Stroud, Gloucestershire, UK: Sutton Publishing, 2000.

Gershenhorn, Suki. "History and Materiality of Rustic Cement Sculptures," MS in Historic Preservation, Columbia University, 2015, 17. https://doi.org/10.7916/D89G5M91

Gothein, Marie Luise. Walter P. Wright, ed. *A History of Garden Art,* vol. II. New York: Hacker Art Books, 1966.

Graham, Joe S. "Tejano Folk Arts and Crafts in South Texas, Artesanía Tejana." Kingsville: Texas A&I University, September 1989. Catalogue for a travelling exhibit from the John E. Connor Museum prepared by The University of Texas at San Antonio Institute of Texan Cultures Initiative.

Gromicko, Nick, and Kenton Shepard. "The History of Concrete," International Association of Certified Home Inspectors. Accessed December 24, 2016, https://www.nachi.org/history-of-concrete.htm

Harris, Cyril M., Ed. *Illustrated Dictionary of Historic Architecture.* New York: Dover Publications, 1977.

Hembrook Family of Websites. "The Lost City of Pompeii, Italy." Accessed March 11, 2017, http://www.hembrook.com/travel/it/pompeii

Jasper, Pat, and Kay Turner, Eds. *Art Among Us: Mexican American Folk Art of San Antonio,* with photographs by Kathy Vargas. San Antonio: San Antonio Museum Association, 1986. Catalog for the exhibit at the San Antonio Museum of Art, April 27-June 15, 1986.

Komara, Ann. "Concrete and the Engineered Picturesque: The Parc des Buttes-Chaumont (Paris, 1867)." *Journal of Architectural Education,* 58, n0.1, September 2004, 5–12. doi.org/bh9smq

Light, Patsy. *Capturing Nature: The Cement Sculpture of Dionicio Rodríguez.* College Station, TX: TAMU Press, 2008.

Macauley-Lewis, Elizabeth. "Greek and Roman Gardens," August 31, 2015. Accessed March 5, 2017, https://doi.org/fwd4

Mack, Daniel. *Making Rustic Furniture.* Asheville, NC: Lark Books, 1992, 100.

Magalhães, Cristiane Maria. "Rustic Works and Ornaments: The Technique of Rockery and its Craftsmen in the Gardens and Urban Parks of Brazil at the Turn of the Twentieth Century." Translated by David Yann Chaigne. *Anals do Museu Paulista: Historia e Cultura Material, 25*(3), 19–57.

Newby, Frank, Ed. *Early Reinforced Concrete: Studies in the History of Civil Engineering.* Burlington, VT: Ashgate Publishing, 2001.

Oettinger, Marion Jr. *The Folk Art of Latin America: Visiones del Pueblo.* New York: Dutton Studio Books in association with the Museum of American Folk Art, 1992.

Pruitt, Sarah. "The Secrets of Ancient Roman Concrete," June 21, 2013, updated August 29, 2018. Accessed July 19, 2019, https://www.history.com/news/the-secrets-of-ancient-roman-concrete

Purnell, Carolyn. "War of the Roses: The French vs. English Garden," April 3, 2012. Accessed December 4, 2016, https://www.apartmenttherapy.com/a-war-of-roses-the-french-vs-english-garden-168600

Racine, Michel. *Jardins "au naturel" Rocailles, grotesques et art rustique.* Arles, France: Actes Sud, 2001.

Rio Bravo–Rio Grande Valley Newsletter. Reynosa: propuestas de recuperación patrimonial de "Orizatlán" y del "Indian Market." June 15, 2018: vol. 5, no. 18. URL: https://newsletterbbrgv.wordpress.com/category/localidad/bajo-bravo/reynosa/page/2/ Website: https://newsletterbbrgv.wordpress.com/category/localidad/bajo-bravo/reynosa/

Rivera, Jesús. "Reynosa-Orizatlán: La historia en concreto." *La Prensa.mx,* September 20, 2010. www.laprensa.mx/notas.asp?id=27332

Rogers, Elizabeth Barlow. *Landscape Design: A Cultural and Architectural History.* New York: Harry Abrams, 2001.

Ross, David (Ed.). "Capability Brown Biography." Britain Express: Passionate about British Heritage. Accessed November 26, 2016, https://www.britainexpress.com/History/bio/brown.htm

Rutherford, Sarah. *Capability Brown and His Landscape Gardens.* London: National Trust Books, 2016.

Saborio, Gladys. "Creating Art; Michigan's Trabajo Rústico." *Michigan History Magazine,* 92 no. 4, July–Aug. 2008, 32–44.

Schávelzon, Daniel. El Árbol de cemento: Arquitecturas de rocallas en Argentina y América Latina. Buenos Aires, Centro de Arqueologia Urbana, 2019.

Schávelzon, Daniel, and Francisco Girelli. "Grutas, rocallas y árboles de cemento: otra arquitectura desaparecida de Buenos Aires (1880–1910)." *Anales del Instituto de Arte Americano E Investigaciones Estéticas,* 44 no. 2, July 2014, 205–224. Accessed January 26, 2015, http://www.scielo.org.ar/scielo.php?script=sci_arttext&pid=S2362-20242014000200009

Sellers, Vanessa Bezemer. "The Eighteenth Century: From Geometric to Informal Gardens." In Heilbrunn Timeline of Art History. New York: The Metropolitan Museum of Art, 2000–October 2003. http://www.metmuseum.org/toah/hd/gard_3 /hd_gard_3.htm

Spoerl, Joseph S. *A Brief History of Iron and Steel Production.* Accessed February 23, 2020, https://www.academia.edu/31060927/A_Brief_History_of_Iron_and_Steel_Production

Symes, Michael. Introduction and commentary to Thomas Whately's *Observations on Modern Gardening: An Eighteenth-Century Study of the English Landscape Garden* (1770). Rochester: Boydell Press, 2016, 2.

Thecker, Christopher. *The History of Gardens.* Berkley: University of California Press, 1985.

Tucker, Donald. *An Introduction to Sculpting Ferro-cement Faux Bois.* Scotts Valley, CA: CreateSpace Independent Publishing Platform, 2010.

Urrutia, Dr. A. A. *Boda de Oro del Doctor Aureliano Urrutia.* San Antonio, TX: Artes Graficas, 1946.

Urrutia, Dr. A. A. *Pintocoteca.* San Antonio, TX: possibly self-published, n.d.

Vaux, Calvert. *Villas and Cottages: A Series of Designs Prepared for Execution in the United States.* New York: Harper and Brothers, 1864. Reprint Dover Publications, 1970.

Watkin, David. *The English Vision: The Picturesque in Architecture, Landscape and Garden Design.* New York: Harper & Row, 1982.

Westkaemper, Sarah C. "The Twentieth Century Gardens: A Heritage of Excellence in San Antonio." MA thesis, Louisiana State University, 1985.

Wild, Andrew M. (2013). "Capability Brown, the Aristocracy, and the Cultivation of the Eighteenth-Century British Landscaping Industry." *Enterprise & Society,* 14 no. 2 (2013), 237–270. doi:10.1093/es/kht018

Woods, May. *Visions of Arcadia; European Gardens from Renaissance to Rococo.* London: Aurum 1996, 166–167.

Woodward, George E., and F. W. Woodward. *Woodward's Architecture and Rural Art: Landscape Gardening and Rural Art,* 2 vols. New York: Palala Press, 2015. Vol. 1: 1, 68.

Yegul, Fikret. Review of Principles of Roman Architecture (2001) by Mark Wilson Jones. https://www.academia.edu/14746298/Fikret_Yegul_review_of_Principles_of_Roman_Architecture

Index

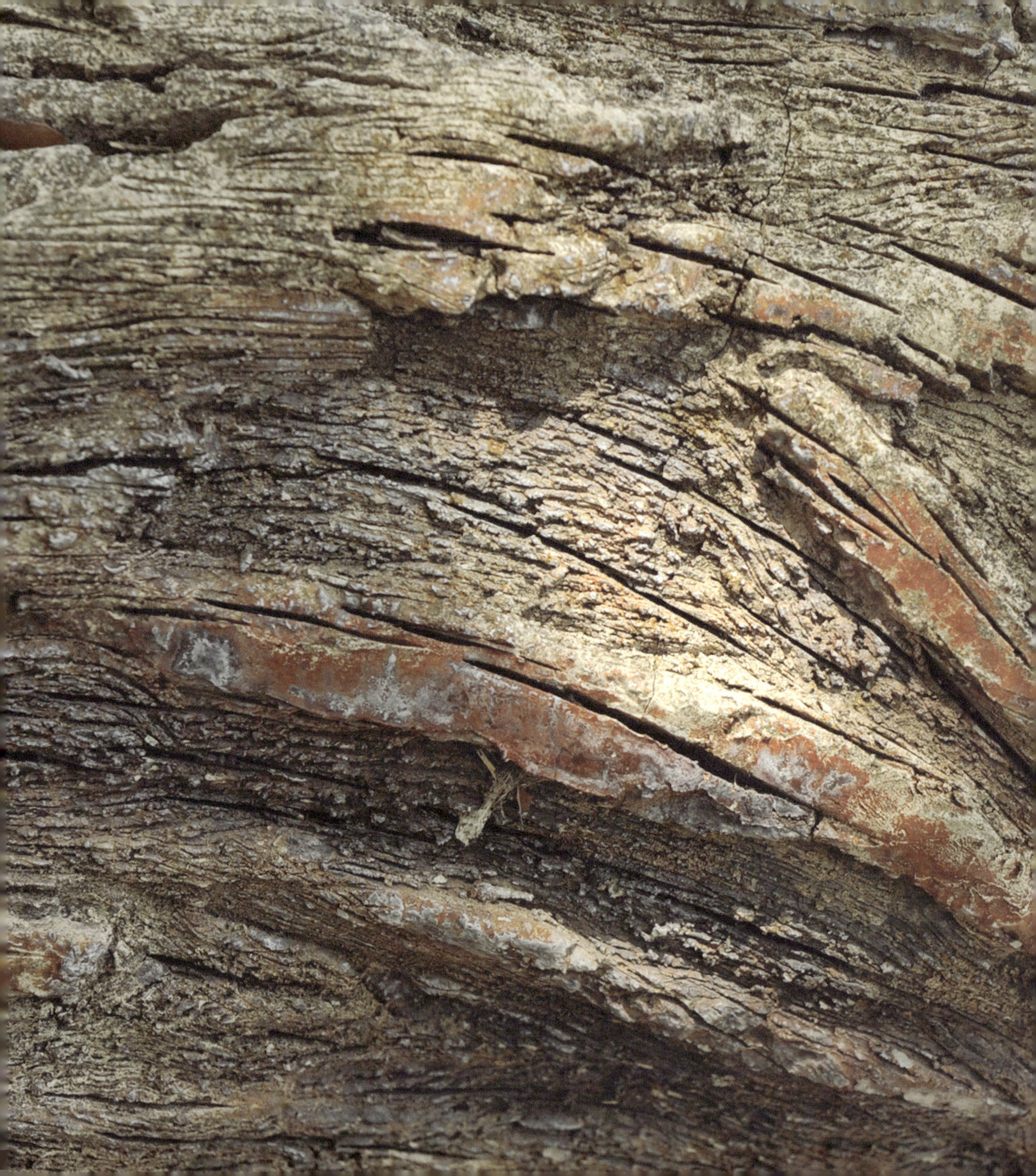